IMISCOE Research Series

This series is the official book series of IMISCOE, the largest network of excellence on migration and diversity in the world. It comprises publications which present empirical and theoretical research on different aspects of international migration. The authors are all specialists, and the publications a rich source of information for researchers and others involved in international migration studies. The series is published under the editorial supervision of the IMISCOE Editorial Committee which includes leading scholars from all over Europe. The series, which contains more than eighty titles already, is internationally peer reviewed which ensures that the book published in this series continue to present excellent academic standards and scholarly quality. Most of the books are available open access.

Letizia Palumbo

Taking Vulnerabilities to Labour Exploitation Seriously

A Critical Analysis of Legal and Policy Approaches and Instruments in Europe

Springer

IMISCOE

Letizia Palumbo
Department of Philosophy and Cultural Heritage
Ca' Foscari University of Venice
Venice, Italy

ISSN 2364-4087 ISSN 2364-4095 (electronic)
IMISCOE Research Series
ISBN 978-3-031-55423-0 ISBN 978-3-031-55424-7 (eBook)
https://doi.org/10.1007/978-3-031-55424-7

This work was supported by IMISCOE

This Springer imprint is published by the registered company Springer Nature Switzerland AG
The registered company address is: Gewerbestrasse 11, 6330 Cham, Switzerland

Paper in this product is recyclable.

To Rosa and Alessandro

Introduction

> *Inevitably, one of us will be killed someday, and then they will realise that we exist.* Jerry Essan Masslo[1] (Umtata, South Africa, 4 December 1959—Villa Literno, Campania, 25 August 1989)

In Europe, diverse labour sectors rely on the employment of workers who frequently face exploitative conditions, which can range from the violation of contract provisions or regulations on working conditions to cases of severe abuse and trafficking in human beings (see, for instance, Amnesty International, 2012, 2014; FRA, 2015, 2021; UNODC, 2022). These dynamics of labour exploitation primarily affect migrant workers. Yet, this situation risks jeopardising the rights of all workers, leading to an erosion of labour and human rights.

Until a few years ago exploited migrant labour in European countries comprised mainly undocumented workers. Today many migrant workers experiencing exploitation are also third-country migrant individuals with a residence permit such as for seasonal work, beneficiaries of international protection, asylum seekers, and EU-nationals from the least prosperous EU countries (Lewis & Waite, 2015; Dwyer et al., 2016; Osservatorio Placido Rizzotto & FLAI-CGIL, 2020, 2022; Palumbo et al., 2022). Indeed, this migrant workforce—which is ethnicised, racialised, and gendered—is composed of labourers with different nationalities and legal statuses.

The transformation in the composition of migrant labour has mirrored the changes in migratory movements to and within Europe, especially since the first decade of the 2000s. In addition to EU enlargement and the related increase in intra-EU mobility, changes have been mainly due to the narrowing of legal entry channels for third-country nationals, in particular for those considered 'low- and medium-skilled' workers (Martin et al., 2015; Geddes et al., 2020). The parallel spread of conflicts and wars in various countries has produced an increase in the number of migrant people who, in a context of progressively militarised and externalised

[1] Jerry Essan Masslo, a South African refugee farmworker, was killed in 1989 in a mugging by Italian teenagers in the shanties of Villa Literno (Campania) where he lived.

borders, have been forced to go through dangerous routes, such as the Mediterranean Sea, to reach Europe (see, for instance, Amnesty International, 2017; Sciurba, 2021).

The diversification and stratification of the migrant labour force—in terms of legal status, nationality, and gender—characterising the labour market in many European countries has challenged any rigid distinction between 'economic migration' and 'forced migration' as well as the idea that labour exploitation primarily occurs in the context of irregular migration (Triandafyllidou & Bartolini, 2020; Garofalo Geymonat et al., 2022). Moreover, it has led to new forms of exploitation which rely on the combination of diverse factors—legal, social, economic, and cultural—thus prompting vulnerabilities among migrant workers (Waite et al., 2015; Palumbo & Sciurba, 2018).

Simultaneously, in the process of European market unification, there has been an expanding use of atypical forms of employment, such as temporary agency work and posted work, that go beyond the reach of most national labour laws. As research has highlighted, workers involved in these types of employment are particularly exposed to forms of exploitation, including severe exploitation, which mainly rely on the loopholes of European and national legal frameworks. This reveals a tension between economic competition rules and the protection of workers (Schiek et al., 2015; Novitz & Andrijasevic, 2020; Arnholtz & Lillie, 2020).

Against this context, most institutional and political attention focuses on extreme cases of exploitation—such as trafficking in human beings—and adopts mainly a criminal law response to target abusive employers and traffickers. Yet, as underlined by several legal and social scholars (see, for instance, Chuang, 2017; Fudge, 2018; Siegmann et al., 2022; Giammarinaro, 2022), this approach tends to neglect those forms of exploitation that are less sensational and conspicuous but are endemic in labour market sectors, including agriculture, domestic work, construction, and the textile industry (FRA, 2015, 2021). At the same time, it tends to overlook the impact of inconsistencies in EU and national legislation and policies concerning migration, asylum, and labour rights, as well as legislation and policies addressing exploitation and its severe forms (Corrado et al., 2018; Mantouvalou, 2018; Giammarinaro, 2022).

The impact of these factors emerged more noticeably during the global health crisis triggered by the Covid-19 pandemic, which shed light on both the 'essential' role played by migrant workers for the functioning of core sectors—such as agriculture and domestic and care work—in European countries and the exploitative conditions and related situations of vulnerabilities experienced by these workers, revealing the structural character of dynamics of exploitation (Triandafyllidou, 2022; Palumbo et al., 2022). In this sense, the pandemic drew attention to the issue of which labour shortages are genuine (Anderson et al., 2023) and which are connected to a shortage of dignified job opportunities (Corrado & Palumbo, 2022).

All this gives rise to the question as to whether the EU and national legislation and policies aimed at protecting labour and migrants' rights and preventing/addressing exploitation, including severe exploitation, achieve their objectives.

This book intends to contribute to the debate on migrant labour exploitation by exploring the extent to which the EU and national legal and policy frameworks provide and uphold standards for protecting migrant workers. It moves from a socio-legal and theoretical perspective to build on critical studies on vulnerability (Butler, 2004, 2015; Fineman, 2008; Mackenzie et al., 2014), exploitation (Marks, 2008; Mantouvalou, 2018; LeBaron, 2020), trafficking (O' Connell Davidson, 2010; Andrijasevic, 2010; Shamir, 2012; Kotiswaran, 2017), labour, and migration regimes (Mezzadra & Neilson, 2013; Fudge, 2018), along with relevant feminist theories—including theories on social reproduction (Fortunati, 1981; Picchio, 1992; Bhattacharya, 2017; Rigo, 2022). By mobilising the concept of 'situational vulnerabilities' (Palumbo, 2022b, 2023; Giammarinaro & Palumbo, 2021), the book investigates the assemblage and interaction of factors producing and amplifying migrant workers' vulnerabilities to exploitation, paying special attention to the crucial sectors of agriculture and domestic and care work.

Relevant literature (for instance, Anderson, 2010; Costello & Freedland, 2014; Waite et al., 2015) has highlighted how specific features inherent to migrant workers' experiences render them vulnerable to exploitation even in the case of regular migration. On the other hand, scholars examining exploitation and its worst forms, including forced labour and trafficking, have focused on criminal law and victims' rights (see, for instance, Chaudary, 2011; O'Neill, 2011; Kyriazi, 2015; Stoyanova, 2016; Borraccetti, 2017; Weatherburn, 2021). There are only a few studies that, by adopting an integrated and comprehensive approach, have contextualised and examined the issue of labour exploitation in the framework of the EU and European countries' laws and policies, taking into account the various fields involved (see, for instance, Rijken & de Lange, 2018). This book contributes to bridging this gap, exploring relevant European and national legislation and policies in the ambit of migration, labour, and social rights, as well as those directed at preventing and combatting exploitation, including its severe forms (such as trafficking). The aim is to illuminate how situations of vulnerability to exploitation are generated and exacerbated by legal and policy frameworks, questioning and underlining the tensions, continuities, and ambiguities between different regimes, such as those aimed at combatting exploitation and those regulating labour migration.

Through a critical examination of definitions informing relevant international, European, and national legal instruments, as well as significant case law of the European Court of Human Rights (ECtHR), the book will engage in an analysis of the concepts of slavery, forced labour, trafficking, labour exploitation, and vulnerability. In particular, drawing on relevant legal, social and philosophical literature (for instance, Sample, 2003; Allain, 2009; Shamir, 2012; Chuang, 2014; Pieper et al., 2015; Santoro, 2020), Chaps. 1 and 2 unpack the legal and theoretical conceptions of these notions, devoting special attention to the relationships between vulnerability, consent to exploitation, and the related concept of human dignity. As argued in this study, exploitation shall be considered in its systemic dimension and as a continuum (Skrivankova, 2010) that encompasses various forms and degrees of exploitation and has a structural nature as it is intricately connected to relevant regulatory regimes and social hierarchies, including those related to the distinction between production and social reproduction (Picchio, 1992; Rigo, 2022).

Viewing exploitation as a continuum underscores the vulnerabilities of exploited people within their situational dimension. Far from seeing vulnerability as something fixed and static, the book sheds light on how, along this continuum, forms of exploitation are associated with different situational vulnerabilities produced by the interplay of personal and structural elements in line with the gender and intersectional approach supported by feminist scholars such as Kimberlé Crenshaw (1991). Informed by feminist analyses of the notion of vulnerability, including the works of Martha Fineman (2008) and Judith Butler (2004), the situational understanding of vulnerability mobilised in this volume does not negate or oppose individual agency. Instead, it acknowledges the specificities of the context and related economic, social, and power relationships in which subjects operate and make choices, taking into account the complex ways—as highlighted by the work of Anthony Giddens (1984)—in which the dimensions of social structures and individuals' agency interact and mutually shape each other.

Building on this theoretical framework, the book critically examines relevant EU legal and policy regimes on labour migration as well as on exploitation and trafficking. In particular, Chap. 3 looks at the EU legal and policy framework regarding labour migration of non-EU migrant workers considered 'low-skilled' and intra-EU labour mobility. It explores the areas, including the social reproduction dimension, where migrant workers' rights are compressed, fostering situations of vulnerability to exploitation.[2] Chapter 4 delves into both positive aspects and shortcomings or ambiguities in the EU instruments, such as Directive 2009/52/EC (the Employer Sanctions Directive) and Directive 2011/36/EU (the Anti-Trafficking Directive), and related policies and approaches. It discusses the limitations and risks associated with reducing the complex dimension of exploitation—including its severe forms such as trafficking—to mere exceptional and pathological relationships between exploiters and victims.

The volume then focuses, in Chaps. 5 and 6, on Italian legislation and policies, assessing the impact and effective capacity of the national legal and policy framework to face and prevent contemporary forms of exploitation in their full complexity.

Italy is an emblematic case study for several reasons. First, its geographical location and the fact of being the point of arrival of many people crossing dangerous routes, such as the Mediterranean Sea, have rendered it a significant place, a laboratory as it were, from which to look at the ongoing transformation in the composition of migration movements—with a significant presence of refugees and asylum seekers as well as intra-EU migrants. Second, and related to the first point, Italian policies on migration and asylum have been particularly focused on stringent and selective measures, paying much less attention to the protection of the fundamental rights of migrant people (Chiaromonte & Federico, 2021; Sciurba, 2021). Third, the Italian labour market is highly segmented along nationality, legal status, gender, and

[2] It is worth noting that the term 'migrant' in this volume refers to people residing in a country of which they are not citizens, whether they are from the EU or a third country, and irrespective of their legal status (e.g., asylum seekers, long-term residents, etc.). Therefore, the term 'EU migrant' is used to refer to citizens of an EU Member State.

age and is characterised by particularly high rates of irregularity in employment, especially in sectors such as domestic work and agriculture (see, for instance, IDOS, 2023).

On the other hand, Italy is considered a model for the protection system for victims of exploitation and trafficking, particularly regarding the system under Article 18 of the Consolidated Act on Immigration (Legislative Decree 286/1998). In 2016, the country adopted Law No. 199 that has approached labour exploitation as a stand-alone offence and brought institutional attention to this issue, primarily in agriculture. However, as discussed in Chap. 6, protection measures for victims of exploitation have displayed several shortcomings, resulting in many exploited migrant people not receiving adequate assistance and support (GRETA, 2018; Corrado & Palumbo, 2022; Palumbo, 2017, 2022a, Santoro, 2022).

Although there is extensive research on the working conditions of migrant workers in Italy, only a few studies have examined the national legal and policy framework relating to exploitation in all its complexity, taking into account the various legal and political fields involved (see, for instance, Rigo, 2015; Sciurba, 2015; Corrado et al., 2018; Santoro, 2020, 2023). Hence, the book would contribute to covering this gap.

While centring on Italy as a case study, this volume, in Chaps. 7 and 8, also takes a comparative look at the relevant legal and policy framework on labour migration and exploitation in the UK. The decision to focus on the UK, made prior to its official exit from the EU, was motivated by the intent to explore a country with a migration history and related regulatory regime, as well as labour market laws and policies, that are significantly distinct from Italy—while also experiencing high instances of labour exploitation.

Unlike Italy, which has a historical tradition of emigration and only a recent history of immigration, the UK, along with other European countries such as Germany and France, has traditionally been a destination for migrant people (King et al., 2000). Furthermore, the UK has been marked by a liberal market economy, characterised by low state intervention and a promotion of deregulation and flexibility (Hall & Soskice, 2001). According to the Organisation for Economic Co-operation and Development (OECD) indicators, the UK is among the OECD countries with the lowest levels of employment regulation (OECD, 2019). Its labour market also shows significant gendered and racialised segmentation (see, for instance, Diamond, 2021; Baglioni et al., 2020).

On the other hand, there has been some national legislative progress in the field of severe exploitation and trafficking—in particular the 2015 Modern Slavery Act—that has contributed to the UK being lauded as one of the 'world leaders' in the fight against modern slavery. Furthermore, the UK has been one of the first countries to establish a regulatory body—the Gangmasters and Labour Abuse Authority (GLAA)—for the activities of labour providers (gangmasters) through a licensing scheme aimed at protecting workers in some sectors, including agriculture.

The UK legal and policy framework, however, still does not provide adequate protection to victims of exploitation and does not address the high risk of abuse faced by migrant workers in sectors such as domestic work and agriculture (see, for instance, Kalayaan, 2019; FLEX, 2021). Furthermore, the national points-based immigration system, built on a sponsorship model and extended to EU citizens in 2021, significantly restricts routes for those considered 'low-skilled' migrant workers and ties workers to employers and specific jobs (Alberti & Cutter, 2022). In a context of an increasingly hostile migration environment (Sigona et al., 2021), like Italy, the UK too has introduced progressively restricted migration and asylum policies that have fostered and amplified migrant workers' vulnerabilities to exploitation.

While examining the dynamics of labour exploitation involving migrant workers and the implementation of relevant laws and policies in national contexts, the book looks at two labour market sectors, notably agriculture and domestic work, and related regulatory frameworks. It will focus on the agriculture-migration nexus (Kings et al., 2021; Corrado et al., 2023) and domestic work-migration nexus (Marchetti, 2022; Kofman, 2022) as connected systems with multiple relationships, highlighting the reciprocal links between agriculture and migration and domestic work and migration that co-construct and shape one another. It is worth clarifying that the term domestic work is considered in this volume as consistent with the broad definition adopted by the International Labour Organization (ILO) in the Domestic Workers Convention No. 189 of 2011 as 'work performed in and for a household or households' (Art. 1). Sometimes this study will also refer to care work to pay attention to care-related activities covered by the notion of domestic work.

Both agriculture and domestic work are key sectors of occupation for migrant workers in Europe and, especially in the case of domestic and care work, for women migrant workers. Furthermore, similar features make them particularly prone to abusive employment practices, including severe exploitation such as trafficking (FRA, 2015, 2018; Palumbo et al., 2022; Giammarinaro, 2022).

As Kitty Calavita (2005, p. 73) argues, domestic work and agriculture are embedded in the 'global, post-Fordist economy' but simultaneously retain 'essentially pre-Fordist labour relations'. Diverse similar aspects—such as isolation, coincidence between working space and the space where workers live (especially in the case of live-in domestic workers and farmworkers living on the farms), dependency on employers, and widespread irregularity—characterise both sectors. This shapes and affects labour relations and makes them particularly susceptible to abusive employment practices. Furthermore, gendered and racialised representations inform these sectors considered 'low-skilled'. In domestic and care work, which is a domain of women migrant employment par excellence (Triandafyllidou & Marchetti, 2014), the emotional labour and skills of migrant domestic workers tend to be rendered invisible due to the historical undervaluation of reproductive work and 'the idea of a predisposition for it among women of certain nationalities and racialised backgrounds' (Garofalo Geymonat et al., 2022, p. 214; see also Marchetti, 2014). In agriculture too skills and tasks are highly gendered and racialised, often according to specific body characteristics and stereotypes (Piro, 2021; Palumbo, 2022b).

Moreover, in both sectors, women workers experience sexual blackmail and abuse (Sciurba, 2015; Hellio, 2016; Palumbo & Sciurba, 2018). The book delves into these gendered dimensions of exploitation experiences, exploring how they are (or are not) addressed and prevented by relevant policies and practices. Naturally this approach also considers how gender is intertwined with issues of class, race, and nationality-based discrimination in fostering situations of exploitation.

This volume is grounded in ten years of research conducted especially in Italy from 2014 to 2023. Adopting a legal, social, and theoretical perspective, in addition to relevant literature, I examined pertinent legal and policy documents, and judicial decisions. I also engaged in extensive fieldwork on agricultural work in the rural area of Ragusa (Sicily) and researched domestic and care work in various regions of Italy. Over these years, I conducted participant observation, informal conversations, and interviews with 110 stakeholders, including migrant workers, social workers, experts, trade union members, lawyers, magistrates, and judges. Through this comprehensive fieldwork, I had the opportunity to delve deeper into the complexity of contemporary forms and dynamics of labour exploitation and how legal and policy discourses and regimes construct, foster, and address the situations of vulnerability of migrant workers. In particular, the opportunity to engage in dialogue with numerous migrant workers, listening to their perspectives and insights, has allowed me to understand and question how the law, policies, and practices operate in reality. Of course, this book does not claim to represent the voices of these workers. Their perspective is employed here to problematise and critically reflect on the interplay of the factors producing vulnerabilities. Utilising a gender and intersectional approach, my research paid special attention to the impact of relevant migration, labour, and social policies on the working and living conditions of migrant women, exploring how the compression of the social reproduction sphere and related family responsibilities play a crucial role in the dynamics of exploitation.

Between 2016 and 2023, I also interviewed 40 stakeholders in the UK, including social workers, experts, trade union representatives, lawyers, and policymakers. The variation in empirical research and related methodologies conducted in the two countries is reflected in the data collected and the analysis provided in this book, with the primary focus being on Italy. However, even though the fieldwork in the UK was not as extensive as that conducted in Italy, the testimonies collected allow for insights into similar trends and approaches, as well as differences between the two countries.

Participants for this study have been identified and met thanks to the trusting relationships with stakeholders I have built during these years of research. All the interviews conducted were generally recorded, transcribed, and analysed jointly with fieldnotes. Participants' names are provided in this text only for those interviewees who asked to be identified when their quotations are reported.

By combining a legal and theoretical perspective with empirical fieldwork, this book intends to shed light on how the material conditions created and strengthened by relevant EU and national legislation and policies determine situations of vulnerability that curtail individuals' freedom of choice and undermine the related principle of human dignity, viewed in its social dimension (Rodotà, 2012). This perspective, as underlined in the last chapter (Chap. 9), can help to revisit relevant and different regulatory and policy frameworks within which exploitation occurs, with a view to preventing situations in which migrant individuals are led to 'accept' work in exploitative conditions as the only feasible choice.

References

Alberti, G., & Cutter, J. (2022). Labour migration policy post-Brexit: The contested meaning of regulation by old and new actors. *Industrial Relations Journal, 53*, 430–445.

Allain, J. (2009). The definition of slavery in international law. *Howard Law Journal, 52*, 258–261.

Amnesty International. (2012). *Exploited labour. Migrant workers in Italy's agricultural sector*. Amnesty International.

Amnesty International. (2014). *Exploited labour two years on*. Amnesty International.

Amnesty International. (2017). *A perfect storm: The failure of European policies in the Central Mediterranean*. Amnesty International.

Anderson, B. (2010). Migration, immigration controls and the fashioning of precarious workers. *Work, Employment and Society, 24*(2), 300–317.

Anderson, A., Khadka, U., & Ruhs, M. (2023). Demand for migrant workers: Institutional system effects beyond national borders. *Journal of Ethnic and Migration Studies*, https://doi.org/10.1080/1369183X.2023.2279741

Andrijasevic, R. (2010). *Migration, agency and citizenship in sex trafficking*. Palgrave Macmillan.

Arnholtz, J., & Lillie, N., (Eds.) (2020). *Posted work in the European Union. The political economy of free movement*. Routledge.

ASGI. (2015). *La tutela delle vittime di tratta e del grave sfruttamento: il punto della situazione oggi in Italia*. Report, Associazione per gli studi giuridici sull'immigrazione [online], www.asgi.it/notizia/look-out-report-sfruttamento-lavorativo-tratta-italia/ (Last Access Apr 2024).

Baglioni, S., Calò, F., & Lo Cascio, M. (2020). Covid-19 and labour migration: Investigating vulnerability in Italy and in the UK. *Quaderni Di Economia Del Lavoro, 111*, 109–129.

Bhattacharya, T. (Ed.) (2017). *Social reproduction theory: Remapping class, recentering oppression*. Pluto.

Borraccetti, M. (2017). Human trafficking, equality, and access to victims' rights. In L. Rossi, & F. Casolari (Eds.). *The principle of equality in EU law* (pp. 281–293). Springer.

Bosma, A., & Rijken, C. (2016). Key challenges in the combat of human trafficking: Evaluating the EU trafficking strategy and EU trafficking directive. *New Journal of European Criminal Law, 7*(3), 315–330.

Butler, J. (2004). *Undoing gender*. Routledge.

Butler, J. (2015). *Notes toward a performative theory of assembly*. Harvard University Press. Cambridge: Cambridge University Press.

Calavita, K. (2005). *Immigrants at the margins: Law, race, and exclusion in Southern Europe* (Cambridge Studies in Law and Society).

Caprioglio, C., & Rigo, E. (2020). Lavoro, politiche migratorie e sfruttamento: la condizione dei braccianti migranti in agricoltura. *Diritto, Immigrazione e Cittadinanza, 3*, 32–56.

Castagnone, E., Salis, E., & Premazzi, V. (2013). *Promoting integration for migrant domestic workers in Italy*. FIERI.

Chaudary, S. (2011). Trafficking in Europe: An analysis of the effectiveness of European Law. *Michigan Journal of International Law, 33*(1), 77–99.

Chiaromonte, W., & Federico, V. (2021). The labour market needs them, but we don't want them to stay for good: The conundrum of migrants, refugees and Asylum Seekers' integration in Italy. In V. Federico, & S. Baglioni (Eds.), *Migrants, refugees and Asylum Seekers' integration in European labour markets* (pp. 193–212). IMISCOE Research Series. Springer

Chuang, J. A. (2014). Exploitation creep and the unmaking of human trafficking law. *American Journal of International Law, 108*, 609–649.

Chuang, J. A. (2017). Contemporary debt bondage, "self-exploitation," and the limits of the trafficking definition. In P. Kotiswaran (Ed.), *Revisiting the law and governance of trafficking, forced labour, and modern slavery* (pp. 112–133). Cambridge University Press.

Collins, H., Ewing, K. D., McColgan, A. (2012). *Labour law: Law in context*. Cambridge University Press.

Corrado, A., & Palumbo, L. (2022). Essential but exploitable: Migrant agri-food workers in Italy and Spain. *European Journal of Migration and Law, 24*, 193–216.

Corrado, A., F. Caruso, M. Lo Cascio, M. Nori, L. Palumbo, & A. Triandafyllidou (2018). *Is Italian agriculture a 'pull factor' for irregular migration; and, if so, why?* European Policy Institute, Open Society Foundation Report.

Corrado, A., Pisacane, L., & Alarcón Ferrari, C. (2023). The agrifood-migration nexus: migration regimes and the politics of labour shortages in Italy and Sweden. *Journal of Ethnic and Migration Studies, 50*(5), 1252–1276.

Corrado, A. Caruso, F. S., Lo Cascio, M., Nori, M., Palumbo L., & Triandafyllidou, A. (2018). *Is Italian agriculture a 'pull factor' for irregular migration—And, if so, why?* Open Society European Policy Institute.

Costello, C., & Freedland, M. (Eds.) (2014). *Migrants at work: Immigration and vulnerability in labour law.* Oxford University Press.

Crenshaw, K. (1991). Mapping the margins: Intersectionality, identity politics, and violence against women of color. *Stanford Law Review, 43*(6), 1241–1299.

Diamond, A. (2021). Race and colonialism in the construction of labour markets and precarity. *Industrial Law Journal, 50*(4), 506–531.

Dwyer, P., Hodkinson, S., Lewis, H., & Waite, L. (2016). Socio-legal status and experiences of forced labour among asylum seekers and refugees in the UK. *Journal of International and Comparative Social Policy, 32*(3), 182–198.

Fineman, M. A. (2008). The vulnerable subject: Anchoring equality in the human condition. *Yale Journal of Law and Feminism, 20*(1), 177–1911.

FLEX. (2021). Focus on Labour Exploitation (FLEX) (2021), *New report highlights risks of human trafficking on UK Seasonal Workers Pilot*, Report [online], https://labourexploitation.org/news/new-report-highlights-risks-of-human-trafficking-on-uk-seasonal-workers-pilot/ (Last Access Apr 2024).

Fortunati, L. (1981). *L'arcano della riproduzione. Casalinghe, prostitute, operai e capitale.* Marsilio.

FRA. (2015). *Severe labour exploitation: Into the European Union. States' obligations and victims' rights*. European Union Agency for Fundamental Rights.

FRA. (2018). *Out of sight: Migrant women exploited in domestic work.* European Union Agency for Fundamental Rights.

FRA. (2021). *Protecting migrants in an irregular situation from labour exploitation—Role of the Employers Sanctions Directive*. European Union Agency for Fundamental Rights.

Fudge, J. (2018). Modern slavery, unfree labour and the labour market: The social dynamics of legal characterization. *Social & Legal Studies, 27*(4), 414–434.

Garofalo Geymonat, G., Marchetti, S., & Palumbo, L. (2022). Migrant women workers in Europe: Forms of irregularity and conditions of vulnerability. In I. Va Liempt, J. Schapendonk, & A. Campos-Delgado (Eds.), *Research handbook on irregular migration* (pp. 215–226). Edward Elgar Publishing.

Geddes, A. Hadj-Abdou, L., & Brumat, L. (2020). *Migration and mobility in the European Union* (2nd edn). Red Globe Press.

Giammarinaro, M. G. (2022). Understanding severe exploitation requires a human rights and gender-sensitive intersectional approach. *Frontiers in Human Dynamics, 4* [online], https://www.frontiersin.org/journals/humandynamics/articles/10.3389/fhumd.2022.861600/full (Last Access Apr 2024).

Giammarinaro, M. G., & Palumbo, L. (2021). Vulnerabilità situazionale, genere e diritti umani. Analisi della normativa e della giurisprudenza italiana e sovranazionale sullo sfruttamento lavorativo. In G. Gioffredi, V. Lorubbio, & A. Pisanò (Eds.), *Diritti umani in crisi? Emergenze, disuguaglianze, esclusioni* (pp. 45–62). Pacini Giuridica.

GRETA. (2018). *Report concerning the implementation of the Council of Europe convention on action against trafficking in human beings by Italy*. Council of Europe, Group of Experts on Action against Trafficking in Human Beings.

Guga, S. (2016) *Romanian migrants in the EU: The struggle for decent work and dignity*. LabCity Country Report [online], http://migrationonline.cz/romania_country_report.pdf (Last Access Apr 2024).

Hall, P. A., & Soskice, D. (2001). *Varieties of capitalism: The institutional foundations of comparative advantage*. Oxford University Press.

Hellio, E. (2016). 'They know that you'll leave, like a dog moving into the next bin'. Undocumented male and seasonal female workers in the agricultural labour market of Huelva, Spain. In A. Corrado, C. De Castro, & D. Perrotta (Eds.), *Migration and agriculture: Mobility and change in the Mediterranean area*. Routledge.

IDOS. (2023). *Dossier statistico immigrazione*. Centro studi e ricerche IDOS. Inprinting srl.

Kalayaan. (2019). *Dignity, not destitution. The impact of differential rights of work for migrant domestic workers referred to the national referral mechanism*. Kalayaan Justice for Domestic Workers.

King, R., Lazaridis, G., & Tsardanidis, C. (Eds.) (2000). *Eldorado or fortress? Migration in Southern Europe*. Palgrave Macmillan.

King, R., Lulle, A., & Melossi, E. (2021). New perspectives on the agriculture–Migration Nexus. *Journal of Rural Studies, 85*, 52–58.

Kofman, E. (2022). Scale and spaces of global labor markets. In U. Mense-Petermann, T. Welskopp, & A. Zaharieva (Eds.), *In search of the global labor market*. Brill.

Kotiswaran, P. (Ed.) (2017). *Revisiting the law and governance of trafficking, forced labour, and modern slavery*. Cambridge University Press.

Kyriazi, T. (2015). Trafficking and slavery, the emerging legal framework on trafficking in human beings—Case-law of the European Court of human rights in perspective. *International Human Rights Law Review, 4*, 33–52.

LeBaron, G. (2020). *Combatting modern slavery: Why labour governance is failing and what we can do about it*. Polity.

Lewis, H., & Waite, L. (2015). Asylum, immigration restrictions and exploitation: Hyperprecarity as a lens for understanding and tackling forced labour. *Anti-Trafficking Review, 5*, 49–67.

Mackenzie, C., Rogers, W., & Dodds, S. (2014). Introduction: What is vulnerability and why does it matter for moral theory? In C. Mackenzie, W. Rogers, & S. Dodds (Eds.), *Vulnerability: new essays in ethics and feminist philosophy* (pp. 1–29). Oxford University Press

Marchetti, S. (2014) *Black girls: Migrant domestic workers and colonial legacies*. Brill.

Martín, I., Di Bartolomeo, A., De Bruycher P., Renaudiere, G., Salamońska, J., & Venturini, A. (2015). *Exploring new avenues for legislation for labour migration to the European Union*. Study for the LIBE Committee, European Union.

Mantouvalou, V. (2018). Legal construction of structures of exploitation. In H. Collins, G. Lester, & V. Mantouvalou (Eds.), *Philosophical foundations of labour law*. Oxford University Press.

Mantouvalou, V. (2023). *Structural injustice and workers' rights*. Oxford University Press.

Marchetti, S. (2022). *Migration and domestic work*. IMISCOE Short Reader. Springer.

Marks, S. (2008). Exploitation as an international legal concept, in international law on the left. Re-examining Marxist legacies. In S. Marks (Ed.), *International law on the left: Re-examining Marxist legacies* (pp. 281–307). Cambridge University Press.

Mezzadra, S., & Neilson, B. (2013). *Border as method, or, the multiplication of labor.* Duke University Press.

Middelburg, M. J., & Rijken, C. R. J. J. (2011). Combating trafficking in human beings for labour exploitation. In C. R. J. J. Rijken (Ed.), *Combating trafficking in human beings for labour exploitation*. Wolf Legal Publishers.

Novitz, T., & Andrijasevic, R. (2020). Reform of the posting of workers regime—An assessment of the practical impact on unfree labour relations. *JCMS: Journal of Common Market Studies*, *58*, 1325–1341.

O'Connell Davidson, J. (2010). New slavery, old binaries: Human trafficking and the borders of 'freedom.' *Global Networks*, *10*, 244–261.

OECD. (2019). *Detailed description of employment protection legislation, 2019 OECD Countries*. OECD [online], www.oecd.org/els/emp/OECD2019-EPL.pdf (Last Access Apr 2024).

O'Neill, M. (2011). The EU legal framework on trafficking in human beings: Where to from here—The UK perspective. *Journal of Contemporary European Research*, *7*(4), 452–467.

Osservatorio Placido Rizzotto & FLAI-CGIL (Eds.) (2020). *Agromafie e caporalato—V Rapporto*. Futura-Ediesse.

Osservatorio Placido Rizzotto & FLAI-CGIL (Eds.) (2022). *Agromafie e caporalato—VI Rapporto*. Futura-Ediesse.

Palumbo, L. (2017). Exploiting for care: Trafficking and abuse in domestic work in Italy. Journal *of Immigration and Refugee Studies*, *15*(2), 171–186.

Palumbo, L. (2022a). Exploitation in the agri-food sector in Europe: A comparative analysis of the impact of migration and labour regimes in producing migrants' vulnerabilities. *European Journal of Migration and Law*, *24*(2), 287–312.

Palumbo, L. (2022b). Sfruttamento lavorativo e vulnerabilità in un'ottica di genere. Le condizioni di vita e di lavoro delle lavoratrici migranti nelle serre del Ragusano. *L'Altro Diritto Rivista*, *6*, 229–194.

Palumbo, L. (2023). Vulnerability to exploitation through the lens of intersectionality: A critical analysis of instruments and approaches to identify and support exploited and trafficked migrants seeking protection. *European Journal of Migration and Law*, *25*(4), 421–448.

Palumbo, L., & Sciurba, A. (2018). *The vulnerability to exploitation of women migrant workers in agriculture in the EU: The need for a human rights and gender based approach*. European Parliament Study, Policy Department for Citizens' Rights and Constitutional Affairs. European Union.

Palumbo, L., Corrado, A., & Triandafyllidou, A. (2022). Migrant labour in the agri-food system in Europe: Unpacking the social and legal factors of exploitation. *European Journal of Migration and Law*, *24*(2), 179–192.

Picchio, A. (1992). *Social reproduction. The political economy of the labour market*. Cambridge University Press,

Pieper, N., Segrave, M., & Moore, R. N. (2015). Editorial: What's in a name? Distinguishing forced labour, trafficking and slavery. *Anti-Trafficking Review*, *5*, 1–9.

Piro, V. (2021). *Migrant farmworkers in 'plastic factories'. Investigating work-life struggles*. Palgrave Macmillan.

Rodotà, S. (2012). *Il diritto di avere diritti*. Editori Laterza.

Rigo, E. (Ed.) (2015). *Leggi, migranti e caporali. Prospettive critiche e di ricerca sullo sfruttamento del lavoro in agricoltura*. Quaderni de L'Altro diritto, Pacini Giuridica.

Rigo, E. (2022). *La straniera. Migrazioni, asilo, sfruttamento in una prospettiva di genere*. Carocci Editori.

Rijken, C., & de Lange, T. (Eds.) (2018). *Towards a decent labour market for low waged migrant workers*. Amsterdam University Press.

Ruhs, M., & Anderson, B. (2013). Migrant workers: Inevitability or policy choice? In J. W. Holtslag, M. Kremer, & E. Schrijvers (Eds.), *Making Migration Work. The future of labour migration in the European Union* (pp. 69–82). Amsterdam University Press.

Sample, R. J. (2003). *Exploitation: what it is and why it's wrong*. Rowman & Littlefield.

Santoro, E. (2020). Vulnerability between political theory and normative texts: A new language to repeat old things or a new tool to problematize differences in social power? *Revista de Estudos Constitucionais, Hermenêutica e Teoria do Direito,* 12(3), pp. 311–334
Santoro, E. (2022) Lo sfruttamento lavorativo e la protezione delle sue vittime. In Centro studi e ricerche Idos (Ed.), *Dossier statistico immigrazione 2022* (pp. 284–290). Stampa.
Santoro, E. (2023), From 'refugeeization' of labour exploitation to debtbondage: Developing the subversive content of protecting the victims of exploitation. *Revista de Estudos Constitucionais, Hermenêutica e Teoria do Direito* (RECHTD), *15*(1), 2–21.
Schiek, D., Oliver, L., Forde, C., & Alberti, G. (2015). *EU social and labour rights and EU internal market law.* Study for the European Parliament's Committee on Employment Affairs, European Union.
Sciurba, A. (2015). Chi protegge il diritto d'asilo in Europa? Un confronto tra il recente orientamento giurisprudenziale della Corte di Strasburgo e la narrazione umanitaria delle politiche europee. In L. Zagato (Ed.), *Introduzione ai diritti di cittadinanza* (pp. 189–218). Libreria Editrice Cafoscarina.
Sciurba, A. (2021). *Le parole dell'asilo: un diritto di confine.* Giappichelli.
Shamir, H. (2012). A labour paradigm for human trafficking. *UCLA Law Review*, *60*, 76–136.
Siegmann, K. A., Quaedvlieg, J., & Williams, T. (2022). Migrant labour in Dutch agriculture: Regulated Precarity. *European Journal of Migration and Law*, *24*(2), 217–240.
Sigona, N., Kato, J., Kuznetsova, I. (2021). Migration infrastructures and the production of migrants' irregularity in Japan and the United Kingdom. *CMS*, *9*, 31.
Skrivankova, K. (2010). *Between decent work and forced labour: Examining the continuum of exploitation.* JRF programme paper: forced labour. Joseph Rowntree Foundation.
Stoyanova, V. (2016). *Human trafficking and slavery reconsidered. Conceptual limits and states' positive obligations in European law.* Cambridge University Press.
Triandafyllidou, A. (2022). *Migration and pandemic. Spaces of solidarity and spaces of exception.* Springer.
Triandafyllidou, A., & Marchetti, S. (2014). *Employers, agencies, and immigration: Paying for care.* Routledge.
Triandafyllidou, A., & Bartolini, L. (2020). Understanding irregularity. In S. Spencer, & A. Triandafyllidou (Eds.), *Migrants with irregular status in Europe* (pp. 11–31). IMISCOE Research Series. Springer.
UNODC. (2022). *Global report on trafficking in persons,* United Nations Office on Drugs and Crime.
Wagner, I. (2018). *Workers without borders: Posted work and precarity in the EU.* Cornell University Press.
Waite, L., Craig, G., Lewis, H., & Skrivankova, K. (Eds.) (2015). *Vulnerability, exploitation and migrants.* Palgrave Macmillan.
Waite, L., Lewis, H., Dwyer, P., & Hodkinson, S. (2015). Precarious lives: Refugees and Asylum seekers' resistance within unfree labouring. *ACME: An International Journal for Critical Geographies*, *14*(2), 479–491.
Weatherburn, A. (2021). *Labour exploitation in human trafficking law.* Intersentia.

Acknowledgements

This book would never have seen the light of day without the support, conversations, discussions, and meetings with numerous academics, scholars, colleagues, experts, and friends throughout the years of research and writing this manuscript. Here, I will mention some of them, knowing that the list of people to thank should undoubtedly be much longer. Certainly, any limitations, shortcomings, and errors in this book are to be attributed solely to me.

The first person I would like to thank is Anna Triandafyllidou, to whom I am infinitely grateful for her constant presence, support, encouragement, and trust. I truly thank her for involving me in different research activities at the European University Institute (EUI) between 2015 and 2019, providing me with the opportunity to engage in vibrant European and international research and academic contexts. Her innovative and brilliant perspective and insights have been a constant source of inspiration for my research.

I would like to thank Emilio Santoro for supporting and encouraging me throughout the research, and for having patiently read various drafts of this book. The stimulating discussions with him and his incisive and attentive suggestions have always given me food for thought. I thank him for consistently providing me with new perspectives to interpret social reality and strive to change it, integrating research with concrete field experience, with the aim of enhancing the effectiveness and the protection of the rights of marginalised people.

I would like to thank Sabrina Marchetti and Giulia Garofalo Geymonat, with whom I currently have the fortune to work at the Department of Philosophy and Cultural Heritage of Ca' Foscari University of Venice, for their always inspiring and helpful input, and for the time they spent reading and commenting on sections of this book with keen suggestions. I am particularly grateful to Sabrina Marchetti for her constant support, for her understanding throughout the writing process of this manuscript, for our enriching exchange of reflections and her ever-brilliant insights, which have been fundamental for the development of my research.

My sincere gratitude also goes to Antonello Miranda for involving me in his research group at the Department of Political Sciences and International Relations of the University of Palermo. I am extremely grateful for his unwavering commitment to reading and providing precious comments on my work, for his constructive and important advice and critiques, for his support and for guiding me into the field of comparative law.

In these years of research, I have had the fortune of sharing reflections and working with Maria Grazia Giammarinaro. In addition to the time she dedicated to reading and commenting on some drafts of the chapters, I am thankful for her valuable insights, analyses, and our fruitful exchange, which significantly shaped and contributed to development of my research. Her unique perspective and intuition have consistently prompted me to question and examine issues related to exploitation, vulnerability, and gender from different and always thrilling angles.

My deep gratitude also goes to Alessandra Sciurba because it is with her—and thanks to her—that I went to the greenhouses in Ragusa for the first time in 2014, to research the living and working conditions of women migrant farmworkers in that context. I am extremely grateful to Alessandra not just for her time dedicated to accurately reading and commenting on several sections of this book but also for her stimulating insights into migration and asylum issues as well as her perspective on law-related research as an important instrument for promoting social justice. Our continuous exchange, countless conversations, and friendship have always been a source of encouragement and strength.

I am also profoundly grateful to Alessandra Corrado, with whom I have had the opportunity to work on various research projects, exchanging ideas, and addressing challenges. I hugely thank Alessandra for reading and providing valuable feedback on the draft of this book, for our always inspiring discussions, and for her consistent presence and support as a colleague and friend.

Special thanks go to Marco Brigaglia for providing invaluable advice; his constant encouragement and accurate suggestions have helped me significantly to address several challenges throughout my research. I also express my heartfelt gratitude to Isabel Trujillo for her important support and our fruitful exchange since she supervised my doctoral research in Human Rights at the University of Palermo (2008–2012).

My gratitude goes also to Gabriella Alberti for having read and commented on some sections of the book and for her significant suggestions. I deeply thank her for the help and long-lasting friendship.

I am profoundly grateful to all the other academics and researchers with whom I have had the opportunity to discuss, from different perspectives, the topics addressed in my research in these years. Their essential insights greatly helped me in shaping and writing this book. Many thanks, among others, to Francesco Carchedi, Dany Carnassale, Francesco Caruso, Salvatore Casabona, Alberto Di Martino, Yasmine Ergas, Sheila Foster, Andrew Geddes, Andrea Iossa, Prabha Kotiswaran, Giulia Laganà, Luc Leboeuf, Martina Lo Cascio, Maria Rosaria Marella, Sandro Mezzadra, Martina Millefiorini, Michele Nori, Francesco Parisi, Manoela Patti, Alessandra Pera, Francesca Raimondo, Alexandra Ricard-Guay, Enrica Rigo, Serena Romano, Martin Ruhs, Jan Schneider, Karin Siegmann, Guido Smorto, and Maria (Milli) Virgilio.

I will never cease to say thank you to Diane Shugart and Nicholas Gledhill who accurately, patiently, and with high professionalism copyedited the book, providing me with constant assistance, understanding the difficulties, and continually encouraging me.

I express my sincere gratitude to Lucila Granada and Kate Roberts from Focus on Labour Exploitation (FLEX), Rita Gava and Avril Sharp from Kalayaan Justice for migrant domestic workers, and Robyn Phillips from Human Trafficking Foundation for the careful reading and comments of those sections of the book related to the UK context. I truly thank them for sharing their experience and for the insightful conversations on labour exploitation issues and relevant UK policies in this field. The exchange with other stakeholders and experts based in the UK—including Bev Clarkson from Unite the Union; Claire Falconer, former co-founder and Legal Director of FLEX; and Roger Plant, former head of the ILO Special action programme to combat forced labour—has also been crucial for the research for this book.

Many thanks to Maurizio Braglia and Cristina Falaschi from the project Oltre la Strada (Emilia Romagna Region); Francesca Nicodemi from the Association for Juridical Studies on Immigration (ASGI); Consuelo Bianchelli from la Casa delle donne per non subire la violenza in Bologna; Teresa Cecere, Grazia Moschetti, and Isabella Orfano from ActionAid Italy; Giuliana Mesina from the trade union FP-CGIL (previously from FILCAMS-CGIL); and Jean-Rene Bilongo, Raffaele Falcone, and Giovanni Mininni from the trade union FLAI-CGIL. I am grateful to all of them for the time they dedicated to me, sharing their different experiences in the field of labour exploitation in Italy and engaging in stimulating discussions.

Special thanks go to the community of experts, social workers, activists, and other stakeholders who have welcomed me in the context of Ragusa (Sicily), sharing their work, involving me in their activities, and trusting and supporting my research. In particular, I am deeply indebted, among others, to Giuseppe Scifo from the trade union CGIL; Ausilia Cosentini, Michele Mililli, Gina Scibilia, Massimo Scribano, and Ivana Tumino from the Proxima Cooperative; Vincenzo La Monica, Domenico Leggio, and Lucia Nicosia from the Caritas Diocesana-Ragusa; Andrea Gentile from the Diaconia Valdese Ragusa; and Francesca Commissari. Their remarkable work and steadfast commitment to bring changes to such a complex territory have given me invaluable insights into the structural dimension of labour exploitation and the complexity of the situations of vulnerability of migrant workers involved in these dynamics.

I would like to acknowledge the Horizon I-CLAIM project (GA No. 101094373) for hosting my research from September to December 2023. The research conducted for this book received funding also from the following projects: the Horizon 2020 VULNER project (GA No. 870845), from 2020 to 2022; two projects on labour exploitation funded by Open Society European Policy Institute (OSEPI), from 2018 to 2020, under the auspices of the EUI's Global Governance Program and Migration Policy Centre; the DemandAT project (GA No. FP7/612869/EU), from 2014 to 2015; and a post-doctoral research fellowship at the Department of

Political Science and International Relations of the University of Palermo, from 2013 to 2016.

I deeply thank all my friends for the encouragement, help, laughter, and understanding throughout every phase of my research and the book-writing process. Many thanks, in particular, to Elena Baglioni, Caterina Briguglia, Matteo Cavalleri, Pietro Denaro, Emilio Distretti, Chiara Pancaldi, Manoela Patti, Marianna Pino, Giulia Rodeschini, Maria Romano, Serena Romano, Maria Sammartano, Simona Valenza, and Elian Weizman. I am hugely thankful to my parents, Loredana and Giorgio, for their trust, love, help, and their extraordinary way of being grandparents. I truly thank my dad for always reading my work and providing invaluable and incisive suggestions. I am also grateful to my brothers, Enrico, Gabriele, Pietro and Stefano, my sister/cousin Letizia, my aunt Annamaria, my uncle Pietro, and all other family members, including Giuditta, Claudia, Fabiana, Lucia, Carlo, Marilia, and Ildo, for their constant support and presence. My endless gratitude goes to Alessandro and our daughter Rosa, who have patiently handled the rhythms and challenges of these years of research, consistently making me feel their love. I would never cease to thank Rosa for her big and comforting hugs.

My greatest thanks are reserved for the migrant workers, and particularly the women migrant workers, whom I met during the years of research for this book and who dedicated their time to conversing with me, challenging and shaping my thinking and perspectives. I thank all of them for sharing their stories, their living and working experiences, their situations of vulnerability, their strength and challenges, their strategies of resistance, and their visions for change. I will be forever grateful to them for this.

Contents

About the Author

Letizia Palumbo is a Researcher at Ca' Foscari University of Venice, Department of Philosophy and Cultural Heritage. She is currently working in the ambit of the Horizon I-Claim project 'Improving the living and labour conditions of irregularised migrant households in Europe' (GA: 101094373). Her research focus takes a socio-legal and gender perspective on migrant labour, exploitation, trafficking, women's rights, and migrant workers' rights, especially with regard to agricultural and domestic work sectors. Her work has been published in several peer-reviewed journals, papers, and reports. Dr Palumbo has served as a research consultant for NGOs and international and European organisations and institutions including the European Parliament, Council of Europe, Food and Agricultural Organisation (FAO), and International Labour Organization (ILO).

Chapter 1
Slavery, Forced Labour, and Trafficking

Labour exploitation is specifically addressed and defined in regional and national legal frameworks, including for instance EU and Italian legislation, but not clearly defined by any international legal instruments. However, the notion of labour exploitation is part of the international legal framework concerning offences such as 'forced labour', 'slavery', and 'trafficking'.

This chapter provides an overview of relevant international legal instruments concerning forced labour, slavery, and trafficking, and related definitions that have guided relevant policy and legislation on exploitation at the European and national levels. The two first sections focus on the notions of slavery and forced labour in international legal instruments, referring also to the understanding of these concepts in relevant cases of the European Court of Human Rights (ECtHR). The chapter then focuses on the legal definition of trafficking, closely tracing the main stages that marked the development of relevant international instruments on this issue. This specific attention on trafficking is due primarily to the fact that the internationally-agreed definition of trafficking, contained in the 2000 UN Protocol to Prevent, Suppress and Punish Trafficking in Persons, especially Women and Children (also known as the Palermo Protocol), provided—for the first time at international level—a broad notion of exploitation. Furthermore, in recent years the issue of trafficking for labour exploitation has achieved increasing attention at the global, European, and national levels. As a result, severe exploitation, such as forced labour and slavery, has tended to be conflated with trafficking, causing what has been defined as 'exploitation creep' (Chuang, 2017) to describe this trend of collapsing the meaning of trafficking into the element of purposes, namely exploitation in its extreme forms. The chapter concludes by highlighting the porous boundaries between legal notions of slavery, forced labour, and trafficking, and points to the need to also consider forms of exploitation that are less severe and do not amount to these specific crimes.

L. Palumbo, *Taking Vulnerabilities to Labour Exploitation Seriously*, IMISCOE Research Series, https://doi.org/10.1007/978-3-031-55424-7_1

1.1 Slavery and Similar Practices in the International Legal Framework

The prohibition of slavery in times of both peace and war is today unanimously considered to be customary rule of international law and has also achieved the level of peremptory norm of international law (*jus cogens* rules), as affirmed by international bodies.[1]

The international legal framework concerning slavery primarily consists of the 1926 League of Nations' Slavery, Servitude, Forced Labour and Similar Institutions and Practices Convention (known as the 'Slavery Convention') and the 1956 Supplementary Convention on the Abolition of Slavery, the Slave Trade, and Institutions and Practices Similar to Slavery—known as the 'Supplementary Slavery Convention'.[2] The 1926 Slavery Convention was the first treaty to address slavery and the slave trade. This Convention obliges states to abolish slavery in all its forms and defines slavery as 'the status or condition of a person over whom any or all of the powers attaching to the right of ownership are exercised' (Art. 1). The Convention also defines the slave trade as 'all acts involved in the capture, acquisition or disposal of a person with intent to reduce him to slavery; all acts involved in the acquisition of a slave with a view to selling or exchanging him; all acts of disposal by sale or exchange of a slave acquired with a view to being sold or exchanged, and, in general, every act of trade or transport in slaves' (Art. 1).

The Slavery Convention requires States Parties to abolish slavery 'progressively…in all its forms' and to 'prevent and suppress' the slave trade (Art. 2). Furthermore, it obliges States Parties to assist one another in securing the abolition of slavery and the slave trade (Art. 4); adopt laws and regulations giving effect to the purpose of the Convention; and introduce severe penalties for those who infringe these (Art. 6). However, while it calls for the abolition of slavery, the 1926 Convention does not contain any provisions concerning states' assistance and protection of the slaves. This is indeed left to individual states. Furthermore, the Convention did not create any body to assess and monitor the measures implemented by States Parties or compliance with the obligations set out in the Convention (Dottridge, 2017, p. 68).

The 1956 Supplementary Slavery Convention was adopted by the UN in the post-second world war period to address those abusive practices such as debt bondage and serfdom, 'facing developing and newly independent countries which were breaking free from colonialism and seeking to reform their agrarian and labour system accordingly' (Plant, 2017, p. 427). Though similar to slavery, these practices

[1] These include, for instance, the UN International Law Commission. See in this regard United Nations, 1963 and Bassiouni, 1999.

[2] It is also worth mentioning the 1953 Protocol 'Amending the Slavery Convention', 182 U.N.T.S. 51, entered into force 7 December 1953, which allowed the bodies of the UN, in particular the Secretariat of the UN and the International Court of Justice to acquire the duties and functions previously held by the organs of the League of Nations.

were not covered by the 1926 Convention, and the Supplementary Slavery Convention extended its reach to practices such as debt bondage, serfdom, servile forms of marriage, and child exploitation. In particular, Article 1 of the Convention affirms that States Parties shall 'take all practicable and necessary legislative and other measures to bring about progressively and as soon as possible the complete abolition or abandonment' of the aforementioned institutions and practices similar to slavery, 'where they still exist and whether or not they are covered by the definition of slavery contained in Article 1 of the Slavery Convention signed at Geneva on 25 September 1926'. Thus, if these practices and institutions manifest any or all the powers attached to the right of ownership they might amount to slavery. If they do not involve this element, they would be considered 'practices similar to slavery' under the 1956 Convention (Allain, 2008; Members of the Research Network on the Legal Parameters of Slavery, 2012).[3]

Article 1 of the Supplementary Slavery Convention goes on to define these practices and institutions similar to slavery:

(a) Debt bondage, that is to say, the status or condition arising from a pledge by a debtor of his personal services or of those of a person under his control as security for a debt, if the value of those services as reasonably assessed is not applied towards the liquidation of the debt or the length and nature of those services are not respectively limited and defined;
(b) Serfdom, that is to say, the condition or status of a tenant who is by law, custom, or agreement is bound to live and labour on land belonging to another person and to render some determinate service to such other person, whether for reward or not, and is not free to change his status;
(c) Any institution or practice whereby:
    (i) A woman, without the right to refuse, is promised or given in marriage on payment of a consideration in money or in kind to her parents, guardian, family, or any other person or group; or
    (ii) The husband of a woman, his family, or his clan, has the right to transfer her to another person for value received or otherwise; or
    (iii) A woman on the death of her husband is liable to be inherited by another person;
(d) Any institution or practice whereby a child or young person under the age of 18 years is delivered by either or both of his natural parents or by his guardian to another person, whether for reward or not, with a view to the exploitation of the child or young person or of his labour.

The persons subjected to any of the above-mentioned institutions or practices are referred to as persons having a 'servile status' (Art. 7 of the Supplementary Slavery Convention). Like the 1926 Slavery Convention, the Supplementary Slavery

[3] It must be noted that where these practices and institutions similar to slavery manifest powers attached to the right of ownership, they would be covered by both the 1926 Convention and the 1956 Supplementary Convention (Allain, 2008, p. 19).

Convention does not contain specific provisions regarding the states' assistance and protection of these victims but leaves such measures to the respective states' discretion.

The prohibition on holding a person in slavery, servitude, or forced labour is found in human rights law in Article 4 of the 1948 Universal Declaration of Human Rights, Article 8 of the 1966 International Covenant on Civil and Political Rights (ICCPR), and Article 11 of the 1990 International Convention on the Protection of the Rights of All Migrant Workers and Members of their Families (ICRMW). At the regional level, this prohibition is also included in the 1950 European Convention on Human Rights (ECHR) (Art. 4), the 2000 Charter of Fundamental Rights of the European Union (Art. 5), the 1969 American Convention on Human Rights (Art. 6), and the 2004 Arab Charter on Human Rights (Art. 10.1).

Slavery is also addressed in international criminal law. Article 7(2)(c) of the1998 Rome Statute of the International Criminal Court (ICC) defines enslavement identically to slavery in the 1926 Slavery Convention, with an additional reference to trafficking in human beings as the process that might lead to situations of enslavement. According to the Statute, if enslavement is committed as part of an intentional attack direct against civil population, it constitutes a crime against humanity.[4] The Elements of Crimes to the Rome Statute further elaborates that exercising any or all powers attaching to the right of ownership over one person includes:

> purchasing, selling, lending, or bartering such a person or persons, or by imposing on them a similar deprivation of liberty…It is understood that such deprivation of liberty may, in some circumstances, include exacting forced labour or otherwise reducing a person to a servile status as defined in the Supplementary Convention on the Abolition of Slavery, the Slave Trade, and Institutions and Practices Similar to Slavery of 1956. It is also understood that the conduct described in this element includes trafficking in persons, in particular women and children.

As Paulo Pinto de Albuquerque, former Judge of the European Court of Human Rights (ECtHR), has clearly underlined in his concurring opinion in the case *J. and Others v. Austria* (Application No. 58216/12, 17 January 2017), by comparing the concept of slavery set out in international law and the concept of enslavement in international criminal law, it emerges that the powers attaching to the right of ownership is the '*sine qua non* element' of the concept of slavery or enslavement in international law: 'both the de jure possession or the de facto exercise of these powers suffices to define the concept' (Ibid., para. 16).[5]

---

[4] Enslavement has also been identified as a crime against humanity in the statutes of some ad hoc tribunals, such as the 1945 Charter of the International Military Tribunal of Nuremberg (Art. 6(c)), the 1946 Charter of the International Military Tribunal for the Far East (Art. 5 (c)), the 1993–1994 Statutes of the International Criminal Tribunals for Ex-Yugoslavia and Rwanda (respectively Arts. 5(c) and 3(c)), the 2000 Statute of the Special Court for Sierra Leone (Art. 2(c)), and the 2003 UN-Cambodia Agreement Concerning the Prosecution of Crimes Committed during the Period of Democratic Kampuchea (Art. 9).

[5] See also United Nations Economic and Social Council, *Slavery, the slave trade and other forms of servitude*, Report of the Secretary-General, 27 January 1953, E/2357, p. 28.

While the notion of servitude is widely used in international human rights law and international human trafficking law, international law does not provide a definition. Nonetheless, today it is generally argued that, at the international level, servitude corresponds with the four institutions and practices prohibited by the 1956 Supplementary Slavery Convention, which—as mentioned above—identifies victims of 'practices similar to slavery' (debt bondage, serfdom, servile forms of marriage, and sale or adoption of children for exploitation) as 'persons of servile status'. As the Explanatory Report on the 2005 Council of Europe Trafficking Convention clarified, '[s]ervitude is to be regarded as a particular form of slavery, differing from it less in character than in degree. Although it constitutes a state or condition and is a "particularly serious form of denial of freedom"...it does not have the ownership features characteristic of slavery' (Council of Europe, 2005, p. 17).

Such an understanding of the relationship between slavery and servitude has been followed by the ECtHR, especially in its landmark judgment *Siliadin v. France* (Application No. 73316/01, 26 July 2005), concerning a case of forced labour and servitude in domestic work. This was the first decision where the Court ruled that there had been a violation of Article 4 of the ECHR. In *Siliadin*, the ECtHR identified a graduation between servitude and slavery, holding that 'servitude means an obligation to provide one's services that is imposed by the use of coercion, and is to be linked with the concept of "slavery"' (ibid., paras. 123–124). While finding that the applicant's treatment breached the prohibition of servitude, the Court stated that the deprivation of personal autonomy is not itself sufficient to amount to slavery according to the 1926 Slavery Convention, which refers to the 'classic meaning of slavery as it was practiced for centuries' (ibid., para. 122). In particular, the Court claimed that 'although the applicant was, in the instant case, clearly deprived of her personal autonomy, the evidence does not suggest that she was held in slavery in the proper sense, in other words that Mr and Mrs B. exercised a genuine right of legal ownership over her, thus reducing her to the status of an object' (para. 33). This ECtHR ruling has been criticised for suggesting a very narrow understanding of the 1926 definition of slavery as requiring the existence of a legal right to ownership over another person, while the Slavery Convention also includes the de facto condition of being subjected to the exercise of a power similar to ownership (Allain, 2013; Stoyanova, 2017b).

In *Rantsev v. Cyprus and Russia* (Application No. 25965/04, 7 January 2010) concerning a case of trafficking for sexual exploitation, the ECtHR diverged from the conception of slavery in its ruling on *Siliadin*. By referring to *Prosecutor v. Kunarac* et al. (Case No. IT-96-23-T & IT-96-23/1-T, 22 February 2001) before the International Criminal Tribunal for the former Yugoslavia (ICTY), the ECtHR underlined that the 'traditional concept of "slavery" has evolved to encompass various contemporary forms of slavery based on the exercise of any or all of the powers attaching to the right of ownership' (para. 280). In *Rantsev*, the Court importantly expanded the scope of the ECHR's Article 4, affirming that trafficking in human beings, being based on 'the exercise of powers attaching to the right of ownership' falls within the scope of this provision. The judges in Strasbourg did not provide a clear explanation about how trafficking falls within the meaning of Article 4.

Furthermore, in a certain sense, they overlapped the concepts of trafficking and slavery. However, the importance of this groundbreaking decision concerns the fact that by widening the scope of Article 4 to include trafficking, the ECtHR made a significant interpretative operation that is innovative with respect to the letter of the ECHR, which indeed does not refer to trafficking.

A further important contribution in the understanding of the concept of slavery has been provided by the Inter-American Court of Human Rights (IACtHR) in its 2016 decision in the case *Trabajadores de la Hacienda Brazil Verde vs Brazil* (Series C No. 318, 20 October 2016). The case concerned 85 workers at a privately-owned estate (including some minors) who claimed to be victims of slavery under Article 6 of the American Convention on Human Rights. The IACtHR found a breach of this article affirming that deception, fraud, control of movement, and physical and psychological forms of coercion against these workers in situations of vulnerability amounted to a 'situation of slavery' (*situación de esclavitud*), despite the fact that such a situation did not entail that victims could be regarded as being property *stricto sensu* of an owner (De Sena, 2019).

1.2 Forced Labour in the International Legal Framework

The 1930 Forced Labour Convention No. 29 and the 1957 Convention on the Abolition of Forced Labour N. 105 are the principal International Labour Organisation (ILO) instruments aimed at prohibiting and eliminating forced labour. As affirmed in the 1998 ILO Declaration on Fundamental Principles and Rights at Work (Art. 2), all ILO Member States have an obligation—even if they have not ratified these two ILO Conventions—to respect, promote, and realise the principle of the elimination of all forms of forced or compulsory labour.

The 1930 Forced Labour Convention No. 29 defined forced or compulsory labour as 'all work or service which exacted from any person under the menace of any penalty and for which the said person has not offered himself voluntarily' (Art. 2.1). This definition contains three key elements. The first refers to the expression 'work or service' through which the Convention means that forced labour includes any work, service, or employment occurring in any activity, industry, or sector and irrespective of the worker's employment status 'being in either a formal or informal employment relationship' (ILO, 2012a, p. 12). The second is the element of 'menace of any penalty', which indicates the wide range of coercive measures used to force someone to perform work or service. These include 'penal sanctions and various forms of direct and indirect coercion, such as physical violence, psychological threats, or the non-payment of wages' (ILO, 2016, p. 5). Finally, the third is the related element of 'offered voluntarily' through which the Convention refers to the free and informed consent of a person to enter into an employment relationship and their freedom to leave at any time (ILO, 2016). This means that even if a worker has accepted a job, their consent becomes irrelevant if forms of coercion or deception have been used (ILO, 2012a).[6] As Beate Andrees (2008, p. 2) noted, the 'key indicator to distinguish free from un-free labour is the possibility of the worker to always revoke a labour agreement without losing any rights or privileges. This could include the right to receive a promised wage'.

With the 1957 Convention on the Abolition of Forced Labour (N. 105)—which was adopted in the context of the Cold War when the international community paid increasing attention to the 'mass imposition of forced labour by states mainly for ideological and political purposes' (Plant, 2017, p. 427)—the ILO aimed primarily at addressing forced labour imposed by states as a means of political coercion, i.e., as a punitive mechanism as well as an exploitative practice. More precisely, the 1957 Convention called for the immediate and complete abolition of forced or compulsory labour as: (a) a means of political coercion or education or as a punishment for holding or expressing political views or views ideologically opposed to the established political, social, or economic system; (b) a method of mobilising and using labour for purposes of economic development; (c) a means of labour discipline; (d) a punishment for having participated in strikes; and (e) a means of racial, social, national or religious discrimination.

It is worth noting that while today the concept of forced labour concerns practices imposed by both state and non-state actors, in recent decades the ILO has mainly focused on the latter (Dottridge, 2017). Furthermore, since the second half of the twentieth century, the ILO has adopted a series of other Conventions that have consolidated a legal framework on forced labour, delineating the fundamental principles and rights at work and thus ensuring a decent work environment (Andrees & Aikman, 2017).[7]

The ILO Domestic Workers Convention No. 189 and Recommendation No. 201, adopted in 2011, strengthened this legal framework by introducing important standards for the protection of the rights of domestic workers. Furthermore, in 2014, the ILO introduced the Protocol to the 1930 Forced Labour Convention N. 29 (ILO, 2014) and Forced Labour (Supplementary Measures) Recommendation N. 203[8] to bolster ILO standards against forced labour and address gaps in the 1930 Forced Labour Convention, which—adopted decades before the UN's two human rights

[6] The 1930 Convention provides for certain exceptions that do not constitute forced labour, including: work exacted under compulsory military service for the necessity of national defence; prison labour after conviction in a court of law and carried out under the control of a public authority; and work in cases of emergency such as war or other calamities (Art. 2.2).

[7] These Conventions include, for instance: the 1948 Freedom of Association and Protection of the Right to Organise Convention No. 87; the 1949 Right to Organise and Collective Bargaining Convention No. 98; the 1973 Minimum Age Convention No. 138; the 1951 Equal Remuneration Convention, No. 100; the 1958 Discrimination (Employment and Occupation) Convention, No. 111; the 1999 Worst Forms of Child Labour Convention No. 182. With regard to migrant workers' rights, it is worth mentioning, among others, the 1990 International Convention on the Protection of the Rights of All Migrant Workers and Members of their Families (ICRMW).

[8] The Recommendation is non-binding and builds on the Protocol's provisions, thus these instruments should be read in conjunction.

covenants[9]—lacks provisions to protect victims and their human rights. By addressing this shortcoming, the 2014 ILO Protocol has firmly situated forced labour within a human rights framework, explicitly recognising that 'forced or compulsory labour violates the human rights and dignity of millions of women and men, girls and boys'.[10] Far from solely focusing on repressive measures, both instruments – the 2014 ILO Protocol and Recommendation No. 203 – identify prevention, protection of victims, and remedies as essential actions in addressing forced labour (Andrees & Aikman, 2017; Swepston, 2017).

The 2014 ILO Protocol reaffirms the definition of forced labour set out in the 1930 Forced Labour Convention. Furthermore, the Protocol highlights the link between forced labour and trafficking in all its forms, affirming that 'the context and forms of forced or compulsory labour have changed and trafficking in persons for the purposes of forced or compulsory labour, which may involve sexual exploitation, is the subject of growing international concern' (ILO, 2014).

As discussed below in Sect. 1.4, the ILO has not been clear on the essential differences between the concepts of forced labour and trafficking, sometimes suggesting that trafficking is a subset of forced labour, other times the reverse (ILO, 2005, 2007). Beyond this debate, however, it should be noted that, as underlined by Judge Pinto de Albuquerque, according to the ILO, a forced labour situation is determined by the nature of the relationship between a worker and the 'employer' and 'not by the type of activity performed, the legality or illegality of the activity under national law, nor its recognition as an "economic activity"' (Pinto de Albuquerque concurring opinion in *J. and Others v. Austria* (cited above, para 9)). The exaction of labour under the threat of a penalty—which includes various forms of direct and indirect coercion—is the distinguishing feature of a worker/employer relationship in a forced labour situation (ibid.). In this light, forced labour also includes, as the ILO has explicitly affirmed (ILO, 2007, p. 42), forced begging, forced criminal activity, coercive sexual exploitation, and forced prostitution. On the other hand, as the ILO has also underlined, the mere failure to respect labour laws and working conditions (such as the failure to pay a worker the statutory minimum wage) does not in itself constitute forced labour (ILO, 2005, p. 19).

It is worth noting that the ECtHR has gradually developed a growing body of case law on forced labour, taking the definition set out in the 1930 Forced Labour Convention as 'a starting point' (Van der Mussele v. Belgium, Application No. 8919/80, 23 November 1983, para. 32) for its interpretation of Article 4(2) of the ECHR prohibiting forced labour. Especially on 'the menace of any penalty' in the

---

[9] The 1996 International Covenant on Economic Social and Cultural Rights (ICESCR), and the 1966 International Covenant on Civil and Political Rights (ICCPR).

[10] Importantly, the 2014 ILO Protocol explicitly and formally abolished the so-called transitional proposals contained in the 1930 ILO Convention (Art. 1, paras 2 and 3, and Arts. 3 to 24), which provided for the limited use of forced labour, subject to certain regulations, as a transitional measure only. Indeed, the original aim of the 1930 Forced Labour Convention was to progressively abolish forced labour in colonial territories while immediately prohibiting forced labour for private purposes.

definition of forced labour, in the domestic servitude case *C.N. and V. v. France* (Application No. 67724/09, 11 October 2012), the Court took a broad approach in line with that followed by ILO in its global report *The Cost of Coercion* (ILO, 2009). In particular, the Court held that '"penalty" may go as far as physical violence or restraint, but can also take subtler forms, of a psychological nature, such as threats to denounce victims to the police or immigration authorities when their employment status is illegal' (ibid., para. 77). The ECtHR took a similar view in other relevant cases, notably *Chowdury and Others v. Greece* (Application No. 21884/15, 30 March 2017), in which the judges in Strasbourg focused on the threats related to the condition of irregularity of the migrant workers. The ECtHR's judgment in *Tibet Menteş and Others v. Turkey* (Applications Nos. 57818/10 and 4 others, 24 October 2018) further clarified the contours of 'the menace of any penalty' element. The *Tibet Menteş* case concerned some airport shop workers' claims that their unpaid overtime amounted to forced and compulsory labour in breach of ECHR Article 4. The Court highlighted that the applicants agreed to their working conditions willingly, including the work and rest cycle arrangement at the workplace, and there was no indication of any forms of physical or mental coercion. In particular, the judges affirmed that in the absence of any sort of physical or mental coercion, the mere possibility that the applicants could be dismissed in the event of refusal to work overtime did not correspond to the 'menace of any penalty' within the meaning of Article 4 (para. 68).

On the element of 'involuntariness' in the definition of forced labour, the ECtHR has not given decisive weight to the applicant's prior consent to the work or service required to be performed (*Van der Mussele v. Belgium,* cited above, para. 36). Rather, the Court has considered it necessary to examine all the circumstances of the case when determining whether tasks required to be performed fall within the prohibition of 'forced labour or compulsory labour' according to Article 4. This approach has been recently confirmed in *Chowdury and Others v. Greece*, where the Court for the first time applied Article 4(2) of the ECHR to a case of forced labour involving undocumented migrant farmworkers. The Court stressed the issue of voluntariness and consent to exploitation, affirming that, where employers abuse their power or take advantage of workers' vulnerability to exploit them, the latter 'do not offer themselves for work voluntarily' (para 96). In its reasoning, the Court focused on the factors creating the applicants' situations of vulnerability (see Chap. 2) and ruled that their working conditions amounted to human trafficking and forced labour. In this regard, the judges of Strasbourg specified that 'exploitation of labour is one of the forms of exploitation in the definition of trafficking in human beings, which highlights the intrinsic relationship between forced and compulsory labour and trafficking in human beings' (*Chowdury and Others v. Greece,* cited above, para. 93). The ECtHR stressed that, in contrast to servitude, to qualify abuse as forced labour it is not necessary that the victim lives in a 'state of exclusion from the outside world' without any possibility of freely moving and leaving the employment (ibid., para. 99).

Chowdury and Others v. Greece is a landmark in the case law under Article 4 of the ECHR. The ruling contributed to clarifying that the concept of forced labour covers various forms of severe working conditions; the consent of the victims to exploitation is irrelevant; the irregularity of legal status is a crucial factor to take into account when assessing cases of exploitation; and, that a person might be held in forced labour even if not subjected to any form of deprivation of freedom of movement. In this light, as legal scholar Vladislava Stoyanova (2018, p. 2) has emphasised, 'the definitional clarifications offered in the judgment are of importance not only for the future case law in this area, but also for the national legislation of the Council of Europe (CoE) states'. These include, for instance, the 2015 United Kingdom Modern Slavery Act, which does not define the elements of slavery, servitude, and forced labour, and instead refers to Article 4 of the ECHR (see Chap. 8).

1.3 Trafficking in Persons in the International Legal Framework

This section focuses on the legal definition of trafficking. It looks at the development of relevant international legal frameworks and related definitions and understandings of trafficking associated to the main legal instruments. As highlighted above, this chapter pays special attention to the legal conception of trafficking because the international agreed definition offered by the 2000 UN Palermo Protocol on trafficking contained, for the first time at the international level, the reference to a broad notion of exploitation. At the same time, in recent years there has been increasing institutional attention—at global, European, and national levels—to the issue of trafficking (Kotiswaran, 2017). As a result, there has been a tendency to merge the notion of trafficking with that of exploitation, with problematic consequences as discussed in Chap. 2.

1.3.1 Trafficking Conflated into Prostitution

Human trafficking has been addressed as an offence in international law since the early 1900s. However, the first international treaties did not use the term trafficking but 'White slavery' and conflated it with prostitution.[11] The term 'white slavery' was used by the so-called abolitionist movement in their campaigns to eradicate all

[11] The term 'White slavery' was originally adopted by activists as a powerful metaphor to indicate White workers' oppression in England (Roediger, 1991). Following the passage of the Factories Act (1847), also known as the Ten Hours Act because it limited the working hours of women and young persons (aged 13–18) in British factories to roughly 10 h per day, the term 'white slavery' was more narrowly invoked by nineteenth-century 'abolitionist' feminists in their campaign to eradicate all forms of prostitution.

forms of prostitution, whether licensed or unlicensed[12] (Nadelmann, 1990, p. 513). From this perspective, the abolitionist movement also focused on the phenomenon of trafficking of White women from Europe and North America for the purpose of prostitution in the colonial nether regions in Asia, Africa, and South America (Chuang, 2010, p. 1667; Otto, 2006).

Although the 'White slavery' phenomenon was probably 'smaller than popularly depicted' (Nadelmann, 1990, p. 514; see also Guy, 1992),[13] it soon became an object of international treaty-making: the 1904 International Agreement for the Suppression of the White Slave Traffic and the 1910 International Convention for the Suppression of White Slave Traffic. The Conventions were 'limited to the process of recruitment and transportation and did not address the end purposes of trafficking' (Chuang, 1998, pp. 74–75), which was considered a matter of domestic jurisdiction.

As feminist scholars have critically pointed out, the metaphor of 'White slavery', on the one hand, spread the image of the prostitute as a 'woman in chains', leaving no room for voluntary prostitution (Doezema, 2000). On the other hand, the focus on the 'Whiteness' of the victims reflected a Eurocentric approach in most of the abolitionist perspectives on prostitution and trafficking.[14] Feminist scholar Jo Doezema (2000, p. 23) argued that '[t]he narratives of "white slavery" become something other than factual accounts of women's experiences: "white slavery" becomes a metaphor for a number of fears and anxieties in turn of the century European and American society'. The fears and anxieties were about both women's bodies and sexual relationships, as well as the loss of national identity through 'foreigners'—fears and anxieties that were, and still are, strongly intertwined (Yuval-Davis, 1997).

The term 'White slavery' was subsequently replaced in international law documents and discourse with the 'colour-blind' notion of 'traffic of women and children' (Demleitner, 1994). Specifically, under the auspices of the League of Nations, the 1921 International Convention for the Suppression of the Traffic in Women and Children and the 1933 International Convention for the Suppression of the Traffic in Women of Full Age were adopted. The focus was on sexual exploitation; the 1933 Convention, for instance, expanded the scope of trafficking to 'immoral purposes'. However, none of these Conventions contained a definition of trafficking.

The early conventions on trafficking were consolidated in the 1949 UN Convention for the Suppression of the Traffic in Persons and of the Exploitation of the Prostitution of Others, which was the first international treaty to adopt a more gender-neutral approach to trafficking as applying to both women and men. The

[12] In England, the campaigns against 'white slavery' culminated in a rally in London in 1885, which led to the immediate adoption of the Criminal Law Amendment Act (Lammasniemi, 2017).

[13] According to the research of feminist historian Ruth Rosen (1982), 'White slavery' accounted for not more than 10% of all prostitution.

[14] For instance, as feminist historian Donna Guy (1992) illustrated, nineteenth-century abolitionist campaigns against the 'White slave trade' from Britain to Argentina were not concerned about the situation of native-born prostitutes.

1949 Convention requires States Parties to punish 'any person who, to gratify the passions of another: (1) procures, entices or leads away, for the purpose of prostitution, another person, even with the consent of that person; (2) exploits the prostitution of another person, even with the consent of that person'. This offence shall not need to be transnational, but it can be cross-border or internal within one country. The Convention also requires States Parties to punish any person who 'keeps or manages, or knowingly finances or takes part in the financing of a brothel; knowingly lets or rents a building or other place or any part thereof for the purpose of the prostitution of others' (Art. 2).

It is worth underlining that the 1949 Convention does not define trafficking. Yet, trafficking is conceived as an offence necessarily linked to prostitution, overlooking therefore that it also occurs for purposes other than sexual exploitation. Significantly, the 1949 Convention criminalises the 'exploitation of prostitution' and does not criminalise or prohibit prostitution *per se*. However, the document does not provide a definition of 'exploitation'; nor does it clarify any distinction between 'forced' and 'voluntary prostitution'. Rather, it has an ambivalent approach to prostitution: while its title refers to 'exploitation of prostitution', the text tends to speak only of prostitution (Demleitner, 1994). Moreover, its preamble reveals a moral and non-neutral stance of the Convention to prostitution by declaring that 'prostitution and the accompanying evil of the traffic for the purpose of prostitution are incompatible with the dignity and worth of the human person and endanger(ed) the welfare of the individual, the family and the community'. As Anne Gallagher (2010, p. 59) notes, this ambiguous approach to prostitution was 'no doubt an attempt to forge consensus between those countries that outlawed prostitution and those that tolerated it under certain conditions, thereby ensuring the widest possible ratification'.

In general, the 1949 Convention has been the object of critiques by scholars and experts for failing to take a solid rights-based approach and for stigmatising trafficked persons, especially women. As the UN Special Rapporteur on Violence against Women significantly pointed out in 2000:

> The 1949 Convention has proved ineffective in protecting the rights of trafficked women and combating trafficking. The Convention does not take a human rights approach. It does not regard women as independent actors endowed with rights and reason; rather, the Convention views them as vulnerable beings in need of protection from the 'evils of prostitution' (Coomaraswamy, 2000).

1.3.2 Trafficking as a Form of Gender-Based Violence

Combatting trafficking began to emerge in the late 1970s in the context of the UN actions to address violence against women. The adoption of this new framework must be considered in the light of the UN's engagement to specifically address women's related issues and gender equality.[15] A milestone in this period was the adoption by the Convention on the Elimination of All Forms of Discrimination Against Women (CEDAW) by the UN General Assembly in 1979. The 30 Articles of this wide-ranging document establish detailed norms on matters of equality and opportunity, bringing 'together, in a comprehensive, legally binding form, internationally accepted principles on the rights of women' (Boutros-Ghali, 1995, p. 41). Yet, the Convention does not mention rape, domestic or sexual abuse, or any other instance of violence against women (Keck & Sikkink, 1998). The only exception is Article 6, which requires States Parties to take all 'appropriate measures including legislation, to suppress all forms of traffic in women and exploitation of prostitution of women'. Like the 1949 Convention on trafficking, the CEDAW does not define either the notion of traffic/trafficking or that of 'exploitation of prostitution'. But, unlike the 1949 Convention, the CEDAW refers to 'all forms of traffic', seeming to suggest that it also covers trafficking for purposes other than for sex work. However, from a review of the *travaux preparatories*, it emerges that the drafters of the Convention aimed to address primarily trafficking for sex work (Chuang, 2011).

Nonetheless, the CEDAW Committee has supported a broader conception of trafficking than that conceived by the drafters of the CEDAW (ibid.). The CEDAW Committee's General Recommendation No. 19 of 1992 recognises trafficking as a form of gender-based violence that 'impairs or nullifies the enjoyment by women of human rights and fundamental freedoms' including, amongst others, the right to life, the right to liberty and security of person, the right to equal protection under the law; the right to equality in the family; the right to the highest standard attainable of physical and mental health; the right to just and favourable conditions of work (para. 7).[16] The document explicitly affirms that forms of trafficking also involve sex tourism, domestic labour, and organised marriages.

In line with Recommendation No. 19 of 1992, other UN documents on gender violence, in particular the 1993 UN Declaration on the Elimination of Violence against Women and the 1995 UN Beijing Declaration and Platform for Action, identified trafficking as a form of gender-based violence. This framework has been successively confirmed in the 2011 Council of Europe Convention on Preventing and Combating Violence Against Women and Domestic Violence, known as the Istanbul Convention. This Convention represents the most far-reaching international legal instrument that tackles violence against women from a holistic approach, recognising its structural nature and indirectly addressing trafficking through its comprehensive perspective on violence against women (De Vido, 2016; Niemi et al., 2020).

[15] Since 1975, the UN has organised three World Conferences—in Mexico City (International Women's Year, 1975), Copenhagen (1980), and Nairobi (1985)—that spanned the UN Decade for Women and served as locations to build and connect an international network of women's rights and as a forum for drawing attention to key women's issues, including trafficking (Miller, 2004).

[16] General Recommendation No. 19 defines 'gender-based violence' as 'violence that is directed against a woman because she is a woman or that affects women disproportionately'. It includes acts that inflict physical, mental, or sexual harm or suffering, threats of such acts, coercion and other deprivations of liberty" (para. 6).

As feminist scholars have underlined, the thematic of violence against women has played a crucial role in building alliances between women globally. This has contributed to bring gender-based violence—including trafficking framed as a form of gender violence—to the fore and into the human rights discourse and shed light on its systemic character (Miller, 2004; Giammarinaro, 2022). On the other hand, as critical legal feminist scholars and postcolonial feminist scholars have pointed out (Kapur, 2002; Halley et al., 2006; Munro, 2013), so-called radical or structuralist feminist theories on violence against women—for instance, legal scholar Catharine Mackinnon's analysis (Mackinnon & Dworkin, 1988)—has had controversial impact on the conceptualisation and understanding of issues such as trafficking and exploitation. Indeed, although radical feminist theories have brough to light the structural dimension of gender-based violence and power relationships, they also have supported an extensive use of the notion of violence, that, for instance, comes to embrace all forms of sexual labour and prostitution. Simultaneously, they have tended to depict women as perpetually victimised and subordinated, conveying gendered and cultural stereotypes discourses (Kapur, 2002), representing women as inherently vulnerable and without agency, and 'flattening important distinctions in the grades and modalities of victimisation that might be encountered by different women at different times...and in different contexts' (Munro, 2013, p. 238). This narrative, in turn, has served for supporting the use of a repressive and carceral apparatus as the main approach to addressed gender-based violence (Bullimer, 2008), regardless of the wishes of victims and the impact that these interventions may have on them (Munro, 2013, p. 243; see also Hoyle & Sanders, 2000).

At the same time, this controversial narrative supported by radical/structuralist feminists has fostered a misleading understanding of trafficking (Chuang, 2010). In line with the restrictive approach of the 1949 Convention on trafficking, this has tended to conflate trafficking with prostitution/sex work, which is always considered as a form of violence, and primarily depicted in terms of personal-level coercion and abuse by traffickers/abusers, thereby mainly supporting criminalisation measures without addressing the root causes of dynamics of exploitation (Aradau, 2008; Andrijasevic, 2010). This controversial approach is the basis of the so-called neo-abolitionist approach to prostitution/sex work and trafficking that affected the UN negotiations for the 2000 Protocol on trafficking (Chuang, 2010) and still significantly impacts international, European, and national policies on trafficking and prostitution/sex work (Kotiswaran, 2017; Rubio Grundell, 2023; see Chap. 4).

Nevertheless, the gender-based violence approach supported by the above-mentioned international instruments represents a fundamental tool to address women's vulnerabilities and their systemic dimensions. Importantly, for instance, the 1993 Declaration on the Elimination of Violence against Women recognised violence against women as a 'violation of the rights and fundamental freedoms of women' and as 'a manifestation of historically unequal power relations between men and women, which have led to domination over and discrimination against women' (Premable). Along this perspective, trafficking is therefore considered a form of systemic gender-based violence.

1.3.3 Trafficking as a Problem of Irregular Migration and Organised Crime

Trafficking has drawn increasing political attention at the national and international levels since the 1990s due to the focus by the women's rights movement on violence against women and female exploitation and global concern over HIV/AIDS transmission through migration, in particular sex workers (Wijers & Lap-Chew, 1999). In this context, feminist activists and neo-abolitionist organisations have been crucial in defining the parameters and issues in the discourse (Chuang, 2010).

At the same time, as a result of extensive liberalisation of financial and labour markets in the developed countries and a rise in international migration, trafficking became part of the debate on stemming irregular migration of persons to be employed at lower and often unregulated sectors of labour markets (Aradau, 2008; Gallagher, 2010; Plant, 2017). In particular, in Europe, attention to trafficking was fostered by a significant increase in number of women migrating from the countries of central and eastern Europe to west European countries, and mainly employed in sex work or domestic/care work (Vianello, 2019; Andrijesevic, 2010; Parrenas, 2001; Hochschild, 2002). As feminist scholars have highlighted, similarly to the era of the 'White slavery', the female migration of the 1990s tended to be viewed in dominant discourse only in terms of dangers and risks, portraying women, together with children, as potential victims of trafficking and organised crime groups (Doezema, 2000; Gallagher, 2010).[17]

In this context, growing concern regarding trafficking as an irregular migration and border-security issue—which, as discussed in later chapters, continues to be a dominant frame in European and national policies on migration and trafficking—became intertwined with the perceived threat posed by criminal groups organising irregular migration movements in both sender and destination countries (ICMPD, 1999; Plant, 2017).[18] In 1994, the UN General Assembly, in its Resolution on trafficking in women and girls, condemned the

> the illicit and clandestine movement of persons across national and international borders, largely from developing countries and some countries with economies in transition, with the end goal of forcing women and girl children into sexually or economically oppressive and exploitative situations, for the profit of recruiters, traffickers and crime syndicates, as well as other illegal activities related to trafficking, such as forced domestic labour, false marriages, clandestine employment and false adoption.

Although the focus was on women and children, this Resolution revealed the shift to attention on trafficking in sectors other than sex industry. As the UN Secretary General's 1995 report noted, trafficking started to be addressed in terms of: '(a) its human rights dimension, including as discrimination against women and violence

[17] Traffic in women and girls: resolution/ adopted by the General Assembly UN General Assembly (49th sess.: 1994–1995).

[18] UN Secretary-General (1996).

against women; (b) migration and its regulation; (c) crime prevention; and (d) social services'.[19] There clearly emerged the need for an internationally-agreed definition of trafficking that grasped and delineated the nature and the scope of an evolving phenomenon with a complex framework involving diverse and interrelated issues.

1.3.4 The Broad Legal Conception of Trafficking in the UN Palermo Protocol

The above illustrates how the relevant international framework and approaches on trafficking developed. It provides a picture of some of the main competing issues and frames related to trafficking in persons, as well as the background against which the UN Protocol to Prevent, Suppress and Punish Trafficking in Persons, especially Women and Children—known as the Palermo Protocol—was drafted. This overview helps us to understand the inherent tensions within the Protocol and their impact on relevant European and national policies and legislation on trafficking.

It is worth mentioning that the UN's efforts to adopt a proposal for an international convention on transnational organised crime dates back to the mid-1990s. In parallel, trafficking was also addressed at the regional level. For instance, in 1997 the Council of the European Union issued a Joint Action on trafficking, focusing on sexual exploitation.[20] In October 2000, the US adopted the Trafficking Victims Protection Act (TVPA) containing a gender-neutral and broad definition of trafficking, which was in part reflected in the wording of the definition of this offence introduced successively by the Palermo Protocol (Gallagher, 2010, p. 22).

The Palermo Protocol supplemented the *UN Convention Against Transnational Organised Crime*,[21] entering into force in 2003. It was adopted in 2000 after long and intense negotiations—the 'Vienna Process'—involving government and UN officials as well as NGO lobbyists representing feminist stances (Chuang, 2010). The Protocol was agreed in the framework of the fight against transnational organised crime, and trafficking was mainly conceived as a problem of (irregular) migration (Scarpa, 2018, p. 27). Focused on whether trafficking should be defined by the nature of the work involved or by the use of coercion or deception or both, the discussion largely became a battlefield for the prostitution-as-violence versus prostitution-as-work debate (Ditmore & Wijers, 2003). One bloc, led by the Coalition Against Trafficking in Persons (CATW), advocated the neo-abolitionist approach that trafficking concerned both 'consensual' and 'forced'/non-consensual prostitution, questioning the 'false' distinction between 'forced' and 'voluntary

[19] UN General Assembly, Traffic in Women and Girls: Report of the Secretary-General, UN Doc. A/50/369, 24 August 1995, para. 45.

[20] It is worth also mentioning the 1994 Inter-American Convention on International Traffic in Minors.

[21] The United Nations Convention against Transnational Organised Crime, adopted by General Assembly resolution 55/25 of 15 November 2000.

prostitution' (Chuang, 2010). Opposite this, the International Human Rights Caucus—an alliance of human rights, anti-trafficking, and sex workers' rights activists—argued that prostitution is a job and supported a definition of trafficking that could not be used to obstruct or penalise consensual sex work. The Caucus advocated for a broad and inclusive definition covering different ambits and focusing on the use of deceptive or coercive means or purposes rather than on the nature of work (Ditmore & Wijers, 2003, p. 82). This position was also supported by UN Office of the High Commissioner for Human Rights (UNOHCHR), the ILO, and UNICEF (Ditmore & Wijers, 2003).

Finally, after prolonged debate, trafficking was defined in Art. 3 of the Protocol as

(a) 'Trafficking in persons' shall mean the recruitment, transportation, transfer, harbouring or receipt of persons, by means of the threat or use of force or other forms of coercion, of abduction, of fraud, of deception, of the abuse of power or of a position of vulnerability or of the giving or receiving of payments or benefits to achieve the consent of a person having control over another person, for the purpose of exploitation. Exploitation shall include, at a minimum, the exploitation of the prostitution of others or other forms of sexual exploitation, forced labour or services, slavery or practices similar to slavery, servitude or the removal of organs;
(b) The consent of a victim of trafficking in persons to the intended exploitation set forth in subparagraph (a) of this article shall be irrelevant where any of the means set forth in subparagraph (a) have been used.

According to this definition, trafficking consists of three structural components: the act required for trafficking (e.g. recruitment, transportation, transfer, harbouring, or receipt of persons); the means by which it is obtained (e.g. threat or use of force or other forms of coercion, the abuse of power or of a position of vulnerability, and so on.); and, the purpose, namely exploitation. The presence of these three elements is necessary to constitute a situation of trafficking; the only exception is when children are victims, when the 'means' requirement does not apply (Art. 3 [c, d]).

This definition was viewed as a compromise; the use of terms such as 'the abuse of a position of vulnerability' and related 'irrelevance of the consent' represented a way to respond to different and opposing views (Jordan, 2002). Neo-abolitionists emphasised the inclusion of these elements to point out that all migration for sex work is in the framework of trafficking. They also considered the inclusion of terms evoking the 1949 Trafficking Convention such as 'sexual exploitation' and 'exploitation of prostitution others' as acknowledging the strong correlation between trafficking and exploitation of prostitution (Chuang, 2010, p. 1676; Raymond, 2001, p. 5). Conversely, non-abolitionist groups saw the inclusion of the coercion requirement as highlighting the exclusion of consensual migration for sex work from the definition of trafficking. They argued that the element of the irrelevance of consent was introduced to avoid that the victim's consent could be used by traffickers to escape punishment (Chuang, 2010). Furthermore, they stressed that the terms 'exploitation of prostitution of others' and 'sexual exploitation'—which are not defined anywhere else in international law—were left undefined to allow all governments to sign the Palermo Protocol 'including countries that have laws criminalising adult sex work and countries that have laws decriminalising and/or regulating adult sex work' (Jordan, 2002, p. 9).

Marking an important change with respect to the earlier international agreements, the Protocol provided a broad and comprehensive definition of trafficking that is gender-neutral ('persons'), refers to victims irrespective of their legal status (undocumented or documented migrants, as well as citizens), and encompasses different forms of exploitation, including forced labour or services, slavery, or practices similar to slavery. In this regard, the Protocol is a key shift in the frame of the notion of exploitation, which ceases to be linked only to the sexual dimension and refers instead to a wide range of exploitative practices (see Chap. 2). Moreover, as already highlighted above, the Protocol affirms the irrelevance of the victims' consent to exploitation where any of the above-mentioned means have been used (Art. 3(b)).

The Palermo Protocol, therefore, provided the first internationally agreed-upon definition of trafficking, which was then integrated into regional and national legal frameworks in the field. For instance, this definition has been successively incorporated in the 2005 Council of Europe Convention on Action against trafficking in human beings (hereafter Council of Europe Convention on Trafficking), and in EU Directive 2011/36 on 'preventing and combatting trafficking in human beings and protecting its victims', which made some important additions with respect to the illicit purposes, by explicitly including 'begging' and 'exploitation of criminal activities', bringing, therefore, the attention to new forms of trafficking (Giammarinaro, 2012, p. 21).

It is worth mentioning that according to Art. 1 of the Palermo Protocol, its provisions shall be interpreted together with the UN Convention against Transnational Organised Crime. This has spurred debate about whether the Protocol requires States Parties to collaborate against trafficking only in situations involving a transnational movement or a criminal organisation or both. However, as the UNODC clarified in its 2004 Legislative Guide, the offence of trafficking 'shall be established in the domestic law of each State Party, independently of the transnational nature or the involvement of an organised criminal group' (UNODC, 2004). This has been successively confirmed by the 2005 Council of Europe Convention on Trafficking, which expressively recognises that the definition of trafficking covers both internal and cross-border trafficking (Art. 2). The notion of 'internal trafficking' has since also been explicitly adopted by the UNODC in several of its official documents, affirming that the Palermo Protocol's definition of trafficking encompasses both trafficking across the borders and within a country (UNODC, 2018, 2020).

The Palermo Protocol has undoubtedly contributed to an advance in the understanding of a complex phenomenon such as trafficking and provided a broad and more structured definition covering multiple forms of exploitation. At the same time, this has led to harmonisation of national legislation and enabled a 'dialogue' among States Parties. However, several studies highlighted how its interpretation remains contentious and often occurs in restrictive terms, especially at the national level (UNODC, 2012; Scarpa, 2013; Kotiswaran, 2017; Weatherburn, 2021). Such a narrow approach to what constitutes trafficking is somewhat paradoxical given the broad scope of its definition, which aims to address evolving and contemporary forms of exploitation that could be not addressed by the UN Conventions on slavery or the ILO Convention on forced labour. The UNODC has underlined that one of the main causes of this restrictive approach to the definition of trafficking concerns the level of vagueness of key aspects, such as the concepts of vulnerability and the irrelevance of the consent and exploitation (UNODC, 2013, 2018, 2020). This helps foster hesitancy in authorities and practitioners evaluating cases of trafficking, with the consequent focusing, for instance, on vitiated consent and emphasis on the movement element rather than on exploitation (Gallagher, 2017, p. 105). As several reports and studies have underlined, such restrictive interpretations of trafficking's definition results in widespread impunity as well as denial of victims' rights and justice for them (see, for instance, Gallagher, 2017; Giammarinaro, 2020).

Another salient point is that Part II of the Palermo Protocol contains some provisions concerning the protection and support of victims. However, there are only very few obligations for states, which are left to decide if and how to address the assistance and protection of victims (Jordan, 2002). Indeed, being part of a wider UN instrument on Transnational Organised Crime, the Protocol constitutes primarily a transnational criminal law treaty. It is therefore an instrument heavily influenced by the principles of crime control and prevention, security, and border control, with scant attention to victims and the protection of their human rights (Allain, 2013, p. 361).

To promote and facilitate the integration of a human rights perspective into national, regional, and international anti-trafficking laws, policies, and interventions, in 2002 the Office of the High Commissioner for Human Rights adopted the Recommended Principles and Guidelines on Human Rights and Human Trafficking. Although it is not a binding instrument, this document constitutes an important tool to frame and interpret, from a human rights approach, international and regional legal instruments dealing with trafficking. Such a human rights approach has been followed by the 2005 Council of Europe Convention on Trafficking, which dedicates special attention to the assistance of victims and the protection of their human rights, and EU Directive 2011/36/EU on trafficking.

At the same time, developments in international and national case law, including for instance that of the ECtHR, have helped establish states' obligations to protect victims' rights. Notably, in *Rantsev,* discussed earlier, the Court for the first time applied the definition of trafficking offered by the Palermo Protocol within the scope ECHR Article 4. Specifically, the ECtHR affirmed that the UN Palermo Protocol and the Council of Europe Convention on Trafficking (and accordingly EU Directive 2011/36) express the need for a comprehensive approach to address trafficking that includes measures to (a) prevent the phenomenon; (b) protect victims; and, (c) punish traffickers. The Court also underlined that the Member States' positive obligations under Article 4 of the ECHR must be construed in the light of the

Council of Europe Convention on Trafficking (see *Chowdury and Others v. Greece* (cited above, para. 104)).

1.3.5 The Fine Line between Trafficking and Smuggling

The UN Convention against Transnational Organised Crime is supplemented by the Protocol against the Smuggling of Migrants by Land, Sea, and Air, which aims 'to prevent and combat migrant smuggling, to promote international cooperation to that end, and to protect the rights of smuggled migrants' (Art. 2). The Protocol defines the smuggling of migrants as 'the procurement, in order to obtain, directly or indirectly, a financial or other material benefit, of the illegal entry of a person into a State Party of which the person is not a national or a permanent resident' (Art. 3).

While the key distinguishing element of human trafficking is its purpose (i.e., exploitation) and the irrelevance of their consent, the key element of human smuggling is the irregular crossing of borders and the consent of the smuggled person. In this perspective, smuggling is seen as a crime against a state, while trafficking is a crime against a person (Gallagher, 2010; see also Miranda, 2009). Accordingly, the relationship between the person and the smuggler is considered to be that of client and a service provider, while the relationship between the migrant and the trafficker is considered to be that of victim and exploiter. However, as several scholars have pointed out, these interpretations appear reductive in respect to the complicated context within which 'migrant and migration broker interact with one another' (Alpes, 2017, p. 117), where solidarity and violence, deception, and trust can occur simultaneously (Achilli, 2018; Sanchez, 2020). The same can be said about the relationships between 'trafficked' persons and 'traffickers', which again involve violence, abuse, fraud, but also help, and support (Andrijesevic, 2010).

On the other hand, as an extensive body of literature demonstrates, the same boundaries distinguishing between trafficking and smuggling tend to blur and overlap in practice. Certainly, there are cases that conform to the definitions offered by trafficking and smuggling Protocols. But as legal scholar Jacqueline Bhabba (2005) points out 'the available evidence suggests that most transported undocumented migrants consent in some way to an initial proposition to travel, but that, on route or on arrival in the destination country, circumstances frequently change'. Indeed, often a path that started as irregular migration with the help of a *passeur*—a person who, upon payment of money, facilitates the irregular crossing of borders—and therefore fits into the smuggling framework evolves into a situation of 'trafficking' (Giammarinaro, 2012). This may be caused, for instance, by a situation of debt-bondage, such as a debt contracted for the trip.

Legal scholar Emilio Santoro (Santoro, 2023) has underlined how the classification of debt bondage as a 'practice comparable to slavery' in the 1956 UN Supplementary Slavery Convention questioned the trafficking/smuggling dichotomy, which was subsequently codified in the UN Protocols. Defining debt bondage as a 'practice comparable to slavery' opened the way to also consider as trafficking those migratory experiences that begin in a negotiated way and terminate with the compulsion to pay an agreed debt. This view has recently evolved to include, as emerged for instance in Italy (ibid.), those cases in which the debt bondage could arise not only from travel, but also from agreements stipulated in the country of destination to pay for food, accommodation, or (illegal) intermediaries who favour migrant workers to find a job. In this context, the complexity and exploitative experiences and variety of migration paths and strategies challenges any neat categorisation and legal definition.

Moreover, as some feminist scholars have further emphasised, the trafficking/smuggling distinction tends to be imbued by gendered assumptions and narratives that smuggled persons are men while most trafficked persons are women and children (Chuang, 2010). Therefore, while men are generally viewed as active subjects capable of making independent and voluntary decisions, women are seen as passive and powerless agents in situations of vulnerability to exploitation (O'Connell Davidson, 2015). In line with this misleading narrative built on a gendered victimisation of migrant women, exploited migrant women are more commonly viewed as 'victims of trafficking' whereas exploited migrant men are frequently deemed smuggled persons or irregular migrants and often do not receive adequate assistance and protection.

1.4 The Boundaries Between Notions of Trafficking, Forced Labour, and (Modern) Slavery

This overview of the relevant international legal framework and definitions of slavery, forced labour, and trafficking sheds lights on the background and related issues affecting the delineation and meaning of these concepts and, accordingly, the linked states' obligations. Moreover, it highlights how these notions are strongly related. For instance, slavery, servitude, and forced labour are the examples of the exploitative practices in the purpose element of the definition of trafficking provided by the Palermo Protocol. However, trafficking occurs even if exploitation—in the forms of forced labour, servitude, slavery, and so on—has not actually been committed (UNDOC, 2013; Stoyanova, 2017a, p. 295). Indeed, the purpose of exploitation—in addition to the acts and means elements—is sufficient to constitute trafficking. Since trafficking refers to a process, there can be trafficking even without subsequent exploitation. This latter point represents one of the significant aspects distinguishing the notion of trafficking from slavery and forced labour. Furthermore, with specific regard to the relationship between forced labour and trafficking, forced labour does not encompass the removal of organs, and trafficking often does not entail the forced labour of prisoners.

Apart from these distinguishing elements, defining a clear distinction, for example, between forced labour and trafficking, is highly controversial in most cases as they tend to overlap (Piper et al., 2015), Although the ILO has produced some operational instruments such as the 2009 Operational Indicators of Trafficking in Human Beings that provide support in the identification of cases of forced labour and trafficking, the boundaries between these notions tend to blur. The ILO itself, in its soft-law documents such as its 2012 *Global Estimate of Forced Labour* affirmed that 'human trafficking can also be regarded as forced labour', and therefore 'captures the full realm of human trafficking for labour and sexual exploitation' (ILO, 2012b). In other documents, the ILO seems to suggest that forced labour is a subset of trafficking (ILO, 2013).

Certainly, changes in the features and common understanding of trafficking and forced labour have contributed to their convergence. In the immediate wake of the Palermo Protocol, trafficking was viewed essentially as associated with exploitation in the context of sex work; more recently, especially since the 2010s, there has been growing attention, at both international and national levels, to trafficking for labour exploitation beyond the sex industry. As legal scholar Prabha Kotiswaran (2017, p. 18) has argued, labour organisations ranging from the ILO to trade unions or other workers' groups have started to form networks with anti-trafficking NGOs and use a broad conception of trafficking and related vocabularies and frames.

At the same time, there has been an increase in the share of cases of 'internal' trafficking, i.e., cases of persons trafficking within national borders (UNODC, 2018), with the consequent weakening of the transnational dimension in trafficking dynamics. The recognition of internal trafficking has also been supported by the fact that, as UNODC explicitly clarified, according to the Palermo Protocol trafficking does not always require the movement element. Movement is just one possible way the 'action' element can be satisfied. Notions such as 'receipt' and 'harbouring' mean that trafficking does not refer solely to the process whereby a person is moved into a situation of exploitation but also extends 'to include the maintenance of that person in a situation of exploitation' (UNODC, 2013, p. 7). Trafficking, as the UNDOC argued, 'is rooted in the exploitation of victims, and not necessarily their movement' (UNODC, 2018, p. 13).

Internal trafficking has also been recognised by the ECtHR in *S.M. v. Croatia* (Application No. 60561/14, 25 June 2020) in which the Grand Chamber of the Court found a violation of Article 4 of the ECHR in a case of trafficking within the country for the purpose of sexual exploitation.[22] In this regard, it is worth mentioning that in *S.M. v. Croatia,* as well as in its previous case law (for instance, *Rantsev v. Cyprus and Russia* and *Chowdury and Others v. Greece* (cited above)) in which the ECtHR affirmed that trafficking itself falls within the scope of Article 4 of the ECHR, the Court did not focus on explaining the relationships between the concept of trafficking, on the one hand, and the concepts of slavery, servitude, and forced labour, explicitly included in Article 4, on the other. For this reason, some legal scholars and experts have stressed that the Court has fostered some conceptual confusions (see, for instance, Stoyanova, 2017a), and have also questioned the utility of

[22] See, in this regard, the NGO L'altro Diritto's intervention submitted to the ECtHR in the case *S.M. v. Croatia* and written by Letizia Palumbo and Emilio Santoro (see L'Altro Diritto onlus, 2019).

including human trafficking in Article 4, when this provision might already refer to notions of slavery, forced labour, or servitude to cover relevant abuses (Stoyanova, 2017b).

Conversely, it might be pointed out that, although the Court has not provided an articulated explanation of the relationships between the notion of trafficking and those explicitly covered by Article 4—and even suggested an overlap between them—in *Rantsev* the judges of Strasbourg have been clear in underlining their position in this respect by affirming that the global phenomenon of trafficking in human beings runs counter to the spirit and purpose of Article 4 and that:

> in view of its obligation to interpret the Convention in light of present-day conditions, the Court considers it unnecessary to identify whether the treatment about which the applicant complains constitutes 'slavery', 'servitude' or 'forced [or] compulsory labour'. Instead, the Court concludes that trafficking itself, within the meaning of Article 3 (a) of the Palermo Protocol and Article 4 (a) of the Anti-Trafficking Convention, falls within the scope of Article 4 of the Convention. (*Rantsev*)

Moreover, in the cases following *Rantsev*, such as *J. and Others v. Austria* and *Chowdury and Others v. Greece*, the Court has sought to provide some explanation of how the phenomenon of human trafficking falls within the scope of Article 4 of the ECHR. For instance, in *Chowdury and Others v. Greece*, the Court has stressed that 'exploitation through work is one of the forms of exploitation covered by the definition of human trafficking, and this highlights the intrinsic relationship between forced or compulsory labour and human trafficking'. Successively, in *S.M. v. Croatia*, the Court has further clarified that

> the notion of 'forced or compulsory labour' under Article 4 of the Convention aims to protect against instances of serious exploitation, such as forced prostitution, irrespective of whether, in the particular circumstances of a case, they are related to the specific human-trafficking context...the question whether a particular situation involves all the constituent elements of 'human trafficking' (action, means, purpose) and/or gives rise to a separate issue of forced prostitution is a factual question which must be examined in the light of all the relevant circumstances of a case (para. 303).

In this light, the importance of including human trafficking in Article 4 relies on the broad extension of the definition of trafficking that, in comparison to those of slavery and forced labour, aims—at least in the intention of the negotiators of the Palermo Protocol—to have a wider application scope enabling to cover different and evolving forms of exploitation. On the other hand, this does not mean that slavery and forced labour always involve trafficking. Indeed, as the same judge of the ECtHR, Pinto de Albuquerque, has underlined in his concurring opinion in the case *J. and Others v. Austria* (cited above), 'not all forced labour is trafficking, just as not all trafficking is slavery', and these assumptions are manifestation of the 'exploitation creep', which must be avoided (para. 40).

The term 'exploitation creep' has been introduced by legal scholar Janie Chuang to underline the widespread tendency by institutions, relevant stakeholders, and, in general, mainstream discourses to collapse the meaning of trafficking as defined in the Protocol into the element of purposes, namely exploitation, and especially forced labour and slavery. As Chuang (2017, p. 112) argues, while this view 'has had the benefit of bringing long overdue scrutiny to nonsexual labour exploitation, it has also raised challenging practical and normative concerns regarding which forms of exploitation warrant the application of anti-trafficking laws and policies'. Given national authorities' tendency to interpret trafficking on restrictive terms and the criminal justice paradigm characterising anti-trafficking responses, 'exploitation creep' has had the controversial impact of legitimising legal and policy actions embedded primarily in criminal law and repressive paradigms, overlooking the dimensions of prevention and protection of human rights of the persons involved and the factors creating their situations of vulnerability. Moreover, as discussed in Chap. 2, this dominant attention to trafficking has conveyed the idea that labour exploitation mainly consists of acute and exceptional situations, neglecting the routine patterns involving different exploitative practices.

This tendency has been further supported by the recent trend in the UK, the US, and Australia to use the generic term of 'modern slavery' to cover a much wider array of exploitation than included in the Slavery Conventions (Dottridge, 2017). For instance, as discussed in Chap. 8, in 2015 the UK adopted the Modern Slavery Act, which does not provide a definition of 'modern slavery' but refers, in its sections 1, 2, and 3, to slavery, servitude, forced labour, and trafficking. In this context, 'modern slavery' is used as an umbrella notion 'while continuing to focus on the crime of human trafficking as defined by the Trafficking Protocol' (ibid., p. 76).

Lacking an agreed definition of 'modern slavery', some international organisations, including UNODC, have expressed some doubts concerning the usefulness and impact of this notion. As UNODC (2016) argues, this term

> has an important advocacy impact and has been adopted in some national legislation to cover provisions related to trafficking in persons, however the lack of an agreed definition or legal standard at the international level results in inconsistent usage.

Concerns have been also raised by legal experts and scholars about the impact of the term's widespread institutional use, emphasising that the notion of modern slavery is too often used for its 'emotive effects, rather than its technical accuracy' (Dottridge, 2017, p. 77; Le Baron, 2019). In general, as Mike Dottridge (2017) has argued, similarly to the dominant narrative concerning the notion of trafficking, the frame of 'modern slavery' contributes to give the impression of exceptional situations of exploitation, overlooking its systemic character, which as discussed in Chap. 2, undertakes different forms and graduations.

1.5 Concluding Remarks

This chapter has focused on the notions of slavery, forced labour, and trafficking in the relevant international legal framework. It highlighted how these definitions have not emerged in a vacuum but in a context in which different and competing issues and perspectives are at stake, including for instance gender- and women rights-related issues. In particular, the chapter has focused on the context and inherent tensions against which the UN Palermo Protocol was drafted and adopted, underlining the innovative character of the definition of trafficking provided by this international instrument. Indeed, the Palermo Protocol has introduced a broad, comprehensive, and gender-neutral definition of trafficking, encompassing a wide range of exploitative practices. This definition has been then incorporated in relevant European instruments, in particular in the 2005 Council of Europe Convention on Trafficking and EU Directive 2011/36.

While the international legal framework provides the definitions of the notions of slavery, forced labour, and trafficking, the contours of these legal concepts are porous (Piper et al., 2015). On the one hand, the boundaries between trafficking and smuggling tend to blur in increasingly evident ways, especially in cases of migratory and exploitation experiences concerning debt-bondage. On the other hand, the changes in the understanding of trafficking and its features have increased the proximity and overlap between this notion and those of slavery and forced labour. Indeed, if in the early years after the adoption of the Palermo Protocol in 2000, trafficking was primarily framed in terms of trafficking for sexual exploitation, since the second decade of the 2000s there has been closer attention, at both international and national levels, to trafficking for labour exploitation. This has reduced the conceptual distance between trafficking, forced labour, and slavery. The increase in the awareness and identification of cases of internal trafficking—and in the related awareness that trafficking does not always require the movement element—has also contributed to lower such a conceptual distance. Moreover, in recent years, in some countries, such as the UK, legal interventions have begun referring to the generic and undefined concept of 'modern slavery' despite primarily focusing on trafficking.

In this scenario, given the broad scope of its definition, trafficking has become the dominant frame to address exploitation, albeit overlooking that there can be trafficking without subsequent exploitation and there can be exploitation—including forced labour and slavery, but also less severe forms of exploitation—without trafficking. This conceptual approach, which has been defined as 'exploitation creep', has had some controversial consequences for the understanding and response to exploitation in legal and political terms. As discussed in this volume, a dominant narrow interpretation of the main elements of trafficking (e.g. the irrelevance of consent and the abuse of a position of vulnerability) and the criminal justice paradigm characterising anti-trafficking responses have resulted in support for repressive measures, including restrictive migration policies, while neglecting the complexity of trafficking and exploitation in general as well as their structural underpinnings. This, in turn, overlooks all those less severe cases of exploitation that do not amount to a specific crime (such as trafficking, forced labour, or slavery) or consist of labour law infractions that may be subject to another legal regime (Mantouvalou, 2017).

By framing exploitation from a more articulated perspective—which also takes into account those exploitative practices that are less severe and evident, and do not amount to crimes of trafficking, forced labour, or slavery—the next chapter focuses on the concept of exploitation and the related notion of vulnerability, highlighting relevant legal and theoretical perspectives that underlie this book's analysis. In addressing the issue of exploitative practices experienced by migrant workers, my intention is not to focus on juridical qualification of some cases (i.e., if they amount to some crimes rather than others), but instead on the interplay of structural factors contributing to produce the situations of vulnerability on which dynamics of exploitation rely.

References

Achilli, L. (2018). The 'good' smuggler': The ethics and morals of human smuggling. *The Annals of the American Academy of Political and Social Science, 676*(1), 77–96.

Allain, J. (2008). *Slavery conventions: The Travaux Préparatoires of the 1926 league of nations convention and the 1956 United Nations convention*. Brill.

Allain, J. (2013). *Slavery in international law: Of human exploitation and trafficking*. Martinus Nijhoff Publishers.

Alpes, M. J. (2017). Papers that work: Migration brokers, state/market boundaries, and the place of law. *PoLAR, 40*(2), 262–277.

Andrees, B. (2008). *Forced labour and trafficking in Europe: how people are trapped in, live through and come out*. ILO Working Papers 994017183402676, International Labour Organisation.

Andrees, B., & Aikman, A. (2017). Raising the Bar: The adoption of new ILO standards against forced labour. In P. Kotiswaran (Ed.), *Revisiting the law and governance of trafficking, forced labour, and modern slavery* (pp. 359–394). Cambridge University Press.

Andrijesevic, R. (2010). *Migration, agency, and citizenship in sex trafficking*. Palgrave Macmillan.

Aradau, C. (2008). *Rethinking trafficking in women. Politics out of security*. Macmillan Palagrave.

Bassiouni, C. M. (1999). *International Criminal Law: Crimes*. Transnational Publishers.

Bhabha, J. (2005). Trafficking, smuggling, and human rights. *Migration Information Source: Special Issue on Migration and Human Rights* [online], https://documentation.lastradainternational.org/lsidocs/424%20migration_funda_1007.pdf

Boutros-Ghali, B. (1995). Introduction. In UNDPI, *The United Nations and the Advancement of Women, 1945–1996* (pp. 3–72). UN Department of Public Information. United Nations.

Bullimer, K. (2008). *In an abusive state: How neo-liberalism appropriated the feminist movement again sexual violence*. Duke University Press.

Chuang, J. A. (1998). Redirecting the debate over trafficking in women: Definitions, paradigms, and contexts. *Harvard Human Rights Journal, 11*, 65–108.

Chuang, J. A. (2010). Rescuing trafficking from ideological capture: Prostitution reform and anti-trafficking law and policy. *University of Pennsylvania Law Review, 158*(6), 1655–1728.

Chuang, J. (2011). Commentary on CEDAW Article 6. In M. A. Freeman, C. Chinkin & B. Rudolf (Eds.), *The UN Convention on the Elimination of All Forms of Discrimination Against Women: A Commentary*. Oxford University Press.

Chuang, J. A. (2017). Exploitation creep and the unmaking of human trafficking law. *The American Journal of International Law, 108*(4), 609–649.

Coomaraswamy, R. (2000). Report of the Special Rapporteur on violence against women, its causes and consequences, Ms. Radhika Coomaraswamy, on trafficking in women, women's migration and violence against women, submitted in accordance with Commission on Human Rights resolution 1997/44. E/CN.4/2000/68, 29 February.

Council of Europe. (2005). *Explanatory report to the Council of Europe Convention on action against trafficking in human beings*. Council of Europe Treaty Series, No. 197 [online], https://rm.coe.int/16800d3812 (Last Access Apr 2024).

De Sena, P. (2019). Slaveries and new slaveries: Which role for human dignity? *Questions of International Law, 64*, 7–17.
De Vido. S. (2016). *Donne, Violenza e Diritto internazionale. La Convenzione di Istanbul del Consiglio d'Europa del 2011*. Mimesis.
Demleitner, N. V. (1994). Forced prostitution: Naming and international offense. *Fordham International Law Journal, 18*(1), 163–196.
Ditmore, M., & Wijers, M. (2003). The negotiations on the UN protocol of trafficking in persons: Moving the from morality to actual conditions. *Nemesis, 4*, 79–88.
Doezema, J. (2000). Loose women or lost women? The re-emergence of the myth of white slavery in contemporary discourses in trafficking in women. *Gender Issues, 18*(1), 23–50.
Dottridge, M. (2017). Trafficked and exploited: The urgent need for coherence in international law. In P. Kotiswaran (Ed.), *Revisiting the law and governance of trafficking, forced labor and modern slavery* (pp. 59–82). Cambridge University Press.
Gallagher, A. T. (2010). *The international law of human trafficking*. Cambridge University Press.
Gallagher, A. T. (2017) The international legal definition of 'trafficking in persons': Scope and application. In P. Kotiswaran (Ed.), *Revisiting the law and governance of trafficking, forced labour, and modern slavery* (pp. 83–111). Cambridge University Press
Giammarinaro, M. G. (2012). La direttiva 2011/36/UE sulla prevenzione e la repressione della tratta di esseri umani e la protezione delle vittime. *Diritto, immigrazione e cittadinanza, 1*, 15–33.
Giammarinaro, M. G. (2020). *Beyond law enforcement, towards social justice: A human rights based-approach to trafficking in persons*. Report of the Special Rapporteur on trafficking in persons, especially women and children. A/HRC/44/45. United Nations [online], https://documents-dds-ny.un.org/doc/UNDOC/GEN/G20/086/90/PDF/G2008690.pdf?OpenElement (Last Access Apr 2024).
Giammarinaro, M. G. (2022). L'influenza trasformativa delle prospettive femministe. Vulnerabilità e agency. *Rivista di filosofia del diritto, 2*, 339–352.
Guy, D. J. (1992). 'White slavery,' citizenship, and nationality in Argentina. In A. Parker et al. (Eds.), *Nationalisms and sexualities* (pp. 201–215). Routledge.
Halley, J., Kotiswaran, P., Thomas, C., & Shamir, H. (2006). From the international to the local in feminist legal responses to rape, prostitution/sex work, and sex trafficking: Four studies in contemporary governance feminism. *Harvard Journal of Law & Gender, 29*(2), 335–423.
Hochschild, A. R. (2002). Love and gold. In B. Ehrenreich & A. R. Hochschild (Eds.), *Global woman. Nannies, maids, and sex workers in the new economy* (pp. 15–30). Metropolitan Books.
Hoyle, C., & Sanders, A. (2000). Police responses to domestic violence: From victim choice to victim empowerment. *British Journal of Criminology, 40*(1), 14–36.
ICMPD. (1999). *The relationship between organised crime and trafficking in aliens*. International Centre for Migration Policy Development.
ILO. (2005). *Human trafficking and forced Labour exploitation: Guidelines for legislation and law enforcement*. International Labour Organisation.
ILO. (2007). *Eradication of forced Labour: General survey concerning the Forced Labour Convention, 1930 (no. 29), and the Abolition of Forced Labour Convention, 1957 (no. 105)*. Report of the Committee of Experts on the Application of Conventions and Recommendations (Articles 19, 22 and 35 of the Commission. International Labour Conference (96th session). International Labour Organisation.
ILO. (2009). The cost of coercion. *Global report under the follow-up to the ILO declaration on fundamental principles and rights at work*. International Labour Organisation.
ILO. (2012a). *Hard to see, harder to count: Survey guidelines to estimate forced labour of adults and children*. International Labour Organisation.
ILO. (2012b). *Global estimate of forced labour. Results and methodology*. International Labour Organisation.

ILO. (2013). *Report and conclusions of the tripartite meeting of experts on forced labour and trafficking for labour exploitation*. International Labour Organisation.
ILO. (2014). *P029–Protocol of 2014 to the Forced Labour Convention, 1930*. International Labour Organisation.
ILO. (2016). *ILO standards on forced labour. The new protocol and recommendation at a glance*. International Labour Organisation.
Jordan, A. D. (2002). *The annotated guide to the complete UN trafficking protocol*. International Human Rights Law Group.
Kapur, R. (2002). The tragedy of victimization rhetoric: Resurrecting the 'native' subject in international/post-colonial feminist legal politics. *Harvard Human Rights Journal, 15*(1), 1–38.
Keck, M. E., & Sikkink, K. (1998). *Activists beyond borders: Advocacy networks in international politics*. Cornell University Press.
Kotiswaran, P. (Ed.) (2017) *Revisiting the law and governance of trafficking, forced labour, and modern slavery*. Cambridge University Press.
L'Altro Diritto onlus (2019). *Third party intervention in the case S.M. v. CROATIA* (Application No. 60561/14), written by Letizia Palumbo and Emilio Santoro [online], https://www.adir.unifi.it/odv/sportello/tpi/trafficking/trafficking-en.pdf (Last Access Apr 2024).
Lammasniemi, L. (2017). 'White slavery': The origins of the anti-trafficking movement. *Open Democracy*", 16 November 2017 [online], www.opendemocracy.net/en/beyond-trafficking-and-slavery/white-slavery-origins-of-anti-trafficking-movement/ (Last Access Apr 2024)
Langille, B. (2011). Labour law's theory of justice. In G. Davidov & B. Langille (Eds.), *The idea of labour law* (pp. 101–119). Oxford University Press.
Le Baron, G. (Ed.) (2019). *Researching forced labour in the global economy: Methodological challenges and advances*. (Proceedings of the British Academy). Oxford University Press.
MacKinnon, C., & Dworkin, A. (1988). *Pornography & civil rights: A new day FOR Women's equality*. Organizing Against Pornography.
Mantouvalou, V. (Ed.). (2017). *The right to work: Legal and philosophical perspectives*. Hart Publishing.
Members of the Research Network on the Legal Parameters of Slavery. (2012). *Bellagio-Harvard Guidelines on the Legal Parameters of Slavery'* [online], law.qub.ac.uk (Last Access Apr 2024)
Miller, A. M. (2004). Sexuality, violence against women, and human rights: Women make demands and ladies get protection. *Health and Human Rights, 7*(2), 16–47.
Miranda, A. (2009). The private law answers to a criminal attitude: The human trafficking and smuggling in a new Italian perspective. *The Cardozo Electronic Law Bulletin, 15*, 1–7.
Munro, V. (2013). Violence against women, 'victimhood', and the (neo)liberal state. In M. Davies & V. Munro (Eds.), *The Ashgate research companion to feminist legal theory* (pp. 233–248). Ashgate.
Nadelmann, E. A. (1990). Global prohibition regimes: The evolution of norms in international society. *International Organization, 44*(4), 479–526.
Niemi, J., Peroni, L., & Stoyanova, V. (Eds.). (2020). *International law and violence against women: Europe and the Istanbul convention* (1st ed.). Routledge.
O'Connell Davidson, J. (2015). *Modern slavery: The margins of freedom*. Palgrave Macmillan.
Otto, D. (2006). Lost in translation: Re-scripting the sexed subjects of international human rights law. In A. Orford (Ed.), *International law and its others* (pp. 318–356). Cambridge University Press.
Parrenas, R. S. (2001). *Servants of globalization: Women, migration, and domestic work*. Stanford University Press.
Piper, N., Segrave, M., & Napier-Moore, R. (2015). Editorial: What's in a name? Distinguishing forced labour, trafficking, and slavery. *Anti-Trafficking Review, 5*, 1–9.
Plant, R. (2015). *Modern slavery: The concepts and their practical implications*. International Labour Organisation.
Plant, R. (2017). Combating trafficking for labour exploitation in the global economy: The need for a differentiated approach. In P. Kotiswaran (Ed.), *Revisiting the law and governance of trafficking, forced labour and modern slavery* (pp. 422–442). Cambridge University Press.

Raymond, J. G. (2001). *Guide to the new UN trafficking protocol.* Coalition Against Trafficking in Women. [online], https://catwinternational.org/wp-content/uploads/2019/09/Guide-to-the-New-UN-Trafficking-Protocol.pdf

Roediger, D. R. (1991). *The wages of whiteness: Race and the making of the American working class.* Verso.

Rosen, R. (1982). *The lost sisterhood: Prostitution in America 1900–1918.* Johns Hopkins University Press.

Rubio Grundell, L. (2023). *Security meets gender equality in the EU: The politics of trafficking in women for sexual exploitation.* Palgrave Macmillan.

Sanchez, G. (2020). Who is a smuggler? In S. Carrera, D. Courtin, & A. Geddes (Eds.), *20 year anniversary of the Tampere Programme: Europeanisation dynamics of the EU area of freedom, security and justice* (pp. 183–195). European University Institute.

Santoro, E. (2023). From 'refugeeization' of labour exploitation to debtbondage: Developing the subversive content of protecting the victims of exploitation. *Revista de Estudos Constitucionais, Hermenêutica e Teoria do Direito (RECHTD), 15*(1), 2–21.

Scarpa, S. (2013). The definition of trafficking in adult persons for various forms of exploitation and the issue of consent: A framework approach that respects peculiarities. *Groningen Journal of International Law, 1*(2), 154–163.

Scarpa, S. (2018). *Contemporary Forms of Slavery.* European Union [online], https://www.europarl.europa.eu/RegData/etudes/STUD/2018/603470/EXPO_STU(2018)603470_EN.pdf (Last Access Apr 2024).

Stoyanova, V. (2017a). *Human trafficking and slavery reconsidered: Conceptual limits and States' positive obligations in European law.* Cambridge University Press.

Stoyanova, V. (2017b). Irregular migrants and the prohibition of slavery, servitude, forced labour & human trafficking under article 4 of the ECHR. *EJIL:Talk!*, 26 April [online], www.ejiltalk.org/irregular-migrants-and-the-prohibition-of-slavery-servitudeforced-labour-human-trafficking-under-article-4-of-the-echr/ (Last Access Apr 2024).

Stoyanova, V. (2018). Sweet taste with bitter roots: Forced labour and 'Chowdury and others v. Greece'. *European Human Rights Law Review, 1*, 67–75.

Swepston, L. (2017) Trafficking and forced labour: Filling in the gaps with the adoption of the supplementary ILO standards, 2014. In P. Kotsiwaran (Ed.), *Revisiting the law and governance of trafficking, forced labour and modern slavery.* (pp. 395–421). Cambridge University Press.

UN Secretary-General (1995). *Traffic in women and girls: Report of the Secretary-General,* A/50/369, Last Access 24 Aug 1995.

UN Secretary-General (1996). *Traffic in women and girls. Report of the Secretary-General,* A/51/309, Last Access 27 Aug 1996..

United Nations. (1963). *Yearbook of the International Law Commission.* Vol. I, United Nations.

UNODC. (2004). *Legislative guide for the implementation of the United Nations convention against transnational organized crime and the protocols thereto* (1st edn). United Nations Office on Drugs and Crime.

UNODC. (2012) *Global report on trafficking in persons.* United Nations Office on Drugs and Crime.

UNODC. (2013). *Abuse of a position of vulnerability and other 'means' within the definition of trafficking in persons.* United Nations Office on Drugs and Crime.

UNODC. (2016). *Global report on trafficking in persons.* United Nations Office on Drugs and Crime.

UNODC. (2018). *Global report on trafficking in persons.* United Nations Office on Drugs and Crime.

UNODC. (2020). *Legislative guide on the trafficking in persons protocol only, 2020 update.* United Nations Office on Drugs and Crime.

Vianello, F. A. (2019). *Migrando sole. Legami transnazionali tra Ucraina e Italia.* Franco Angeli.

Weatherburn, A. (2021). *Labour exploitation in human trafficking law.* Cambridge University Press.

Wijers, M., & Lap-Chew, L. (1999). *Trafficking in women: Forced labour and slavery-like practices in marriage, domestic labour, and prostitution*. Foundation Against Trafficking in Women.
Yuval-Davis, N. (1997). *Gender and nation*. SAGE Publications Ltd.

Chapter 2
Labour Exploitation as a Continuum, Human Dignity, and Vulnerability

This chapter focuses on the notion of labour exploitation, following on from the previous chapter's examination of the notions of slavery, forced labour, and trafficking in the international legal framework. While international and European instruments provide definitions of slavery, forced labour, and trafficking, the boundaries between these legal concepts are porous. At the same, institutional attention at both international and national levels on the issue of trafficking or so-called modern slavery has increased in recent years, with the risk of overlooking the complexity of labour exploitation, which can take on different shapes and gradations.

Building on these considerations, Chap. 2 aims to specifically focus on the concept of labour exploitation, unpacking the legal and theoretical conceptions of this notion and the related concepts of human dignity and vulnerability. In particular, it explores these notions in relevant international and European legal instruments, as well as in significant case law of the European Court of Human Rights (ECtHR), while drawing on relevant legal and social literature on this matter. In so doing, Chap. 2 – in line with Chap. 1 – highlights the conceptual framework and perspectives underlying the analysis carried out in this book.

The first section focuses on the meaning of labour exploitation as a violation of human dignity, seeing this latter notion in its social dimension as social human dignity. At the same time, this section looks at the structural continuum nature of exploitation, highlighting how forms of exploitation are associated with different 'situational' vulnerabilities along this continuum. The second section discusses the notion of vulnerability, illustrating the main theoretical perspective on this concept and how this notion has been incorporated in relevant international and European legislation on labour exploitation. By highlighting the importance of a situational conception of vulnerability to exploitation, the section examines how this notion has been incorporated in relevant ECtHR case law. The chapter then explores the complex relationship between vulnerability, power bargaining, and consent to exploitation. Finally, it underlines the need for an intersectional and gender-based approach to exploitation and vulnerability.

L. Palumbo, *Taking Vulnerabilities to Labour Exploitation Seriously*, IMISCOE Research Series, https://doi.org/10.1007/978-3-031-55424-7_2

2.1 Exploitation and Its Legal and Theoretical Conceptions

The notion of labour exploitation is at the heart of legal frameworks concerning offences such as 'forced labour' and 'trafficking'. However, the notion of exploitation is not defined by any international legal instruments. At regional and national levels, only some legal frameworks, including those of the EU and Italy, contain a definition of labour exploitation as such (Di Martino, 2019; Iossa & Selberg, 2022). In many other cases, labour exploitation is seen as the outcome or intent of crimes such as trafficking, albeit without defining this notion. In an issue paper on this topic, the UNODC (2015) underlines the lack of a clear definition of labour exploitation – in both international law and the national legislation of many countries, with the consequent risk that those forms of labour exploitation that do not amount to severe exploitation such as trafficking, forced labour, or slavery go unnoticed or tend to be normalised.

2.1.1 Labour Exploitation in Relevant International and European Instruments

Before the adoption of the 2000 UN Palermo Protocol, relevant international documents in the ambit of slavery, forced labour, trafficking, or in general concerning the protection of workers' rights did not refer to the notion of exploitation as such.[1] For instance, relevant ILO documents of the last century mainly used the notion 'exploitation' for specific categories, such as indigenous peoples[2]; people with disabilities[3]; or migrant workers.[4] Moreover, it might be argued that, in these texts, the attention is not to the dynamics of exploitation per se but to the specific (considered intrinsic?) conditions of vulnerability of certain categories that may expose them to exploitation. As legal scholar Susan Marks has importantly highlighted, in these exceptional contexts in which the word 'exploitation' is used, it seems to be difficult to detach labour standards from the long history of paternalism towards specific groups, such as 'indigenous peoples, people with disabilities, and other groups represented by the authorities as incapable, helpless, and touchingly innocent of the ways of the world' (Marks, 2008, p. 299).

Relevant international documents on trafficking adopted before the Palermo Protocol, such as the early international Conventions on trafficking (see Chap. 1), focused instead on sexual exploitation,[5] especially with respect to prostitution, in

[1] For an interesting reconstruction of the notion of exploitation in international law see Marks (2008).

[2] Para. 36, 1957 ILO Indigenous and Tribal Populations Recommendation (No. 104).

[3] Para. 11, 1983 Vocational Rehabilitation and Employment (Disabled Persons) Recommendation (No. 168).

[4] Para. 43(b), 1984 Employment Policy (Supplementary Provisions) Recommendation (No. 169).

[5] For instance, the UN 1949 Convention for the Suppression of the Traffic in Persons and of the Exploitation of the Prostitution of Others.

line with the feminist 'abolitionist' view of prostitution always being a form of 'sexual exploitation' (Chuang, 2010). Alongside these international treaties referring to sexual exploitation, the term 'exploitation' appeared mainly in international legal provisions concerning children.[6]

Interestingly, among other relevant international texts, the 1990 UN International Convention on the Protection of the Rights of All Migrant Workers and Members of their Families, which sets out the rights of migrant workers across a wide range of spheres, contains a section (Art. 11) on slavery, servitude, and forced labour. Yet, the notion of exploitation is not used in these provisions.[7]

In 2000, with the Palermo Protocol, exploitation appears as a new legal concept (Allain, 2015, p. 347) more broadly than the sexual dimension to include various types of labour market exploitation. Importantly, as already underlined in Chap. 1, the Protocol does not define the notion of exploitation. However, the document offers some examples, for instance 'the exploitation of the prostitution of others or other forms of sexual exploitation, forced labour or services, slavery or practices similar to slavery, servitude or the removal of organs' (Art. 3). The Protocol therefore provides an open list of forms of exploitation, leaving relevant actors with the important role of filling it with ever more examples of exploitative practices.

The Palermo Protocol does not expressively refer to 'labour exploitation' in Article 3.

In fact, during the Protocol's drafting process, the ILO proposed including a clear reference to 'labour exploitation' as an exploitative purpose (UNODC, 2018, p. 15; Weatherburn, 2021, pp. 66–67). Despite such a proposal, there was no explicit reference to this term, while the Protocol kept the broader language of 'other forms of sexual exploitation'. This choice – as legal scholars like Prabha Kotiswaran (2015) and Marjan Wijers (2015) have suggested – confirms that the 'means' and 'action' elements of trafficking definition received more attention than the 'exploitation' element during the negotiation and drafting of the Protocol. At the same time, the decision to single out exploitation of prostitution and other forms of sexual exploitation as separate from labour exploitation (i.e., forced labour) reflected controversies around the approach to prostitution and women's sexuality that dominated during the drafting (Chuang, 2010) (see Chap. 1). Feminist scholars and experts have highlighted the damaging effects of these differentiations. In particular, separating sexual exploitation from labour exploitation/forced labour conveys the false idea that sex work cannot be deemed as work and, moreover, that sexual

[6] The 1956 Supplementary Convention on the Abolition of Slavery, the Slave Trade and Institutions and Practices Similar to Slavery identified among these practices the 'exploitation of the child or young person of his labour' (Art. 1(d)); furthermore, the 1966 International Covenant on Economic, Social and Cultural Rights declares that '[c]hildren and young persons should be protected from economic and social exploitation'; and the 1989 Convention on the Rights of the Child affirms that States Parties 'shall take all appropriate legislative, administrative, social and educational measures to protect the child from…exploitation, including sexual abuse' (Art. 19(1)).

[7] This Convention refers to exploitation only with reference to access to housing, especially regarding protection of migrant workers against exploitation in respect to rents (Art. 43(d)).

exploitation does not amount to forms, for instance, of forced labour (Wijers, 2015; Palumbo & Sciurba, 2015), while even before the adoption of the Palermo Protocol, the ILO had identified exploitation of sexual labour as a form of forced labour (Wijers, 2015; Plant, 2007; ILO, 2012a).

Despite these considerations and limitations, the innovative aspect of the legal concept of exploitation found in the Palermo Protocol is its framing and extent, which is not limited to some specific categories/groups and goes beyond the sexual dimension to include, for instance, forced labour. This finds confirmation in the Model Law against Trafficking in Persons (UNODC, 2009) – a soft-law instrument produced by UNODC to assist states in implementing the provisions of the Palermo Protocol – which noted that although the term exploitation is not defined in the Protocol, it is generally 'associated with particularly harsh and abusive conditions of work', or 'conditions of work inconsistent with human dignity' (ibid., p. 28).

With specific regard to EU secondary law, in addition to the conception of exploitation contained in relevant EU Directives on trafficking – especially Directive 2011/36/EU, which reflects that found in the Palermo Protocol's definition of trafficking – the notion of labour exploitation appears in Directive 2009/52 on Employers' Sanctions[8] (here after Employer Sanctions Directive). By reflecting relevant provisions of the EU Charter of Fundamental Rights, Directive 2009/52 defines 'particularly exploitative working conditions' as:

> working conditions, including those resulting from gender based or other discrimination, where there is a striking disproportion compared with the terms of employment of legally employed workers which, for example, affects workers' health and safety, and which offends against human dignity (Art. 2 (i)).

This definition of labour exploitation targets situations that do not constitute forced labour, but that 'still amount to very serious violations of a worker's right to decent working conditions under Article 31 of the Charter' (FRA, 2015, p. 42). Furthermore, by conveying the idea of assuming a complex conception of exploitation attentive to social, gendered, and contextual power relationships, this definition pays attention to exploitative working conditions built on gender-based and other discriminations. In addition, it 'points to a proportionality analysis and severity threshold as tools for assessing exploitative circumstances' (Stoyanova, 2017, p. 72) and takes respect for the principle of human dignity as the main criterion to be considered.

As Stoyanova points out, due to the intent not to affect labour rights regulations of the Member States, one of the main limitations of the definition of 'exploitative working conditions' contained in the Employers Sanctions Directive is that the Directive supposes that 'the terms of employment of legally employed workers' are good in all sectors. Unfortunately, this is not always true. Indeed, in certain occupations, especially those where migrant workers are predominant (such as agriculture, domestic work etc.), the terms of employment might be bad with very little

[8] Directive 2009/52/EC of the European Parliament and of the Council of 18 June 2009 providing for minimum standards on sanctions and measures against employers of illegally staying third-country nationals.

protection. In these cases, as Stoyanova (ibid.) has noted, the proportionality method adopted in definition of 'particularly exploitative working conditions' provided by the Employers Sanction Directive, might be not useful as in those sectors no migrant worker 'is treated disproportionately badly since all of them are treated badly or some are simply treated worse' (Stoyanova, 2017, p. 72).

The concerns raised by Stoyanova are shareable. Additionally, by referring to 'particularly exploitative working conditions,' the Employers Sanction Directive seems to allude to a specific feature of exploitation, effectively leaving this concept undefined. On the other hand, it can be argued that the Directive has the merit of having introduced an agreed notion of labour exploitation at the European level, thus placing exploitation within the framework of an employment relationship and framing it as a violation of human dignity. This notion has then been reflected in the definition of labour exploitation contained in some legislation of European countries. In particular, as discussed in Chap. 6, Art. 603bis of the Italian Criminal Code (CC) provides an innovative definition of labour exploitation referring to some indicators – in relation to pay, working hours and rest, safety, working conditions, methods of surveillance and 'degrading' housing situations – that fall within the broader horizon of the protection of human dignity.

2.1.2 Labour Exploitation and Human Dignity

Since the 2000s, following the adoption of the Palermo Protocol, the notion of labour exploitation has been progressively incorporated in international, regional, and national legal texts and documents. This has led to a sort of conceptual shift as the notion no longer has only a strict Marxist economic connotation as an extraction of surplus labour (Elster, 1997) and, at the same time, has ceased to be primarily considered, in relevant legal discourses and texts, as related to the sexual dimension. In this scenario, exploitation has started to be also understood as a violation of fundamental rights and a violation of human dignity.

As highlighted in Chap. 1, the language of human dignity permeates international and European legal frameworks on slavery, forced labour, and trafficking (De Sena, 2019; Scarpa, 2019). Since the first decade of the 2000s, this language has begun being used to specifically assess and ban labour exploitation. This clearly emerges in international soft law instruments, such as the above-mentioned Model Law against Trafficking in Persons and EU secondary law, in particular in the Employers Sanction Directive, which, as mentioned earlier, frames exploitation as a breach of human dignity. The language of human dignity has also permeated the legal conception of exploitation in the national legislation of some European countries, even before the adoption of relevant EU Directives. For example, in Belgian legislation exploitation is defined in the provision concerning the offence of trafficking as work or labour conditions contrary to human dignity (Belgian Criminal

Code Criminal Code), Article 433quinquies (1) (3)).[9] French legislation contains the offence of 'subjecting a person, whose vulnerability or dependence is obvious or known to the offender, to working or living conditions incompatible with human dignity' (Art. 225–14 of the French Criminal Code).[10] In Italy, although relevant legislation – Art. 603bis of the Italian Criminal Code, concerning the crime of 'illegal gang-mastering and labour exploitation' introduced in 2011 and revised in 2016 – does not explicitly refer to exploitation as violation of human dignity,[11] the offence of labour exploitation is included in the Criminal Code's section concerning crimes against individual freedom. This confirms the legislator's will to identify the juridical good to be safeguarded in the human dignity (of the worker).[12] Furthermore, as discussed in Chap. 6, Art. 603bis of the Italian Criminal Code contains some indicators of exploitation that refer to working and living conditions contrary to human dignity according to the Italian Constitution, especially Arts. 3 and 36.

To understand the conceptual shift that has led to framing the legal notion of exploitation in the language of human dignity, it is worth underlining that since the twentieth century – especially after the end of the second world war – the concept of human dignity has been progressively incorporated in international, regional, and national legislation and legal documents (McCrudden, 2008; Resta, 2014). More specifically, the notion of dignity made a clear appearance in the 1945 UN Charter and 1948 Universal Declaration of Human Rights, which also refers to human dignity to enhance the protection of economic, social, and cultural rights and, in particular the right to a 'just and favourable' remuneration. The centrality of the respect for human dignity in the 1948 Universal Declaration has notably contributed to make it a shared normative basis in international and regional human rights, humanitarian law, and criminal law texts (McCrudden, 2008; Scarpa, 2019), including those specifically regarding slavery, forced labour, trafficking, and fair working conditions (De Sena, 2019; Somavia, 2013).

As legal scholar Stefano Rodotà (2012, p. 184) notes, while the 'revolution of equality' marked the age of modernity, the 'revolution of dignity', as a result of twentieth-century tragedies, has marked a turning point in which dignity has become 'an inescapable common denominator' defining 'a new status of the person and a new framework of constitutional duties'.[13]

Against this background, the reference to the principle of human dignity with respect to the definition of labour exploitation has shed light on the issue of the

---

[9] Article 433quinquies (1) (3) of the Belgian Criminal Code referred to the concept of human dignity, in the definition of exploitation contained in the trafficking definition even before the transposition of the Employer Sanctions Directive and Directive 2011/36/EU on trafficking into national legislation.

[10] This provision of the French Criminal Code (Art. 225-4-1) referred to human dignity even before the transposition of the Employer Sanctions Directive and Directive 2011/36/EU on trafficking into national legislation.

[11] This point will be addressed in Chap. 5.

[12] See, in this regard, the decision of the Tribunal of Prato, 4 November 2019, R.G. N. 5690/2018.

[13] My translation in English.

irreducibility of labour to mere commodity and of the worker to object (ibid., 192). The principle of human dignity thus constitutes not only a criterion to assess working conditions, but also a measure of what can respond to economic logics and what is incompatible with these (Rodotà, 2012; Santoro, 2020). This latter conception explicitly emerges, for instance, in Art. 36 of the Italian Constitution affirming that workers must be paid a salary that enables them to meet their own needs and that of their families and to have a free and dignified existence, and in Art. 41 affirming that private economic initiative cannot be carried out 'in a manner that could damage safety, liberty, and human dignity'.[14]

The notion of human dignity and its operational use have been the subject of an intense scholarly debate that has critically focused on the dichotomy between its objective and subjective dimensions and its role as constraint or as empowerment (Brownsword, 2013; Hennette-Vauchez, 2011; Resta, 2014; Viola, 2013). With specific regard to exploitation, building on the Kantian view that 'human beings are ends in themselves' and cannot be treated as a means to an end, philosophical scholars such as Ruth Sample (2003) argue that a human dignity approach to exploitation requires the application of a duty to respect themselves and others. Such a duty, according to Sample, needs awareness and restraint to preserve persons' dignity. This human dignity-based approach to exploitation emphasises the personal and relational aspects of the exploited party by also considering their condition of vulnerability. However, while providing significant insights, Sample's perspective builds on a 'morally thick standard' that is difficult to apply in contexts of competing interests and to address material conditions in which individuals act and make their choices (Weatherburn, 2021, p. 37). Above all, it seems to suggest an abstract and heteronomous conception of human dignity that risks imposing a scale of values – not necessarily accepted and shared – and in tension with individual freedom and autonomy.

This concern is one of the main issues highlighted by some legal and theoretical scholars discussing the use of the principle of human dignity in general – not with specific regard to labour exploitation – and stressing that this notion risks supporting an 'oppressive moral' (see, for instance, Whitman, 2003) and disciplining order that limits persons' freedom and autonomy (see, for instance, Brownsword, 2013). Relevant in this debate has been important European and national case law (Resta, 2014, pp. 31–60). This includes the famous decision of the French *Conseil d'Etat* (27 October 1995) outlawing the spectacle of dwarf-throwing (*lancer de nain*)[15] as it represented a threat to the respect for human dignity, which is considered a constituent of public order. This decision has been criticised for conveying an abstract and 'authoritarian' conception of human dignity. In particular, the *Conseil d'Etat* embraced a conception of human dignity as constraint, arguing that the dwarf-throwing might compromise the dwarf's dignity and, consequently, the dignity of

---

[14] My translation in English.

[15] Conseil d'Etat (27 October 1995) req. nos. 136–727 (Commune de Morsang-sur-Orge) and 143–578 (Ville d'Aix-en-Provence).

fellow humans in contemporary France (Resta, 2014). In this view, human dignity is conceived as an overriding value standing over and above individual choice and consent, and which accordingly shall be respected by all members of human society (Cayla, 1998).

A similar approach was adopted in a recent decision of the Italian Constitutional Court (Decision N.14, 7/06/2019). Building on an understanding of human dignity as a meta-moral concept imposing itself as a postulate (Parisi, 2019), the decision considered sexual labour as incompatible with human dignity, in line with a feminist 'neo-abolitionist' approach to prostitution (Giammarinaro, 2022a). Such an abstract and objective conception of dignity – as Giammarinaro argued commenting on this decision of the Italian Constitutional Court – hinders a balancing act between fundamental rights, including sexual self-determination, and justifies not the limitation of the rights of third parties but, instead, the restriction of the right to self-determination of the individual involved, including in the sphere of sexuality (ibid.).

By challenging such a limiting conception of human dignity, Italian legal scholars Stefano Rodotà (2012) and Maria Rosaria Marella (2007), among others, have highlighted the socially embedded dimension of dignity, which opposes any paternalistic or 'authoritarian' visions that exclude the individual's ability to self-determine with respect to their life choices. By supporting a social view on human dignity, they have stressed that this notion should not be considered as a static and abstract principle, but as a guarantee of those 'minimum living conditions that allow the person to actively participate in social life and the public sphere' (Marella, 2007).[16] Dignity is not limited to an innate quality of a person, but is the 'result of a construction that moves from the person, examines and integrates personal relationships and social ties, [and] requires consideration of the overall context within which existence unfolds'[17] (Rodotà, 2012, p. 233). In this perspective, therefore, human dignity refers to the materiality of social relationships and, accordingly, encompasses the needs and material living conditions of individuals (Marella, 2007).

This social conception of dignity arises in the Constitutions of several European countries, including the Italian Constitution (Arts 3(1), 36 and 41), the Belgian Constitution (Art. 23), as well as in the EU Charter of Fundamental Rights. For example, Article 3 (para. 1) of the Italian Constitution affirms that 'all citizens have equal social dignity', emphasising a context and system of relationships in which persons are located in conditions of freedom and equality. Furthermore, as mentioned above, Art. 36 affirms that the worker must be paid a salary that enables them to meet their own needs and those of their family and to have a free and dignified existence. As Rodotà (2012) has pointed out, the social conception of dignity found in the Italian Constitution sheds light on the notion of dignity as combining the principle of equality, which recognises the equal social dignity of all people, and the principle of self-determination. At the same time, such a conception of dignity entails an obligation on states to build and guarantee the necessary conditions for

[16] My translation.

[17] My translation.

each person to make decisions in conditions of freedom and responsibility (ibid., p. 209). Such a view on human dignity therefore relates to a more elaborate idea of private autonomy that builds on human rights law; consequently, it 'goes beyond negative freedom from interference to place a duty on the state to promote conditions that enable individuals to realize their own conceptions of a worthwhile life' (Collins, 2012, p. 43), in a context – it is important to stress this again – characterised by substantial equality.

This obligation on states to guarantee that nobody falls below a 'dignified' level of existence has been also expressly recognized by the ECtHR, including in decisions regarding migrants' rights,[18] and by national constitutional courts[19] (Resta, 2014, p. 40; Marella, 2007). Furthermore, at the national level, in particular in Italy, the protection of the right to a dignified existence is at the centre of important Italian case law in the field of international protection and former humanitarian protection (former art. 5(6) of Legislative Decree 286/1998), including decisions concerning the protection of exploited migrant workers (Giammarinaro & Palumbo, 2021).

With specific regard to working conditions, therefore, the principle of human dignity – considered in its social dimension – ensures that all persons must enjoy fundamental rights, regardless of position occupied in the social hierarchy, and have the right to work in conditions that allow them to have a free and dignified life. It is therefore worth reminding that as affirmed by the International Covenant on Economic, Social, and Cultural Rights (ICESCR), the right to work 'includes the right of everyone to the opportunity to gain his living by work which he freely chooses or accepts' (Art. 6). The right to work is thus 'essential for realising other human rights and forms an inseparable and inherent part of human dignity. Every individual has the right to be able to work, allowing him/her to live in dignity…In this light, the conception of work provided in Article 6 shall be understood as "decent work"' (UN Committee on Economic, Social and Cultural Rights, 2005, para 1). Indeed, decent work – as the ILO highlights in its documents (see ILO, 1999) – refers to employment that contributes to the social and economic stability of workers and is the foundation of a decent life.

From the perspective highlighting decent work as a specific aspect of (social) human dignity, the principle of dignity entails an obligation of states to guarantee that no person works and lives in exploitative and degrading conditions. This, accordingly, means – as discussed in the subsequent chapters – preventing persons from being and making decisions in situations of vulnerability such as to lead them to 'accept' work in exploitative conditions as one of the few viable practical choices available to them. Building on Rodota's analysis, Emilio Santoro and Diana Genovese (2018, p. 553) argued that 'to ensure the dignity of the individual, one must not deprive the person of their freedom of choice, but rather ensure that their choice is not made under conditions of vulnerability that anyone could exploit'.

[18] See, for instance, the landmark 2011 decision in *M.S.S. v Belgium and Greece*, App no 30696/09.

[19] See, for instance, Italian Constitutional Court., Decision No. 217, 1988, I. and French Constitutional Court, 94–359 DC of 19 January 1995.

Dignity is therefore harmed when a person's freedom of choice is limited or, in severe cases, seriously restricted, so that the person is led to accept exploitative conditions.

Hence, far from referring to a merely abstract and moral conception of human dignity, the normative theoretical understanding of exploitation as a violation of human dignity should drive attention, as discussed below, to the background conditions of injustices and inequality creating and amplifying situations of vulnerability to exploitation from which abusive actors may benefit.

2.1.3 Exploitation as a Structural Continuum

As highlighted so far, since the 2000s, the term exploitation has been progressively incorporated in relevant international, supranational, and national legal texts, and conceived not only with regard to prostitution/sex work but also in other labour sectors. At the same time, the notion of exploitation has been increasingly framed in terms of violation of human dignity. Building on analyses of relevant literature, I have thus emphasised the need to consider the social dimension of human dignity in order to avoid abstract and simple moralistic understandings of this concept and focus instead on the social and relational context in which the persons are located and therefore on the conditions in which they make decisions, such as labour options and circumstances.

However, the gradual use of exploitation in international and national legal texts has not reflected a conceptual clarity of this notion, especially labour exploitation. In contrast to a social human dignity approach, exploitation has tended to be mainly addressed from a criminal justice perspective (Mantouvalou, 2018a, b).

As discussed in Sect. 1.1, labour exploitation is not defined in international law. Only a few pieces of regional and national legislation such as the EU Employers Sanction Directive 2009/52 and the criminal codes of Italy,[20] Sweden,[21] and France[22] include a definition. Some EU Member States, notably Belgium and the Netherlands, apply the crime of trafficking in human beings in a more flexible manner to also cover victims of particularly exploitative working conditions according to the Employers Sanction Directive (FRA, 2021); others introduced provisions criminalising labour exploitation when transposing the Employers Sanction Directive into national legislation, but limited them to third-country nationals in irregular conditions. With regard to non-EU countries, for example the UK,[23] exploitation is addressed in the framework of the 2015 Modern Slavery Act (discussed in Chap. 7),

[20] See Art. 603bis of Italian Criminal Code.

[21] Brottsbalk SFS 1962:700.

[22] Art. 225-14 of the French Criminal Code.

[23] It is worth noting that even while still a member of the EU, the UK had opted out from Employers Sanctions Directive 2009/52.

where the reference to an umbrella term such as modern slavery tends to invoke the worst forms of exploitation (Mantouvalou, 2018a).

Especially in those countries that frame labour exploitation in mainly anti-trafficking and modern slavery laws, legal and political discourses and interventions have tended to consider exploitation primarily in terms of extreme forms, i.e., slavery, forced labour and trafficking (Chuang, 2015; Mantouvalou, 2018b). On the other hand, in countries such as Italy or Sweden where labour exploitation is specifically defined in national legislation, exploitation is primarily conceived and addressed as a criminal justice issue (Caprioglio & Rigo, 2020; Sjödin, 2021). In both cases, exploitation tends to be considered as a kind of contingent pathology (Marks, 2008) connected to a dimension of arbitrariness and individual deviant behaviours requiring a repressive response – an approach many scholars call into question (Mantouvalou, 2018b; Kotiswaran, 2017).

A first concern is that such a view tends to distil the complex nature of exploitation into a simple narrative of crime perpetrated by unscrupulous individuals or organisations and suffered by victims that need to be rescued (O'Connell Davidson, 2010). It follows that this approach overlooks the pervasive and systemic character of labour exploitation, including severe exploitation, in contemporary capitalist systems. As stressed in the introduction to this volume, while developed countries, and particularly in Europe, commit the protection of workers' rights to collective bargaining and a certain degree of re-distribution and social protection measures, exploitation – including in its worst forms – is a structural element of their economic and labour market systems (see, for instance, FRA, 2015; ILO, 2017; UNODC, 2022), characterised by labour deregulation and flexibilisation according to neo-liberal dynamics.

As the scholarship notes, capitalism operates by constantly creating differentiations (Mezzadra & Neilson, 2021; Fraser, 2018; Fraser & Jaeggi, 2018; Bhattacharyya, 2018), resulting in a significant segment of the population having limited rights and scarce social protection. Several aspects of contemporary globalisation align with this process, including neo-liberal policies, dispossession through wars and conflicts, post-colonial processes, structural adjustment policies, ecological disasters, transnational criminal activity, and restrictive migration and social legislation. In particular, as discussed in following chapters, the restriction in regular migratory paths, especially for 'low- and medium-skilled' third-country national workers, and the simultaneous compression of labour and social rights in many countries play a major role, as Maria Grazia Giammarinaro (2022b) argues, in creating an 'edge population' (Bhattacharyya, 2018) – migrant people in situations of vulnerability – that is instrumental for the functioning of economic systems globally. Gendered and racialised discrimination and power dynamics significantly foster and affect these processes, ultimately resulting in marginalisation and exploitation. In this context, as discussed in Sect. 2.1.4, the distinction between the spheres of production and reproduction, mirrored in a gendered and racialised hierarchy of productive and reproductive labour, plays a crucial role (Fraser, 2018; Bhattacharyya, 2018; Rigo, 2022).

Another (and associated) concern linked to viewing exploitation as contingent pathology is that by primarily focusing on interpersonal relations between exploiters and victims and related unequal contractual relationships, the dominant criminal law approach to exploitation tends to overlook the background conditions, and structures – economic, social, and legal factors – that lead to instances of injustice and exploitation at work. In this context, those cases that do not straightforwardly amount to a crime (such as trafficking, forced labour, or labour exploitation) and lack strong elements showing that consent of the person concerned has been vitiated, are often not considered as situations of exploitation. Consequently, this produces a sort of 'normalisation' of less serious or evident forms of exploitation (Palumbo, 2017; Giammarinaro, 2022b). For instance, as Mantouvalou (2018b, p. 1) notes with specific regard to UK Modern Slavery legal and policy actions, the current trend that focuses primarily on the most extreme forms and on situations in which workers' consent to abusive conditions is evidently not genuine 'may appear to legitimise unfair treatment at work, which should also be viewed as exploitative'.

Countering such a narrow and risky approach to exploitation and framing it in a more articulated narrative, significant scholarship (Le Baron, 2020; Mantouvalou, 2017; Fudge, 2017; Rigo, 2015) has underlined the need to consider the structural accounts of exploitation in neo-liberal capitalism, taking into account the impact of market structures, relevant legal and policy frameworks, and social inequalities. Within this prism, exploitation consists of a wide spectrum of forms and relations of commodification and abuse, many of which often have a 'contractual' character (Phillips, 2013).

Klara Skrivankova (2010, p. 5), among others, suggests conceiving exploitation as a continuum of experiences characterised by an increasing level of unfair treatment, deprivation of rights, and restriction of personal autonomy, 'ranging from decent work through minor and major labour law violations, to extreme exploitation in the form of forced labour' or trafficking or slavery. As Skrivankova points out, 'the concept of a continuum comes in to help us understand how the denial of rights to certain categories of workers (allowing for their exploitation) fills the space between the desirable (decent work) and the unacceptable (forced labour)...The continuum of exploitation aids understanding of the persistent problem of the changing reality of work, captures various forms of exploitation and assists in identifying ways of addressing it' (ibid. p. 18).

By challenging exploitation's 'false contingency' (Marks, 2008) as relating mainly to individual pathologic relationships, the paradigm of exploitation as a continuum draws attention to its structural roots and highlights how the difference between forms of exploitation is a matter of degree of 'immobility, devaluation, and coercion' (Allain et al., 2013). Exploitation thus includes cases that, while not necessarily amounting to crimes, are characterised alternatively or cumulatively by harsh or even degrading working and living conditions, low wages, inadequate safety measures, and the absence of basic social protections, especially if involving migrant workers (Giammarinaro, 2022a, b). The diverse situations along the continuum between decent work and serious forms of exploitation may fall under the scope of different legal fields – including criminal law, civil/ labour law, and human rights law – and may require the combined implementation of various legal instruments and measures (Skrivankova, 2010).

Today the continuum approach to exploitation is increasingly adopted in institutional texts and reports (FRA, 2015). Furthermore, although the notion of continuum is not explicitly used, the continuum approach can be found in some national judicial decisions, for instance in Italy,[24] concerning cases of labour exploitation (see Chap. 6).

While recognising the relevance of the continuum approach, some scholars point out that it can risk reinforcing the idea that 'coercion/consent and freedom/unfreedom are antithetical dyads' (see, for instance, Fudge, 2019, p. 117). By contrast, it can be argued that the continuum approach to exploitation should be seen as directing attention to the complexity of persons' experiences at work characterised by combinations of voluntariness and coercion. Approaching exploitation as a continuum thus entails for each case to be considered on its own merits with attention to the spectrum of regimes, pressures, and constraints under which a person acts, accepts, or reacts to different practises and dynamics of exploitation. Such an approach is linked to the frame of exploitation as a violation of social human dignity, which looks to the material conditions that allow a person to have a dignified work and life. All this, in turn, draws attention to situations of vulnerability associated to this exploitation continuum, as discussed in Sect. 2.2.

2.1.4 Labour Exploitation and Social Reproduction

A careful analysis of the complex ways in which exploitation manifests itself today cannot overlook the issue of social reproduction, particularly the traditional distinction between the sphere of production and the sphere of reproduction. Feminist analyses, reflections, and struggles have consistently contested this distinction, which tends to establish a hierarchy between these two areas, obscuring the political and productive nature of tasks traditionally assigned to social reproduction (Picchio, 1992; Bhattacharya, 2017; Toupin, 2018). These activities encompass all the tasks necessary to reproduce human life, from both a material and symbolic perspective (such as cooking, cleaning, raising children, taking care of family members, the elderly, the sick or disabled, but also creating serenity, intimacy, pleasure, and, more generally, supporting social bonds), which are traditionally carried out by women, both unpaid in the domestic-family sphere and in wage-earning form (Picchio, 1992; Brenner & Laslett, 1991).

Italian feminist thought, specifically materialist feminist theories recouping Marxist theory for feminist ends, has since the 1970s offered a significant contribution to the analysis of the role of social reproduction in the capitalist processes of value production. In particular, the important works of Mariarosa Dalla Costa,

[24] See for instance Tribunal of Prato, Decision of 4 November 2019, No. 330.

Leopoldina Fortunati, Silvia Federici, Antonella Picchio, and Alisa Dal Re have revealed how the naturalisation and devaluation of reproductive labour, historically carried out by women, are fundamental to capitalist accumulation processes, allowing for the containment of labour force wages (Dalla Costa, 1972; Fortunati, 1981; Picchio, 1992; Federici, 2004, 2014). Internationally, important insights on this theme have been provided by Selma Jamees (2012) and Maria Mies (2014), and more recently by Tithi Bhattacharya (2017) and Nancy Fraser (2017). All these analyses, although diversified and with different approaches, have the merit of providing a different understanding of the functioning of capitalist society, focusing on the correlation between extractive capitalism and the undervaluation and compression of the conditions of life reproduction in processes of subordination based on gender, class, and racialised inequalities.

In a recent work on social reproduction theory, Tithi Bhattacharya (2017, p. 3) has underlined how feminist theories on social reproduction see and treat forms of oppression (through gender, race, sexuality, ableism, etc.) 'as structurally relational to, and hence shaped by, capitalist production.' In this perspective, such theories are concerned with understanding how categories of oppression – such as gender, race, sexuality, and so on – are simultaneously connected to and generated by the processes of capital accumulation.

In this line, in an influential work on racial capitalism, Gargi Bhattacharyya (2018) has significantly highlighted the continuities between the dynamics of appropriation and devaluation of reproductive labour and racialisation. As the author argues, throughout the historical trajectories of capitalism, racialised subjects have consistently and systematically experienced dispossession and devaluation. This has occurred in ways compatible with processes of extraction and depletion specifically targeting activities and sectors considered as 'non-productive', even though they are fundamental to the sustenance of capitalist life. In this sense, Bhattacharyya sheds light on how, within racial capitalism, individuals are attributed differential and hierarchical positions within capitalist relations in both the spheres of reproduction and production.

Migration regimes play a crucial role in this. The literature on gender and migration has underscored the indispensable contribution of women migrant workers to the reproduction of contemporary societies on a global scale, revealing the gender, racial, and class hierarchies underpinning these process and dynamics (Ehrenreich & Russell Hochschild, 2002; Parreñas, 2001; Anderson, 2000; Kofman & Raghuram, 2015). In particular, by specifically examining the working and living conditions of migrant domestic workers, many studies have explored the dynamics of gender, race, and class discrimination and the subordination experienced by migrant women in the countries of arrival (Parreñas, 2001; Anderson, 2000; Teeple Hopkins, 2017). A common theme in these analyses is the emphasis on the precarious migratory status characterising the conditions of many migrant women employed in social reproduction sectors, particularly in low-skilled areas such as domestic work.

Legal scholar Enrica Rigo (2020, 2022) has provided important insights by specifically examining the interconnections between social reproduction and mobility. It is worth noting here that topic of social reproduction has received attention also within feminist legal scholarship, in diverse legal fields, including family, welfare, international labour, and migration law (see, for instance, Silbaugh, 1996; Halley & Rittich, 2010; Alessandrini, 2018; Kotiswaran, 2023). In Italy, for instance, the works of Maria Rosaria Marella (2018) on family law and Enrica Rigo (2022) on migration have played a significant role in bringing attention to this matter. In particular, Rigo has focused on the connection between processes of social reproduction and migration regulation regimes, highlighting how these regimes are built and simultaneously reproduce a conceptual distinction between production and reproduction. As Rigo underlines, the proliferation and spread of borders constitute a process that 'coercively assigns migrants to hierarchized regimes, not only of labour but also of the reproduction of life itself' (ibid., p. 81). Emblematic in this regard, as discussed in the following chapters, are EU and national legal frameworks concerning low-skilled labour, such as seasonal workers. These frameworks contain workers' mobility, ensuring their temporary status by limiting their rights, especially those concerning their reproductive conditions like access to family reunification. All of this, in turn, has significant effects in terms of gender-based inequalities, discrimination, and forms of exploitation.

As Rigo (2022) argues, the issue of social reproduction is also essential to understanding the forms and dynamics of exploitation in their structural dimension. The regimes of migrants' reproduction represent, indeed, a functional element of a production system based on exploitation that operates through the compression of costs related to the reproductive sphere of the workforce. This is evident in the live-in domestic work sector, as discussed in the following chapters, where cohabitation with employers, often in inadequate conditions, is functional to the compression of the costs of the labour force. Similar dynamics can be observed in the agricultural sector, where the production model relies on the reduction of the reproduction costs related to workers' living conditions, such as accommodation. But emblematic of these dynamics, as will be highlighted in the case of Italy, are also the reception centres for asylum seekers that in many contexts have become reservoirs from which employers and intermediaries can recruit a low-cost labour force. As Caprioglio and Rigo (2020) point out, in the case of reception centres in Italy, there is an externalisation of the costs of reproducing the workforce. These costs are thus shifted onto the reception system and do not burden employers or more generally the supply chain.

These dynamics intensify when it comes to women migrant workers. Many of those migrant women considered 'low-skilled' workers – especially in countries such as Italy with a labour market highly segregated on the basis of gender and nationality – find a job in those sectors necessary for social reproduction such as domestic and care work, sex work, and agricultural work that are characterised by irregularity and exploitative conditions (Garofalo Geymonat et al., 2023). Moreover, as in the Italian case, many of these women workers transit from one of these unprotected sectors to another or engage in them simultaneously (Giammarinaro, 2022a), experiencing a shift from one form of exploitation to another or simultaneous forms of exploitation (Chap. 5). Within these dynamics of overlaps, continuities, and negotiations, forms of exploitation hinge on reducing and limiting costs concerning the reproduction conditions of these women workers.

At the same time, most of these women still bear a greater burden of family and reproductive responsibilities (Giammarinaro, 2022a, b; Sciurba, 2015). This, as discussed in Chap. 5, results in women workers managing a doubly burdensome and stressful workload, combining demanding working conditions and degrading living conditions with the family's reproductive work, along with the associated need for immediate earnings (Palumbo, 2022). Family and reproductive responsibilities thus represent a key element in creating and amplifying situations of vulnerability to exploitation.

2.2 Vulnerability and Its Legal and Theoretical Conceptions

Over recent decades, the notion of 'vulnerability' has become prominent in legal discourses and texts, especially in the ambit of human rights and migration law. Lawmakers and courts, at both international and national levels, have started using this notion with respect to different contexts and different categories of persons (Ippolito, 2020; Santoro, 2020; Timmer et al., 2021). Some legal scholars describe a 'quiet revolution' in the systemic use of this notion by courts, in particular the ECtHR (Timmer, 2013; Peroni & Timmer, 2013), thus expanding the scope of the rights laid down in relevant human rights Conventions, especially with regard to the protection of migrants' rights.

However, this progressive incorporation of the concept of vulnerability in international, European, and national legal texts has been far from being linear in terms of use and interpretation (Timmer et al., 2021; Leboeuf, 2022). When mobilised as part of legal reasoning, vulnerability seeks to ensure that everyone can access their rights on an equal footing and without opposing the universal character of human rights. However, one key contention is that dedicated attention to vulnerable persons in legal reasoning and instruments bears the risk of fostering selection and exclusion dynamics by marking a distinction between those persons/groups considered vulnerable, and therefore deserving of protection, and those who are not.

As Santoro (2020, p. 317) underlines in his analysis retracing how the concept of vulnerability has been incorporated in international and EU legislation on migration and trafficking, the use of this notion in legal discourses has acted, especially in a first stage, as 'a way to re-propose the protection needs of the weakest social groups at a time in history when the lexicon that made it possible to claim and represent them during the second half of the twentieth century seems to be de-legitimized'. The concept of vulnerability has therefore been used to define those migrant persons who for personal characteristics need some specific protection.

As discussed below, the definition of 'position of vulnerability' adopted in relevant international and EU legal instruments on trafficking is particularly innovative as it detaches vulnerability from being associated to categories of persons/groups considered intrinsically weak and ascribes this notion to the social context. Across time there has also been increasing attention, in both relevant supra-national and national case law, to the socio-contextual dimension of vulnerability, including with respect to cases of labour exploitation (Giammarinaro & Palumbo, 2021).

Before looking at the conception of vulnerability in international and European legal instruments concerning exploitation and the challenges in its understanding, the next section focuses, from a theoretical perspective, on the complexity of the notion of 'vulnerability', recently defined as a 'chameleon concept' (Timmer et al., 2021), underscoring the importance of considering its situational dimension.

2.2.1 Vulnerability in Social and Political Philosophy and Its Situational Dimension

Parallel to the progressive incorporation of the notion of vulnerability in legal discourses and texts, this concept has been increasingly debated in various disciplines (Philosophy, Law, Sociology, etc.) and from different perspectives, ranging from feminist scholars to those within the human rights field (Mackenzie et al., 2014; Timmer, 2013; Giolo & Pastore, 2018). It is worth emphasising that vulnerability and related core issues addressed in this theoretical debate (for instance, human fragility and dependency) have long been the subject of philosophical, political, and legal reflections, even if the terminology used has been different. The assumption of human vulnerability is, indeed, at the core of modern political thought (Verza, 2018; Santoro, 2020).[25] Awareness of the condition of vulnerability of human beings, which characterises every person in the name of common mortality and the fear of evil, and the related drive to protect it, in Hobbesian analysis is the key factor for each individual participating in the pact to enter into the social contract and accept their subordination to the Leviathan (Hobbes, 1651). Similarly, the natural rights in John Locke's (1690) theory of the social contract were also conceived as aimed at guaranteeing and protecting against common vulnerability (Verza, 2018).

However, as feminist analyses emphasise, while liberal thought was developed on the assumption of universal vulnerability and the need to protect it from private force and violence, it has incorporated in its own paradigms and assumptions the patriarchal structure of power and domination (Pateman, 1988; Brown, 1995). As feminist political philosopher Carole Pateman (1988, p. 2) argues, while the social contract theory is conventionally thought of as a story about universal freedom, it is instead a story of both freedom and domination: the freedom of autonomous and rational (male) subjects relying on the subordination of the other subjects, in particular women, not taking part in the original contract, but being subject to it.

By relegating to the private sphere 'the vulnerabilising manifestations of patriarchal culture' (Verza, 2018), liberal thought has thus supported a conception of autonomous, capable, and independent (male) subject built on the subjection and

[25] See, in this regard, Santoro (2020), who considers the classical theories of modern political thought through the lens of vulnerability; see also Verza (2018).

marginalisation of those who are considered 'non-autonomous', 'non-self-determining', and 'non-independent' subjects – in particular, women (Brown, 1995).

Within this normative model of (male) autonomous and self-independent subject, vulnerability – no longer read as a condition characterising all persons – has been progressively viewed as a special trait of some specific situations considered in need of protection: a protection that 'has come to be configured in the cold, asymmetrical, and basically stigmatising terms of the *top-down* relationship promoted by performance-based welfare systems'[26] (Verza, 2018, p. 240). In this framework, vulnerability has become an inherent element to some categories of persons perceived as the exception to the (male) norm: in particular, women, children, the elderly, persons with disabilities, poor people, and so on.

This approach has been exacerbated in the neoliberal age. As feminist political philosopher Judith Butler (2004) has powerfully highlighted, in the neoliberal context the vulnerable subjects are those subjects to be protected and assisted, but who cannot claim transformation nor the redistribution of goods and resources; they can only ask to be assisted and taken care of. This is the main dimension of agency accessible to them in line to a corrective justice model, which in neoliberal societies has replaced the redistributive model of justice aimed instead to address the systemic conditions creating vulnerability (Giolo & Pastore, 2018). Moreover, as Butler (2015) has also stressed, in neoliberal societies the vulnerable subjects can also suddenly become the target of restrictive policies in ambit of fundamental rights protection due, for example, to high costs and economic crisis.

It is against this background that the notion of vulnerability has been explicitly at the centre of a vibrant debate fostered by feminist scholars over the last few decades (Fineman, 2008, 2011; Butler, 2004; Mackenzie et al., 2014). By marking what has been defined as a 'vulnerability turn' (Giolo & Pastore, 2018), these scholars have aimed at recovering the complex nature of the concept of vulnerability against those conceptions of this notion that conceal mechanisms of domination and power. In particular, by questioning the liberal 'myth of autonomy' (Santoro, 1991, 2003) and the conception of vulnerability as something static or fixed, intrinsic to specific categories of persons or groups conceived as victims in need only of protection, such a feminist scholarship has significantly underlined the idea of vulnerability as a condition of shared humanity and *simultaneously* as related to the social context and power relationships in which a person is situated (Fineman, 2008; Butler, 2004).

Notably, feminist and legal scholar Martha Fineman (2008) has proposed a universal approach to vulnerability – which, as highlighted above, is at the origin of modern political thought[27] – seeking to overcome the binary idea of vulnerable and

[26] My translation.

[27] In this regard, feminist legal scholar Orsetta Giolo (2018) has criticised Fineman's analysis of vulnerability for not explicitly referring to the notion of vulnerability in the classics of philosophical-juridical and philosophical-political thought that founded the origins of the law and of the institutions of modernity on the assumption of human vulnerability. According to Giolo, in this way Fineman contributes to the drawing a distinction between the 'liberal' conception of vulnerability and what can be described as a 'neoliberal' one (ibid, p. 258).

passive versus non-vulnerable and active persons. As Fineman (2012) posits, vulnerability is constitutive and a common trait of human beings: all human beings are exposed to various forms of harm and injury, although each individual's vulnerability may vary depending on their resources and personal characteristics. While vulnerability, as Fineman (2013, p. 32) argues, 'is conceived as universal and constant on an abstract theoretical level that a construction of the legal and political subject requires, on the individual or experiential level, it is realized in particular, varied and unique ways'. Vulnerability therefore is universal, but also depends on human 'social location': we are all 'differently situated within webs of economic and institutional relationships that structure our options and create opportunities' (ibid., p. 33). Such a conception of vulnerability challenges the liberal model of an autonomous and self-independent subject, suggesting a relational and contextually relative approach to autonomy (on this point, see also Santoro, 2003). From this perspective, in Fineman's (Fineman, 2017, p. 219) view, states play a central role as 'inescapable vulnerabilities argue for a responsive state that ensures equality of opportunities and individuals' access to society institutions'.[28]

Other feminist scholars such as Martha Nussbaum (2006) and Judith Butler (2004), from different perspectives, have also highlighted the conception of vulnerability as a condition of shared humanity and how a person's vulnerability is linked to the inherent sociality of human life, while varying in forms and degrees in people's lives and depending on the social contexts in which a person is situated (Mackenzie et al., 2014). For instance, Butler (2004) notes that the human body 'is constitutively social and interdependent', and it is this corporeal vulnerability that makes human life precarious. Yet, while stressing that precariousness is an ontological condition of human life, Butler (2004, 2015) also highlights that individuals are not all affected by it to the same degree and to same extent; indeed, vulnerability is always related to people's positions in society and power relations.

Therefore, vulnerability is both an inescapable human condition and socially embedded. Such an approach, however, does not equate vulnerability with the absence of persons' capacities and agency. Butler (2004, 2015), for instance, is careful to argue against the association of vulnerability with victimhood and weakness. Far from opposing or excluding agency, this understanding of vulnerability as related to its social dimension recognises how persons act, negotiate, resist and make their choices within contexts marked by structural injustices and inequalities.

In their important work on vulnerability, feminist legal and social scholars Mackenzie, Rogers, and Dodds (Mackenzie et al., 2014) have underlined the need to consider both the ontological character and the social/relational dimension of vulnerability. They have proposed a taxonomy of different sources of vulnerability that takes into account the complex and strongly related dimensions of vulnerability, building on Robert Goodin's (Goodin, 1985, p. 191) considerations that 'any dependency or vulnerability is arguably created, shaped, or sustained, at least in

[28] Fineman's theory of a 'responsive state' has been criticised by a different body of literature (see for instance Giolo, 2018; Morondo Taramundi, 2016; Bernardini, 2022), which has also highlighted its risks in relation to a protective state.

part, by existing social arrangements. None is wholly natural'. In particular, Mackenzie et al. (2014) have proposed the notion of inherent vulnerability to refer to sources that are intrinsic to the human condition and arise from persons' corporality, dependence on others, and their affective and social natures. Furthermore, they have developed the notion of 'situational' vulnerability, shedding light on the social and context-specific dimension of vulnerability caused or accentuated or both by personal, social, political, economic, or environmental situations of individuals or social groups. Situational vulnerability also refers to the impact of abusive interpersonal and social relationships as well as socio-political oppression or injustice caused by institutional structures and policies,[29] highlighting 'the ways that inequality of power, dependency, capacity, or need render some agents vulnerable to harm or exploitation by others' (Mackenzie et al., 2014, p. 6). Situational vulnerability, as Mackenzie et al. emphasise, may be 'short term, intermittent, or enduring' (ibid., p. 8).

Far from being clearly distinct, the inherent and situational dimensions of vulnerability are strongly interconnected. Furthermore, both inherent and situational vulnerability may be dispositional (potential) or occurrent (actual). As Dodds (2014, p. 39) argues, 'the dispositional-occurrent distinction enables us to determine whether an identifiable vulnerability is potential or actual and to distinguish vulnerabilities that are not yet or not likely to become sources of harm from those that place a person at imminent risk of harm'. For example, unaccompanied children are potentially vulnerable to abuse and exploitation; however, whether or not children are actually in a situation of vulnerability to exploitation will depend on social, economic, and legal circumstances.

Vulnerability is therefore conceived as caused or exacerbated by the interaction of personal and structural factors (legal, economic, political, and social elements) rendering some people vulnerable. The structural factors refer to those policies, laws, norms and practices producing those 'structural injustices' that, as political and feminist theorist Iris Marion Young (1990) has argued, place large categories of persons 'under a systematic threat of domination or deprivation of the means to develop and exercise their capacities'. These factors include, as examined in subsequent chapters, restrictive migration policies and related social reproduction regimes (Rigo, 2022) putting large categories of migrants, especially migrant women, in conditions of general disadvantage and vulnerability. Inequalities on the basis, for instance, of gender, class and nationality imbue and intensify these dynamics and processes.

Hence, vulnerability is a socially-embedded condition that is variable in its form and its intensity, depending on the social relations and hierarchies of power characterising the context in which a person is located. In this sense, as discussed in Sect. 2.2.3, the understanding of vulnerability is strongly related to the theory of

[29] Mackenzie, Rogers and Dodds talk in this regard about 'pathogenic vulnerabilities' which is a subset of situational vulnerability (Mackenzie et al., 2014).

intersectionality, introduced and developed by, among others, feminist legal scholar Kimberlé Crenshaw (1989).

Building on this theoretical framework, in this volume I focus on the situational conception of vulnerability, taking into account the interconnection between persons' characteristics and socio/contextual elements. For this reason, I will avoid using the term 'vulnerable' persons. Instead, by adapting and elaborating on the taxonomy proposed by Mackenzie et al. (2014), I will use the notion of 'situational vulnerabilities' or 'situations of vulnerability' to underline the interplay between personal characteristics or conditions and structural circumstances or factors such as policy, legal, economic, and social elements. This situational conception of vulnerability allows us to shift attention to the socio-contextual framework in which persons are situated and, consequently, to the impact of power relationships and institutional dynamics, including relevant states' policies and laws and related practices (Santoro, 2020). Such an approach, in turn, avoids the risk of favouring essentialistic views and perpetuating stigmatisation of some specific individuals or groups considered vulnerable per se, thus reinforcing disempowering dynamics.

Importantly, this situational understanding of vulnerability does not preclude a person's agency, as it recognises the trajectories and dynamics of action and autonomy within a framework of economic, social, affective, and power relationships marked by structural injustices and inequalities. In other words, far from glorifying an abstract idea of persons' agency, a situational view of vulnerability pays attention to the ways in which persons act, negotiate, and make choices in the face of structural conditions and constraints affecting and limiting individual choices and decision-making. In this regard – and paraphrasing Camille Schmoll (2022) – the expression 'agency in tension' can be used to underline the combination of constraint and the pursuit of freedom, exploitation and resistance characterising the dimension of agency and, as discussed for instance in Chap. 5, that emerges from the experiences and life stories of many women workers. Lastly, such a situational approach to vulnerability helps avoid paternalistic responses, instead enabling us to identify actions that both address the systemic framework producing vulnerabilities and which facilitate paths of empowerment and effective social and labour inclusion (Giammarinaro & Palumbo, 2021).

2.2.2 Vulnerability in Relevant International and European Legislation and ECtHR Case Law on Exploitation

As mentioned, over recent years, the notion of vulnerability has been progressively incorporated in international, regional, and national legal instruments in the field of asylum, migration, and exploitation. With specific regard to exploitation, the term 'vulnerability' appeared for the first time in the international legal framework concerning trafficking. In particular, the 'abuse of a position of vulnerability' was added to the list of illicit means in the definition of trafficking of persons contained in the

UN Palermo Protocol at the very final stage of the negotiation of this document. The decision to include this type of means was due to the need to find a compromise – among national official delegations and among feminist groups – between an excessive criminalisation, on the one hand, and underestimating the subtlety of coercive means used by exploiters and traffickers, on the other (Giammarinaro & Palumbo, 2021, p. 47). Indeed, while some organisations, in particular feminist neo-abolitionist groups, pushed for a decisive broadening of the definition of trafficking to include forms of subtle subjugation, other groups, including sex workers' rights organisations, were concerned that excessive enlargement of the area of criminalisation could be used as a pretext for repression of consensual forms of sexual commerce (Chuang, 2010).

A compromise was found by referring to the definition of vulnerability contained in one of the first EU soft law documents on trafficking for sexual exploitation, namely the 1997 Hague Declaration,[30] which was drafted after significant involvement of feminist organisations. However, the Palermo Protocol did not incorporate the definition of vulnerability provided by the 1997 Hague Declaration. It considered its essential content by introducing the concept of 'abuse of a position of vulnerability' in the list of illicit means by which trafficking can occur, applying it to all types of exploitation, not only to sexual exploitation. The definition of vulnerability offered by the Hague Declaration was instead inserted in the *travaux preparatoires* of the Palermo Protocol, specifying that a position of vulnerability 'is understood to refer to any situation in which the person involved has no real and acceptable alternative but to submit to the abuse involved' (UNODC, 2006, p. 347).

Such a definition has subsequently been integrated into relevant EU Directives – first the Framework Decision 2002/629/JHA on combatting trafficking in human beings and subsequently in Directive 2011/36/EU on trafficking (replacing the Framework Decision of 2002). More specifically, Directive 2011/36/EU (known as the Anti-Trafficking Directive) codified in its provisions the definition of position of vulnerability as 'a situation in which the person concerned has no real or acceptable alternative but to submit to the abuse involved' (Art. 2(2)).

This definition of position of vulnerability reflects a situational dimension of this notion (Sciurba & Palumbo, 2018; Santoro, 2020). Indeed, this definition does not limit vulnerability to the person's inherent characteristics such as those vulnerable persons/groups listed in other international and European instruments on migration and asylum (Marchetti & Palumbo, 2021). On the contrary, it draws attention to the constructed nature of vulnerability and in particular to the interplay of personal, circumstantial and structural factors that expose persons to dynamics of exploitation and abuse, leaving them without any concrete and real alternative but to 'accept' being involved in abusive and exploitative relations and conditions. Therefore, especially in the context of judicial interpretation, it would be crucial to question the concept of acceptability, which is closely connected to that of vulnerability. In this

[30] The Hague Ministerial Declaration on European Guidelines for Effective Measures to Prevent and Combat Trafficking in Women for the Purpose of Sexual Exploitation, 1997.

sense, as has been argued (Giammarinaro & Palumbo, 2021), it is important to avoid the use of a 'reasonableness test' based on criteria of 'social normality' as cases of exploitation often concern extreme situations. At the same time, the concept of acceptability shall be integrated with that of the 'reality' of the alternative. In other words, what matters is that the alternative is a real alternative, that is, it presents the characteristics of a non-exploitative job or at least of a job in which exploitation is not associated with coercive or abusive practices and therefore is not incompatible with the realisation of the person's life plan. This 'situational' understanding of vulnerability requires a case-by-case assessment of the interplay of personal and contextual factors producing it.

As Santoro (2020) has rightly underlined, in contrast to a situational approach to vulnerability, Anti-Trafficking Directive 2011/36/EU (similarly to the previous Framework Decision 2002/629/JHA) also provides for reference to categories of individuals/groups considered vulnerable per se (see, for instance, recital 12). In this sense, Santoro points to a 'schizophrenic' and 'ambiguous' approach of the EU legislation, which seems to swing from an understanding of vulnerability as a static condition intrinsic to some persons/categories to one that takes into account the situational dimension of this notion. However, despite these ambiguities, Anti-Trafficking Directive 2011/36/EU undoubtedly has merit having codified, together with Framework Decision 2002/629/JHA, in EU law a situational definition of position of vulnerability.

The other regional and international instruments (including the *travaux preparatoires* of the Palermo Protocol) containing a situational conception of vulnerability are soft law documents. For instance, the *Explanatory Report* of the 2005 Council of Europe Convention on Trafficking[31] incorporates the above-illustrated definition of position of vulnerability included in the Palermo Protocol's *travaux preparatoires*, and successively adopted in Anti-Trafficking Directive 2011/36/EU. Furthermore, the Explanatory report affirms that: 'The vulnerability may be of any kind, whether physical, psychological, emotional, family-related, social or economic. The situation might, for example, involve insecurity or illegality of the victim's administrative status, economic dependence or fragile health. In short, the situation can be any state of hardship in which a human being is impelled to accept being exploited' (para. 83). Therefore, the document refers to both the personal and context-specific elements of vulnerabilities, explicitly recognising that certain situations of vulnerability are created by a lack of economic opportunities or by financial difficulties, as well as by the impact of relevant legislation and policies (involving 'insecurity or illegality of the victim's administrative status').

Regarding the international instruments concerning slavery and forced labour illustrated in Chap. 1, the notion of vulnerability does not explicitly appear in these texts. However, the ILO (2002) supervisory bodies have clarified that psychological coercion – such as threatening to report an undocumented worker to the authorities – can be qualified as threat of penalty according to the ILO definition of forced

[31] Council of Europe (2005), para 83.

labour contained in the 1930 ILO Convention. Such a subtle form of coercion indirectly refers to the notion of vulnerability (Giammarinaro & Palumbo, 2021). Furthermore, the ILO has produced the Survey Guidelines (ILO, 2012b), a soft-law instrument intended to help states measure the problem of forced labour and which directly addresses the abuse of a position of vulnerability in the context of forced labour. The document does not provide a definition of vulnerability, however, its wording reflects a situational approach to vulnerability; the guidelines, for instance, refer to vulnerability resulting from irregular migration status (ibid., p. 75). A broad conception of vulnerability that takes into account its situational dimension also seems to emerge in the 2014 ILO Recommendation on forced labour (No. 203), which focuses on the root causes of vulnerability, shedding light on its contextual character. The same approach is found in the 2019 ILO Violence and Harassment Convention No. 190, which refers to 'situations of vulnerability' – and not to a list of vulnerable groups/individuals – thus revealing an attention to the complexity and context-related aspect of this notion.

Similarly, the 2018 UN Global Compact for Safe, Orderly and Regular Migration (A/RES/73/195) dedicates a specific objective (number 7) to 'address and reduce vulnerabilities in migration', recognising that migrant persons face multiple and intersecting forms of vulnerability (including to labour exploitation and abuse). Furthermore, the document highlights the need to review relevant policies and practices that can create, exacerbate, or increase migrants' vulnerabilities. From this perspective, the UN Global Compact adopts an approach to vulnerability that disentangles it from being only related to personal characteristics and brings it to its social, political, and legal dimensions (Atak et al., 2018).

In recent years, therefore, the notion of vulnerability has begun entering legal texts concerning exploitation, especially its severe forms such as forced labour and trafficking, with increasing attention to the situational dimension of this concept. However, as a 2013 study by UNODC highlighted, the vagueness of the notion of vulnerability and lack of a clear definition often leads to ambiguities that make it difficult to understand and apply: 'it is unclear what "real and acceptable alternative" actually means. It is also unclear whether it is the state of mind of the victim or of the alleged perpetrator that is relevant to a determination of whether vulnerability has been abused' (UNODC, 2013, p. 25).

The 2012 ILO Survey Guidelines also raised critical issues in the interpretation of the notion of vulnerability, and in particular of abuse of a position of vulnerability, affirming that 'the obligation to stay in a job because of the absence of alternative employment opportunities, taken alone, does not equate to a forced labour situation; however, if it can be proved that the employer is deliberately exploiting this fact (and the extreme vulnerability which arises from it) to impose more extreme working conditions than would otherwise be possible, then this would amount to forced labour' (ILO, 2012b, p. 16). Furthermore, the document clarified that with respect to the recruitment process, poverty and a family's need for income are not seen as indicative of coercion. By requiring specific deceit on the employer's part, the ILO's approach to situations of vulnerability appears to be restrictive compared to that adopted in international and EU instruments on trafficking (Giammarinaro &

Palumbo, 2021). Also, regarding recruitment processes, the ILO's formulation tends to underestimate the impact of economic difficulties on positions of vulnerability.

The elements to be considered in identifying situations of vulnerability in cases of exploitation and its severe forms such as trafficking are the subject of intense debate (see, for instance, Stoyanova, 2017; Di Martino, 2019; Weatherburn, 2021). This discussion focuses on recent and relevant case law developments at the European and national levels, including for instance Italian case law (see Chap. 6), that have significantly contributed to a more articulated understanding of the notion of vulnerability, paying special attention to its situational dimension.

With specific regard to the issue of vulnerability to labour exploitation, the ECtHR decision in *Chowdury and Others v Greece* (Application No. 21884/15, 30 March 2017) marked an important step in comprehending the notion of vulnerability in relation to dynamics of exploitation. The case concerned 42 undocumented migrant workers from Bangladesh who worked on a strawberry farm in Greece in severe degrading and exploitative conditions: 12-hour days under the supervision of armed guards and housing in makeshift shacks without toilets or running water. The workers were unpaid and when they demanded their wages – amounting to 22 euros per day – were subjected to violent retaliation. The Court recognised that such workers had been subjected to forced labour and had been victims of trafficking based on Article 3 of the Palermo Protocol and Article 4 of the Council of Europe Convention on Trafficking, and therefore condemned Greece for violation of Article 4(2) of the ECHR. In its reasoning, the Court paid specific attention to the situational dimension of workers' vulnerabilities, considering the interplay of different factors producing a situation of vulnerability that exposes migrant workers to exploitation. The Court focused specifically on the workers' condition of irregularity: 'the applicants began working in a situation of vulnerability as irregular migrants without resources and at risk of being arrested, detained and deported' (para. 97). As the Court noted, 'an attempt to leave their work would no doubt have made this more likely and would have meant the loss of any hope of receiving the wages due to them, even in part' (para. 95).

Central in this regard is the issue of voluntariness and consent. By invoking the disproportionate burden test used in its previous judgment,[32] the ECtHR underlined that 'the validity of the consent must be assessed in the light of all the circumstances of the case' (para. 90). In *Chowdury*, the workers were subjected to exploitative conditions; assessing these conditions, the ECtHR emphasised their situations of vulnerability, arguing that where employers abuse their power or take advantage of the vulnerability of workers in order to exploit them, these latter 'do not offer themselves for work voluntarily' (para. 96). The person's consent prior to the abusive conditions is 'not sufficient to exclude the characterisation of work as forced labour' (ibid.) since in a situation of vulnerability, the person has no concrete alternatives and therefore no real choice.

[32] In particular, *Van der Mussele v Belgium* (Application No. 8919/80, 23 November 1983).

The Court highlighted three concurrent factors creating vulnerability: the condition of irregularity as undocumented workers; the consequent risk of being arrested, expelled, and deported; and the lack of economic resources. In doing so, the judges in Strasbourg focused on the structural conditions fostering the situations of vulnerability on which dynamics of exploitation rely. Yet, the Court neglected to consider an important element converging in the production of vulnerability, that is, the forms of discrimination concerning the national and ethnic origin of the applicants – who were all citizens of Bangladesh – in a labour market system marked by genderisation and racialisation dynamics.

However, despite these limitations, it can be argued that the ECtHR's innovative approach gives consideration to the situations of vulnerability and related forms of exploitation in a complex frame that focuses on the interplay of different personal and structural elements causing vulnerability. At the same time, such a frame underlines not only the nature of pathologic exploitation in terms of the abusive relationship between the employers and workers, but also systemic exploitation facilitated by the impact of relevant legal and policy framework on migration.

Such an approach to vulnerability, and accordingly to dynamics of exploitation, has been confirmed by the ECtHR in the more recent judgment *Zoletic and others v. Azerbaijan* (Application No. 20116/12, 7 October 2021), concerning a group of workers recruited in Bosnia and Herzegovina by the Serbaz construction company that brought these workers to Azerbaijan, confiscated their passports, and forced them to work in exploitative conditions and live in unsafe conditions. Even in this case, the Court has affirmed the violation of the prohibition of forced labour, despite the initial consent of the exploited workers. In particular, in line with the decision in *Chowdury*, the Court stressed the 'situation of the applicants' particular vulnerability as irregular migrants without resources', affirming that 'allegations concerning physical and other forms of punishments, retention of documents and restriction of movement explained by threats of possible arrests of the applicants by the local police because of their irregular stay in Azerbaijan (without work and residence permits) were indicative of possible physical and mental coercion and work extracted under the menace of penalty' (para. 166).

2.2.3 Situational Vulnerability, Bargaining Weakness, and Consent to Exploitation

In the cases discussed above, particularly in *Chowdury*, the ECtHR decisions are in line with principle of the irrelevance of consent contained in international and European instruments on trafficking and forced labour. The ECtHR highlighted that taking advantage of a person's vulnerability for the purpose of exploitation excludes voluntariness, even when the person has initially consented. In these cases, although the coercion mechanisms are not immediately identifiable, the freedom of the persons involved is seriously affected due to the lack of alternatives to exploitation.

Yet, it is important to underline that affirming the principle of the 'irrelevance of consent' – and thus the legal ineffectiveness of consent to exploitation – does not mean affirming the exploited person's inability to make decisions and choices; it does not exclude their agency. Rather, it affirms the principle of punishment of the conduct despite the possible acceptance of exploitation by the victim (Giammarinaro, 2021). In other words, it states that the consent of the victim cannot be invoked by exploiters/traffickers to exempt themselves from responsibility.

The issue of consent is, therefore, the other side of vulnerability to exploitation. Indeed, if viewed as a continuum, exploitation is characterised by varying degrees of submission or acceptance or both to certain exploitative practices, depending on the different situations of vulnerability of the persons involved.

It might be argued that in the ECtHR decisions discussed above, the situational dimension of vulnerability to exploitation appears to be easily ascertainable as it is linked mainly to the status of irregularity of the persons involved. In these cases, the situation of vulnerability seems to clearly reflect the definition provided by the Anti-Trafficking Directive 2011/36/EU as being the absence of an effective and acceptable alternative, if not that of submitting to abuse.

Difficulties may however emerge in those cases, increasingly on the rise in the national labour markets in Europe, that do not clearly amount to crimes such as forced labour and trafficking (FRA, 2015; Palumbo, 2022; Siegmann et al., 2022; Mantouvalou, 2020). These often lack strong indications of specific situations of vulnerability to exploitation and, therefore, that the consent of the person concerned has been vitiated. Examples of such cases include situations where workers 'accept' a deprivation of rights and unfair treatment (such as being underpaid, not having a contract, living in degrading conditions) because of their weak bargaining power and limited alternative options. Far from being easily solved, the issue at stake here concerns the complex relationships between agency/autonomy of persons, situations of vulnerability, weak bargaining power, and consent to forms of exploitation.

As scholars, in particular from Critical Legal Studies, discussing freedom of contract have significantly underlined, the persons' behaviours in bargaining and the equilibrium achieved within the negotiation depend on the structure of power relationships – and the resources each one actually has – in a context marked by 'class division, patriarchy and racialism' (Kennedy, 1982, p. 566). In this framework, deciding where coercion and unfair pressure end and freedom begins can be difficult. Even distinguishing wrongful threats from permissible offers might be challenging (McGregor, 1988).

In line with this perspective, focusing on the specific conditions of workers, Santoro (2020) highlighted how already a century ago Max Weber, in his work on freedom of contract, stressed that freedom of contract always allows 'the more powerfully party in the market, i.e., normally the employer…to set the terms, to offer the job "take it or leave it," and, given the normally more pressing economic need of the worker, to impose his terms upon him' (Weber, 1954, pp. 189–190). In this context, the sphere left to free bargaining leads to the power of stronger parties, while the weaker parties are instead forced to 'consent' to conditions imposed within an asymmetrical negotiation, according to a *coactus voluit* dynamics, as Weber pointed out (Santoro, 2020, pp. 330–331).

Today the protection of workers' rights in developed countries, and particularly in Europe, is committed to collective bargaining, a certain degree of re-distribution, and social protection measures. However, globally and in most European countries, exploitation – including severe exploitation – is part of economic and labour market systems, involving primarily those persons who are in particular situations of vulnerability such as many migrant people who are deprived of several (if not, all) rights and social protections and whose wages are just sufficient to ensure their survival and eventually the survival of their families. Thus, considering that any specific transaction/contractual relationship entails some imbalance of bargaining power, and that exploitation is a continuum entailing different forms and degrees of exploitation tending to blur, account must be taken of the conditions/elements determining that an imbalance of power, built on situations of vulnerability, amounts to exploitation.

This issue brings us to some theoretical debates about exploitation. For instance, according to political philosopher Alan Wertheimer (1999), exploitation involves *A* unfairly benefitting from an interaction with *B*: 'A must benefit from the transaction…In addition, A exploits B only when the transaction is harmful or unfair to B'. In this account, the wrong in question, as Wertheimer pointed out, should be examined against what fairness requires in a specific transaction, paying attention to a person's consent and considering the 'fair price' of the transaction. While background conditions may be relevant, according to Wertheimer it is important to focus on individual transactions as this would also take into account those cases in which exploitation may be mutually beneficial and not harmful (ibid.).

Other theoretical scholars such as Robert Goodin and Adrian Wood have focused on the dimension of vulnerability in dynamics of exploitation. Goodin (1985), for instance, has pointed out that exploitation means 'playing for advantage in situations where it is inappropriate to do so' and entails a violation of the moral norm of 'protecting the vulnerable'. According to Goodin, this norm applies 'regardless of the particular source of vulnerability' (ibid., p. 187). Building on the Kantian idea of respect of persons, Wood (2016) considers exploitation as 'playing on some weakness or vulnerability' which is humiliating and degrading, but not necessarily unfair. Similarly, Ruth Sample (2003, p.57) argues that rather than unfairness being a moral element of exploitation, the wrong of exploitation concerns the inherent lack of respect for others: exploitation thus consists of 'interacting with another being for the sake of advantage in a way that fails to respect the inherent value in that being'. This, in her opinion, would also include failing to respond appropriately to the unmet basic needs of others. While these analyses, especially Sample's, provide relevant insights on exploitation and violation of human dignity, they mainly rely on a moral understanding of the wrongness of exploitation, overlooking the impact of structural circumstances and inequalities and, consequently, the social character of human dignity as well as the social-context-specific (situational) dimension of vulnerability.

More significant in our analysis appears instead the approach to vulnerability and exploitation suggested by legal scholars Virginia Mantouvalou (2018b) and Jonathan Wolff (2018). By focusing specifically on workers' situations of vulnerability – but distancing themselves from both the transaction approach to exploitation followed by Wertheimer and from the Kantian approach followed by analyses above – Mantouvalou and Wolff have highlighted that structural inequalities causing situations of vulnerability should be the principal focus when seeking to identify the elements of exploitative dynamics and relationships. Building on Marxist insights to exploitation, Mantouvalou (2018b) argued that any understanding and assessment of situations of exploitation should not be limited to analysing the fairness required in a specific transaction/contractual relationship, but should also focus on examining such a transaction against the 'background conditions of fairness'. Accordingly, attention should be paid to the impact of legal, political, and economic structures in creating conditions of vulnerability to exploitation, from 'which either private employers or the state itself may benefit' (ibid., p. 18). Therefore, in line with a conception of exploitation as a continuum and with a situational understanding of vulnerability, Mantouvalou suggests not to focus only on interpersonal relations between individual exploiters and innocent victims, but to frame these relations in the systemic context in which these relationships occur.

Along this perspective, attention should be paid – as Steinfeld (2009, p. 12) has stressed in his work on US court cases concerning 'involuntary servitude' – to the 'choice sets with which individuals are confronted as they make their decisions about conducting their lives' and how these choice sets may be affected and altered by relevant legal arrangements and other frameworks.

In practice, this means that in the context of interpretation to assess a specific form and degree of exploitation, and accordingly to identify the different lenses and legal regimes through which to address it, legal experts and actors should conduct a case-by-case basis assessment, taking into account both personal and external/contextual circumstances relevant to a determined situation. In particular, with regard to those cases in which evident forms of coercion have not been used and in which a person has 'accepted' unfair working conditions (such as, for instance, being underpaid) due to limitations of alternatives, attention should be devoted to assessing – according to a procedural approach – the material conditions in which the concerned person gave their consent to certain exploitative conditions. This means considering the dynamics and contextual elements that may have produced or exacerbated a person's situation of vulnerability, preventing them from not 'accepting' an exploitative job (Giammarinaro & Palumbo, 2021). This assessment should rely on some indicators that consider the sources of situational vulnerability (Weatherburn, 2021),[33] including the impact of specific migration and labour regulation policies.

This approach has been de facto followed by the ECtHR, for instance, in *Chowdury,* which underlined the need to consider the situation as a whole and

[33] Weatherburn (2021), in particular, dedicates specific attention to the role and importance of indicators.

assess every case individually, focusing on the factors creating vulnerabilities to exploitation. A similar perspective has also been followed by some national courts, including in Italy, even with regard to cases in which there were not evident dynamics of exploitation and no criminal proceedings were involved. For example, in two recent decisions of the Tribunal of Milan of 2021[34] that granted humanitarian protection to two asylum seeker victims of labour exploitation in the agri-food sector, the judges highlighted the position of vulnerability caused by the violence and abuses experienced in the countries of origin and during the migratory path (see Chap. 6). Furthermore, the judges identified as a crucial element of vulnerability the absence of alternatives for these persons, given the impossibility for them to find a non-exploitative job in Italy (Giammarinaro & Palumbo, 2021).

Another important Italian judicial decision to note is a recent ruling of the Tribunal of Prato (Italy) concerning a case of labour exploitation in the textile industry (Tribunal of Prato, Sez. GIP/GUP, Decision of 4 November 2019, No. 330/2019). While this case will be examined in detail in Chap. 6, interestingly in his reasoning the judge highlighted the distinction between the legal conception of vulnerability in relation to severe forms of exploitation, such as trafficking and slavery, and the legal conception of 'state of need' (*Stato di bisogno*) in relation to cases of labour exploitation not amounting to those crimes. Building on relevant international and EU legal instruments and related national legislation, the judge affirmed that while the legal notion of vulnerability in relation to trafficking and slavery refers to the lack of a real and acceptable alternative than to submit to the abuse, the notion of 'state of need' refers to a less pressing and cogent situation, which does not annihilate in an absolute way any freedom of choice but constitutes instead 'an impellent worry' (*assillo impellente*) (Tribunal of Prato, Sez. GIP/GUP, Decision of 4 November 2019, para. 75). Such a situation is 'not necessarily nor tendentially irreversible' but could also consist of a temporary and contingent state that is such as to affect the ability of the exploited person to 'autonomously determine the contractual relationship' (ibid.).[35]

The perspective suggested by the judge of Prato (and successively also adopted by The Italian Supreme Court of Cassation in two recent decisions[36]) is in line with a conception of exploitation as a continuum, including a range of diversified forms of compression of personal freedom, reaching the highest and most severe grades in the cases of forced labour, trafficking, or slavery. At the same time, while it is true that the judge of Prato makes a distinction between the legal notion of vulnerability in the context of trafficking and that of 'state of need' in the case of labour exploitation, this distinction, in my opinion, can be read in line with a situational conception of social vulnerability to exploitation. Indeed, such a situational conception shifts attention to the different forms and degrees of situations of vulnerability, which vary

34 Tribunal of Milan, Decision of 12.5.2021, RG. 42440/2019; Decision of 12.5.2021, RG. 57114/2018.

35 My translation in English.

36 Criminal Court of Cassation, Sez. 4, decision 45615/2021; Criminal Court of Cassation, Sez. 4, decision 24441/2021.

according to social relationships and the hierarchies of power characterising the context in which a particular person is located. This means that the notion of vulnerability can take on various connotations from a legal perspective: at times, for example, it can coincide with the 'state of need' and therefore consists of an 'impellent worry' that affects the freedom of choice of the people concerned; at other times, it can have a more serious and incisive connotation and correspond to the 'lack of a real and acceptable alternative' in line with the definition of a position of vulnerability offered by international and EU legislation on trafficking.

On the basis of all these considerations, the perspective on the situational dimension of vulnerability and its link to exploitation, viewed as a continuum, sheds light on those factors producing situations of vulnerability that lead a person to be involved in or to 'accept' conditions of exploitation because of their weak bargaining power and limited alternatives or lack of these. Cases of exploitation often concern situations in which the persons find themselves facing arduous, sometimes even 'impossible', choices between incomparable needs (Sciurba, 2015): subsistence (of themselves and of their families) or dignified work; choices that no persons should be faced with in a democratic society that should guarantee social human dignity.

In this light, the concept of situational vulnerability is strongly related to the notion of social human dignity, viewed as a guarantee of those basic conditions allowing a person to freely determine their own life project – including making decisions concerning working conditions – in a context of freedom and equality. Indeed, the greater the conditions are for the realisation of a person's social dignity, the lower the situations of vulnerability to dynamics of exploitation – and vice versa.

2.3 Exploitation and Vulnerability from an Intersectional and Gender-Based Perspective

The above considerations on exploitation as a continuum, the situational dimension of vulnerability, and related notion of social human dignity are strongly connected with the analytical framework of intersectionality (Atrey, 2019). This final section will dedicate a few words on an intersectional approach to a situational conception of vulnerability, as this approach underlies the analysis presented in this book.

Although an intersectional approach has long been 'in gestation in Black Feminist thought as well as in the toil and struggles of black working women in the United States' (Mezzadra, 2021a, b; see also Carastathis, 2016; Collins, 1990), the notion of intersectionality has been formally elaborated since the 1980s within US legal scholarship, defined as critical race feminism, in response to the theoretical and normative inadequacies in understanding and addressing black women's experiences of discrimination (Atrey, 2019). By contesting the law's pretence of universality, this scholarship – including among others Kimberlé Crenshaw (1991), who is usually credited to have developed the notion of 'intersectionality' – pinpointed the need to shed light on the experiences of disadvantage and discrimination endured, for instance, by black women on the intersecting grounds of sex, race, and class. Crenshaw paid special attention to the US anti-discriminatory law and its judicial enforcement, highlighting the inadequacies of recognising 'combined race and sex discrimination', relying on the erroneous assumption that the 'boundaries of sex and race discrimination are defined respectively by White women's and Black men's experiences' (Crenshaw, 1989, p. 143). This – as Crenshaw stressed – led to overlooking and obscuring the specific experiences of those persons, such as black women workers, placed at the intersection of multiple grounds of discrimination. Furthermore, the law's failure to take into account these specificities further exacerbated disadvantages and inequalities. Intersectional subordination 'is frequently the consequence of the imposition of one [normative] burden that interacts with pre-existing vulnerabilities to create yet another dimension of disempowerment' (Crenshaw, 1991, p. 1249).

Looking at the experiences of discrimination from an intersectional approach therefore means that the ways women experience gender oppression, for instance, qualify differently when crossed by the lines of subordination on the basis of class, race, nationality, ethnic origin, migrant status, dis/ability, age, and so forth. The power of this approach lies in its capacity to illuminate the complexity of experiences and situations of vulnerability, recognising how the overlapping of forms of oppression and domination result in persons experiencing distinct and compounded forms of discrimination, vulnerability, and subordination. As Shreya Atrey (2019, p. 41) has explained, within the intersectionality frame, oppression, subordination, domination, violence, and other kinds of 'disadvantage' are 'defined not by isolated and stray incident but by systemic and structural nature' thus considering their historical and social motifs.

The intersectionality approach has been increasingly mobilised in scholarly debates even beyond the legal field (Domaas, 2021), as well as by institutional and political authorities,[37] as a conceptual and methodological frame to reach a better understanding of the multiple elements and structures producing inequalities and oppression; how they interact taking into account the different axes along race, sex, gender, class etc.; and how they perpetuate in the shadow of legal and policy remedies (Crenshaw, 1989; Fredman, 2016; Marini, 2021). In this sense, as legal scholar Enrica Rigo underlined, intersectionality can be seen as an 'heuristic device' (Bello, 2020), playing a crucial role in the 'critical deconstruction of norms and in the reconstruction of that "normative challenge" aimed to their discursive transformation'[38] (Rigo, 2022, p. 75).

With specific regard to labour exploitation and related situational vulnerabilities, relevant literature (Giammarinaro, 2022b) – although not extensive – has highlighted how an intersectional approach to vulnerability with regard to labour

[37] For instance, in its 2020–2025 Gender Equality Strategy, the European Commission clearly refers to the need to adopt an intersectional perspective to understand and address gender discrimination.

[38] My translation in English.

exploitation is essential to understand how 'any person's life, at the crossroad of different identities, is affected by multiple discrimination factors resulting in various forms...of exploitation' (ibid.). At the same time, an intersectional approach helps to consider how contemporary capitalist systems take advantage of these specific situations of vulnerability and simultaneously aggravate these, resulting in different forms of exploitation. In fact, exploitative practices and dynamics leverage social roles, legal status, bodies, and sexuality. This is intensified by discourses and ideologies of racialisation and gender imbuing relevant legal and policy frameworks (Bhattacharyya, 2018).

Indeed, as feminist (and especially materialist feminist) scholars have pointed out (Federici, 2004; Fudge, 2014; Fraser, 2017; Giammarinaro, 2022a, b; Rigo, 2022), women workers' situations of vulnerability and the structural dimension of exploitation cannot be understood without considering how patriarchal norms – and in particular the division between production and social reproduction – pervade political and legal frameworks, intertwining with other social hierarchies and discrimination grounds, such as race, class, nationality, and legal status. In particular, the division between production and social reproduction and related hierarchies have been exacerbated by neo-liberal policies (Fraser, 2018), with the consequence that 'the entire area of social reproduction is tailored to serve productive [male] workers' interests' (Giammarinaro, 2022b). As highlighted above and further discussed in subsequent chapters, labour migration and social rights regimes play a crucial role in this context as they help foster the dichotomy between productive and reproductive labour (Rigo, 2022). This is functional to dynamics of exploitation, which rely on the compression of the costs of social reproduction (housing, food, etc.) of workers.

Far from perpetuating and strengthening traditional and patriarchal stereotypes of an intrinsic 'weakness' linked to female subjects, a gender-sensitive intersectional approach to vulnerability and exploitation should look at the interplay of factors creating situational vulnerabilities, considering the differences in the experiences of women, men, and transgender people from a systemic perspective. This involves focusing on the structural and simultaneous functioning of gendered, racialised, classed, and so on systems of oppression and subordination (Yuval-Davis, 2015; Atrey, 2019). In this frame, various dynamics of coercion, negotiation, and individual agency exist and combine in different ways along the lines of different degrees of vulnerability within a continuum of exploitation (Giammarinaro & Palumbo, 2021).

It is worth underlining that such a gender and intersectional approach has been recently followed in some relevant judgments by regional and national courts (Palumbo & Pera, 2021; Giammarinaro & Palumbo, 2021; Mantouvalou, 2023). These include, for example, the decision of the ECtHR in *BS v Spain* (Application No. 47159/08, 24 July 2012), where the Court followed, for the first time, an intersectional interpretation of discrimination (La Barbera & Cruells López, 2019). It is worth also mentioning a recent decision of the Constitutional Court of South Africa, *Mahlangu & another v Ministry of Labour and others* (CCT306/ 19) of November 2020. This latter case involved a domestic worker, Ms. Mahlangu, who drowned in her employer's pool while carrying out her work. After Ms. Mahalangu's death, her daughter, who at the time depended on her economically, petitioned the Department of Labour for compensation. However, she was informed that she could not receive compensation because of the exclusion of domestic workers from South Africa's Compensation for Occupational Injuries and Diseases Act (COIDA). With a powerful and well-articulated decision, the Constitutional Court of South Africa declared that the provision excluding domestic workers from benefits under COIDA is unconstitutional because it breaches both Article 9(1) of the Constitution, which provides for equality before the law, and Article 9(3) prohibiting unfair discrimination by the state.

In its reasoning, the Constitutional Court of South Africa specifically focused on the violation of the prohibition of unfair discrimination by the state, expressively referring to the notion of intersectionality and the work by Crenshaw. The innovative and strong aspect of the intersectional approach – as the Court argued– 'lies in its capacity to shed light on the experiences and vulnerabilities of certain groups that have been erased or rendered invisible' (paras 79 and 87). This approach, according to the Court, 'helps us to understand the structural and dynamic consequences of the interaction between these multiple forms of discrimination' (para. 90). This means that the judicial authorities must consider the contextual factors that produce vulnerability, including 'the nature and context of the individual or group at issue, their history, as well as the social and legal history of society's treatment of that group' (para. 95).

The Court of South Africa has thus underlined how the marginalisation that domestic workers experience in South Africa has its roots in the historical regime of Apartheid, during which this category of workers was excluded from fair labour standards such as compensation for workplace injuries, minimum wage standards, and unemployment insurance. These dynamics of marginalisation intersect with those historically suffered by Black women in South Africa. According to the Court, these women 'found themselves at the intersection or convergence of multiple oppressions…the indignities they face can tell us something about the "grand design" or brutality of apartheid' (para. 102). The intertwinement of these forms of subordination and marginalisation has resulted 'in a situation where domestic workers have for decades into our democracy, had to bear work-related injuries or death without compensation…been rendered invisible' (para. 103). Lastly, the Court underlined how the exclusion of domestic workers from the COIDA undermines their human dignity, revealing not only the persistent devaluation of domestic work, but also the fact that this activity is still not considered 'real work' (para. 108), due to its gendered and racialised nature' (para. 110).

Following expressly the perspective adopted for instance by the ECtHR in *BS v. Spain,* but unlike the European judges clearly referring to the term 'intersectional discrimination', the Court of South Africa therefore discussed, in a powerful and effective way, the intersection of the historical and social factors that create the vulnerability of domestic workers in South Africa. The Court has thus shed light on the experiences of discrimination suffered by these women due to the interaction of various axes of power and subordination (relating to gender, nationality, skin colour, class), framing this in a structural and systemic picture. As legal scholars

Mantouvalou and Sedacca (2020) have pointed out in this regard, the Court has significantly showed that 'despite the specifically tragic nature of Ms Mahlangu's case, the judgment does not seek to treat her poor treatment as a domestic worker as exceptional. Instead, it contextualises Ms Mahlangu's situation as one manifestation of a broader, ongoing structural disadvantage that dates back to apartheid and has not been adequately addressed to date'. Such an approach followed by the Court of South Africa, attentive to the structural dimension of oppression and subordination factors, is in line with the approach that highlights the need to consider the systemic and structural nature of exploitation, going beyond a conception that limits it to an exceptional and contingent phenomenon.

2.4 Concluding Remarks

This chapter provides an overview of the theoretical framework underlying the analysis carried out in this book. By highlighting the absence of a clear definition – especially at the international level – of exploitation, the first section has shed light on the need to operate a conceptual shift, framing exploitation from a broader approach to avoid flattening it to a purely economic conception or to associate it only with its severe forms according to a criminal law approach. From this perspective, the chapter focused on the conception of exploitation as a violation of human dignity, as formulated in several international, EU, and national legal instruments. In particular, I underlined the importance of considering the notion of dignity in its social/contextual dimension and, accordingly, as a guarantee of minimum living conditions that allow a person a dignified life. Such a social conception of dignity – which considers the material conditions in which persons act and make choices – entails, in turn, an obligation on states to guarantee that nobody lives and works in exploitative and degrading conditions. Moving along this perspective, I then underlined the conception of exploitation as a continuum that covers different forms and degrees of exploitation and has a structural nature as it is linked to relevant regulatory frameworks and social hierarchies, including those related to the distinction between production and social reproduction.

This understanding of exploitation as a continuum, in turn, highlights the situations of vulnerability of the exploited persons, conceived in their situational dimension. Indeed, along this continuum, forms of exploitation are associated with different 'situational' vulnerabilities produced by the interplay of personal and structural elements in line with an intersectional approach. This generates situations where the individual's choices are so limited that they are led to 'accept' exploitation. Especially in cases of severe exploitation, this is often the only alternative available to support themselves and their families.

Such a situational conception of vulnerability can be found in the definition of 'position of vulnerability' contained in Anti-Trafficking Directive 2011/36/EU. Furthermore, over recent years, the ECtHR and national case law, including Italian, have paid increasing attention to the situational dimension of vulnerability in relation to labour exploitation. From the analysis of this case law, it emerges how vulnerability, being socially embedded, varies in forms and degrees, depending on the combination of the various individual and structural elements placing a person in a condition that can be easily exposed to dynamics of exploitation. This means that, especially in severe cases such as trafficking or slavery, vulnerability coincides with the absolute lack of alternative; in other cases of less severe forms of exploitation, vulnerability probably consists of a condition of need that however does not absolutely eliminate any freedom of choice.

It is worth emphasising that this situational understanding of vulnerability in relation to exploitation does not exclude a person's agency – without glorifying the independence and autonomy of the persons experiencing exploitation because this may be naïve or even callous (Bhabha, 2005). What is important to underline here is that the situational understanding of vulnerability recognises how persons act, negotiate, and make their choices within contexts marked by structural injustices and inequalities.

Building on this conceptual and legal framework, and paying specific attention to the situations of vulnerability of migrant persons to labour exploitation in Europe, the next chapters will explore relevant European and national legislation and policies in the ambit of migration, labour, and social rights, as well as those aimed at preventing and combatting exploitation, including its severe forms (such as trafficking). The aim is to highlight how situations of vulnerability to exploitation are also generated and exacerbated by legal and policy frameworks, underlining the tensions and ambiguities between different regimes, such as those aimed at combatting severe exploitation and those aimed facilitating regular labour migration.

References

Alessandrini, D. (2018). Of value, measurement and social reproduction. *Griffith Law Review, 27*(4), 393–410.

Allain, J. (2015). *The law and slavery: Prohibiting human exploitation*. Brill.

Allain, J., Crane, A., LeBaron, G., & Behbahani, L. (2013). *Forced labour's business models and supply chains. Report*. Joseph Rowntree Foundation.

Anderson, B. (2000). *Doing dirty work? The global politics of domestic labour*. Zed Books.

Atak, I., Nakache, D., Guild, E., & Crepeau, F. (2018). *'Migrants in vulnerable situations' and the global compact for safe and orderly migration*. Queen Mary School of Law Legal Studies Research Paper No. 273. [online], https://papers.ssrn.com/sol3/papers.cfm?abstract_id=3124392 (Last Access Apr 2024).

Atrey, S. (2019). *Intersectional discrimination*. Oxford University Press.

Bello, B. G. (2020). *Intersezionalità. Teorie e pratiche tra diritto e società*. Francoangeli.

Bernardini, M. G. (2022). Vulnerable capacity. Notes on a quiet legal revolution. *International Journal for the Semiotics of Law, 36*, 1415–1442.

Bhabha, J. (2005). Trafficking, smuggling, and human rights. *Migration Information Source: Special Issue on Migration and Human Rights*. [online], https://www.migrationpolicy.org/print/4698 (Last Access Apr 2024).

Bhattacharya, T. (Ed.). (2017). *Social reproduction theory: Remapping class, recentering oppression*. Pluto.

Bhattacharyya, G. (2018). *Rethinking racial capitalism. Questions of reproduction and survival.* Rowman & Littlefield International.
Brenner, J., & Laslett, B. (1991). Gender, social reproduction, and women's self-organization: Considering the U.S. welfare state. *Gender and Society, 5*(3), 311–333.
Brown, W. (1995). *State of injury: Power andfreedom in late modernity*. Princeton University Press.
Brownsword, R. (2013). Human dignity, human rights, and simply trying to do the right thing. In C. McCrudden (Ed.), *Understanding human dignity* (pp. 345–358). Oxford University Press.
Butler, J. (2004). *Undoing gender*. Routledge.
Butler, J. (2015). *Notes toward a performative theory of assembly*. Harvard University Press.
Caprioglio, C., & Rigo, E. (2020). Diritto, migrazioni e sfruttamento nell'agricoltura italiana. In I. Ippolito, M. Perrotta, & T. Raeymaekers (Eds.), *Braccia rubate dall'agricoltura, Pratiche di sfruttamento del lavoro migrante* (pp. 39–64). Edizioni SEB27.
Carastathis, A. (2016). *Intersectionality: Origins, contestations, horizons*. Nebraska University Press.
Cayla, O. (1998). Le coup d'État de droit? *Le Débat, 100*, 108–133.
Chuang, J. A. (2010). Rescuing trafficking from ideological capture: Prostitution reform and anti-trafficking law and policy. *University of Pennsylvania Law Review, 158*(6), 1655–1728.
Chuang, J. A. (2015). The challenges and perils of reframing trafficking as 'modern-day slavery'. *Anti-Trafficking Review, 5*, 146–149.
Collins, P. H. (1990). *Black feminist thought: Knowledge, consciousness and the politics of empowerment*. Routledge.
Collins, H. (2012). *On the (In)compatibility of Human Rights Discourse and Private Law.* LSE Law, Society and Economy Working Papers, 7 [online], https://www.lse.ac.uk/law/research/working-paper-series/2007-08/WPS2012-07-Collins.pdf (Last Access Apr 2024).
Council of Europe. (2005). *Explanatory Report to the Council of Europe Convention on Action against Trafficking* [online], https://rm.coe.int/16800d3812%3E
Crenshaw, K. (1989). Demarginalizing the intersection of race and sex: A black feminist critique of antidiscrimination doctrine, feminist theory and antiracist politics. *University of Chicago Legal Forum, 1*, 139–167.
Crenshaw, K. (1991). Mapping the margins: Intersectionality, identity politics, and violence against women of color. *Stanford Law Review, 43*(6), 1241–1299.
Dalla Costa, M. (1972). *Potere femminile e sovversione sociale*. Marsilio.
De Sena, P. (2019). Slaveries and new slaveries: Which role for human dignity? *Questions of International Law, Zoom-in, 64*, 7–17.
Di Martino, A. (2019). *Sfruttamento del lavoro. Il valore del contesto nella definizione del reato.* II Mulino.
Dodds, S. (2014). Dependence, care, and vulnerability. In C. Mackenzie, W. Rogers, & S. Dodds (Eds.), *Vulnerability. New essays in ethics and feminist philosophy* (pp. 181–203). Oxford University Press.
Domaas, N. (2021). More than a migration status: Examining intersectionality and its effects on the experiences of migrant women in France. *Journal of Immigrant & Refugee Studies, 21*(3), 249–262.
Ehrenreich, B., & Russell Hochschild, A. (2002). *Global woman: Nannies, maids, and sex workers in the new economy*. Holt Paperbacks.
Elster, J. (1997). Exploitation, freedom, and justice. In K. Nielsen & R. Ware (Eds.), *Exploitation*. Humanities Press.
Federici, S. (2004). *Caliban and the witch: Women, the body and primitive accumulation*. Automedia.
Federici, S. (2014). *Il punto zero della rivoluzione. Lavoro domestico, riproduzione e lotta femminista*. Ombrecorte.
Fineman, M. (2008). The vulnerable subject: Anchoring equality in the human condition. *Yale Journal of Law & Feminism, 20*(1), 8–40.

Fineman, M. (2011). Vulnerability, equality, and the human condition. In J. Jones, A. Grear, R. A. Fenton, & K. Stevenson (Eds.), *Gender, sexualities, and law* (pp. 53–62). Routledge.
Fineman, M. (2012). 'Elderly' as vulnerable: Rethinking the nature of individual and societal responsibility. *The Elder Law Journal, 20*, 101–141.
Fineman, M. (2013). *Vulnerability: Reflections on a new ethical foundation for law and politics*. Routledge.
Fineman, M. (2017). Vulnerability and inevitable inequality. *Oslo Law Review, 4*, 133–149.
Fortunati, L. (1981). *The Arcane of reproduction: Housework, prostitution, labour and capital*, trans. H. Creek & J. Fleming (ed.). Autonomedia, 1995.
FRA. (2015). *Severe labour exploitation: Workers moving within or into the European Union*. European Union Agency for Fundamental Rights.
FRA. (2021). *Protecting migrants in an irregular situation from labour exploitation – Role of the Employers Sanctions Directive*. European Union Agency for Fundamental Rights.
Fraser, N. (2017). Crisis of care? On the social-reproductive contradictions of contemporary capitalism. In T. Bhattacharya (Ed.), *Social reproduction theory: Remapping class, recentering oppression* (pp. 21–36). Pluto Press.
Fraser, N. (2018). From exploitation to expropriation: Historic geographies of racialized capitalism. *Economic Geography, 94*(1), 1–17.
Fraser, N., & Jaeggi, R. (2018). *Capitalism. A conversation in critical theory*. Polity Press.
Fredman, S. (2016). *Intersectional discrimination in EU Gender equality and non-discrimination law*. European Commission
Fudge, J. (2014). Feminist reflections on the scope of labour law: Domestic work, social reproduction, and jurisdiction. *Feminist Legal Studies, 22*(1), 1–23.
Fudge, J. (2017). The future of the standard employment relationship: Labour law, new institutional economics and old power resource theory. *Journal of Industrial Relations, 59*(3), 374–392.
Fudge, J. (2019). (Re)conceptualising unfree labour: Local labour control regimes and constraints on workers' freedoms. *Global Labour Journal, 10*(2), 108–122.
Garofalo Geymonat, G., Marchetti, S., & Palumbo, L. (2023). Sfruttamento e riproduzione sociale: donne migranti nel lavoro agricolo, sessuale e di cura. In B. Coccia, G. Demaio, & M. P. Nanni (Eds.), *Le migrazioni femminili in Italia. Percorsi di affermazione oltre le vulnerabilità* (pp. 151–158). Centro Studi e Ricerche Idos.
Giammarinaro, M. G. (2021). *The Victim's consent in international law and case-law*. Keynote speech. Vienna, 8 November 2021 [online], https://giammarinaro.net/en/home-2/ (Last Access Apr 2024).
Giammarinaro, M. G. (2022a). L'influenza trasformativa delle prospettive femministe. Vulnerabilità e agency. *Rivista di filosofia del diritto, Journal of Legal Philosophy, 2*, 339–352.
Giammarinaro, M. G. (2022b). Understanding severe exploitation requires a human rights and gender-sensitive intersectional approach. *Frontiers in Human Dynamics, 4*. https://doi.org/10.3389/fhumd.2022.861600
Giammarinaro, M. G., & Palumbo, L. (2021). Vulnerabilità situazionale, genere e diritti umani. Analisi normativa e della giurisprudenza italiana e sovranazionale sullo sfruttamento lavorativo. In G. Gioffredi, V. Lorubbio, & A. Pisanò (Eds.), *Diritti umani in crisi? Emergenze, disuguaglianze, esclusioni* (pp. 45–62). Pacini Giuridica.
Giolo, O. (2018). La vulnerabilità neoliberale. Agency, vittime e tipi di giustizia. In O. Giolo, & B. Pastore (Eds.), *Vulnerabilità. Analisi multidisciplinare di un concetto* (pp. 252–273). Carocci Editore.
Giolo, O., & Pastore, B. (Eds.) (2018). *Vulnerabilità. Analisi multidisciplinare di un concetto*. Carocci Editore.
Goodin, R. (1985). *Protecting the vulnerable: A reanalysis of our social responsibilities*. University of Chicago Press.
Halley, J., & Rittich, K. (2010). Critical directions in comparative family law: Genealogies and contemporary studies of family law exceptionalism. *The American Journal of Comparative Law, 58*(4), 753–775.

Hennette-Vauchez, S. (2011). A human *dignitas*? Remnants of the ancient legal concept in contemporary dignity jurisprudence. *International Journal of Constitutional Law, 9*(1), 32–57.
Hobbes, T. (1651). *Leviatano*, trans. it., Laterza, 2001.
ILO. (1999). *Report of the Director-General: Decent work.* Paper presented at the 87th Annual International Labour Conference. International Labour Organisation.
ILO. (2002). *Report of committee of experts on the application of convention and recommendations*. International Labour Organisation.
ILO. (2012a). *Hard to see, harder to count: Survey guidelines to estimate forced labour of adults and children*. Special Action Programme to combat Forced Labour (SAP-FL) and International Programme on the Elimination of Child Labour (IPEC). International Labour Organisation.
ILO. (2012b). *Survey guidelines to estimate forced labour of adults and children*. International Labour Organisation.
ILO. (2017). *Global estimates of modern slavery*. International Labour Organisation.
Iossa, A., & Selberg, N. (2022). Socio-legal aspects of labour market segmentation in the agri-food sector in Sweden: Spatio-temporal dimensions. *European Journal of Migration and Law, 24*, 241–264.
Ippolito, F. (2020). *Understanding vulnerability in international human rights law*. Editoriale Scientifica.
James, S. (2012). *Sex, race and class—The perspective of winning: A selection of writings 1952–2011*. PM Press.
Kennedy, D. (1982). Distributive and paternalist motives in contract and tort law, with special reference to compulsory terms and unequal bargaining power. *Maryland Law Review, 41*(4), 563–658.
Kofman, E., & Raghuram, P. (2015). *Gendered migrations and global social reproduction*. Palgrave Macmillan.
Kotiswaran, P. (2015). Protocol at the crossroads: Rethinking anti-trafficking law from an Indian labor law perspective. *Anti-Trafficking Review, Special Issue on '15 Years of the UN Trafficking Protocol, 4*, 33–55.
Kotiswaran, P. (Ed.). (2017). *Revisiting the law and governance of trafficking, forced labour, and modern slavery*. Cambridge University Press.
Kotiswaran, P. (2023). Laws of social reproduction. *Annual Review of Law and Social Science, 19*, 145–164.
La Barbera, M. C., & Cruells López, M. (2019). Toward the implementation of intersectionality in the European multilevel legal praxis: *B. S. v.* Spain. *Law & Society Review, 53*, 1167–1201.
Le Baron, G. (2020). Gender and forced labour: Understanding the links in global cocoa supply chains. *The Journal of Development Studies, 56*(6), 1095–1117.
Leboeuf, L. (2022). The Juridification of 'vulnerability' through EU asylum law: The quest for bridging the gap between the law and asylum applicants' experiences. *Laws, 11*(3), 45.
Locke, J. (1690). *Il secondo trattato sul governo*, trans. it. BUR, 2001.
Mackenzie, C., Rogers, W., & Dodds, S. (Eds.). (2014). *Vulnerability: New essays in ethics and feminist philosophy*. Oxford University Press.
Mantouvalou, V. (Ed.). (2017). *The right to work: Legal and philosophical perspectives*. Hart Publishing.
Mantouvalou, V. (2018a). The UK Modern Slavery Act 2015 three years on. *The Modern Law Review, 81*, 1017–1045.
Mantouvalou, V. (2018b). Legal construction of structures of exploitation. In H. Collins, G. Lester, & V. Mantouvalou (Eds.), *Philosophical foundations of labour law* (pp. 188–204). Oxford University Press.
Mantouvalou, V. (2020). Structural injustice and the human rights of workers. *Current Legal Problems, 73*(1), 59–87.
Mantouvalou, V. (2023). Structural injustice and workers' rights. *Oxford Labour Law*.
Mantouvalou, V., & Sedacca, N. (2020). The human rights of domestic workers: *Mahlangu v Ministry of Labour* and the Transformative Nature of the South African Constitution, UK. *UK*

Labour Law [online], https://uklabourlawblog.com/2020/12/11/the-human-rights-of-domestic-workers-mahlungu-v-ministry-of-labour-and-the-transformative-nature-of-the-south-african-constitution-by-virginia-mantouvalou-and-natalie-sedacca/ (Last Access Apr 2024).

Marchetti, S., & Palumbo, L. (Eds.). (2021). Vulnerability in the asylum and protection system in Italy: Legal and policy framework and implementing practices. *VULNER Research Report, 1*. https://doi.org/10.5281/zenodo.5518933

Marella, M. R. (2007). Il fondamento sociale della dignità umana. Un modello costituzionale per il diritto europeo dei contratti. *Rivista Critica del Diritto Privato, XXV*(1), 67–103.

Marella, M. R. (2018). Family-relations law between 'stratification' and 'resistance': Housework and family law. In R. Sarti, A. Bellavitis, & M. Martini (Eds.), *What is work? Gender at the crossroads of home, family, and business from the early modern era to the present. International studies in social history* (pp. 295–325). Berghahn Books.

Marini, G. (2021). Intersezionalità: genealogia di un metodo giuridico. *Rivista critica del diritto privato 4*, 473–502.

Marks, S. (2008). Exploitation as an international legal concept. In S. Marks (Ed.), *International law on the left: Re-examining Marxist legacies* (pp. 281–308). Cambridge University Press.

McCrudden, C. M. (2008). Human dignity and judicial interpretation of human rights. *European Journal of International Law, 19*(4), 655–724.

Mcgregor, J. (1988). Bargaining advantages and coercion in the market. *Philosophy Research Archives, 14*, 23–50.

Mezzadra, S. (2021a). Intersectionality, identity, and the riddle of class. *Papeles del CEIC, 2*(3), 1–10.

Mezzadra, S. (2021b). Challenging borders. The legacy of postcolonial critique in the present conjuncture. *Soft Power, 7*(2), 21–44.

Mezzadra, S., & Neilson, B. (2021). The geopolitics of labour. In L. Weber & C. Tazreiter (Eds.), *Handbook of migration and global justice* (pp. 14–25). Elgar.

Mies, M. (2014). *Patriarchy and accumulation on a world scale: Women in international division of labour*. Zed Books.

Morondo Taramundi, D. (2016). ¿Un nuevo paradigma para la igualdad? La vulnerabilidad entre condición humana y situación de indefensión. *Cuadernos Electrónicos de Filosofía del Derecho, 1*(34), 205–221.

Nussbaum, M. (2006). *Frontiers of justice: Disability, nationality, species membership*. Harvard University Press.

O'Connell Davidson, J. (2010). New slavery, old binaries: Human trafficking and the borders of 'freedom'. *Global Networks, 10*(2), 244–261.

Palumbo, L. (2017). Exploiting for care: Trafficking and abuse in domestic work in Italy. *Journal of Immigrant & Refugee Studies, 15*(2), 171–186.

Palumbo, L. (2022). Exploitation in the agri-food sector in Europe: A comparative analysis of the impact of migration and labour regimes in producing migrants' vulnerabilities. *European Journal of Migration and Law, 24*(2), 287–312.

Palumbo, L., & Pera, A. (2021). Donne migranti e diritto all'unità familiare. Fattori di vulnerabilità e forme di tutela nella giurisprudenza italiana ed europea. In G. De Marzo & F. Parisi (Eds.), *Diritto e Immigrazione. Un quadro aggiornato delle questioni più attuali e rilevanti* (pp. 253–274). Il Foro Italiano - LaTribuna.

Palumbo, L., & Sciurba, A. (2015). Vulnerability to forced labour and trafficking: The case of Romanian women in the agricultural sector in Italy. *Anti-Trafficking Review, 5*, 89–110.

Parisi, F. (2019). Il bene della dignità umana in soccorso della legge Merlin? Sulla Sentenza 141/2019 della Corte Constituzionale in materia di favoreggiamento e reclutamento della prostituzione. *La Legislazione Penale*, 1–50.

Parreñas, R. S. (2001). *Servants of globalization: Women*. Stanford University Press.

Pateman, C. (1988). *The Sexual contract*. Polity Press

Peroni, M., & Timmer, A. (2013). Vulnerable groups: The promise of an emerging concept in European Human Rights Convention Law. *ICON-International Journal of Constitutional Law, 11*(4), 1056–1085.

Phillips, N. (2013). Unfree labour and adverse incorporation in the global economy: Comparative perspectives on Brazil and India. *Economy and Society, 42*(2), 171–196.

Picchio, A. (1992). *Social reproduction. The political economy of the labour market*. Cambridge University Press.

Plant, R. (2007). *Forced labour, slavery and poverty reduction: Challenges for development agencies*. Presentation to UK High-Level Conference to Examine the Links between Poverty, Slavery and Social Exclusion. Foreign and Commonwealth Office and DFID, London, 30 October. International Labour Organisation.

Resta, G. (2014). *Dignità, Persone, Mercati*. Giappichelli.

Rigo, E. (Ed.). (2015). *Leggi, migranti e caporali: Prospettive e critiche di ricerca sullo sfruttamento del lavoro in agricoltura*. Pacini Editore.

Rigo, E. (2020). La straniera. Mobilità, confini e riproduzione sociale oltre lo straniero di Simmel. *Teoria Politica, X*, 263–275.

Rigo, E. (2022). *La straniera. Migrazioni, asilo, sfruttamento in una prospettiva di genere*. Carocci editore.

Rodotà, S. (2012). *Il diritto di avere diritti*. Editori Laterza.

Sample, R. J. (2003). *Exploitation: What it is and why it's wrong*. Rowman & Littlefield Publishers.

Santoro, E. (1991). Per una concezione non individualistica dell'autonomia individuale. *Rassegna Italiana di Sociologia, 3*, 267–311.

Santoro, E. (2003). *Autonomy, freedom and rights. A critique of liberal subjectivity*. Kluwer Academic Publishers.

Santoro, E. (2020). Vulnerability between political theory and normative texts: A new language to repeat old things or a new tool to problematize differences in social power? *Revista de Estudos Constitucionais, Hermenêutica e Teoria do Direito, 12*(3), 311–334.

Santoro, E., & Genovese, D. (2018). L'articolo 18 (t.u. immigrazione) e il contrasto allo sfruttamento lavorativo: la fantasia del giurista tra libertà e dignità. *Giornale di diritto del lavoro e di relazioni industriali, 159*, 543–579.

Scarpa, S. (2019). Conceptual unclarity, human dignity and contemporary forms of slavery: An appraisal and some proposals. *Questions of International Law, Zoom-in, 64*, 19–41.

Schmoll, C. (2022). *Le dannate del mare. Donne e frontiere nel mediterraneo*. Astarte Edizioni.

Sciurba, A. (2015). *La cura servile, la cura che serve*. Pacini Editore.

Sciurba, A., & Palumbo, L. (2018). *The vulnerability of women migrant workers in agriculture and the EU: The need for a Human Rights and Gender based approach*. Study commissioned by the European Parliament's Policy Department for Citizens' Rights and Constitutional Affairs. PE 604.966 (May).

Siegmann, K. A., Quaedvlieg, J., & Williams, T. (2022). Migrant labour in Dutch agriculture: Regulated precarity. *European Journal of Migration and Law, 24*(2), 217–240.

Silbaugh, K. (1996). Turning labor into love: Housework and the law. *Northwestern University Law Review, 91*(1), 1–86.

Sjödin, E. (2021). Criminalisation as a response to low wages and labour market exploitation in Sweden. *European Labour Law Journal, 12*(4), 529–546. https://doi.org/10.1177/2031952521110380

Skrivankova, K. (2010). *Between decent work and forced labour: Examining the continuum of exploitation*. Report. Joseph Rowntree Foundation.

Somavia, J. (2013). *The meaning of decent work: A struggle for human dignity*. International Labour Organisation.

Steinfeld, R. (2009). *Coercion/consent in labour. COMPAS working paper No. 66*. University of Oxford Centre on Migration, Policy and Society.

Stoyanova, V. (2017). *Human trafficking and slavery reconsidered: Conceptual limits and states' positive obligations in European law*. Cambridge University Press.

Teeple Hopkins, C. (2017). Mostly work, little play: Social reproduction, migration, and paid domestic work in Montreal. In T. Bhattacharya (Ed.), *Social reproduction theory: Remapping class, recentering oppression* (pp. 131–147). Pluto.

Timmer, A. (2013). A quiet revolution: Vulnerability in the European court of human rights. In M. Fineman & A. Grear (Eds.), *Vulnerability: Reflections on a new ethical foundation for law and politics* (pp. 147–170). Ashgate.

Timmer, A., Baumgärtel, M., Kotzé, L., & Slingenberg, L. (2021). The potential and pitfalls of the vulnerability concept for human rights. *Netherlands Quarterly of Human Rights, 93*(3), 190–197. https://doi.org/10.1177/09240519211048009

Toupin, L. (2018). *Wages for housework: A history of an international feminist movement, 1972–1977*. Pluto press.

UN Committee on Economic, Social and Cultural Rights. (2005). *General Comment No. 18, art. 6 of the International Covenant on Economic, Social and Cultural Rights*.

UNODC. (2006). *Travaux préparatoires for the organized crime convention and protocols*. United Nations Office on Drugs and Crime.

UNODC. (2009). *Global report on trafficking in persons*. United Nations Office on Drugs and Crime.

UNODC. (2013). *Abuse of a position of vulnerability and other 'means' within the definition of trafficking in persons*, Issue paper, United Nations Office on Drugs and Crime.

UNODC. (2015). *The concept of 'Exploitation' in the trafficking in persons protocol*, Issue paper, United Nations Office on Drugs and Crime. United Nations.

UNODC. (2018). *The international legal definition of trafficking in persons: Consolidation of research findings and reflection on issues raised*. United Nations Office on Drugs and Crime.

UNODC. (2020). *Legislative guide on the trafficking in persons protocol only, 2020 update*. United Nations Office on Drugs and Crime.

UNODC. (2022). *Global report on trafficking in persons*. United Nations Office on Drugs and Crime.

Verza, A. (2018). Il concetto di vulnerabilità e la sua tensione tra colonizzazioni neoliberali e nuovi paradigmi di giustizia. In O. Giolo & B. Pastore (Eds.), *Vulnerabilità. Analisi multidisciplinare di un concetto* (pp. 229–252). Carocci.

Viola, F. (2013). Lo statuto normativo della dignità umana. In A. Abignente & F. Scamardella (Eds.), *Dignità della persona. Riconoscimento dei diritti nelle società multiculturali* (pp. 283–295). Editoriale Scientifica.

Weatherburn, A. (2021). *Labour exploitation in human trafficking law*. Cambridge University Press.

Weber, M. (1954). *Max Weber on law in 'Economy and Society'*. Edited and translated by Max Rheinstein. Twentieth Century Legal Philosophy Series 6. Harvard University Press.

Wertheimer, A. (1999). *Exploitation*. Princeton University Press.

Whitman, J. Q. (2003). From fascist 'honour' to European 'dignity'. In C. Joerges & N. Ghaleigh (Eds.), *The darker legacy of European law: Perceptions of Europe and perspectives on a European order in legal scholarship during the era of fascism and national socialism* (pp. 243–266). Hart.

Wijers, M. (2015). Purity, victimhood, and agency: Fifteen years of the UN trafficking protocol. *Anti-Trafficking Review*, (4). https://doi.org/10.14197/atr.20121544.

Wolff, J. (2018). Structures of exploitation. In H. Collins, G. Lester, & V. Mantouvalou (Eds.), *Philosophical foundations of labour law* (pp. 175–187). Oxford University Press.

Wood, A. (2016). Unjust exploitation. *The Southern Journal of Philosophy, 54*(51), 92–108.

Young, I. M. (1990). *Justice and the politics of difference*. Princeton University Press.

Yuval-Davis, N. (2015). Situated intersectionality and social inequality. *Raisons Politiques, 58*, 91–100.

Chapter 3
EU Legal and Policy Frameworks Regarding Labour Market Access for EU and Non-EU Migrants: Preventing, Protecting, or Creating Situational Vulnerabilities?

As underlined in the Introduction, the composition of migratory movements—and consequently of labour migratory movements—to and within Europe has changed profoundly in recent years, especially since the end of the first decade of 2000s, due to the interplay of several factors. On the one hand, EU countries have significantly reduced legal entry channels for third-country nationals, in particular for low- and medium-skilled workers, with some exceptions for seasonal workers and for family reunification (even if this latter avenue has become difficult because of diverse income and housing prerequisites). On the other hand, the spread of asymmetric conflicts and new wars have produced an increase in migrant people who, in the absence of legal paths and increasingly militarised and externalised borders, are forced to go through dangerous routes such as the Mediterranean Sea (Amnesty International, 2017; Sciurba, 2017b, 2021a).

The statistics on residence permits issued in the European Union are revealing. Although this process began before the so-called refugee crisis, which peaked in 2015 (Martin et al., 2015), it was during this period, especially between 2013 and 2016, there was an increase in residence permits issued for international protection (Eurostat, 2023). The same data show that while permits for family reasons tend to remain fairly stable over the years, it is the fluctuations between permits for employment-related reasons and those for other reasons (including international protection) that determine the percentage variation. In 2016, for example, residence permits for other reasons (including international protection) exceeded those for employment reasons (ibid.). From 2017, however, there has been a reverse trend, with a rise in work permits, likely due to the drop in asylum seekers' arrivals because of the closure of external borders with Turkey and in the central Mediterranean, and at the same time due to increasingly restrictive and selective national asylum policies (Sciurba, 2021b; Atak & Crépeau, 2022).

L. Palumbo, *Taking Vulnerabilities to Labour Exploitation Seriously*, IMISCOE Research Series, https://doi.org/10.1007/978-3-031-55424-7_3

The other major group of migrants in the EU is EU nationals,[1] especially from eastern Member States (primarily Romania), who can easily cross the borders and who are 'forced' to leave their country because of the gap between average salaries and the rising cost of living (Corrado et al., 2018; Siegmann et al., 2022; Sciurba, 2015).

All these changes in migrations to and within Europe are reflected in the composition of the migrant labour force, especially in low-paid and less protected sectors such as agriculture and domestic work (see, for instance, Garofalo Geymonat et al., 2023). This, in turn, fosters new forms and situations of vulnerability for migrants, significantly affecting the dynamics of labour exploitation in European countries.

Building on the legal and conceptual framework illustrated in previous chapters, and paying specific attention to structural factors creating the situational vulnerabilities of migrant workers, this chapter critically examines the EU legal and policy frameworks concerning labour market access for EU and non-EU migrants, with a particular focus on those workers considered low-skilled. With regard to non-EU migrants, the chapter focuses on the Seasonal Workers Directive, shedding light on its innovative elements as well as its shortcomings. Attention is also given to the EU regulation of labour market access for beneficiaries of international protection and asylum seekers. The chapter scrutinises the rights and protection granted to these different migrant workers, analysing those aspects that contribute to preventing or instead fostering situations of vulnerability to exploitation.

3.1 The Fragmented EU Legal Framework on Labour Migration

The evolution of EU policies in the field of migration has mainly followed two distinct yet related trajectories. On the one hand, institutional attention has concentrated on developing a common policy on asylum and on the joint control and strengthening of the EU's external borders aimed at containing migrants' mobility. This has led to migration being framed primarily within the domain of security (Guild, 2009). In this sense, some literature sees a 'securitisation of migration', that is, the extreme politicisation of migration and its portrayal as a security threat (Huysmans, 2006). Such a securitarian approach has also gradually become the predominant framework for addressing 'forced migration',[2] especially since the 2015 'refugee crisis'. Prior to that, EU and national policies assumed a clear distinction between 'economic' and 'forced' migrants, criminalising the former while admitting the latter, albeit often after a restrictive and selective process (De Genova,

[1] As underlined in the Introduction, in this volume, the term 'migrant' refers to people residing in a country of which they are not citizens – whether they are from the EU or a third country – irrespective of their legal status (e.g. asylum seekers, long-term residents, etc.).

[2] Several critical migration scholars have criticised this distinction. See, for instance, Mezzadra (2013) and D'Onghia (2019).

2013). With the 'refugee crisis', asylum seekers have also become subjects of EU and national border and migration containment policies (Sciurba, 2017a; Atak & Crépeau, 2022). As Sciurba (2021b, p. 93) points out, the criminalisation of migration has engulfed the right to asylum, 'completely ignoring the issue of refugees, the rights of those fleeing from violence and wars, and the corresponding international legal obligations of states'.

On the other hand, a common EU policy on labour migration has been belatedly developed and continues to face significant challenges (De Bruycker, 2019; Favilli, 2020a) to the extent that some scholars have recently raised the issue of a 'EU labour migration crisis' (Minderhoud, 2021). This has resulted largely from the reluctance of Member States, particularly those that have historically relied on migrant labour, to relinquish their prerogatives in an area considered crucial for their national policies and economy. The EU regulatory dimension has thus remained 'suspended between the European and national level, even though it is firmly anchored to the latter' (Calafà, 2020, p. 73). Indeed, EU competencies in the ambit of labour migration by non-EU nationals have been always very limited (Evola, 2018).

Given these substantial limitations, since the 1990s there have been EU-level developments leading to a fragmented legal framework on labour migration (Minderhoud, 2021; Verschueren, 2016a). It is worth mentioning that in 2000, the European Commission defined the guidelines on the migration policy that the Community should develop in the framework of the principles established by the 1999 Tampere Programme (European Commission, 2000). In this Document, the Commission dealt with the issue of a common labour migration policy, recognising that 'the "zero" immigration policies of the past 30 years are no longer appropriate' (ibid., p. 3). The Commission noted that 'many economic migrants have been driven either to seek entry through asylum procedures or to enter illegally' (ibid., p. 13). This 'allows for no adequate response to labour market needs and plays into the hands of well-organised traffickers and unscrupulous employers' (ibid., p. 9).

The Commission highlighted the importance of incorporating the issue of labour migration into discussions on the development of EU economic and social policy. Labour migration, it argued, provides an opportunity to 'reinforce policies to combat irregular work and the economic exploitation of migrants which are at the present fuelling unfair competition in the Union' (ibid., p. 14). The Commission further underlined that an economic immigration policy must ensure employers' compliance with existing national labour legislation to guarantee equality with respect to 'wages and working conditions' as this is 'not only in the interests of the migrants, but of the society itself which then both benefits fully from the contribution migrants make to economic and social life' (ibid., p. 14).

The Commission, therefore, significantly proposed the development of policy for common labour migration measures. This approach certainly marked a new direction compared to the former migration policies at EU-level. However, as Daniel Wilsher (2001, p. 178) noted, 'the difficulty not addressed by the Commission is the acknowledged need for different migration volumes at the national level, which militates against any policy of granting further rights of residence to third-country nationals'.

Building on this Communication, in 2001 the Commission published a proposal for a Directive on the conditions of entry and residence of third-country-national workers and self-employed persons (European Commission, 2001). Refugees, posted workers, third-country-national family members of EU citizens, and those covered by the then-pending proposal for a Directive on family reunification were excluded. In line with the dominant approach of Member States to migration, the proposed Directive relied on the labour market test as the main prerequisite for admitting third-country national workers (Evola, 2018).

Although the proposed Directive aimed to harmonise legislation on labour migration into the EU, it provided Member States with ample power in regulating labour migration. As Bjarney Friðriksdóttir (2017, p. 102) stressed, the approach suggested by the proposal 'mainly focused on the facilitation of the procedures to admit labour migrants that were identified as needed to fill gaps in the national labour markets of the Member States' and did not challenge Member States' authority to control admission into their territory.

Yet, despite their wide discretionary power, Member States were reluctant with regard to this proposed Directive. The horizontal criteria for admission worried Member States because 'the comprehensive approach and the absence of a distinction between highly and semi- or low-skilled migrants' diverged 'from the labour market-oriented labour migration policies of the Member States' (Wiesbrock, 2010, p. 148). Member States such as Germany hesitated to allow any EU interference in establishing a common labour migration policy (Groenendijk, 2014). As a consequence, the 2001 proposal was withdrawn in 2005 and the Commission opted for a selective and sectoral approach, targeting specific categories of workers.

It is worth noting that during that time, there was not only a shift from a horizontal to a sectoral approach to labour migration but also a change in how the issue of migrant labour exploitation was framed. Indeed, while the Commission's 2000 Communication aimed at creating a common labour migration policy to also address irregular and exploitative labour conditions, shortly thereafter, with the adoption of the Employer Sanctions Directive in 2009[3] (Chap. 4), the focus shifted toward addressing irregular migration and exploitation mainly through a criminal law approach. It is true that the Employer Sanctions Directive[4]—and subsequently the Seasonal Workers Directive—includes measures to protect workers' rights. However, their implementation and impact are limited, as discussed below (see also Chap. 4).

[3] It is interesting to note that in 2001 the Commission adopted a communication on a Common Policy on Illegal Migration in which, addressing the causes of irregular migration, it argued that 'demand for illegal workers is especially caused by their employers'. In this sense, the Commission announced that it would 'examine the opportunity of tabling a proposal for a Directive on the illegal residents from third countries' (p. 23). While the Commission significantly focused on sanctioning employers, no attention was given in this policy document to the rights of irregularly present third-country nationals (see Friðriksdóttir, 2017, pp. 99–100).

[4] Directive 2009/52/EC providing for minimum standards on sanctions and measures against employers of illegally staying third-country nationals

Returning to the EU legal framework on labour migration, after the withdrawal of the horizontal and comprehensive approach of the 2001 proposal, a patchwork of several Directives was introduced focusing on specific segments of EU labour migration around the entry into force of the Treaty of Lisbon in 2009. In particular, a horizontal Directive—Directive 2011/98/EU, the Single Permit Directive[5]—was adopted, which nevertheless has a limited scope, excluding for instance third-country family members of EU citizens, posted workers, seasonal workers, intra-corporate transferees, au pairs, long-term residents under Directive 2003/109, self-employed workers, asylum seekers, and beneficiaries of protection in accordance with national law, international obligations or the practice of a Member State. Additionally, four specific sectorial Directives were adopted: Directive 2005/71/EC on researchers,[6] later repealed by Directive 2016/801/EU on researchers and students; Directive 2009/50/EC on highly skilled workers (Blue-Card Directive),[7] later repealed by Directive 2021/1883/EU (recast Blue-Card Directive); Directive 2014/36/EU on seasonal workers (Seasonal Workers Directive)[8]; and Directive 2014/66/EU on intra-corporate transferees (Intra-Corporate transferee Directive).[9]

As Herwig Verschueren (2016a, p. 379) noted, through these Directives the EU was 'only fragmentally and gradually able to develop an arsenal of rules of its own in this field, still leaving a lot of leeway for the Member States to implement them'. It is thus worth noting that the 2007 Treaty of Lisbon reaffirmed the national prerogative to determine the annual number of entries for third-country migrant workers, thereby limiting the exercise of the EU of its shared legal competence related to labour migration. Indeed, according to Article 79(5) of the Treaty on the Functioning of the European Union (TFEU), the provisions of the Treaty 'do not affect the right of Member States to determine the volume of admission of third-country nationals coming from third countries to their territory in order to seek work, whether employed or self-employed'.[10] As a consequence, Member States are, in practice, free to establish the criteria and requirements, even very stringent and complex ones, for the admission of third-country migrant workers, including not setting any entry quotas (Nunin, 2020; Minderhoud, 2021).

---

[5] Directive 2011/98/EU on a single application procedure for a single permit for third-country nationals to reside and work in the territory of a Member State and on a common set of rights for third-country workers legally residing in a Member State

[6] Directive 2005/71/EC on a specific procedure for admitting third-country nationals for the purpose of scientific research.

[7] Directive 2009/50/EC on the conditions of entry and residence of third-country nationals for the purpose of highly qualified employment.

[8] Directive 2014/36/EU on the conditions of entry and stay of third-country nationals for the purpose of employment as seasonal workers.

[9] Directive 2014/66/EU on the conditions of entry and residence of third-country nationals in the framework of an intra-corporate transfer.

[10] As Minderhoud (2021, p. 33) highlights, this provision was 'especially added at the request of Germany which only accepted the institutional change of the Lisbon Treaty by an explicit limitation of EU powers on this point'.

As discussed below, the Seasonal Workers Directive is emblematic of the EU's fragmented and sectorial approach to labour migration, which aims primarily at addressing Member States' evolving economic and labour market needs. This was also affirmed by the 2015 European Agenda on Migration and subsequently by the 2020 Pact on Migration and Asylum.

The 2015 European Agenda on Migration, adopted during the so-called refugee crisis, did not address the EU labour migration regime's inadequacies. Focused instead on border enforcement, effective returns, and actions against criminal networks of traffickers and smugglers as the principal incentive for irregular migration, the Agenda did not dedicate attention to the issue of entry channels for work-related reasons. Despite the significant presence of third-country migrant workers in low-paid and low-prestige economic sectors, the Agenda only emphasised the need for 'an attractive EU-wide scheme for highly qualified third-country nationals' (European Commission, 2015, p. 15), suggesting a revision of the Blue Card Directive on high-skilled workers. This again made evident the limitations of EU policies and associated legal instruments in addressing the complexities of contemporary migration processes, particularly labour migration.

The EU Pact on Migration and Asylum adopted in September 2020 reflected this limited approach by not addressing the gaps and deficiencies in EU policies on labour migration (Favilli, 2020b; Minderhoud, 2021). The Pact confirms the policy of migration and border control through cooperation with countries of origin and transit, further enhancing collaboration in combatting trafficking and, consequently, containing and hindering migrations, including those for asylum (Favilli, 2020b; Borraccetti, 2021). The section of the Pact addressing the issue of labour migration focuses on reviewing, revising, or intensifying existing instruments: the EU Blue Card Directive, the Long-Term Residence Directive, and the Single Permit Directive. The Pact, therefore, reasserted the disjointed nature of the EU legal framework on labour migration. More generally, as Chiara Favilli (2020b) argued, 'it once again confirmed that the Union's inability to produce a credible policy for managing migration is a direct responsibility of the governments of the Member States, capable of significantly influencing the Commission's direction'.[11]

It is important to mention that in October 2021, the recast Blue Card Directive (Directive 2021/1883/EU) was adopted to make the Blue Card scheme more attractive to employers and to improve migrant workers' rights, especially concerning family reunification, intra-EU mobility, and access to long-term residence and circular migration (De Lange and Vankova, 2022). With specific regard to the 2022 proposal for revising the Single Permit Directive, its aim is to simplify and clarify the Directive's scope and enhance migrant workers' protection against exploitation. The scope is broadened by simply removing the exclusion of beneficiaries of protection (current Art. 3(2)(h)). The proposal also focuses on improving migrant workers' rights to file complaints, change employers and receive protection. However, as Tesseltje de Lange (2022) points out, 'the Single Permit Directive

[11] My translation.

remains focused on streamlining national entry procedures and migrant worker rights and does not...deal with entry conditions for low- and medium-skilled labour migrants'.

3.1.1 Migrant Seasonal Workers' Rights and Protection Under the Seasonal Workers Directive

The fragmented and sector-specific EU legal framework on labour migration established so far relies on a system based on skills as a key selection criterion and on a differentiated legal regime that provides diverse categories of migrant workers with different rights according to the type and duration of the residence permit. Within this system, migration has been increasingly '"commodified" as part of a utilitarian discourse focusing on the purported economic "value" of migrants' (De Haas et al., 2018, p. 354). As discussed in Sects. 3.1.1 and 3.1.2, the Seasonal Workers Directive highlights the paradigms informing this approach, ultimately fostering the situational vulnerabilities of seasonal workers and, more broadly, of those considered low-skilled workers, to exploitation.

The adoption of the Seasonal Workers Directive in 2014 marked a significant step in the development of EU legislation on labour migration as it was the first—and still only—EU legal instrument aimed at regulating the conditions of entry and stay of low-skilled third-country workers into the EU and defining their rights (Art. 1). In the 2010 proposal for this Directive, the Commission recognised that EU economies have a structural need for seasonal work 'for which labour from within the EU is expected to become less and less available' (European Commission, 2010a, p. 2). At the same time, it underlined significant evidence of cases of exploitation and substandard working conditions among third-country seasonal workers (ibid.). According to the Commission, establishing 'swift and flexible admission procedures and securing a legal status for seasonal workers can act as a safeguard against exploitation and also protects EU citizens who are seasonal workers from unfair competition' (European Commission, 2010a, p. 3).

Based on these considerations, the Directive's final text, which was ultimately adopted after three-and-a-half years of negotiations, addresses multiple goals: responding to seasonal fluctuations in the economy and offsetting labour shortages; protecting seasonal workers; and contributing to the development of third countries, among others. The Directive defines a seasonal worker as a third-country national whose principal place of residence is in a third country and who 'stays legally and temporarily in the territory of a Member State to carry out an activity dependent on the passing of the season, under one or more fixed-term work contracts concluded directly between that third-country national and the employer established in that Member State' (Art. 3(b)). As Lydia Medland (2017) has pointed out, the seasonal worker's legal status is thus defined in reference to the objective nature of the employment ('seasonal work'), the worker's subjective identity ('the seasonal worker'), and their specific rights and obligations (temporary status). Such a definition constructs the status and the presence of seasonal workers as temporary, meeting the concern of Member States—clearly expressed during the negotiations of the Directive—to avoid that these workers can obtain a permanent permit.

The Seasonal Workers Directive concerns only third-country nationals residing outside the territory of the Member States and who apply to be admitted or who have been admitted to the territory of a Member State as seasonal workers (Art.2(1)).[12] As a consequence, several categories, including for instance undocumented migrants, are excluded from its scope, and it does not offer a solution for those third-country nationals who are in a precarious situation and already working (often in irregular ways) in a Member State (Zoeteweij-Turhan, 2017).[13]

The Directive notably allows seasonal workers to extend their stay (provided not beyond the maximum period of 9 months) and to be hired by a different employer (Art.15.4). This latter provision, as the preamble makes clear, aims to 'reduce the risk of abuse that seasonal workers may face if tied to a single employer' (para. 52). However, it is not mandatory: Member States have the discretion to decide whether to implement this provision or not. This is a significant limitation, as it does not serve as an effective instrument to prevent situations in which abuse and exploitation of seasonal workers are primarily rooted in the worker's dependency on the employer resulting from the connection between the right to stay and work permits (Rijken, 2015, p. 449).

The Directive introduces a 'controlled admission system' (Hunt, 2014) that requires workers to have sufficient resources to support themselves before admission (Art.5). Furthermore, according to the Directive, the seasonal work permit shall be granted for a minimum of 5 months and maximum of 9 months in any 12-month period. Once that period has expired, the workers must leave the territory of the Member State 'unless the Member State concerned has issued a residence permit under national or Union law for purposes other than seasonal work' (Art. 14(1)). The Directive does not include any provisions concerning access to long-term resident status after consecutive years of seasonal work (Guild, 2014).

By seeking to encourage circular migration, the Seasonal Workers Directive includes some provisions concerning Member States' facilitation of the re-entry of seasonal workers admitted to that Member State at least once within the previous 5 years and who complied with migration law during their stay.[14] Yet, even in this case, the Directive grants a significant amount of discretion to Member States,

---

[12] Third-country-based agencies or other third-country-based service providers are also not in the Directive's scope. Yet, under Recital 12, 'where a Member State's national law allows admission of third-country nationals as seasonal workers through employment or temporary work agencies established on its territory and which have a direct contract with the seasonal worker, such agencies should not be excluded from the scope of this Directive'.

[13] See also in this regard European Parliament (2011), p. 16

[14] These include a simplified application process, an accelerated procedure, the issuing of several seasonal worker permits in a single administrative act, and priority for previous seasonal workers in examining application for admission as a seasonal worker (Art. 16).

without fostering harmonisation of the rules for facilitating re-entry of third-country seasonal workers and, in general, the mobility of these workers (Fudge & Olsson, 2014).

The Seasonal Workers Directive contains important provisions for seasonal workers' rights and protection with regards to accommodation (Art. 20), compensation (Art. 17),[15] and facilitation of lodging complaints against employers directly or through third parties (Art. 25). It also includes sanctions for employers failing to fulfil their obligations (Art. 17).

On accommodation, the Directive requires Member States to ensure that seasonal workers benefit from housing that meets adequate living standards according to national law (Art. 20). In particular, it affirms that where accommodation is provided by the employer, the rent shall not be excessive compared with the worker's net remuneration and cannot be automatically deducted from the worker's wage. As highlighted in the chapters dedicated to the national contexts in Italy and the UK, seasonal agricultural workers are often provided with substandard, inadequate, and isolated accommodations that foster their situational vulnerability to exploitation (FRA, 2015). The compression of the costs related to their accommodation—and therefore to their reproductive dimension—is part of the dynamics of exploitation of migrant workers, especially in sectors such as agriculture (Rigo, 2022; Palumbo, 2022). In this context, the Seasonal Workers Directive's provisions on accommodation are of utmost importance, reflecting a human rights- and social dignity-based approach; an adequate standard of living is one of the fundamental social rights addressed in both international and European conventions (see, for instance, the 1966 International Covenant on Economic, Social and Cultural Rights (Arts. 6 and 11) and the 1961 European Social Charter (Art. 31)).

Yet, as Rijken (2015, p. 448) has rightly noted, one of the shortcomings of the Directive is the absence of a provision stating that when the employer arranges accommodation, the seasonal worker cannot be obliged to stay in it. Furthermore, some terms used in the Directive's accommodation provisions, such as 'excessive rent', are generic and allow Member States (and employers) broad discretion (Zoetewei,j 2018, p. 136; European Migration Network, 2020, p. 32).

The Directive provides for equal treatment of seasonal workers with EU nationals in core areas including terms of employment (like minimum working age) and working conditions (such as pay and dismissal, working hours, leave, and holidays) and health and safety requirements in the workplace; the right to strike and freedom of association; back pay; some social security provisions; equal treatment regarding education and vocational training; recognition of diplomas, certificates, and other professional qualifications; and, tax benefits (Art. 23). However, Member States are

[15] With regard to compensation, the Directive also addresses the issue of liability in subcontracting chains, establishing that in cases where the contractor and intermediary subcontractors have not undertaken due diligence with respect to a subcontractor's infringement of the Directive, they may be subject to sanctions and may also be liable to pay any compensation due to seasonal workers (Art. 17).

allowed to restrict equal treatment, for instance, with regard to social security benefits[16] (Art. 23(1)(d)), such as family and unemployment benefits.

In practice, this means that Member States may prevent seasonal workers from enjoying social security supports, such as unemployment and family benefits, even if they meet the conditions provided for their nationals and even if they or their employers pay social security contributions (Verschueren, 2016a, p. 389). This is the case in Italy, where the exclusion of non-EU seasonal agricultural workers from unemployment benefits encourages, as discussed in Chap. 5, dynamics of abuse and irregularity involving migrant seasonal workers.

Furthermore, according to the Seasonal Workers Directive, non-EU migrant seasonal workers cannot rely on the right of family reunification (recital 46). This provision, as well as those regarding restriction of equal treatment, is in line with the circular and temporary dimension of seasonal migration supported by this EU legal instrument. Indeed, in its preamble, the Directive clearly affirms that the establishment of fair and transparent rules for the admission and stay of seasonal workers and the definition of their rights should be accompanied by 'incentives and safeguards to prevent overstaying or temporary stay from becoming permanent' (Preamble, para. 7). As the Commission underlined in the *Impact Assessment* accompanying the Proposal for the Directive, 'seasonal work is by definition temporary work' (European Commission, 2010b, p. 11). Consequently, seasonal workers are not supposed to stay in the host state after having finished their work.

It is worth mentioning that the Seasonal Workers Directive (Art. 23(1)) stipulates that statutory pensions should be transferred to the third country where the seasonal worker resides, subject to identical conditions and rates as those applicable to nationals of the Member States moving to a third country. Some Member States, including Italy, have a framework in place to enable this transfer (European Migration Network, 2020). However, as emerges, for example, from the Italian case, the requirement that migrant workers must wait until reaching the statutory retirement age set for Italian workers (67 years old) to receive a pension can act as an incentive for irregular dynamics. Indeed, it is common for (predominantly young) seasonal workers to prefer earning more while in Italy, even through irregular practices, rather than benefiting from a meagre pension in the distant future (Ravelli, 2020, pp. 201–202).

A recent study by the European Migration Network (2020, p. 32) assessing the implementation of the Seasonal Workers Directive has revealed how seasonal workers' rights and protection are still inadequate 'mainly due to the short duration of their stay in the Member States'. A great number of Member States have made use of the possibility to restrict seasonal workers' access to unemployment benefits and family benefits (ibid.). Furthermore, in some national contexts, for instance Sweden, the transposition of the Seasonal Workers Directive has challenged a migration regime applying to all labour migrants by re-introducing a sectorial legal entry route for agricultural and forestry work (Palumbo, 2022). Through the application of

[16] The list of social security benefits for which Member States may make an exception to the principle of equal treatment can be found in Article 3 of the Regulation 883/2004 on the coordination of social security systems.

different collective agreements, depending on whether the employer is a Swedish-based company or a foreign or Swedish-based temporary work agency, this has paradoxically contributed to the fragmentation and segmentation of the national labour market and the precariousness of migrant workers (Iossa & Selberg, 2022). This, in turn, has increased seasonal workers' situations of vulnerability to exploitation.

3.1.2 Vulnerabilities of Migrant Seasonal Workers: Between Temporariness and Social Reproduction Limitations

By supporting a temporary and circular mobility for seasonal workers, the Seasonal Workers Directive embraces the approach of temporary labour migration programmes (TLMPs) that today are the main mechanisms for the recruitment of migrant workers. In particular, since the 2000s, TLMPs have been especially recommended for lower-skilled workers (World Bank, 2006; UNDP, 2009; OECD, 2014). The 2018 Global Compact on Migration, for instance, endorsed labour mobility schemes for 'temporary, seasonal, circular, and fast-track programs in areas of labour shortages'. The EU's 'New Pact on Migration and Asylum' in 2020 also called for expanded cooperation between EU and non-EU countries on schemes to 'match people, skills and labour market needs through legal migration' (European Commission, 2020).

In general, the adoption of temporary labour migration programmes finds justification in the notion that such schemes produce a 'triple win' for host countries, migrants, and their countries of origin (Bauböck & Ruhs, 2021): for host countries the ability to quickly fill labour shortages; for the countries of origin the possibility of reducing work surpluses and, thanks to the cyclical return of migrants, injecting the local labour market with new skills and capital flows; for migrants the opportunity to gain experience and receive higher remuneration while maintaining links with the country of origin.

However, especially in the case of recruitment of low-skilled workers, temporary labour migration programmes provide migrant workers with limited rights, in particular with regard to free choice of employment, access to social security benefits, and opportunities for family reunification (Deepa et al., 2012; Shamir, 2017; Mantouvalou, 2023). Restrictive temporary labour migration programmes are adopted in many countries in Europe, including the UK (Mantouvalou, 2023).

As Mantouvalou (ibid., p. 31) has noted, the true 'winners' of these programmes are the host states (and employers), which benefit from utilising a temporary and flexible labour force, and the workers' countries of origin, which benefit from workers' remittances. In contrast, migrant workers often find themselves trapped in a state of temporariness and dependence on employers, making them more vulnerable to dynamics of control, exploitation, and abuse (Shamir, 2017; Mantouvalou, 2023).

Similar considerations have been made about the legal regime established by the EU Seasonal Workers Directive (Zoeteweij, 2018; Papa, 2020). Indeed, the Directive supports an employer-driven mechanism, tethering migrants' temporary legal permissions to working and residing in the host state to employers' needs, making workers dependent on employers and exposing them to forms of exploitation. These dynamics can worsen in cases where the entry visa is issued under a contract with a recruitment agency, as many agencies operate through irregular and exploitative practices (Fudge & Strauss, 2014; Palumbo & Corrado, 2020; Siegmann et al., 2022).

Two related aspects regarding the Seasonal Workers Directive, in particular, give rise for concern. One is the differential legal regime that applies to third-country seasonal workers compared to national workers and other non-EU workers (Zoeteweij, 2018). The other is related to how this regime is based on controlling and managing the social reproduction of migrant seasonal workers, with significant effects in terms of gender-based inequalities, discrimination, and forms of exploitation.

Regarding the first aspect, as highlighted above, the Seasonal Workers Directive encourages what social scholar Anna Triandafyllidou (2022) terms a 'permanent temporariness' for seasonal workers, even when there is a long-term and structural need for them in specific sectors. Indeed, as the Commission underlined in the *Impact Assessment* accompanying the Proposal for the Directive, 'there is a permanent need in the EU for such temporary, seasonal work, but no need for permanent labour in the temporary (seasonal) sector of the economy' (European Commission, 2010b, p. 11). Accordingly, the Commission further stressed that 'admission of foreign workers on a temporary basis is attractive for enhancing the flexibility, availability, and willingness of sufficient numbers of workers to work at prevailing wages of the labour market without involving permanent settlement by the workers' (European Commission, 2010a, p. 12). Therefore, the main premise behind the Directive is that there is a systemic need for temporary seasonal workers but this does not imply prospects of long-term integration in the host Member States. Indeed, due to the temporary nature of their stay and employment, seasonal workers are expected to maintain their principal place of residence in a third country.

As Zoeteweij (2018, p. 132) argues, the Seasonal Workers Directive can be considered 'the schoolbook example of migration law that transforms people into economic inputs who depart when their labour is no longer necessary'. The economic-focused approach of this legislation is reflected in the limited rights granted to seasonal workers, especially regarding social security benefits and family reunification, thus preventing their social integration in the host Member State and compelling them to leave when their work is completed. As Martin Ruhs (2013) has underlined, the restrictive and economic-oriented approach to low-skilled migrant workers relies on the idea that limitations on certain rights is a sort of 'price' that they have to pay for the chance to migrate regularly to higher-income countries. In this context, more rights could come at the cost of a more stringent admission policy on the part of the host countries.

However, as some scholars have highlighted, it is questionable whether Member States implementing laws that create unequal treatment regarding social security for non-EU temporary workers, and in particular seasonal workers, is in line with relevant EU and international law (Zoeteweij, 2018; Bogoeski & Rasnača, 2023). Currently, there is no case law by the Court of Justice of the European Union (CJEU) in relation to the provisions on social benefits in the Seasonal Workers Directive (Verschueren, 2023). However, it is worth noting that, with respect to the right of equal treatment in the Single Permit Directive, the CJEU has pointed out that exceptions to the principle of equal treatment should be interpreted strictly (*Martinez Silva*, C-449/16 and *INPS v WS*, C-302/19). In line with an approach attentive to the material conditions ensuring a social human dignity (Rodotà, 2012), the Court has stressed that one of the main objectives of the right to equal treatment is to support the integration in the host Member States of the third-country national in question (Verschueren, 2023). Such an interpretation followed by the Court is consistent with the prohibition of discrimination outlined in international human rights treaties such as the European Convention on Human Rights. Indeed, as the ECtHR has repeatedly stated in this regard, the difference of treatment regarding social security, based exclusively on the ground of nationality, is only possible if justified by 'very weighty reasons'.[17]

The limited access to social benefits provided for the Seasonal Workers Directive certainly, as Margarite Helena Zoeteweij (2018) has pointed out, does not guarantee that the treatment of migrant seasonal workers is equivalent to that of nationals or other non-EU migrant workers considered 'more economically valuable', such as high-skilled workers under the Blue Cards Directive. Moreover, unlike for instance Blue Card Holders, migrant seasonal workers cannot rely on the right to family reunification. As many scholars have underlined (Zoeteweij, 2018; Verschueren, 2023), this differential legal regime providing for limited rights to seasonal workers reinforces the precarious situations of these workers and increases their vulnerabilities to exploitation and abuse.

In particular, Zoeteweij noted how this differential legal regime among categories of third-country citizens is based on their different perceived 'economic value' to the host Member States. Indeed, despite the 'permanent need' for seasonal work, often devalued as 'unskilled,' its economic value tends to be seen as considerably lower than that of Blue Card holders. Consequently, seasonal workers are granted fewer rights and impeded from settling in the host Member States. This disparity also reflects differing social perceptions and attitudes regarding these categories of workers: unlike highly skilled workers, low skilled/seasonal workers are frequently seen as potential irregular migrants (Zoeteweij, 2018) and, therefore, as a 'threat' (Herzfeld Olsson, 2016) to national society that needs to be contained. This attitude towards low-skilled workers, persisted even during the Covid-19 pandemic (Corrado & Palumbo, 2021).[18]

---

[17] See, for instance, ECtHR, *Gaygusuz v. Austria*, Application no. 17371/90, 16 September 1996, para. 42; also ECtHR, *Andrejeva v. Latvia*, Application no. 55707/00, 18 February 2009, para. 87.

[18] Despite the rhetoric lauding migrant seasonal workers or domestic workers as key workers, the main national responses during the pandemic, such as in Italy have been temporary and primarily focused on addressing the economic and labour market needs rather than the protection of these workers' rights in a solid and long-term perspective (Corrado & Palumbo, 2021).

Another important consideration concerns the role played by social reproduction regimes. As discussed in Chap. 2, feminist social and legal scholars have shed light on the nexus between social reproduction and migration regimes. In particular, Enrica Rigo (2022, p. 81) underscores how the proliferation of borders is a process that assigns migrants to hierarchical systems, 'not only in terms of work but also in the reproduction of life itself'. This perspective is crucial for comprehending the differential legal regime supported by the Seasonal Workers Directive where management and control of seasonal workers' reproduction sphere play a fundamental role. Indeed, the limited rights granted to seasonal workers under this regime, based on their perceived low 'economic value', impacts these workers' social reproduction dimension, constraining and containing it. This, in turn, contributes to processes of subordination of the migrant labour force based on gender, nationality/ethnicity, and class.

The absence of the right to family reunification for migrant seasonal workers is a clear representation of this dynamic. Through this provision, which resembles the approach of guest worker programmes implemented in Europe 1950s and 1970s (Zoeteweij, 2018; Castles, 1986; Walzer, 1983), control over seasonal workers' mobility is exercised by constraining the conditions related to their social reproduction and affecting their related family and care responsibilities. The lack of the right to family reunification prompts workers to go back to the country of origin and prevents their social integration in the host Member States. The same could be said for the restrictions on migrant seasonal workers' access to social security benefits, such as family and unemployment benefits. All these provisions have a significant gender impact on the dynamics of migrant mobility, situations of vulnerabilities, and related forms of exploitation.

It is worth noting that the Seasonal Workers Directive overlooks the adoption of a gender perspective to address the protection seasonal workers' rights. Gender is never mentioned in the text of this legal instrument, conveying the idea it is gender neutral. However, as feminist legal scholars have emphasised, the gender neutrality of law is always open to question. As feminist legal scholar Catharine Mackinnon (1989) argues, 'gender neutrality is a deeply biased standard' covering and simultaneously fostering gendered power dynamics. In this light, despite its gender-neutral approach, the Seasonal Workers Directive's provisions facilitate labour market segmentation, discrimination, and forms of exploitation on the basis of gender, nationality/ethnicity and class, responding to the economic and labour market needs of EU countries.

Given that reproductive work and related family responsibilities in the domestic/family sphere are still primarily assigned to women, the fact that the Directive does not provide for the right to family reunification for seasonal workers is 'inherently disadvantageous' for women (Zoeteweij-Turhan, 2017, p. 40) and can have a substantial impact on their choice to move as seasonal workers in EU countries. As Zoeteweij (ibid.) has rightly argued, 'whereas the Directive is not directly discriminatory, when one considers that in most societies—and especially in the societies of countries that source unskilled seasonal workers—women have maintained primary responsibility for the direct care of children, it is obvious that it will be mainly men that are able and willing to leave their families behind for periods of up to nine months per calendar year to go and take up seasonal work in one of the Member States of the EU'.

On the other hand, the lack of the right to family reunification for seasonal workers, and therefore their inability to bring their children or other family members with them, can serve as an assurance for national governments that these seasonal workers will return to their country of origin once their employment ends. Consequently, this may lead to a preference for workers with family responsibilities, particularly women workers, as these responsibilities make their return to their home countries after the contract expires even more likely. This is the case of the Spanish temporary migration programme '*contratación en origen*'—the main tool of the Spanish admission system to recruit third-country seasonal workers (especially women workers) within the framework of bilateral agreements with the countries of origin such Morocco (Molinero, 2018). This is considered good practice internationally thanks to its 'triple win' focus and has inspired the approach of the Seasonal Workers Directive (López-Sala, 2016). However, this model has been criticised for creating a strong worker dependency on employers and fostering gender exploitative dynamics, violating relevant international and EU legal instruments safeguarding fundamental rights, workers' rights, and gender equality.[19] Indeed, within this system, preference has been formally given to women migrant workers with children as the fact of having left children to be cared for in their country of origin guarantees their return to their countries at the end of the harvest. Under this system, therefore, care and family responsibilities have become elements used for the recruitment of flexible and 'docile' women seasonal workers, increasing their situational vulnerabilities to abuse, gender violence, and exploitation (Palumbo & Sciurba, 2018; Hellio, 2016).

3.2 Access to Work for Beneficiaries of International Protection and Asylum Seekers in EU Law: Rights, Protection, and Vulnerabilities to Exploitation

As emphasised in this chapter's introduction, in recent years, even as a consequence of increasingly restrictive national migration policies, migrant people have significantly turned to channels such as asylum. Given the significant presence in countries such as Italy of refugees and asylum seekers employed in unprotected sectors such as agriculture, it is important to take into account EU regulations on labour market access for beneficiaries of international protection and asylum seekers.

[19] For instance, the Charter of Fundamental Rights of the European Union (Articles 21 and 23) and Gender Equality Directive 2006/54/EC on the implementation of the principle of equal opportunities and equal treatment of men and women in matters of employment and occupation, 2006 OJ L204/23.

Again, the attention here is to assess whether the legal regime addresses and prevents or rather contributes to situational vulnerabilities to exploitation.

It is worth noting that the above-mentioned EU Directives on labour migration, including the Single Permit Directive, the former Blue Card Directive, the Seasonal Workers Directive and the Researchers and Students Directive, do not apply to beneficiaries of international protection or asylum seekers. However, the recently adopted recast Blue Card Directive has extended access to the Blue Card scheme to beneficiaries of international protection. This significantly contributes to bridging the divide between labour migration law and asylum law in the EU context (De Lange & Vankova, 2022), although asylum seekers are still excluded from the Directive's scope. In a similar way, as noted earlier, the current proposal for the revision of the Single Permit Directive provides for extending its scope by removing the exclusion of beneficiaries of protection, making the Directive's provisions on procedures and equal treatment apply to them (De Lange, 2022). This is an important aspect of the proposal. However, the envisaged scope of the Single Permit Directive is still narrow (ibid.).

Directive 2011/95/EU,[20] known as the Qualification Directive and recasting Directive 2004/83/EC, requires Member States to authorise beneficiaries of international protection to engage in employed and self-employed activities immediately after protection has been granted (Art. 26). Member States shall also ensure that activities such as employment-related education opportunities for adults are offered to beneficiaries of international protection under equivalent conditions as nationals. Furthermore, Member States shall ensure beneficiaries of international protection access to education, healthcare, and accommodation under equivalent conditions as nationals. The Directive also requires Member States to ensure that beneficiaries of international protection receive 'the necessary social protection' as provided to the nationals of that Member State (Art. 29(1)). Member States are required to apply this provision to the family members of beneficiaries of international protection (Art. 23(2)).

In this regard, the CJEU has explicitly recognised the direct effect of this provision (see case *Shah Ayubi*, C-713/17) (Verschueren, 2023; Biondi Dal Monte, 2019). In particular, the Court has clarified that Article 29 of the Qualification Directive means that the host Member States may not impose different conditions for the allowance of these benefits than those applicable to their own nationals (*Alo and Osso*, C-443/14 and C-444/14). According to the Court, the word 'necessary' does not imply that Member States are allowed to restrict the allowance of social rights to a mere minimum (Verschueren, 2023). The CJEU made its argument in the same vein regarding the Directive's provision (Art. 29.2) concerning Member States' possibilities to limit social assistance granted to beneficiaries of subsidiary protection to 'core benefits which will then be provided at the same level and under the same eligibility conditions as nationals' of that Member State (*Alo and Osso*, Cases C-443/14 and C-444/14, para. 49). As Recital 45 of the Directive affirms, the

[20] Standards for the qualification of third-country nationals or stateless persons as beneficiaries of international protection, for a uniform status for refugees or for persons eligible for subsidiary protection, and for the content of the protection granted.

possibility to limit such assistance to core benefits is to be understood as encompassing 'at least minimum income support, assistance in the case of illness, or pregnancy, and parental assistance, in so far as those benefits are granted to nationals under national law' (*Shab Ayubi*, C-713/17). Following Verschueren's (2023) analysis, it can be argued that, in the light of relevant CJEU case law, core benefits are those that address basic needs, guaranteeing a decent existence, in accordance with the principles outlined in the EU Charter of Fundamental Rights (Art. 34).

This CJEU case law is important as it highlights how the objective of the Qualification Directive—especially its provisions regarding equal treatment in terms of employment, social assistance, healthcare, and housing—is to facilitate and support the integration of beneficiaries of international protection in the host countries, ensuring them a decent standard of working and living conditions (Verschueren, 2023).

However, as numerous studies have documented, in many European countries refugees face significant challenges in accessing the labour market, often experiencing dynamics of discrimination and exploitation. Additionally, and related to this, many lack access to adequate accommodation and social services (see, for instance, Martin et al., 2016; EPRS, 2018; Corrado et al., 2018; Della Puppa & Sanò, 2021). The conditions are frequently even more dire for asylum seekers, as their prolonged condition of uncertainty amplifies and exacerbates their situations of vulnerability (Sciurba, 2021a; De Lange, 2018; Lewis & Wait, 2015; Slingenberg, 2014).

Directive 2013/33/EU (Art. 15), known as the Reception Conditions Directive[21] and repealing Directive 2003/9/EC, regulates, among other aspects, the employment conditions of asylum seekers. It requires Member States to ensure that applicants have access to the labour market no later than 9 months from the date when the application for international protection was lodged (Art. 15). Member States shall decide the conditions for granting access to the labour market for the applicants, in accordance with national law. They shall ensure that applicants have effective access to the labour market. As De Lange (2018, p. 171) underlined, 'access in a purely legal sense without practical access will not suffice'. For reasons related to their labour market policies, Member States may opt to prioritise EU citizens and regularly resident third-country nationals. Furthermore, according to the Directive (Art. 15), access to the labour market shall not be withdrawn during appeals procedures, if the appeal has suspensive effect, until such time as a negative decision on the appeal is notified.

Member States are, therefore, free to decide how to implement these provisions of the Reception Conditions Directive in their national laws. Consequently, asylum seekers' access to the labour market varies from one country to another. For example, in Sweden asylum seekers may work immediately upon filing the asylum application. In Italy they can work after 2 months, in Germany after 3 months, in Belgium after 4 months, and in the Netherlands after 6 months.

[21] Directive 2013/33/EU of the European Parliament and of the Council of 26 June 2013 lays down standards for the reception of applicants for international protection, OJ L 180.

Importantly, in the preamble, the Directive highlights that it is essential to establish clear rules regarding applicants' access to the labour market to promote 'the self-sufficiency of applicants and to limit wide discrepancies between Member States' (preamble 23). Furthermore, Member States shall establish standards for the reception of applicants that are adequate 'to ensure them a dignified standard of living and comparable living conditions' (preamble 11).

Reality, however, falls far short of these provisions. In fact, in many European countries, those migrants who manage to reach the first country of asylum surpass the initial 'screening' in confinement and filtering systems (Tazzioli, 2023) such as hotspots and detention centres and apply for asylum, then face protracted and complicated asylum procedures. Additionally, many are accommodated in inadequate institutional reception conditions and structures (Sciurba, 2021b; Carnassale & Marchetti, 2022; Saroléa et al., 2021; Schmoll, 2022) or live in informal settlements, as is the case in Italy and Greece (Busetta et al., 2021).

In its landmark decision *M.S.S. v Belgium and Greece* (Application No. 30696/09, 21 January 2011), the ECtHR held the Greek authorities responsible for the violation of Article 3 of the ECHR, which establishes the prohibition of inhuman and degrading treatment, 'because of their inaction, for the situation in which [the applicant] has found himself for several months, living on the street, with no resources or access to sanitary facilities, and without any means of providing for his essential needs. It considers that such living conditions, combined with the prolonged uncertainty in which he has remained and the total lack of any prospects of his situation improving, have attained the level of severity required to fall within the scope of Article 3 of the Convention' (para. 263). In line with a situational conception of vulnerability, the Court highlighted the interplay of factors creating a situation of vulnerability in which many asylum seekers find themselves in 'circumstances wholly dependent on state support' (para. 253).

The situation of vulnerability described by the Court extends far beyond the specific case considered in its decision and applies to the experiences of asylum seekers across several European countries. Many asylum seekers, indeed, find themselves trapped in a state of uncertainty and precariousness that fosters their vulnerabilities and, consequently, exposes them to various forms of abuse and exploitation. These situations of vulnerability are further exacerbated by the need to repay debts accumulated during their journeys and generate income to support themselves and their families with them or in the countries of origin (Santoro, 2021). Indeed, reproductive and family-related responsibilities play a crucial role in these dynamics.

With regard to the income acquired by asylum seekers involved in the reception system, Article 17 of the Reception Conditions Directive requires Member States to ensure that material reception conditions provide an adequate standard of living for applicants, guaranteeing their subsistence and protecting their physical and mental health. Furthermore, according to the Directive, Member States may require applicants to cover or contribute to the cost of material reception and healthcare if they have sufficient resources, 'for example if they have been working for a reasonable period of time' (Art. 17(4)).

In this case as well, Member States have implemented the Directive differently. For example, the Netherlands provides asylum seekers with a material means of existence but seeks reimbursement for room and board once an asylum seeker starts to earn income (De Lange, 2018). However, the Dutch regulation does not take into account whether the income is steady or merely occasional and therefore leaves little discretion to the national competent asylum authorities (ibid.) This, in turn, discourages asylum seekers, especially those with families, living in an asylum reception centre from seeking paid work. Moreover, delays in settling amounts connected to the reimbursement cause asylum seekers to leave the reception centre still carrying debts to the national asylum authorities and 'this makes them vulnerable to abuse and exploitation' (ibid., p. 183).

By contrast in Italy, national regulations[22] provide that asylum seekers lose accommodation in dedicated reception centres when their annual income exceeds the annual social assistance allowance, which currently amounts to €6.947,33. In addition to likely conflicting with the Reception Conditions Directive, this provision paradoxically pushes asylum seekers to accept irregular working conditions (without a regular contract or with a contract reporting fewer hours than those effectively performed by the workers) to avoid the risk of having their admission to reception measures revoked (L'Altro Diritto & FLAI CGIL, 2022). It is worth underscoring that in Italy, as discussed in Chap. 5, many reception centres have turned into a source of low-cost and exploitable labour for abusive employers and intermediaries. This allows for an externalisation of the costs of reproduction of workers that are shifted onto the national reception system and do not fall on the employers and, more broadly, on the production supply chain (Caprioglio & Rigo, 2020; Palumbo, 2022).

3.3 Intra-EU Labour Mobility, Equal Treatment, and Tensions

This section focuses on the EU legal framework for EU nationals' access to the national labour markets in the European context. It highlights the main issues, tensions, and challenges concerning the protection of the rights of mobile EU workers and the factors amplifying their vulnerabilities to exploitation. Even in this scenario, access to social rights and, more broadly, to those rights related to the social reproduction spheres of the EU migrant workers, plays a crucial role in the management of labour mobility and increasing situations of vulnerability.

Free movement of workers, in particular the right of EU nationals to work in another Member State, lies at the foundations of Europe as a free-trade area (Geddes et al., 2020, p. 136). It represents an essential means of the realisation and

[22] See, in particular, Art. 14 of the Legislative Decree 142/2015 concerning the rules on the reception of applicants for international protection.

development of the internal market as it contributes to guaranteeing that labour is allocated where it is most needed while enhancing economic productivity (Jacqueson & Pennings, 2019). As De Lange and Rijken (2018, p. 13) underline, while the worker's 'social advancement' was explicitly mentioned as one aim of free movement of workers in the former Regulation 1612/68,[23] it was subsequently abolished in Regulation 492/2011,[24] 'tipping the balance of interests involved towards the interests of employers and their need for work force over the migrants' interest in "social advancement" through working elsewhere in the EU'.

As established in Article 45 of the TFEU and further detailed in secondary legislation, such as Art. 7 Regulation 492/2011, workers from other Member States must be treated equally compared to national workers as regards employment, remuneration, and other conditions of work and employment. Equal treatment with nationals of the host Member States also covers social security benefits within the meaning of Regulation 833/2004 (Art. 4) on the coordination of social security systems.[25] If the principle of equal treatment is not upheld, free movement of workers would be undermined, with economic and social consequences, for both migrant and local workers as well as for Member States. As Jacqueson and Pennings (2019, p. 66) point out, if EU workers are not entitled to the same pay and working conditions as the nationals of the host state, they may not make use of the freedom of movement. At the same time, violating this principle would result in a downward pressure on wages and social contributions, fostering dynamics of social dumping.

In its relevant case law, the CJEU has argued that it is sufficient that a person performs an economic activity, even small, to deserve equal treatment (Case C-542/09, *Commission v The Netherlands*). According to the CJEU, the fact that migrant workers participate in the employment market establishes 'in principle, a sufficient link of integration with the society of that Member State, allowing them to benefit from the principle of equal treatment, as compared with national workers' (C-542/09, *Commission v. the Netherlands*, para. 65). Indeed, by paying taxes and social security contributions in the host Member State, by virtue of their employment, migrant workers contribute to the economy of that state (ibid., para. 66).

In the absence of a clearly stated definition of 'worker' under EU law, the CJEU has supported a broad interpretation of the term. By relying on the traditional separation between productive and reproductive spaces (Rigo, 2022), in its first relevant decisions the Court defined as a worker any person who performs activities that are 'effective' and 'genuine', to the exclusion of activities on such a small scale that they are purely marginal and ancillary (Case 53/81 Levi 1986, *Lawrie-Blum*, Case 66/85 Blum 1986). The essential element of an employment relationship is 'that for a certain period of time a person performs services for and under the direction of

[23] Regulation (EEC) No. 1612/68 of the Council of 15 October 1968 on freedom of movement for workers within the Community, OJ L 257.

[24] Regulation (EU) No 492/2011 of the European Parliament and of the Council of 5 April 2011 on freedom of movement for workers within the Union Text with EEA relevance.

[25] Regulation (EC) 883/2004 of the European Parliament and the Council of 29 April 2004 on the coordination of social security systems, OJ 2004, L 200/1.

another person in return for which he receives remuneration' (*Lawrie-Blum*, Case 66/85, Lawrie-Blum, para. 17). Following the adoption of Directive 2004/38[26](the Citizens' Rights Directive), the notion of 'worker' has been further broadened by the Court to include persons who work for a very short period or in a job with minor income (see C-83/17, *Tarola*) (Jacqueson & Pennings, 2019).

It is important to note that, despite being a broad definition with regard to remunerated activities, by identifying the requirement of remuneration as a key element, the CJEU's definition of 'worker' excludes unpaid activities such as unremunerated reproductive work within the family from its scope (O' Brien, 2009). As noted by Rigo (2022, p. 33), 'the quality of being a worker remains linked to the condition that the individual has occupied or can occupy a productive space that enables them to procure sufficient resources for their sustenance'.[27] In other words, even though this definition is more encompassing, it still draws a distinction between 'productive' and 'reproductive' activities, creating a differentiation between work considered valuable and work seen as less valuable (Picchio, 2008). This distinction has significant implications for the protection and rights of those (especially women) engaged in unpaid domestic and care labour within the family.

However, the 'broad' conception of 'work' provided by the CJEU has not always been followed by national authorities as some national interpretations are more restrictive, introducing higher requirements, for instance, in terms of earnings thresholds or hours of work (Jacqueson & Pennings, 2019). This, in turn, results in unequal treatment of EU citizen migrants regarding their access to social rights, undermining the protection of EU workers and increasing their situations of vulnerability, particularly among EU mobile citizens from economically disadvantaged eastern EU countries.

Behind this restrictive approach is many Member States' fear that admitting EU workers with short-term employment could become a burden for the host countries. Free movement has become particularly contested after Eastern enlargement (Editorial Comments, 2014). Indeed, while intra-EU mobility has been supported as the cornerstone of the EU (Donaghey & Teague, 2006), many Member States have become concerned about this, tending to view free movement of workers and more generally EU citizens' right to move to any Member State—especially those from new Member States—as a potential threat rather than a benefit. Some governments have argued that free movement of persons can lead to the phenomenon of 'welfare tourism' or 'benefit tourism', with intra- EU migrants moving from countries with less developed welfare state systems to states offering more generous social protection. Concerns about 'unrestricted' free movement of persons and 'welfare shopping' have been mainly supported by right-wing anti-immigration parties (Geddes et al., 2020) and significantly influenced the UK's choice to leave the EU, as discussed in Chap. 7.

---

[26] Directive 2004/38 on the right of EU citizens and their families to move and reside freely within the EU.

[27] My translation in English.

At the same time, such a concerned approach has been reflected in some leading case law of the CJEU regarding access to social benefits for economically inactive EU citizens.[28] In relevant case law (Case C-333/13 *Dano,* Case C-67/14 Alimanovic and Case C-299/14 Garcia-Nieto), the CJEU held a very restrictive approach to access to social rights that limits the mobility of EU citizens to economically active persons, excluding those who are economically inactive and indigent.

The well-known decision in the Dano case involved a young mother from Romania who was refused a German unemployment benefit ('Basic income support for job seekers', job-seeker allowance) since according to German law foreign nationals are excluded from social assistance for jobseekers when the right of residence arises solely from the search for employment. The CJEU first highlighted that Ms. Dano had never worked in Germany or Romania and that nothing showed that she had been seeking employment (Ms Dano and her son lived with the woman's sister, who provided for them). The Court then held that EU citizens can claim equal treatment with nationals in accessing benefits in the host Member State only if their residence fulfils the conditions of the Citizens Rights' Directive. This decision has been characterised as the 'failure of citizens' rights beyond the single market', revealing the absence of a 'thick' conception of social justice at the European level (Thym, 2016; see also Kramer, 2016; Giubboni, 2018a; Pera, 2019). As legal scholar Dion Kramer (2016) argues, EU citizenship has manifested itself as 'earned social citizenship'. In this scenario, economically inactive and poor EU citizens have been confined to the margins of EU citizenship, prevented from enjoying full access to social benefits in the host Member States. This contributes to increasing their situations of vulnerability, with the consequent risk of exposing them to forms of abuse and exploitation.

As De Lange and Rijken (2018, p. 14) argue, 'the differences in wages, labour conditions, and opportunities to work throughout the EU are a constant incentive for people living in the EU where wages and conditions are low, to try to improve these in other EU Member States where wages and labour conditions are high'. However, they often accept working at lower employment and wage conditions than natives. Indeed, in Italy (Chap. 5) and other EU countries, in reality EU migrants encounter significant obstacles when seeking employment and ensuring the continuity of their stay. These hurdles are notably prominent in labour markets marked by significant fragmentation and segregation based on gender, nationality/ethnicity, and socio-economic class, alongside the prevalence of precarious employment contracts (Palumbo & Corrado, 2020; Siegmann et al., 2022; Iossa & Selberg, 2022). Eastern EU migrant workers (particularly Poles, Romanians, and Bulgarians) represent an important pillar of low-protected sectors such as agriculture and domestic work, and are particularly exposed to abuse and exploitation, including severe cases of trafficking (Palumbo, 2020). Indeed, the ability of these workers to easily cross EU

[28] It is worth mentioning that while economically active persons are clearly entitled to social benefits in the host Member States under the principle of equal treatment with nationals, questions arise about economically inactive persons as the Citizens' Rights Directive provides for the possibility of different treatment for them.

internal borders produces a 'circular migration' that facilitates their exploitation in a context of competition on labour costs within the European internal market as well as an ongoing erosion of workers' rights, particularly those concerning their social reproduction sphere. These conditions disproportionately impact workers, particularly women, who have family and reproductive responsibilities, rendering them even more dependent on abusive employers and intermediaries.

The rhetoric depicting eastern EU citizens as potential abusers of the welfare system of the host Member States and supporting restrictive approaches and policies should be overturned by stronger EU social policy and labour protection. The so-called Social Pillar could play an important ambit in this regard.

3.4 Intra-EU Mobility, Freedom to Provide Services, and Spaces for Exceptions and Abuse

As numerous studies have pointed out, in a context of the labour market's flexibilisation and deregulation there has been an increase in the recourse to temporary work agencies, subcontracting, or posted work as a way of circumventing relevant EU and national legislation to hire cheap labour (Arnholtz & Lillie, 2020). Companies use relevant EU and national legal frameworks to create 'spaces of exception' (ibid.) around their work arrangements and enhance their competitiveness by compressing the rights of workers, especially social rights (Cremers, 2011; Houwerzjil & Berntsen, 2020).

The rights of temporary agency workers are protected under Directive 2008/104/EC[29] (the Temporary Agency Workers Directive), which applies to workers under a contract of employment or employment relationship with a temporary-work agency and who are temporarily placed at the disposal of user undertakings (Art. 1(1)). The purpose of the Directive is threefold: to ensure the protection of temporary agency workers, improve the quality of temporary agency work by ensuring the principle of equal treatment, and recognise temporary work agencies as employers (Art. 2). Regarding equal treatment, the Directive provides that the working and employment conditions of temporary agency workers should be at least those that would apply if they had been recruited directly by the user undertaking to occupy the same job (Art. 5). Furthermore, the rules in the undertaking are extended to certain areas including equal treatment for men and women as well as any action to combatt any discrimination based on sex, race or ethnic origin, religion, beliefs, disabilities, age, or sexual orientation. The Directive also provides that Member States shall take appropriate measures, in accordance with national law or practice, with a view to preventing misuse in the application of the provision concerning equal treatment

[29] Directive 2008/104/EC of the European Parliament and of the Council of 19 November 2008 on temporary agency work, OJ L 327.

and, in particular, to prevent successive assignments designed to circumvent the provisions of this Directive.

The Temporary Agency Workers Directive establishes a regulatory framework for temporary agency work, guided by the principles of non-discrimination, transparency, and proportionality. As Giuseppe Bronzini (2022) argues, the Directive is aimed at granting 'minimal rights, especially those that are anti-abusive and anti-discriminatory, to give substance to Article 31 of the Charter of Fundamental Rights, which, in its title, establishes 'fair and just working conditions' for all categories of employment'. However, as observed by certain scholars, the regulatory framework is minimal and, in some instances, ambiguous (see, for instance, Giubboni 2021). Indeed, similar to other European and national legislative instruments regarding 'atypical' employment, the Temporary Agency Workers Directive has been criticised for contributing to a 'flexicurity' model prioritising flexible forms of work at the expense of worker and employee protections and rights (Schiek, 2004).

An important criticism regards some derogations to the principle of equal treatment provided by Temporary Agency Workers Directive (Art. 5.4).[30] Another critical point concerns the concept of the 'temporary' nature of the service as the Directive does not impose a maximum duration for the worker's assignment nor a maximum number of consecutive assignments with the same user company. On this matter, the CJEU has recently intervened with its decision of 14 October 2020, in *JH v. KG, C-681/2018* and with the more recent decision on 17 March 2022 in *Daimler AG, Mercedes-Benz, Werk Berlin, C-232/20*. With this latest ruling in particular, the Court affirmed that an abusive use of temporary agency work may occur when multiple consecutive assignments of the same worker with the same user company result in a duration of employment with that company that exceeds what can reasonably be considered temporary, taking into account the circumstances of the case, the specificities of the sector, and the national legal framework. For this purpose, the Court said, Member States may establish a maximum duration beyond which an assignment cannot be considered temporary or time-limited. In cases where national regulations do not specify a maximum duration, it is the responsibility of national judges to determine it on a case-by-case basis, with consideration for the sector's specificities. These two CJEU decisions are inclined toward a more principled stringency regarding atypical employment in favour of better protection for workers hired through temporary agencies (Bronzini, 2022).

The Temporary Agency Workers Directive's shortcomings in terms of protecting workers employed through agencies are at the heart of the proposal put forth by the European Federation of Food, Agriculture and Tourism Trade Unions (EFFAT) for

[30] The Directive established that 'provided that an adequate level of protection is provided for temporary agency workers, Member States in which there is either no system in law for declaring collective agreements universally applicable or no such system in law or practice for extending their provisions to all similar undertakings in a certain sector or geographical area, may, after consulting the social partners at national level and on the basis of an agreement concluded by them, establish arrangements concerning the basic working and employment conditions which derogate from the principle' of equal treatment (Art. 5(4)).

a Directive on labour intermediation and fair conditions along subcontracting chains.[31] Among the proposal's objectives are ensuring genuine equal treatment throughout subcontracting chains by implementing rules that more effectively address abusive practices; strengthening principles of transparency and accountability; and providing increased safeguards for workers. Indeed, in many European countries, including Italy, migrant workers often access the labour market through subcontracting firms under substandard and exploitative conditions in terms of working hours, wages, and accommodations (Palumbo & Corrado, 2020; Olivieri, 2016). In practice, subcontracting is progressively employed as a business strategy to cut labour force costs and evade employer liability. This is partly due to the complexity of subcontracting chains, which makes monitoring and enforcement more challenging.

Similar strategies to circumvent relevant EU and national regulations resulting in situations of abuse and exploitation also occur in the case of posted workers. Posted workers are sent by their employers 'to carry out a service in another EU Member State on temporary basis, in the context of services, an intra-group posting or a hiring out through a temporary agency'.[32]

In the landmark judgment *Rush Portugusa*, the CJEU ruled that posted workers are not workers within the meaning of Article 45 of the TFEU as they do not access the labour market of the host Member State; they fall under the scope of providing services in other Member States, i.e., in free movement of services (Art. 56 of the TFEU). This has raised the question of when free circulation of services should take precedence and when labour law rules should legitimately protect workers (Houwerzijl & Verschueren, 2019).

The employment rights and working conditions of posted workers are regulated by Directive 96/71/EC (the Posted Workers Directive), Directive 2014/67/EU, and Directive 2018/957/EU. The cornerstone of employment protection for posted workers is that they remain employed with the sending company and, as a result, are subject to the law applicable to their employment contract, which often corresponds to the law of their home Member State. However, the Posted Workers Directive, as revised in 2018 by Directive 2018/957/EU, provides core terms and conditions of employment that are applied according to the regulations of the host Member State when they offer greater protection than the employment law of the home state (or the law applicable to the employment contract). In particular, the Directive ensures non-discrimination between national workers and posted workers regarding remuneration, maximum work periods and minimum rest periods, and conditions of hiring-out workers (particularly the supply of workers by temporary employment undertakings), health, safety and workplace hygiene, paid minimum leave, accommodations provided by the employer, equal treatment between men and women and other provisions on non-discrimination, and allowances or reimbursements for travel, food, and lodging expenses for workers who are away from home for

[31] See EFFAT (2023).

[32] Employment, Social Affairs and Inclusion: [online], https://ec.europa.eu/social/posted-workers

professional reasons. Also, the Directive provides that where the effective duration of posting exceeds 12 months, all the host Member State's applicable terms and conditions of employment, laid down by law or by collective agreements, must be guaranteed.

Despite the significant measures introduced in 2018 by the Directive 2018/957/EU, posted workers still have more limited rights when it comes to social security as they continue to be subject to the social security system of their home state.[33] Additionally, these workers do not benefit from all labour legislation applicable in the host state (Costamagna, 2019).

Before the Directive's revision in 2018, the EU legal framework had proved to be inadequate for finding a balance between the promotion of the free circulation of services, on the one hand, and the preservation of host states' competence to impose their own labour standards and the protection of the rights of posted workers, on the other (Costamagna, 2019, p. 9; Verschueren, 2016b; Houwerzijl & Verschueren, 2019; Novitz & Andrijasevic, 2020). This has been further compounded by well-known 2007–2008 CJEU case law, the 'Laval quartet',[34] which, in line with a market-friendly approach, interpreted the provisions of the Posted Workers Directive in a highly restrictive manner, prioritising the need not to hinder the free provision of services over the protection of workers and ensuring fair competition. As legal scholar Francesco Costamagna (2019, p. 10) argued, these CJEU judgements transformed the Posted Workers Directive from an instrument aimed 'at curbing regulatory competition in the social domain into a tool fostering it'.

This has often led to the instrumental use of posted workers who mostly come from eastern EU countries and are recruited through subcontractors and transnational employment agencies so they can be employed under the conditions of their home countries. These conditions typically involve lower-level social security systems, thereby bypassing the regulations of the host country (Houwerzjil & Berntsen, 2020; Houwerzijl & Verschueren, 2019). This has, in turn, contributed to the creation of a vast grey area where employers and businesses twist the law and profit from loopholes and ambiguities in the relevant EU and national laws, giving rise to dynamics of social dumping, irregularities, and exploitation in sectors such as construction, logistics, and the agri-food industry (Cremers & Dekker, 2018).

In Italy, for example, the recourse to posted work, even as a practice to skirt relevant legislation, occurs in sectors such as construction or manufacturing, and less in the agri-food sector (Dorigatti et al., 2022). The recourse to posted work in agri-food systems, especially as a method to compress labour costs, circumventing relevant EU and national legislation, is instead quite widespread in northern European countries. For instance, as Siegmann et al. (2022) underline, in the Netherlands a common technique among businesses is to create letter-box companies or affiliates in Member States where labour costs are low, such as Poland, and then post workers

[33] Art. 12(1) Regulation 883/2004.

[34] Cases of *Viking* (C-438/05), *Laval* (C341/05), *Ruffert* (C-346/06) and *Commission vs. Luxembourg* (C-319/06).

to Dutch client firms. This provides employers with the opportunity to bypass relevant labour and social security regulations, compressing the rights of workers, in particular of EU mobile workers. This, in turn, causes unfair competition and social dumping dynamics within the European internal market while also eroding workers' rights. Furthermore, these practices often involve cases of severe exploitation, including trafficking (ELA, 2023).

It is worth emphasising that reproduction conditions of posted workers—such as transportation, meals, and accommodation—depend on the employer/company. Furthermore, posted workers often lack knowledge of their rights in the host state. This condition of isolation and dependence on the employer hinders their access to justice and, consequently, amplifies their situational vulnerabilities, further exposing them to dynamics of abuse and exploitation. Situations of exploitation and disciplining of workers also seem to be exacerbated in the case of women workers by prevailing gendered norms and power relations (Palumbo & Corrado, 2020).

Furthermore, as Silvia Borelli (2020) notes, in cases of abusive posting practices involving third-country nationals[35] access to justice is made even more challenging by the fact that 'if they complain about the non-compliance with posting regulations, they change their status from that of a regular migrant in the home country to that of an irregular migrant in the host country'.[36] Consequently, there is the risk they cannot benefit from the sanctioning regime and, therefore, cannot obtain compensation for the damages suffered. Furthermore, according to relevant EU law, they can obtain a residence permit only if they are victims of labour exploitation according to the Employer Sanctions Directive 2009/52 or victims of trafficking according to Directive 2004/81 (see Chap. 4). As Borelli highlighted, the lack of clear and robust protection for third-country migrant posted workers often discourages them from reporting instances of abuse and exploitation as this may jeopardise their status as regular migrant workers and potentially their chances of securing better employment opportunities.

3.5 Recent EU Policies on Fair Labour Mobility and Conditions: A New Social Shift?

In an attempt to raise the profile of the EU's social policy, in 2017 the European Pillar of Social Rights was jointly approved by the European Parliament, the Council, and the European Commission to provide a 'counterweight' (Barnard &

[35] In the *Vander Elst* case, the CJEU confirmed that the option for employers established in one Member State to send their employees to conduct economic activities in another Member State also applies when the posted workers are third-country nationals, provided they are lawfully and regularly employed in the Member State where their employer is based. The CJEU clarified that third-country nationals who are lawfully and regularly employed and then posted to another EU country do not need work permits in the EU Member State where they are posted.

[36] My translation in English.

De Vries, 2019) to the economic dimension of the EU. The Pillar consists of 20 social rights and principles, categorised in three chapters: 'Equal opportunities and Access to the Labour Market'; 'Fair Working Conditions'; 'Social Protection and Inclusion'. While the Pillar is not legally binding, most of the rights and principles that it contains are legally binding by virtue of other European and international legal instruments such as the European Social Charter of the Council of Europe, the EU Charter of Fundamental Rights, and several ILO Conventions (Garben, 2019). As the Commission (2017a) pointed out, the Pillar 'reaffirms the rights already present in the EU and in the international legal acquis and complements them to take account of new realities'. As such, it seeks to render these rights and principles 'more visible, more understandable and more explicit for citizens and for actors at all levels'.

Considered in a broad sense, the Pillar should be understood as a wider process comprising not only rights and principles, but also a range of legislative and non-legislative proposals—some new and some amending existing legal or policy instruments. According to Garben (2019, p. 105), the Pillar's format is particularly reminiscent of the Community Charter of the Fundamental Social Rights of Workers, which is 'declaratory, but it is a source of inspiration for the CJEU, especially in the interpretation of the rights featured in the EU Charter of Fundamental Rights that are based on rights first set out in the Community Charter'.

The Pillar does not aim to assume an autonomous normative value (Giubboni, 2018a) but, as mentioned in its text, to serve 'as a guide towards efficient employment and social outcomes when responding to current and future challenges which are directly aimed at fulfilling people's essential needs, and towards ensuring better enactment and implementation of social rights' (para. 12). Therefore, it seeks to pilot the policy actions of EU institutions and Member States, expressing principles and rights 'essential for fair and well-functioning labour markets and welfare systems in 21st century Europe' (para. 14).

The adoption of the European Pillar of Social Rights has been accompanied by criticism with regard its legal nature and content. In particular, while the tensions between market and social values in the EU constitute the background against which the Pillar has been defined and conceived, this instrument does not (and cannot) solve this constitutional imbalance in the EU (Garben, 2019: 110; Bronzini, 2022; Giubboni, 2018a). Giubboni argues that far from constitutionalising social rights at the EU level, this soft-law instrument represents instead an 'instance of de-constitutionalisation'. At the same time, being shaped along the model of a charter of rights, the Pillar does not provide an adequate framework for adopting concrete policies to address crucial aspects of welfare and labour dynamics and, accordingly, contribute to a (re)politisation of the European social question. For Giubboni (2018b, p. 18), the Pillar represents a 'paradoxical de-costitutionalisation without a (true) re-politisation' of the EU social dimension.

As other scholars have pointed out, the European Pillar of Social Rights is a form of 'adjustment' (Plomien, 2018) rather than an overturn of the imbalance between market and social dimensions. This instrument cannot and does not address the structural asymmetries between social and economic values on which the EU project—especially its economic-financial governance—relies. But it does provide for some corrections of these, combining elements of flexibility and security in the labour market (European Commission, 2016) and, in general, social standards with economic competitiveness. As the Commission (2017b, p. 4) has specified, 'the Pillar should be implemented according to available resources and within the limits of sound budgetary management and Treaty obligations governing public finances'.

In other words, the Pillar outlines the promotion, recognition, and protection of social rights, but doesn't address the fundamental principles of the internal market and economic governance that have historically prioritised the market at the expense of social concerns, leading to the erosion and weakening of these rights.

Nevertheless, even though the Pillar does not offer a comprehensive solution to the shortcomings of the EU's social dimension and its influence on EU hard law appears to be limited, it has, to some extent, sparked renewed attention to social values and rights within the EU. The legal and policy actions adopted and proposed under the Pillar's framework show a new effort and commitment to addressing related social issues. This appears to be a step forward, especially if seen against a background of 'social displacement' in the EU that—as underlined in this chapter—has also been fostered by relevant CJEU case law concerning national social standards of the past decade (Kilpatrick, 2018).

Among the initiatives adopted under the Pillar is Directive 2019/1152 on Transparent and Predictable Working Conditions in the EU, which entered into force in June 2019 and replaced the Written Statement Directive 91/533/ECC. This Directive introduces minimum rights and updates the rules on the information to be provided to workers – including those on atypical contracts—concerning their working conditions. The Directive applies a broad definition of 'worker', preventing Member States from excluding from the scope of its provisions certain categories of workers in non-standard forms of employment (such as, for instance, platform workers, on-demand workers, and voucher-based workers). It is not limited to providing information about obligations but also sets a number of 'material rights' (Barnard & De Vries, 2019). These include, among others, the right to request a job with more predictable and secure working conditions (Art. 12) and the right to compensation if the employer cancels a work assignment after a specific deadline (Art. 10). This new Directive is a step forward for the protection of workers' rights, especially those in more precarious jobs. However, a major shortcoming is that it does not contain concrete obligations for online platforms or prohibit zero-hours contracts. In other words, the Directive looks for solutions to increase the protection to workers in terms of the predictability of their work, but without really addressing the issue of the 'variability of hours' (Piasna, 2019) and, accordingly, effectively limiting the development of new forms of precarious work.

Another relevant instrument adopted under the European Social Pillar is the European Labour Authority (ELA). It was established in July 2019, while its activities started in mid-October 2019,[37] 'to support Member States in implementing EU

[37] The ELA is expected to reach its full operational capacity by 2024.

legislation in the areas of cross-border labour mobility and social security coordination, including free movement of workers, posting of workers and highly mobile services' (Council of the EU, 2018). Far from contributing to substantial policy changes, ELA's role is mainly supporting Member States and stakeholders in strengthening enforcement and monitoring EU rules concerning labour mobility and social security coordination.

The European Strategy on Gender Equality (2020–2025), which pays special attention to the dimension of intersectionality in addressing gender discrimination and inequalities, was also adopted within the framework of the Social Pillar. The Directive (2022/2041) on adequate minimum wages for workers in the EU has also been adopted and there is a proposal for a Directive on corporate sustainability and due diligence to foster sustainable and responsible corporate behaviour throughout global value chains.

Lastly, in connection with this increased focus on the social dimension, a significant development is the introduction of a social conditionality mechanism within the Common Agricultural Policy (CAP) (see, for instance, Canfora & Leccese, 2022). This mechanism links CAP payments to farmers to compliance with labour standards according to relevant international, EU, and national legal instruments, thus placing the protection of workers' rights at the center.

While the effectiveness of all these instruments depends on their implementation at the national level, their introduction can definitely help address the issue of labour exploitation beyond the use of criminal law instruments.

3.6 Concluding Remarks

This chapter offered a critical examination of the EU legal and policy framework on labour market access for EU migrants and non-EU migrants, with a particular focus on those workers considered low-skilled, analysing if its aspects prevent or foster situations of vulnerability to exploitation.

With regard to the fragmented and sectorial EU legal framework on labour migration of third-country nationals, the Seasonal Workers Directive is de facto the main EU instrument regulating the legal migration of low-skilled third country nationals. However, this instrument is premised on an employer-driven approach and provides Member States with wide discretionary powers over implementation of the provisions concerning the rights of seasonal workers, especially with regard to social rights. This chapter highlighted how the legal regime developed by the Seasonal Workers Directive provides for limited rights and protection to migrant seasonal workers compared to national workers and other non-EU workers. It also argued that this differential legal regime is based on containing the social reproduction conditions of migrant seasonal workers—for instance preventing seasonal workers' access to family reunification—with significant effects in terms of gender-based inequalities, discrimination, and forms of exploitation.

Given the significant presence, especially in European countries like Italy, of refugees and asylum seekers employed in unprotected sectors such as agriculture, the chapter also considered EU regulations on labour market access for beneficiaries of international protection and asylum seekers. This chapter underscores the discretion that Member States have when it comes to implementing the provisions of the Reception Conditions Directive regarding asylum seekers' access to the labour market. This leads to a variation in waiting periods for labour market access from one country to another. Even regarding the income earned by asylum seekers within the reception system, the Directive leaves it to the discretion of Member States on how to handle it. However, different national provisions adopted, such as those in Italy and the Netherlands, have the effect of discouraging applicants from seeking employment, as in the Netherlands, or driving them towards irregular work, as in the case of Italy. In both instances, although the implemented provisions differ, asylum seekers resort to these actions to avoid losing their access to the reception system and, consequently, their place to stay and sleep. All this increases asylum seekers' situations of vulnerability to exploitation and abuse.

The chapter's final section critically examined the EU legal framework related to EU labour mobility. It emphasised the tensions between the economic aspects of the free movement of workers and services and the protection of labour and social rights. This tension contributes to amplifying the situations of vulnerability of EU migrant workers, especially those coming from less wealthy eastern EU countries. Furthermore, there is an increasing recourse to temporary work agencies, subcontracting, and posted work to hire cheap labour, thus profiting from loopholes and ambiguities in the relevant EU and national laws. These practices are utilised to minimise labour costs by compressing labour and workers' social rights, especially social security rights. The practices can also include forms of abuse, violence, and severe exploitation.

In the case of both labour migration of non-EU migrant workers and intra-EU mobility, the EU legal framework leaves spaces for limiting equal treatment and compressing workers' rights and protection. The selective and differential inclusion of these workers in the EU legal and social space results in different situations of vulnerability that can be differently exploited in the labour market, as discussed in later chapters. As highlighted here, access to social rights and, more broadly, to those rights related to the social reproduction spheres of migrant workers play a crucial role in this selective and differential inclusion of labour mobility. This, in turn, significantly affects the forms and dynamics of labour exploitation, as discussed in the following chapters.

References

Amnesty International. (2017). *A perfect storm: The failure of European policies in the Central Mediterranean*. Amnesty International.

Arnholtz, J., & Lillie, N. (Eds.). (2020). *Posted work in the European Union. The political economy of free movement*. Routledge.

Atak, I., & Crépeau, F. (2022). Asylum in the twenty-first century: Trends and challenges. In A. Triandafyllidou (Ed.), *Routledge handbook of immigration and refugee studies* (2nd ed.). Routledge.

Barnard, C., & de Vries, S. (2019). The 'social market economy' in a (heterogeneous) social Europe: Does it make a difference? *Utrecht Law Review, 15*(2), 47–63.

Bauböck, R., & Ruhs, M. (2021). *The Elusive Triple Win: Can temporary labour migration dilemmas be settled through fair representation?* RSC Working Paper 2021/60. European University, Institute Robert Schuman Centre for Advanced Studies, Migration Policy Centre.

Biondi Dal Monte, F. (2019). Il diritto all'assistenza sociale dei rifugiati. Riflessioni a partire dalla Corte di Giustizia, sentenza 21 novembre 2018 (C-713/17), *Questione Giustizia*, 8 April 2019 [online], http://www.questionegiustizia.it (Last Access Apr 2024).

Bogoeski, V., & Rasnača, Z. (Eds.). (2023). *Report on the social security rights of short-term third country national migrant workers*. European Trade Union Institute.

Borelli, S. (2020). Il distacco di lavoratori migranti. In W. Chiaromonte, M. D. Ferrara, & M. Ranieri (Eds.), *Migranti e lavoro*. Il Mulino.

Borraccetti, M. (2021). Un nuovo patto per una nuova politica europea dell'immigrazione e dell'asilo. In G. De Marzo & F. Parisi (Eds.), *Diritto e immigrazione. Un quadro aggiornato delle questioni più attuali e rilevanti* (pp. 33–56). Il Foro Italiano - LaTribuna.

Bronzini, G. (2022). Il lavoro in somministrazione e le tutele dell'Unione. Ribadite dalla Corte di giustizia le finalità antiabusive. *Lavoro Diritti Europa, 2*, 2–11.

Busetta, A., Mendola, D., Wilson, B., & Cetorelli, V. (2021). Measuring vulnerability of asylum seekers and refugees in Italy. *Journal of Ethnic and Migration Studies, 47*(3), 596–615.

Calafà, L. (2020). Le migrazioni per motivi non economici nel quadro regolativo dell'Unione Europea. In W. Chiaromonte, M. D. Ferrara, & M. Ranieri (Eds.), *Migranti e lavoro*. Il Mulino.

Canfora, I., & Leccese, V. S. (2022). La sostenibilità sociale nella nuova PAC. *Rivista di Diritto Agrario, 2*, 110–141.

Caprioglio, C., & Rigo, E. (2020). Lavoro, politiche migratorie e sfruttamento: la condizione dei braccianti migranti in agricoltura. *Diritto, Immigrazione e Cittadinanza* (p. 3).

Carnassale, D., & Marchetti, S. (2022). *Vulnerabilities and the Italian Protection System*. VULNER Research Report 2.

Castles, S. (1986). The Guest-Worker in Western-Europe – An Obituary. *International Migration Review, 20*(4), 761–778.

Corrado, A., & Palumbo, L. (2021) Essential farmworkers and the pandemic crisis: Migrant labour conditions, and legal and political responses in Italy and Spain. In A. Triandafyllidou (Ed.), *Migration and pandemics*. IMISCOE Research Series. Springer.

Corrado, A., Caruso, F. S., Lo Cascio, M., Nori, M., Palumbo, L., & Triandafyllidou, A. (2018). *Is Italian agriculture a 'pull factor' for irregular migration—And, if so, why?* Open Society European Policy Institute.

Costamagna, F. (2019). The revision of the posted workers directive as a meaningful war to curb regulatory competition in the social domain? *Sant'Anna Legal Studies, STALS Research Papers No. 2* [online], https://papers.ssrn.com/sol3/papers.cfm?abstract_id=3422858 (Last Access Apr 2024)

Council of the EU. (2018). *European Labour Authority: Council agrees its position*. Press Release, 6 December, 755/18.

Cremers, J. (2011). *In search of cheap labour in Europe: Working and living conditions of posted workers*. CLR/EFBWW/International Books.

Cremers, J., & Dekker, R. (2018). Labour arbitrage on European labour markets: Free movement and the role of intermediaries. In C. Rijken & T. de Lange (Eds.), *Towards a decent labour market for low waged migrant workers* (pp. 109–128). Amsterdam University Press.

D'Onghia, M. (2019). Immigrazione irregolare e mercato del lavoro. Spunti per una discussione. *Rivista Trimestrale di diritto pubblico, 2*, 463–478.

De Bruycker, P. (2019). The EU policy on labour migration: How common it is and should it be? In C. Urbano de Sousa (Ed.), *The relevance of migration for the 2030 agenda for sustainable development*. Universidade Autonoma de Lisboa.

De Genova, N. (2013). Spectacles of migrant 'illegality': The scene of exclusion, the obscene of inclusion. *Ethnic and Racial Studies, 36*(7), 1180–1198.

De Haas, H., Natter, K., & Vezzoli, S. (2018). Growing restrictiveness or changing selection? The nature and evolution of migration policies. *International Migration Review, 52*(2), 324–367.

De Lange, T. (2018). Asylum seekers' limited right to work in The Netherlands. In C. Rijken & T. De Lange (Eds.), *Towards a decent labour market for low waged migrant workers* (pp. 169–185). Amsterdam University Press.

De Lange, T. (2022). Recasting the single permit directive: Furthering the protection of migrants at work in the EU? *EU Immigration and Asylum Law and Policy* [online], https://eumigrationlawblog.eu/recasting-the-single-permit-directive-furthering-the-protection-of-migrants-at-work-in-the-eu/ (Last Access Apr 2024)

De Lange, T., & Rijken, C. (2018). Towards a decent labour market for low-waged migrant workers: An introduction. In T. De Lange & C. Rijken (Eds.), *Towards a decent labour market for low waged migrant workers* (pp. 9–36). Amsterdam University Press.

De Lange, T., & Vankova, Z. (2022). The recast EU blue card directive: Towards a level playing field to attract highly qualified migrant talent to work in the EU? *European Journal of Migration and Law, 24*(4), 489–515.

Deepa, R., Berkowitz, L., Vosko, L. F., Preston, V., & Latham, R. (2012). At the temporary–permanent divide: How Canada produces temporariness and makes citizens through its security, work, and settlement policies. *Citizenship Studies, 16*(3–4), 483–485.

Della Puppa, F., & Sanò, G. (Eds.). (2021). *Stuck and exploited: Refugees and Asylum seekers in Italy between exclusion, discrimination and struggles*. Edizioni Ca' Foscari, Università Ca' Foscari Venezia.

Donaghey, J., & Teague, P. (2006). The free movement of workers and social Europe: Maintaining the European ideal. *Industrial Relations Journal, 37*(6), 652–666.

Dorigatti, L., Pallini, M., & Pedersini, R. (2022). *Posted workers to and from Italy: Facts and figures*. HIVA—Research Institute for Work and Society [online], https://hiva.kuleuven.be/en/news/docs/posted-workers-from-and-to-italy-facts-and-figures.pdf (Last Access Apr 2024).

Editorial Comments. (2014). The free movement of persons in the European Union. Salvaging the dream while explaining the nightmare. *Common Market Law Review, 51*, 729–740.

EFFAT. (2023). *Proposal for a EU Directive on labour intermediaries and fair working conditions across subcontracting chains*, Policy Brief, May 2023 [online], https://effat.org/wp-content/uploads/2023/05/EFFAT-Policy-Briefing-Proposal-EUDirective-on-labour-intermediaries-and-fair-working-conditions-across-subcontracting-chains.pdf

ELA. (2023). *Report on the cooperation practices, possibilities, and challenges between Member States—Specifically in relation to the posting of third-country nationals*. Final Report. European Labour Authority [online], www.ela.europa.eu/sites/default/files/2023-04/ela-report-posting-third-country-nationals.pdf (Last Access Apr 2024).

EPRS. (2018). *The cost of Non-Europe in Asylum Policy*. European Parliamentary Research Service [online], https://www.europarl.europa.eu/RegData/etudes/STUD/2018/627117/EPRS_STU(2018)627117_EN.pdf (Last Access Apr 2024).

European Commission. (2000). *Communication from the Commission to the Council and the European Parliament on a Community Immigration Policy*, COM(2000) 757 final, Brussels, 22 November.

European Commission. (2010a). *Proposal for a Directive of the European Parliament and the Council on the conditions of entry and residence of third-country nationals for the purpose of seasonal employment*, COM (2010), 379, 13 July 2010, 2.

European Commission. (2010b). *Commission Staff Working Document, Impact Assessment accompanying the Proposal for a Directive of the European Parliament and of the Council on the conditions of entry and residence of third-country nationals for the purpose of seasonal employment*, COM (2010), 379 final, p. 11.

European Commission. (2001). *Proposal for a Council Directive on the conditions of entry and residence for the purpose of paid employment and self-employment activities.* COM(2001) 386 final.

European Commission. (2015). *Communication from the Commission to the European Parliament, the Council, the European Economic and Social Committee and the Committee of the Regions. A European Agenda on Migration,* COM (2015), 240.

European Commission. (2016). *Communication from the Commission to the European Parliament, the Council, the European Economic and Social Committee and the Committee of the Regions Launching a consultation on a European Pillar of Social Rights.* COM(2016) 127 final.

European Commission. (2017a). *Communication to the Parliament, Council, the EESC and the Committee of the Regions, establishing a European Pillar of Social Rights.* COM (2017) 250 final.

European Commission. (2017b). *Commission Staff Working Document Accompanying the Document Establishing a European Pillar of Social Rights.* SWD(2017) 201 final.

European Commission. (2020). *Communication from the Commission to the European Parliament, the Council, the European Economic and Social Committee and the Committee of the Regions on a New Pact on Migration and Asylum,* COM/2020/609 final.

European Parliament. (2011). *Draft report on the proposal for a directive of the European Parliament and of the Council on the conditions of entry and residence of third-country nationals for the purposes of seasonal employment,* 2010/0210(COD), Committee on Civil Liberties, Justice, and Home Affairs, Rapporteur Claude Moraes.

European Migration Network. (2020). *Attracting and protecting the rights of seasonal workers in the EU and the United Kingdom.* European Migration Network.

Eurostat. (2023). *Migration and migration population statistics* [online], https://ec.europa.eu/eurostat/statisticsexplained/index.php?title=Migration_and_migrant_population_statistics (Last Access Apr 2024).

Evola, M. (2018). *I lavoratori di Stati Terzi nel Diritto dell'Unione Europea.* Giappichelli.

Favilli, C. (2020a) Il diritto dell'Unione Europea e il fenomeno migratorio. In M. Giovannetti & N. Zorzella (Eds.), *Ius Migranti. Trent'anni di politiche e legislazione sull'immigrazione in Italia* (pp. 55–80). FrancoAngeli.

Favilli, C. (2020b). Il patto europeo sulla migrazione e l'asilo: 'c'e qualcosa di nuovo, anzi di antico'. *Questione Giustizia,* 10 October 2020 [online], https://www.questionegiustizia.it/articolo/il-patto-europeo-sulla-migrazione-e-l-asilo-c-e-qualcosa-di-nuovoanzi-d-antico (Last Access Apr 2024).

FRA. (2015). *Severe labour exploitation: Workers moving within or into the European Union.* European Union Agency for Fundamental Rights.

Friðriksdóttir, B. (2017). *What happened to equality? The construction of the right to equal treatment of third-country nationals in European Union law on labour migration.* Brill | Nijhoff.

Fudge, J., & Olsson, P. H. (2014). The EU seasonal workers directive: When immigration controls meet labour rights. *European Journal of Migration and Law, 16*(4), 439–466.

Fudge, J., & Strauss, K. (2014). *Temporary work, agencies and unfree labour. Insecurity in the New World of work.* Routledge.

Garben, S. (2019). The European pillar of social rights: An assessment of its meaning and significance. *Cambridge Yearbook of European Legal Studies, 21,* 101–127.

Geddes, A., Hadj Adbou, L., & Brumat, L. (2020). *Migration and mobility in the European Union.* Red Globe Press.

Geymonat, G. G., Marchetti, S., & Palumbo, L. (2023). Migrant women workers in Europe: Forms of irregularity and conditions of vulnerability. In I. van Liempt, J. Schapendonk, & A. Campos-Delgado (Eds.), *Research handbook on irregular migration.* Edward Elgar Publishing.

Giubboni, S. (2018a). L'insostenibile leggerezza del Pilastro europeo dei diritti sociali. *Politica del diritto, 4,* 557–578.

Giubboni, S. (2018b). Oltre il Pilastro europeo dei diritti sociali. Per un nuovo riformismo sociale in Europa. In G. Bronzini (Ed.), *Verso un Pilastro sociale europeo* (pp. 16–24). Edizioni Fondazione Basso.

Giubboni, S. (2021). Somministrazione di lavoro e tecniche anti-abusive alla prova del diritto dell'Unione europea, *Ridl*, n. 1/2021.

Groenendijk, K. (2014). Which way forward with migration and employment in the EU. In S. Carrera, E. Guild, & K. Eisele (Eds.), *Rethinking the attractiveness of EU labour immigration policies; comparative perspectives on the EU, the US, Canada and beyond* (pp. 91–100). Centre for European Policy Studies.

Guild, E. (2009). *Security and migration in the 21st century*. Polity Press.

Guild, E. (2014). The EU' internal market and the fragmentary nature of EU labour migration. In C. Costello & M. Freedland (Eds.), *Migrants at work: Immigration and vulnerability in labour law* (pp. 98–118). Oxford University Press.

Hellio, E. (2016). 'They know that you'll leave, like a dog moving onto the next bin'. Undocumented male and seasonal contracted female workers in the agricultural labour market of Huelva, Spain. In A. Corrado, C. De Castro, & D. Perrotta (Eds.), *Migration and agriculture. Mobility and change in the Mediterranean area* (pp. 198–214). Routledge.

Herzfeld Olsson, P. (2016). Introduction to the directives. In R. Blanpain & F. Hendrickx (Eds.), P. Herzfeld Olsson (guest Ed.), *National effects of the implementation of EU directives on labour migration from third countries* (pp. 10–34). Wolters Kluwer.

Houwerzijl, M., & Berntsen, L. (2020). Posting of workers: From a blurred notion associated with 'cheap labour' to a toll for fair labour mobility? In J. Arnholtz & N. Lillie (Eds.), *Posted work in the European Union. The political economy of free movement*. Routledge.

Houwerzijl, M., & Verschueren, H. (2019). Free movement of (posted) workers and applicable labour and social security law. In T. Jaspers, F. Pennings, & S. Peters (Eds.), *European labour law* (pp. 45–131). Intersentia.

Hunt, J. (2014). Making the CAP fit: Responding to the exploitation of migrant agricultural workers in the EU. *The International Journal of Comparative Labour Law and Industrial Relations, 30*, 131–152.

Huysmans, J. (2006). *The politics of insecurity. Fear, migration and asylum in the EU*. Routledge.

Iossa, A., & Selberg, N. (2022). Socio-legal aspects of labour market segmentation in the Agrifood sector in Sweden: Spatio-temporal dimensions. *European Journal of Migration and Law, 24*(2), 241–264.

Jacqueson, C., & Pennings, F. (2019). Equal treatment of mobile persons in the context of a social market economy. *Utrecht Law Review, 15*(2), 64–80.

Kilpatrick, C. (2018). The displacement of social Europe: A productive lens of inquiry. *European Constitutional Law Review, 14*(1).

Kramer, D. (2016). Earning social citizenship in the European Union: Free movement and Access to social assistance benefits reconstructed (22 August) *Cambridge Yearbook of European Legal Studies, 18*, 270–301.

Kramer, D. (2023). EU citizenship: A double-edged sword for European social security. In F. Pennings & G. Vonk (Eds.), *Research handbook on European social security law* (2nd ed.) (pp. 182–203). Edward Elgar.

L'Altro Diritto & FLAI CGIL. (2022). *Quarto rapporto del laboratorio sullo sfruttamento lavorativo e sulla protezione delle sue vittime* [online], http://www.adir.unifi.it/laboratorio/quartorapporto-sfruttamento-lavorativo.pdf (Last Access Apr 2024).

Lewis, H., & Waite, L. (2015). Asylum, immigration restrictions and exploitation: Hyper-precarity as a lens for understanding and tackling forced labour. *Anti- Trafficking Review, 5*, 49–67.

López-Sala, A. (2016). Producing temporariness, (re)producing precariousness: Regulation, rights and non-citizenship status of temporary immigrant workers. *Arbor, 192*(777), 1–4.

Mackinnon, C. (1989). Feminism in legal education. *Legal Education Review, 85*, 85–95.

Mantouvalou, V. (2023). *Structural injustice and workers' rights*. Oxford University Press.

Martín, I., Di Bartolomeo, A., De Bruycker, P., Renaudiere, G., Salamońska, J., & Venturini, A. (2015). *Exploring new avenues for legislation for labour migration to the European Union.* European Parliament [online], https://www.europarl.europa.eu/thinktank/en/document/IPOL_STU(2015)536452 (Last Access Apr 2024).

Martin, I., Arcarons, A., Aumüller, J., Bevelander, P., Emilsson, H., Kalantaryan, S., Maciver, A., Mara, I., Scalettaris, G., Venturini, A., Vidovic, H., Der Welle, V., Inge, W., Michael, W., Rebecca, Z., & Aslan, B. S. (2016). *From refugees to workers : Mapping labour market integration support measures for asylum-seekers and refugees in EU member states. Volume I: Comparative analysis and policy findings.* Bertelsmann Stiftung, Migration Policy Centre [online], https://hdl.handle.net/1814/43504 (Last Access Apr 2024).

Medland, L. (2017). Misconceiving 'seasons' in global food systems: The case of the EU Seasonal Workers Directive. *European Journal of Law, 23*(3.4), 157–171.

Mezzadra, S. (2013). Moltiplicazione dei confine e pratiche di mobilità. *Ragione Pratica,* 41, dicembre.

Minderhoud, P. (2021). Regulation of EU labour migration: At a crossroads after the new pact on migration and asylum. *Utrecht Law Review, 17*(4), 31–44.

Molinero Gerbeau, Y. (2018). La *privatización* de los programas de migración temporal en España como efecto poscrisis. *Anuario CIDOB de la Inmigración, 2018*, 284–306.

Novitz, T., & Andrijasevic, R. (2020). Reform of the posting of workers regime – An assessment of the practical impact on unfree labour relations. *JCMS: Journal of Common Market Studies, 58*, 1325–1341.

Nunin, R. (2020). Le migrazioni per motivi economici nel quadro regolativo dell'Unione Europea. In W. Chiaromonte, M. Ferrara Dolores, & M. Ranieri (Eds.), *Migranti e lavoro* (pp. 49–68). Il Mulino.

O'Brien, C. (2009). Social blind spots and monocular policy making: The ECJ's migrant worker model. *Common Market Law Review, 46*(4), 1107–1141.

OECD. (2014). Managing labour migration: Smart policies to support economic growth. In OECD *International migration outlook*. OECD Publishing.

Oliveri, F. (2016). Giuridificare ed esternalizzare lo sfruttamento. Il caso dei lavoratori immigrati nella vitivinicoltura senese. In E. Rigo (Ed.), *Leggi, migranti, caporali. Prospettive critiche di ricerca sullo sfruttamento del lavoro in agricoltura* (pp. 47–67). Pacini Editore.

Palumbo, L. (2020). Tratta di esseri umani e sfruttamento lavorativo in agricoltura: Il caso dei 'boschetari' nelle serre del Ragusano. In S. Greco & G. Tumminelli (Eds.), *Migrazioni in Sicilia 2019* (pp. 261–272). Mimesis Edizioni.

Palumbo, L. (2022). Exploitation in the agri-food sector in Europe: A comparative analysis of the impact of migration and labour regimes in producing migrants' vulnerabilities. *European Journal of Migration and Law, 24*(2), 287–312.

Palumbo, L., & Corrado, A. (Eds.). (2020). *Are agri-food workers only exploited in southern Europe? Case studies on migrant labour in Germany, The Netherlands and Sweden*. Open Society European Policy Institute.

Palumbo, L., & Sciurba, A. (2018). *The vulnerability to exploitation of women migrant workers in agriculture in the EU: The need for a human rights and gender based approach.* European Parliament Study, 2018/604.966, Policy Department for Citizens' Rights and Constitutional Affairs, European Union.

Papa, V. (2020). Il lavoro stagionale dei migranti. In W. Chiaromonte, M. Ferrara Dolores, & M. Ranieri (Eds.), *Migranti e lavoro* (pp. 279–294). Il Mulino.

Pera, A. (2019). *Un progetto tradito? La cittadinanza europea tra passato e future*. Mimesis Edizioni.

Piasna, A. (2019) *Regulating uncertainty: Variable work schedules and zero-hour work in EU employment policy*. ETUI Research Paper/Policy Brief 5. European Trade Union Institute.

Picchio, A. (2008). *Social reproduction: The political economy of the labour market*. Cambridge University Press.

Plomien, A. (2018). EU social and gender policy beyond Brexit: Towards the European pillar of social rights. *Social Policy and Society, 17*(2), 281–296.

Ravelli, F. (2020). La tutela previdenziale dei migranti. In W. Chiaromonte, M. D. Ferrara, & M. Ranieri (Eds.), *Migranti e lavoro* (pp. 193–209). Il Mulino.

Rigo, E. (2022). *La straniera. Migrazioni, asilo, sfruttamento in una prospettiva di genere*. Carocci Editori.

Rijken, C. (2015). Legal approaches to combating the exploitation of third-country national seasonal workers. *International Journal of Comparative Labour Law and Industrial Relations, 31*(4), 431–451.

Rodotà, S. (2012). *Il diritto ad avere diritti*. Laterza.

Ruhs, M. (2013). *The Price of rights: Regulating international labor migration*. Princeton University Press.

Santoro, E. (2021). La protezione delle vittime di sfruttamento lavorativo: Una pratica sovversiva di alcuni capisaldi della nostra cultura giuridico-politica. *Sociologia del diritto, 3*, 164–189.

Saroléa, S., Raimondo, F., Crine, Z. (2021). *Exploring vulnerability's challenges and pitfalls in Belgian ayslum system*. VULNER Research Report 1.

Schiek, D. (2004). Agency work: From marginalisation towards acceptance? Agency work in EU social and employment policy and the 'implementation' of the draft directive on agency work into German law. *German Law Journal, 5*(10), 1233–1257.

Schmoll, C. (2022). *Le dannate del mare. Donne e frontiere nel mediterraneo*. Astarte Edizioni.

Sciurba, A. (2015). *La cura servile. La cura che serve*. Pacini Editore.

Sciurba, A. (2017a). Misrecognizing asylum. Causes, modalities and consequences of the crisis of a fundamental human right. *Journal of Legal Philosophy, 1*, 141–164.

Sciurba, A. (2017b). Categorizing migrants by disempowering the right to asylum. A focus on the Sicilian implementation of the 'Hotspot approach'. In E. Fontanari, & B. Pinelli (Eds.), Special issue: Subjectivity and control Refugees towards Europe, *Etnografia e Ricerca Qualitativa*, 1, gennaio-aprile (pp. 97–120).

Sciurba, A. (2021a). *Le parole dell'asilo. Un diritto di confine*. Giappichelli.

Sciurba, A. (2021b). Cosi in mare come in terra: cosa resta del diritto d'asilo e dell'orizzonte dei diritti umani. In G. De Marzo & F. Parisi (Eds.), *Il Foro Italiano. Gli speciali. Diritto e immgrazione. Un quadro aggiornato delle questioni più attuali e rilevanti* (pp. 85–102). Il Foro Italiano - LaTribuna.

Shamir, H. (2017). The paradox of 'legality': Temporary migrant worker programs and vulnerability to trafficking. In P. Kotiswaran (Ed.), *Revisiting the law and governance of trafficking, forced labour and modern slavery*. Cambridge University Press.

Siegmann, K. A., Quaedvlieg, J., & Williams, T. (2022). Migrant labour in Dutch agriculture: Regulated precarity. *European Journal of Migration and Law, 24*(2), 217–240.

Slingenberg, L. (2014). Asylum seekers' access to employment: Tensions with human rights obligations in the recast of the directive on reception conditions for asylum seekers. In. C. Matera, & A. Taylor (Eds.), *The Common European Asylum system and human rights: Enhancing protection in times of emergencies* (pp. 93–107). CLEER Working Papers 2014/7. The Hague: Centre for the Law of EU External Relations.

Tazzioli, M. (2023). *Border abolitionism: Migration containment and the genealogies of struggles and rescue*. Manchester University Press.

Thym, D. (2016). Frontiers of EU citizenship. Three trajectories and their methodological limitations. In D. Kochenov (Ed.), *EU citizenship and federalism. The role of rights* (pp. 705–730). Cambridge University Press.

Triandafyllidou, A. (2022). Temporary migration: Category of analysis or category of practice? *Journal of Ethnic and Migration Studies, 48*(16), 3847–3859.

UNDP. (2009). *Overcoming barriers: Human mobility and development. Human development report*. United Nations Development Programme.

Verschueren, H. (2016a). Employment and social security rights of third-country labour migrants under EU law: An incomplete patchwork of legal protection. *European Journal of Migration and Law, 18*(4), 373–408.

Verschueren, H. (2016b). *Residence, employment and social rights of mobile persons. On how EU law defines where they belong*. Intersentia.

Verschueren, H. (2023). Equal treatment as an instrument of integration. The CJEU's case law on social rights for third-country nationals. *European Journal of Social Security, 25*(3), 243–260.

Walzer, M. (1983). *Spheres of Justice: A defense of pluralism and equality*. Basic Books

Wiesbrock, A. (2010). *Legal migration to the European Union*. Martinus Nijhoff.

Wilsher, D. (2001). Economic migration into the European Union: Standing at the crossroads. *Yearbook of European Law, 21*(1), 163–193.

World Bank. (2006). *At home and away: Expanding job opportunities for Pacific islanders through labour mobility*. The World Bank.

Zoeteweij-Turhan, M. H. (2017). The seasonal workers directive: '… but some are more equal than others'. *European Labour Law Journal, 8*(1), 28–44.

Zoeteweij, M. H. (2018). The seasonal workers directive. Another vicious circle? In C. Rijken & T. De Lange (Eds.), *Towards a decent labour market for low waged migrant workers* (pp. 129–148). Amsterdam University Press.

Chapter 4
EU Instruments on Labour Exploitation and Trafficking: Preventing, Protecting, or Amplifying Situational Vulnerabilities?

By considering the situational dimension of migrants' vulnerabilities and viewing exploitation as a continuum, this chapter critically analyses EU instruments addressing labour exploitation and trafficking to protect the rights of victims. It examines the extent to which these instruments protect and prevent vulnerabilities to exploitation and whether they contribute to creating or amplifying them. The chapter focuses on Directive 2009/52/EC providing for minimum standards on sanctions and measures against employers of illegally staying third-country nationals (the Employer Sanctions Directive) and Directive 2011/36/EU on preventing and combatting trafficking in human beings and protecting its victims (the Anti-Trafficking Directive). Here it is worth clarifying that the Employer Sanctions Directive is part of EU legislation regulating labour migration to the EU[1] and therefore falls under the EU Directives on labour migration (Verschueren, 2018). However, the Employer Sanctions Directive also relates to the area of criminal justice and victims' rights (FRA, 2015), which is why it is discussed here and not in Chap. 3 on EU labour migration policy. The intent is to highlight the tensions and ambiguities in instruments aimed at addressing both irregular migration (Employer Sanctions Directive) and trafficking (EU Directives on trafficking) while also protecting the rights of exploited and trafficked persons. Within these tensions and ambiguities, migrants' situations of vulnerability are both generated and exacerbated, and hardly prevented and protected—as discussed in this chapter.

[1] The Directive has its legal basis in Art. 79 Sections 1 and 2(c) of the Treaty on the Functioning of the EU (the former Art. 63.3.b of Title IV of the EC Treaty on Visas, Asylum, Immigration, and Other Policies Related to the Free Movement of Persons).

L. Palumbo, *Taking Vulnerabilities to Labour Exploitation Seriously*, IMISCOE Research Series, https://doi.org/10.1007/978-3-031-55424-7_4

4.1 Addressing Irregular Migration (and Labour Exploitation) by Sanctioning Employers

4.1.1 The Employer Sanctions Directive

While the Employer Sanctions Directive is considered one of the most relevant EU policy instruments designed to combatt irregular employment and labour exploitation, its primary objective is to address irregular migration by prohibiting the employment of irregularly staying third-country nationals (Art. 1). The rationale behind the Directive assumes that the possibility of 'obtaining work in the EU without the required legal status' is one of the key factors encouraging irregular migration into the EU (Preamble 2 of the Directive). This, in turn, can lead to wage depression and poor working conditions and distort competition between businesses (European Commission, 2007a). The Employer Sanctions Directive thus approaches irregular employment as a pull factor for irregular migration 'by targeting the employment of third-country nationals who are illegally staying in the EU'.[2] To achieve this objective, the Directive lays down minimum common standards on sanctions and measures to be applied by the Member States against employers who hire migrant workers who do not fulfil the conditions for stay or residence in that state. As clarified by the European Commission in the proposal, the Directive 'is concerned with immigration policy, not with labour or social policy...It is the employer who will be sanctioned, not the illegally employed third-country national' (ibid., p. 2).

As Peers and colleagues highlighted, the Employer Sanctions Directive was preceded by an important legal instrument, Directive 2001/51/EC (Peers et al., 2012, p. 432).[3] Known as the Carrier Sanctions Directive, this EU legal instrument regulates the issue of carriers transporting undocumented travellers, establishing a sanctioning scheme (Baird, 2017). It is one of the early measures adopted by the EU against commercial entities with respect to migration related-issues and is based on the prior rules set out in the Schengen Convention (Peers et al., 2012, p. 432).[4] These rules significantly 'engaged the private sector, in the execution of its commercial activities, to take an active part in migration control' (ibid.). Indeed, the Carrier Sanctions Directive aims to address irregular migration by harmonising the financial penalties for carriers transporting into the territory of the Member States third-country nationals lacking the necessary admission documents. By attaching responsibilities for the regulation of migration and border controls to the private sector, this Directive has contributed to changing 'the relationship of commercial

[2] COM (2007) 249, 15 May 2007.

[3] Council Directive 2001/51/EC of 28 June 2001 supplementing the provisions of Art. 26 of the Convention implementing the Schengen Agreement of 14 June 1985.

[4] In particular, the Directive supplements Art. 26 of the Schengen Convention implementing the 1985 Schengen Agreement, requiring the carrier to assume responsibility for non-EU nationals it brings to the external border by air, sea, or land.

actor, individual and state official to one where the commercial actor and the state official jointly share responsibility for the disciplining of the individual as regards border controls' (Peers et al., 2012, pp. 432–433; see also Rodenhauser, 2014).[5]

The Employers Sanctions Directive follows this approach and, in a certain sense, goes further, by attaching responsibilities for migration control to private sector actors in the EU, not limited to those involved in transport activities and not only those operating at the EU borders (De Lange, 2011; Peers et al., 2012). Indeed, the Directive concerns all employers, in all their activities within the EU, placing responsibilities on them for ensuring that only those migrant workers 'with permission to be on the territory are engaging in paid employment' (Peers et al., 2012, p. 443).

The Employer Sanctions Directive defines employment as 'the exercise of activities covering whatever form of labour and work regulated under national law or in accordance with established practice for or under the direction and/or supervision of an employer' (Art. 2(c)). Such a definition is in line with that provided by the European Court of Justice (ECJ) recognising that 'the essential feature of an employment relationship is that a person performs services of some economic value for and under the direction of another person in return for which he receives remuneration' (*Lawrie-Blum* C-66/85). As for the notion of employer, the Directive clarifies that it includes 'any natural person or any legal entity, including temporary work agencies, for or under the direction and/or supervision of whom the employment is undertaken' (Art. 2(e)). Moreover, for the purpose of the Directive 'illegal employment' is defined as the 'employment of a third-country national who is staying illegally' (Art. 2(d)). Therefore, 'illegal employment' is determined solely by the residence status of the individual and not by their work status (Peers et al., 2012, p. 437).

The Employers Sanctions Directive stipulates that 'Member States shall prohibit the employment of illegally staying third-country nationals' (Art. 3). It establishes minimum common standards and measures, including criminal and administrative sanctions, to be applied in the Member States against employers who have breached this ban. It is up to the Member States to determine the level of fines, and thus they differ across the EU (Sommarribas et al., 2017). Considering the prevalence of subcontracting in certain relevant sectors, the Directive notably extends liability along subcontractor chains, providing that the contractor and any intermediate subcontractor should be liable to pay financial sanctions and any back pay owed to migrant workers (Art. 8).

According to the Directive, intentional infringement of the prohibition on employing irregularly-staying third-country nationals constitutes a criminal offence when, among other conditions, it is accompanied by 'particularly exploitative working conditions' or when is committed by an employer who uses work or services

[5] A substantial body of literature literature has underlined the impact of carrier sanctions on increasing risks to migrant people in search of protection and having the effect of deterring asylum-seekers and restricting the rights of refugees (see, among others, Rodenhauser, 2014; Baird, 2017).

exacted from an undocumented migrant worker with the knowledge that he/she is a victim of trafficking in human beings (Art. 9).

As noted in Chap. 2, the Employer Sanctions Directive defines 'particularly exploitative working conditions' as:

> working conditions, including those resulting from gender based or other discrimination, where there is a striking disproportion compared with the terms of employment of legally employed workers which, for example, affects workers' health and safety, and which offends against human dignity (para. 22).

As pointed out in Sect. 2.1.1, there are some critical aspects concerning this definition, including, for instance, its proportionality method (Stoyanova, 2017). However, it has the merit of having introduced an agreed notion of labour exploitation at the European level, referring to important elements such as the gender discrimination indicator, the impact on workers' health and safety, and the general clause of contravention to human dignity. As argued in Chap. 2, the latter principle of human dignity gains special relevance when viewed in its social dimension. This means, in alignment with the principles of equality and self-determination, it is considered as ensuring that all persons must enjoy fundamental rights—irrespective of their position in the social hierarchy—and be able to make decisions, including those related to their working conditions, in circumstances of freedom and responsibility (Rodotà, 2012; Santoro, 2020).

The notion of 'particularly exploitative working conditions' provided by the Employer Sanctions Directive has been then reflected in the definition of labour exploitation contained in some legislation of European Countries. In particular, as discussed in Chap. 6, Article 603bis of the Italian Criminal Code (CC) provides an innovative definition of labour exploitation referring to some indicators that fall within the broader context of safeguarding human dignity.

In addition to sanctions against employers who hire irregular migrant workers, the Employer Sanctions Directive includes some provisions aimed at protecting workers' rights. For instance, it requires Member States to ensure that employers are liable for back pay (Art. 6). Specifically, employers must pay any outstanding remuneration,[6] an amount equal to any social security contributions that the employer would have paid had the third-country national been regularly employed, and costs incurred for sending payments back to a returned third-country national worker (Art. 6). Member States must also introduce mechanisms to allow irregularly employed third-country nationals to make a claim against their employer (including in cases in which workers have, or have been, returned) or to call upon

---

[6] As specified in the Directive, the remuneration 'shall be presumed to have been at least as high as the wage provided for by the applicable laws on minimum wages, by collective agreements or in accordance with established practice in the relevant occupational branches, unless either the employer or the employee can prove otherwise, while respecting, where appropriate, the mandatory national provisions on wages' (Art. 6(a)). It is worth noting that the Directive specifies that, to apply the provisions concerning wages owed, there must be a presumption of an employment relationship of at least 3 months 'unless, among other, the employer or the employee can prove otherwise' (Art. 6(3)).

the national authorities to start procedures to recover outstanding remuneration, when these procedures have been already provided by national legislation (Art. 6(2)).

The Directive further stipulates that Member States ensure that irregularly employed third-country nationals are systematically and objectively informed about their rights (Art. 6) and establish effective mechanisms through which these workers may lodge complaints against their employers, either directly or through third parties designated by Member States, including trade unions and NGOs (Art. 13). Where there are criminal proceedings against the employer, Member States shall 'define in national law the conditions under which they may grant, on a case-by-case basis, permits of limited duration, linked to the length of the relevant national proceedings' (Art. 13) to the third-country nationals subjected to particularly exploitative working conditions or who were irregularly employed minors and who cooperate in criminal proceedings against the employer (see also recital 27).

4.1.2 What Kind of Protection for Undocumented Migrant Workers' Rights?

The Employer Sanctions Directive's provisions on the rights of undocumented migrant workers are undoubtably significant tools for preventing and addressing irregular employment and labour exploitation. However, as legal and social literature has underlined and testimonies collected for this study highlight and confirm, several aspects of the Employer Sanctions Directive's relevance and effectiveness in terms of protection of the rights of these workers are controversial. These, as discussed in this section, concern the inadequacies of its protection provisions, the impact of sanctions, and its generally repressive approach on the situations of vulnerability of undocumented workers' and dynamics of labour exploitation.

First, as Peers et al. (2012, p. 442) highlighted, the Employer Sanctions Directive's provision on residence permits for victims of labour exploitation (Art. 13) does not include an obligation to issue residence permits. Therefore, Member States may choose to either grant or not grant such permits. If they choose to do so, they shall define in their national law the conditions under which these permits may be granted. The Directive also specifies that Member States should be free to grant residence permits of limited duration, linked to the length of the relevant national proceedings, and granted under mechanisms similar to those established by Directive 2004/81/EC on the residence permit issued to victims of trafficking.[7] This mechanism is dependent on the victim's cooperation with competent authorities and the progress of proceedings.

While the Employer Sanctions Directive does not expressly require for the residence permit to be linked to the victim's cooperation in criminal proceedings, as emerged from recent reports by FRA (2021) and the European Commission (2021)

[7] This Directive is discussed later in the chapter.

its reference to Directive 2004 has, in practice, led most countries to impose this condition, thus subordinating the victims' protection to the prosecution of criminals. As numerous studies have pointed out, this 'reward-based' approach—which is far from a victim's rights-centred perspective—has proved ineffective (IOM, 2015; Giammarinaro, 2018; Palumbo, 2023). It prevents many people from escaping exploitation and seeking protection as they are unwilling to testify against their exploiters/traffickers and afraid to cooperate or trust the police (FRA, 2021). As emerged from my fieldwork in Italy and has been confirmed by studies in other European countries such as Belgium (Palumbo, 2023), obtaining a residence permit is not necessarily an incentive for victims to denounce the exploiters/traffickers and could potentially increase their vulnerabilities. Indeed, exploited and trafficked migrants are mostly interested in finding a job to earn a living and aware that if they become a police informer they could be even more at risk.

Moreover, a residence permit of limited duration and linked to the length of the relevant national proceedings, as proposed by the Employer Sanctions Directive, fails to recognise how situations of vulnerability arise from the intersection of various factors. These include, for instance, the precariousness of temporary legal status, which tying the residence permit to criminal proceedings de facto further perpetuates (Giammarinaro, 2018; Lidén et al., 2021; Palumbo, 2023). This, in turn, fosters and amplifies situations of vulnerability to exploitation rather than addressing the elements that produce them.

It can, in general, be argued that Employer Sanctions Directive's provisions concerning, for instance, complaint mechanisms and the issuance of a temporary residence permit mainly aim to address abusive employers (and accordingly irregular migration) rather than protect exploited migrants and tackle factors contributing to their situations of vulnerability (such as irregular migration status). It is indicative, in this regard, that in its recital 15, the Directive excluded the possibility for a worker employed irregularly to invoke a right to entry, stay, and access to the labour market based on illegal employment relationships.

In reconstructing the negotiation process that shaped the drafting of the Employers Sanction Directive, Friðriksdóttir (2017) revealed that there had been proposals supporting regularisation measures. For example, the European Parliament suggested adding a preamble in the recital affirming that it 'should not prevent Member States from adopting measures designed to convert undeclared employment relationships into declared employment relationships or from bringing within the law situations of undeclared work' (European Parliament, 2009, p. 32). However, this proposal, like others, was rejected chiefly on the grounds that there was a lack of data on the impact of regularisation programmes and that regularisation could serve as 'a pull factor for illegal immigration and therefore [be] unhelpful in this exercise'(European Commission, 2007b, p. 5). In this light, the choice made was to approach irregular migration—and, in particular, labour exploitation—as primarily criminal matters rather than social issues that should be addressed through regularisation and protection measures, disentangling migrant workers' rights from the criminal law perspective.

In line with this approach, the Employer Sanctions Directive is 'silent on the application of labour law rules other than pay to irregular migrants' (Peers, 2016, p. 418). For instance, it does not include an equal treatment clause guaranteeing irregular third-country nationals equal treatment with nationals of the host Member States as regards employment and social security rights (Dewhurst, 2011; Verschueren, 2016). Therefore, as Verschueren (2018, p. 105) points out, 'the extent of the employment or social security rights such workers have in a Member State fully depends on the domestic legislation of each of the Member States'. Furthermore, although the definition of exploitation makes reference to gender-based discrimination, the Directive does not include any specific measures addressing exploitation and workers' protection from a gender perspective.

Again, from the background documents accompanying the drafting of the Directive, it emerged that during the negotiations the debate among Member States on the provisions concerning workers' protection and rights focused 'on the administrative burdens that they created for national authorities in the Member States and whether or not protection offered based on past employment constituted pull factors for irregular migration' (Friðriksdóttir, 2017, p. 192). In other words, the recognition of certain rights to undocumented migrant workers was based on an assessment of whether this could facilitate or deter irregular migration rather than focusing on the effective protection of the migrant workers themselves.

These critical aspects concerning the approach and provisions of the Employer Sanctions Directive on the protection of undocumented workers' rights are evident in how the Directive has been transposed by Member States into national legislation and applied at the local level. Indeed, as emerged from the Commission's evaluation reports, in most EU countries, including Italy, protection provisions have been inadequately implemented (European Commission, 2021; see also FRA, 2021). Irregular migrant workers face difficulties in using existing complaint mechanisms, and authorities' obligation to ensure that these workers can effectively recover outstanding remuneration is hardly met in practice.

The Employer Sanctions Directive's requirement that Member States create an 'effective complaints mechanism' is unclear (Knockaert, 2017) and does not give any specific indication on how to develop it. Above all, the Directive overlooks that without a clear separation of labour inspections and labour courts from migration control, 'undocumented workers are not in a position to denounce exploitative employers and the exploitative practices are allowed to continue…It remains commonplace to deport undocumented workers instead of or before examining the violation of their labour rights' (PICUM, 2015, p. 11). Indeed, in many European countries, when intercepted by authorities—e.g. during labour site inspections or anti-trafficking operations carried out by law enforcement—undocumented migrants are often subjected to immigration control and risk being detained and deported without previous screening or being informed of their rights as victims or potential victims of exploitation (FRA, 2021; PICUM, 2021).

It can therefore be argued that the Employer Sanctions Directive may contribute to increasing migrant workers' situations of vulnerability to exploitation. Rather than facilitating their escape from exploitation, its provisions may push them to remain in exploitative working arrangements or expose them to more risky situations or both. Consequently, in this context, it is mainly workers who pay the price for the enforcement of employers' sanctions (Bloch et al., 2015).

On the other hand, as is evident in the case of Italy, implementation of the Employer Sanctions Directive at the national level has played a central role in bringing about changes in the composition and legal stratification of the migrant labour force, especially in sectors such agriculture (Corrado & Caruso, 2022). Indeed, the Directive has led to employers hiring migrant workers in regular migration status conditions, albeit still in situations of vulnerability due to the interplay of various factors including nationality, class, precarious legal status, gender, etc. (Corrado et al., 2018; Corrado & Caruso, 2022; Palumbo, 2017). These migrant workers include EU nationals, regular seasonal non-EU migrant workers, asylum seekers, and refugees who, as discussed in later chapters, are also subjected to forms of labour exploitation, including severe exploitation.

At the same time, the significant presence of EU nationals, asylum seekers, and refugees in exploitative conditions has shown the limitations of the Employer Sanctions Directive, especially concerning protection measures, as it only applies to non-EU undocumented migrant workers (Medu, 2015; Palumbo & Corrado, 2020). It is worth mentioning that the European Parliament addressed this aspect in its Resolution of 12 May 2016, calling on, for instance, 'the Member States to ensure that in their national legislation EU nationals who are victims of trafficking are protected from labour exploitation, and relevant sanctions are put in place' (European Parliament, 2016). In Italy, as discussed in Chap. 6, Art. 603-bis of the Criminal Code (CC), as revised by Law 199/2016, is innovative in this regard as it covers all exploited workers, regardless of migration status.

As discussed in later chapters, Anti-trafficking Directive 2011/36 applies to all victims irrespective of their migration status. However, even in this case, there are limits in the protection measures. More generally, as further discussed in Chaps. 6 and 8, limitations concern the impact of the anti-trafficking framework to address cases of labour exploitation in their variety.

4.2 EU Anti-Trafficking Legal and Policy Framework: Changes and Continuities

Directive 2011/36/EU on trafficking is another EU legal instrument related to severe exploitation and protecting victims' rights. The EU has been addressing the issue of trafficking in human beings since the 1990s. Trafficking is prohibited by the EU Charter of Fundamental Rights (Art. 5) and considered a serious form of organised crime by the Treaty on the Functioning of the European Union (Art. 83). Its fight falls within various EU competencies, including 'as an instrument for addressing irregular migration and in the dimension of judicial cooperation in criminal matters' as a serious form of transnational crime (Borraccetti, 2020, p. 686[8]).

Over the past 20 years, the EU has been consolidating its legal and policy framework on trafficking through several instruments in line with the main relevant international treaties: the 2000 UN Protocol on Trafficking and the 2005 Council of Europe Anti-Trafficking Convention (Peers et al., 2012; Borraccetti, 2020; Rijeken, 2011; Krieg, 2009; Askola, 2007). This consolidation occurred within the process of change in institutional and procedural dynamics resulting from the communitarisation of the Area of Freedom, Security, and Justice (AFSJ) with the 2007 Lisbon Treaty.[9] This Treaty subjected all matters of police and criminal cooperation to the ordinary co-decision legislative procedure by formally abolishing the pillar structure. This was a significant shift, considering that 'the issue of judicial cooperation in criminal matters concerns the exercise of policies that are closest to the exercise of state sovereignty' (Borraccetti, 2020 p. 687[10]; Lenaerts, 2010).

While the EU's initial legal and policy interventions focused on trafficking for sexual exploitation, securing prosecutions for this crime, and combatting irregular migration, greater attention is gradually being paid to exploitation in sectors other than sex work. At the same time, there has been a progressive emphasis on adopting a human rights-based, victim-centred, and gender-specific approach as provided by EU Directive 2011/36 on preventing and combatting trafficking and protecting its victims (Giammarinaro, 2012). Yet, as this chapter highlights, the main approach of EU legal and policy interventions on trafficking continues to raise questions and reveals contradictions and shortcomings, especially with regard to the effective protection of trafficked persons' rights.

Since the first EU legal interventions on this topic,[11] trafficking has been framed mainly in terms of addressing irregular migration and combatting organised crime/traffickers. For instance, the Framework Decision on Combatting trafficking in Human Beings (2002/629/JHA), which replaced Council Joint Action 97/154/JHA, had clear targets of criminalisation and harmonisation of penalties (Askola, 2007, p. 99). It paid minimal attention to the issue of protection of the rights of victims and no attention to prevention (Obokota, 2006). Such an approach was also reflected in the policy framework supporting the development of the Area of Freedom, Security, and Justice. For instance, both the Hague programme adopted by the European Council in November 2004 and the Stockholm programme that replaced it in 2009 situated trafficking next to irregular migration, smuggling, terrorism, and other

[8] My translation.

[9] As already mentioned, the 2007 Lisbon Treaty abolished the Third Pillar, which was based on the intergovernmental cooperation and thus generalised the Community method in the AFSJ.

[10] My translation.

[11] The first EU legal response to trafficking was the 1997 Joint Action to Combat Trafficking in Human Beings and Sexual Exploitation of Children (97/154/JHA). Under the action, Member States agreed to review their legislation by making trafficking for sexual exploitation a crime and ensure appropriate penalties through enhanced police and judicial cooperation.

forms of transnational organised crime as newly-urgent security threats (Askola, 2007).

In 2004, the EU adopted an instrument specifically addressing trafficking victims: Council Directive 2004/81/EC[12] (the Residence Permit Directive), which defines 'the conditions for granting residence permits of limited duration, linked to the length of the relevant national proceedings, to third-country nationals who cooperate in the fight against trafficking in human beings or against action to facilitate illegal immigration' (Art. 1). The Directive mandates that Member States provide trafficked people (and smuggled people) with a 'reflection period' to decide whether they wish to cooperate with authorities or not. During this period migrant persons are protected from expulsion, and Member States must ensure they receive appropriate assistance, support, and accommodation. Additionally, the Directive requests that Member States should consider providing trafficked persons (and smuggled persons) who cooperate with authorities with a temporary residence permit for a minimum of 6 months or for the duration of the criminal proceeding (Art. 8 and Art. 9). This permit should also grant them access to the labour market, vocational training, and education during this period (Art. 10).

These provisions of the Residence Permit Directive represent a departure from earlier EU instruments on trafficking. However, as underlined in the Explanatory Memorandum to the Proposal for the Short-Term Residence Permit (European Commission, 2002), the legal basis of the Residence Permit Directive (i.e. former Art. 63(3) of the Treaty establishing the European Community, current Art. 79 TFEU) concerns measures on immigration policy related to the conditions of entry and residence, as well as the fight against irregular immigration and trafficking. Consequently, the purpose of this Directive is to introduce a 'residence permit, with the aim of enhancing measures to combat illegal immigration' (European Commission, 2002, para. 3), not to protect the victims. In line with this perspective, the Directive subordinates the residence permit and related protection and assistance (Art. 7) to the victims' required cooperation with competent authorities. Furthermore, according to the Directive, the residence permit should be valid for at least 6 months or the duration of the criminal proceedings, and if the victim ceases to cooperate or renews contact with the alleged traffickers, the residence permit may be withdrawn (Art. 14). It is worth noting that when withdrawn, the regular alien laws of the respective Member State come into play. This implies that trafficked people may find themselves subject to legal action stemming from any offenses they may have committed while being trafficked. More commonly, they may face expulsion or deportation due to violations of immigration laws (PICUM, 2022; Paasche et al., 2018; Marchetti & Palumbo, 2022).

As legal scholar Heli Askola (2007, p. 94) argues, according to the Residence Permit Directive, those persons who do receive the residence permit are the 'most useful ones, that is "useful" in the sense of agreeing and being able to help and to

[12] Council Directive 2004/81/EC on the residence permit issued to third-country nationals who are victims of trafficking in human beings or who have been the subject of an action to facilitate illegal immigration, who cooperate with the competent authorities.

capture the "real" criminals…those with little reason to cooperate, for instance due to having relatives who have been threatened by traffickers in the country of origin or having the economic imperative to work no matter what, are hardly ideal candidates for success'.

Indeed, far from a human rights-based approach, the Residence Permit Directive endorses the view that the victim must be deserving, i.e., by being cooperative, to receive protection. Such an approach was later reflected in the Employer Sanctions Directive, as discussed below in Sect. 4.1.2. Conditioning protection on cooperation has inherent limitations. Chiefly, victims are often unwilling to report their exploiters to the police or participate in criminal proceedings against them mainly because they fear the consequences or distrust the authorities or both (Giammarinaro, 2018; Marchetti & Palumbo, 2022). In addition, as the Group of Experts on Trafficking in Human Beings of the European Commission (2009)[13] noted in a report, the 2004 Residence Permit Directive provides 'insufficient guarantees concerning a possible right to remain on the territory after relevant national proceedings have been completed, as well as with regard to assistance to victims'. This is an additional factor adversely affecting victims' inclination to cooperate with prosecution and, at the same, contributes to increasing their situations of vulnerability to dynamics of exploitation and trafficking.

It is also worth noting that the Residence Permit Directive's provision linking the residence permit to the victim's cooperation contradicts the principle of unconditional assistance later established by the 2005 Council of Europe Convention on Trafficking (see Chap. 1) and the Trafficking Directive 2011/36/EU (discussed below). In particular, the Council of Europe Convention—ratified by all 27 EU Member States—foresees renewable residence permits in exchange for cooperation with the criminal justice system but also (Art. 14) because of the trafficked person's circumstances. According to the Council of Europe, this implies considering a spectrum of situations that depend on factors such as the victim's safety, health status, family situation, or other relevant circumstances (Council of Europe, 2005, para. 184). In other words, this means taking into account the interplay of the various factors that contribute to and exacerbate the situational vulnerabilities of migrants subjected to exploitation and trafficking.

Furthermore, linking residence permits to cooperation criteria also contradicts EU Member States' obligation to ensure access to justice for victims of crime in accordance with the 2012 Victims' Rights Directive[14] (Directive 2012/29/EU), which applies to all victims of crime, irrespective of their residence status.

Given these considerations, anti-trafficking organisations, experts, and activists have advocated for a revision of the 2004 Residence Permit Directive. They have proposed amending it to allow the issuance of residence permits to trafficked

[13] The expert Group on trafficking in human beings was set up by the European Commission in 2007.

[14] Directive 2012/29/EU of the European Parliament and of the Council of 25 October 2012 establishing minimum standards on the rights, support and protection of victims of crime, and replacing Council Framework Decision 2001/220/JHA.

persons based on their personal situations and, accordingly, considering the different factors creating situations of vulnerability to exploitation and trafficking (Giammarinaro, 2021; La Strada International, 2022; Marchetti & Palumbo, 2022).

However, at the time of writing, the European Commission has proposed a revision not of the Residence Permit Directive, but instead of the EU Anti-Trafficking Directive 2011/36 (see Sect. 4.2.2), which is examined in the following section.

4.2.1 EU Directive 2011/36 on Trafficking: New Approaches for an Old Paradigm?

The Anti-Trafficking Directive, which replaced the Framework Decision 2002/629/GAI, was the first instrument adopted in the Area of Freedom, Justice, and Security (AFSJ) under the new rules established by the 2007 Lisbon Treaty. It was also the first EU legal instrument to take an integrated, holistic, human rights, victim-centred, and gender-sensitive approach to trafficking (Recital 7 of the Directive).

By distancing itself from earlier EU instruments, including the 2004 Residence Permit Directive, the Anti-Trafficking Directive outlines measures that are not solely of criminal nature but also aim at ensuring appropriate support for the victims (Giammarinaro, 2012). Indeed, in line with this holistic approach—supported by the ECtHR in decisions such as *Rantsev v. Cyprus and Russia* (Application No. 25965/04, 7 January 2010)—the Anti-Trafficking Directive does not confine the protection of victims' rights to context of criminal prosecution but provides for coordinated actions aimed at ensuring social assistance, support, and assistance in finding employment opportunities. Furthermore, in accordance with the 2005 Council of Europe Convention on Trafficking, the Anti-Trafficking Directive also recognises the gender-specific features of trafficking and that 'assistance and support measures should also be gender-specific where appropriate' (Recital 3).

The Anti-Trafficking Directive adopts the definition of trafficking found in the UN Palermo Protocol (see Chap. 1), opting for a comprehensive definition that includes all forms of trafficking. In contrast, the definition in the previous Framework Decision 2002/629/GAI distinguished between trafficking for sexual exploitation and trafficking for labour exploitation, thereby excluding other forms of exploitation. Furthermore, the Anti-Trafficking Directive expands on the Protocol's open-ended list of forms of exploitation to include the exploitation of begging and other types of criminal activities,[15] thus drawing attention to 'new forms of trafficking, particularly those involving minors' (Giammarinaro, 2012, p. 21).

[15] The Anti-Trafficking Directive states in its recital that forced begging should be understood as a 'form of forced labour or services as defined in the 1930 ILO Convention No. 29 concerning Forced or Compulsory Labour' (Recital 11). Accordingly, exploitation of begging, 'including the use of a trafficked dependent person for begging' can be classified under the definition of trafficking only when there are all the elements of forced labour and services (Recital 11). This means, therefore, that those cases, for instance, in which begging is a mere survival strategy for a family

As discussed in Chap. 1, the Anti-Trafficking Directive (like the 2002 Framework Decision on trafficking) significantly incorporates the definition of 'position of vulnerability' contained in the Interpretative Note to the 2000 UN Palermo Protocol and the Explanatory Report of the 2005 Council of Europe Convention on Trafficking as 'a situation in which the person concerned has no real or acceptable alternative but to submit to the abuse involved' (Art. 2(1)). This definition reflects a situational conception of the notion of vulnerability: vulnerability is not considered as an inherent quality of certain individuals or groups of individuals, but arises from a complex interplay of personal, circumstantial, and structural factors that leave a person with no alternative but to 'accept' the abusive and exploitative relations and conditions. As Giammarinaro and Palumbo (2021) note, in this definition the concept of acceptability should be complemented with that of the 'reality' of the alternative. Indeed, what matters is that the alternative is a real alternative, that is, it presents the characteristics of a non-exploitative job—or at least of a job in which exploitation is not associated with coercive or abusive practices and therefore is not incompatible with the realisation of the person's life plan. This situational understanding of vulnerability requires a case-by-case assessment of the interplay of personal and structural factors producing it.

The inclusion of this definition of position of vulnerability in the Anti-Trafficking Directive 2011/36 is thus particularly relevant because far from considering vulnerability as something static or fixed, it draws attention to contextual and structural elements, and therefore to the material conditions leading a person to accept abusive and exploitative circumstances.

From this perspective, as emphasised in Chap. 2, a particularly important principle is the concept of the irrelevance of consent, which is found in Art. 3 of the Palermo Protocol, in Art. 4 of the Council of Europe Convention on Trafficking, and integrated into Art. 2 of the Anti-Trafficking Directive. This does not mean that a person cannot consent to exploitation, but that the victim's consent cannot be used by traffickers/exploiters in their defence. The issue of consent is, as mentioned in Sect. 2.2.3, the other side of vulnerability to exploitation. Indeed, if viewed as a continuum, exploitation is characterised by varying degrees of submission or acceptance or both to certain exploitative situations (Giammarinaro & Palumbo, 2021). Along this continuum, forms of exploitation are associated with different situational vulnerabilities. As discussed in the chapters on national contexts, there are cases, quite common in agriculture or domestic work, where the elements of coercion are unclear and individuals accept exploitative dynamics due to challenging economic

---

should not fall within the scope of trafficking (Giammarinaro, 2012, p. 21). As for 'exploitation of criminal activities', according to the Directive this expression should be understood as the exploitation of 'a person to commit, inter alia, pick-pocketing, shop-lifting, drug trafficking, and other similar activities which are subject to penalties and imply financial gain' (Recital 11). Interestingly, in the same Recital the Directive also considers illegal adoption or forced marriage as forms of trafficking 'in so far as they fulfil the constitutive elements of trafficking in human beings' (Recital 11).

circumstances and family responsibilities, often managing to secure limited room for negotiation. In other cases, these margins are significantly reduced.

The Anti-Trafficking Directive also introduces a minimum common threshold of 5 years for the maximum penalty for all trafficking-related offences and elevates the minimum threshold for aggravated offences from 8 years to 10. It also contains provisions regarding prevention that oblige Member States to set up effective measures to prevent offences and deter the demand that fosters forms of exploitation related to trafficking (Art. 18). More importantly, the Directive introduces significant provisions on the protection and assistance of the trafficked persons (Arts 11–17),[16] centring the protection of their human rights (Giammarinaro, 2012; Bosma & Rijken, 2016) in line with the approach of 2005 Council of Europe Convention on Trafficking.

In particular, in cooperation with relevant support organisations, Member States are required to establish appropriate mechanisms aimed at early identification of necessary assistance and support for victims. Furthermore, the Directive establishes that victims shall be provided with assistance and support 'before, during, and for an appropriate period of time after the conclusion of criminal proceedings' (Art. 11(1)). Member States must provide assistance and support to the presumed victims as soon as competent authorities have 'reasonable grounds' for believing that a person was subjected to trafficking and ensure that such assistance and support is not conditional on the victims' willingness to cooperate in the criminal investigation, prosecution, or trial. In line with similar provisions contained in the 2005 Council of Europe Convention on Trafficking and the national legislation of Member States such as Italy (Chap. 6), the Anti-Trafficking Directive adopts the principle of unconditional assistance, affirming that assistance and support cannot be subordinated to the victim's willingness to cooperate with competent authorities.

However, it is important to highlight some critical points hindering the potential of these important provisions. The first concerns the lack of precision concerning the 'reasonable grounds' for indicating that someone has been subjected to trafficking as a criterion for identifying victims. As Bosma and Rijken (2016) have pointed out, this leaves wide discretion to the Member States and, more specifically to assistance providers and law enforcement authorities, with respect to when a person is considered a victim or potential victim of trafficking and therefore when to provide them with assistance and protection. It follows that how the notion of 'reasonable grounds' is understood and interpreted at the respective national levels is decisive in determining the profile of victims and allocating different types of assistance accordingly. The lack of clear indicators can lead Member States to adopt strict categories, potentially leaving those persons who do not meet these criteria without adequate assistance and protection. To prevent this risk, Giammarinaro (2018) emphasises that the identification process should focus on the factors creating vulnerabilities and provide persons with adequate assistance and support according to

[16] Although it is not examined here, it is worth mentioning that Directive 2011/36/EU dedicates specific provisions to the assistance, support, and protection for child victims of trafficking, with special attention to unaccompanied child victims (Arts 13–16).

the different situations and degrees of vulnerability and forms of exploitation experienced (including trafficking or less severe forms of exploitation).

The other critical aspect concerns the issue of unconditional assistance. This principle, which as previously noted prioritises the protection of the rights of victims, benefits trafficked people and may also be more effective for criminal justice purposes. Indeed, when victims feel unconditionally and appropriately assisted and protected, they are more inclined and willing to cooperate with law enforcement and judicial authorities (Giammarinaro, 2012). However, as several studies have highlighted, in most EU countries unconditional assistance is inadequately applied, especially in the case of third-country nationals (Marchetti & Palumbo, 2022; Giammarinaro, 2018). Implementation of this principle is undermined by the fact that, as underlined above, the Residence Permit Directive 2004/81/EC specifies that residence permits should be granted to third-country nationals who cooperate with competent authorities (Art. 8). This reveals a notable incongruity between this Directive and the Anti-Trafficking Directive (Giammarinaro, 2012, p. 18; Borraccetti, 2020; Marchetti & Palumbo, 2022). In turn, it implies an unjustifiable difference of treatment between victims who are nationals or EU citizens, who are provided with unconditional assistance, and third-country nationals, who are instead required to cooperate. In this sense, it is necessary to revise Directive 2004/81/EC on this issue to establish a consistent legal framework (Giammarinaro, 2012; Marchetti & Palumbo, 2022).

The Anti-Trafficking Directive also contains provisions concerning the protection of victims in the framework of criminal investigations and proceedings (Art. 12). These measures apply in addition to the rights set out in the Victims' Rights Directive (2012/29/EU), ensuring better protection to victims of trafficking compared to the protection concerning all victims of crime. More specifically, when trafficked persons cooperate in criminal proceedings, Member States are obligated to ensure that victims promptly gain access to legal counsel and legal representation, which may be provided free of charge if the trafficked individuals cannot afford it.

The Directive dedicates special attention to the issue of compensation, requiring Member States to ensure that victims of trafficking have access to the existing schemes of compensation for victims of violent crimes (Art. 17). Compensation represents an essential right for victims as it is crucial for their social inclusion. However, this provision is scarcely implemented (Cusveller & Kleemans, 2018; Giammarinaro, 2018) because trafficking does not always involve violent means (Giammarinaro, 2021). Indeed, compensation measures should ensure all exploited persons have access to compensation including, for instance, through dedicated and adequate national funds for victims of trafficking and exploitation and expedited procedures that involve trade unions, allowing exploited individuals to reclaim unpaid wages, reimbursements, and compensation.

Following the 2005 Council of Europe Convention on Trafficking (Art. 26), the Anti-Trafficking Directive also contains a provision on the principle of non-punishment of trafficking victims. It provides that Member States shall take the necessary measures to ensure that the 'competent authorities are entitled not to prosecute or impose penalties on victims of trafficking in human beings for their involvement in criminal activities which they have been compelled to commit as direct consequence of being subjected' to any of the acts referred to in the definition of trafficking (Art. 8). However, even this important provision is inadequately implemented at the national level. As Bosma and Rijken (2016, p. 320) point out, 'the scope of this provision remains unclear and the implementation leaves room for discretion'. Some EU countries, for instance Italy, still lack a specific clause concerning the principle of non-punishment of victims, while general provisions such as 'state of necessity' are very rarely applied. In a growing number of European countries, specific legal provisions on the non-punishment principle have been adopted. However, they often do not apply to all types of unlawful acts victims commit under compulsion (Marchetti & Palumbo, 2022). In this sense, the Directive should have foreseen that specific provisions are needed at the national level to ensure that victims are not prosecuted or punished for crimes they have been compelled to commit as a consequence of being trafficked.

Beyond these criticals aspects that may hamper the effectiveness of specific provisions, the Anti-Trafficking Directive is generally innovative in terms of assisting and supporting victims, especially when compared to the legislative instruments that preceded it. As former UN Special Rapporteur on trafficking Maria Grazia Giammarinaro (2012) has argued, the Anti-Trafficking Directive is the first EU instrument that addresses the issue of trafficking in a holistic manner. It does so by, on the one hand, providing for the protection of victims' rights not only within the criminal justice system but by triggering coordinated actions aimed at ensuring assistance and support. On the other hand, it decouples the criteria for accessing assistance from the victims' cooperation in the criminal proceedings.

However, the Directive's progressive character does not seem to be reflected in Member States' respective laws. Indeed, as with the Employer Sanctions Directive, most of the provisions of the Directive regarding victims' identification, assistance, and protection have been inadequately applied or transposed into national legislation. As the EU Commission (2020, p. 17) report assessing implementation of the Directive at the national level underscored, 'when victims receive assistance, support and protection, their needs are not taken into account as regards the forms of exploitation they are subjected to, their gender and age and their specific needs and circumstances...The concerns identified highlight the poor implementation of the Anti-trafficking Directive in Member States, and it needs to be further stepped up'.

Similarly, recent research and reports highlight how many trafficked and exploited people often risk being detained and deported without adequate screening (PICUM, 2020). Most have no access to unconditional assistance, compensation, and remedies or to appropriate support measures that adequately address their situation of vulnerability and related needs (Marchetti & Palumbo, 2022). The principle of non-punishment is either unimplemented or implemented incorrectly (UN Special Rapporteur on Trafficking in Persons, 2021). Furthermore, although the Anti-Trafficking Directive stresses the need for a gender-sensitive approach to trafficking, most countries have not adopted gender-based protocols or indicators for identifying victims of exploitation and trafficking. Relevant actors often overlook the role of family responsibilities, commitments, or dependence on male relatives in creating situations of vulnerability (ibid.; Giammarinaro, 2022). In addition, there is not much awareness of forms of exploitation experienced by women and LGBTQI+ subjectivities in sectors other than the sex industry (e.g. in domestic work or agriculture) or of the fact that men and boys can also be trafficked for sexual exploitation. Overall, there is a lack of instruments aimed at tackling the structural dimension of gender discrimination and violence and related forms of exploitation and trafficking (Rigo & De Masi, 2019). All these shortcomings reveal how exploitation and trafficking are still predominantly considered criminal matters rather than as social issues that should be addressed through a social- and rights-based perspective.

In 2021, the Commission adopted a new EU Strategy on Combatting Trafficking in Human Beings (2021–2025)[17] rooted in the Anti-Trafficking Directive and focused on four areas of action: reducing the demand that fosters trafficking in human beings; breaking the criminal business model of traffickers to halt victims' exploitation; protecting, supporting, and empowering victims, especially women and children; and addressing the international dimension. This Strategy presents some important aspects such as the attention to labour exploitation, abusive recruitment practices, and initiatives to incentivise transparency and due diligence in supply chains. However, it also presents significant deficiencies in terms of protecting the human rights of exploited and trafficked persons. For instance, it does not provide for specific actions to ensure unconditional assistance for victims, delinked from criminal procedures; for greater access to a residence permit beyond criminal procedures and on personal grounds; or for effective complaint mechanisms (La Strada International, 2021; ETUC, 2021). Furthermore, the Strategy focuses on the issue of demand and calls for criminalisation of 'knowing use of exploited services and products from victims', which is actually a non-binding provision of the Anti-Trafficking Directive. Such emphasis is an issue of concern as the attention to demand has mainly focused on clients' criminalisation and, thus, on repressive prostitution interventions. As several studies have noted, these measures, in addition to conflating trafficking and prostitution/sex work, have stigmatising and marginalising effects on sex workers and trafficked people, exposing them to further risks of abusive and exploitative dynamics (see, for instance, Garofalo Geymonat & Selmi, 2022).

In 2022, the European Commission (2022a) called for a revision of the Anti-Trafficking Directive. While this could be an important opportunity to improve and strengthen those aspects hindering the protection of victims' rights, the Proposal for the revision mainly concerns strengthening the provision on demand, stipulating that Member States shall consider measures to criminalise the knowing 'use of services which are the objects of exploitation' (Art. 18(4)), in other words the knowing use of services provided by trafficked persons. As discussed below, this again risks supporting and reinforcing a repressive approach to exploitation and trafficking, particularly in the context of the sex industry, that would likely drive sex work further into hidden and underground channels, increasing sex workers' situation of vulnerability to exploitation and abuse.

[17] The previous EU Strategy on Combatting Trafficking in Human Beings was adopted in 2012 to be implemented by 2016.

4.2.2 The Convergence between Restrictive Migration and Asylum Policies and Anti-trafficking Policies

In one of the first comprehensive commentaries on the Anti-Trafficking Directive, Giammarinaro (2012, p. 32) highlighted its innovative scope and approach while also emphasising that 'no anti-trafficking law can be effective unless accompanied by coherent migration and labour market policies' that reinforce each other and collectively enhance the protection of individuals.

However, it is evident today that the Directive's integrated and human rights approach has not been reflected, or at least supported, by EU and national migration policies. Over recent decades and, especially, since the so-called 2015 refugee crisis, migration policies have been characterised by increasingly stringent and selective measures (see Chap. 3). Trafficking has been addressed predominantly in the context of irregular migration and organised crime, and tackled through restrictive migration policies and externalisation of border control policies to third countries of transit such as Turkey, Libya, and Tunisia (Sciurba, 2021a).

This approach is typified by the already-mentioned 2015 European Agenda on migration that aimed to address the 'root causes of migration' mainly in terms of border control and management, effective returns, and actions against criminal networks of traffickers and smugglers seen as the principal incentive for irregular migrations. The Agenda envisaged a new modality of managing the 'refugee crisis' through the implementation of the system of hotspots (first reception facilities) in Italy and Greece, which has led to constant violations of human rights of migrant people and an erosion of the foundational principles underpinning the right to asylum (Sciurba, 2017b; see also Palumbo & Sciurba, 2018). In line with policies of border externalisation endorsed through the Rabat (2006) and Khartoum (2014) processes (Oette & Babiker, 2017), the Agenda also provided for cooperation and partnerships with third countries of origin and transit to combat trafficking and irregular migration as well as for managing asylum. The Agenda did not address the lack of regular entry channels for 'low-skilled' third-country migrant workers (Minderhoud, 2021). Even when it acknowledged the 'potential source of exploitation' that 'comes from employers inside the EU', this policy document mainly focused on the repressive solution, overlooking the complexity of the phenomenon and merely referring to the necessity of fully implementing the Employer Sanctions Directive without addressing workers' rights and their protection. A similar approach was followed by the 2020 New Pact on Migration and Asylum (Boraccetti, 2020; Minderhoud, 2021).

The Agenda's adoption was followed by the 2016 agreement between the EU and Turkey providing for the indiscriminate return of 'all new irregular migrants and asylum seekers' to Turkey, which was redesignated as a 'safe third country' for this purpose. This deal, as has been extensively argued, violates the principle of *non-refoulment* (which, to be upheld, should encompass an individual assessment of each person's situation) through a notably expansive application of the principles of 'safe third country' and 'first country of asylum' (Sciurba, 2017a; Van Liempt et al., 2017; Amnesty International, 2017). The agreement has 'forced' thousands of migrant people following the 'Balkan route' to change their path to EU countries, making it longer and passing through Serbia, Bosnia, and Belarus, while encountering increasingly militarised frontiers and facing exploitative dynamics by traffickers and abusive actors (Sciurba, 2021a; Astuti et al., 2020).

The 2016 EU-Turkey deal served as explicit inspiration for the 2017 Memorandum of Understanding between Italy and Libya, subsequently renewed in 2020 and 2022. Under this agreement, the so-called Libyan Coast Guard was trained and equipped for the task of intercepting people fleeing Libya across the Mediterranean Sea and returning them to Libya, despite numerous international reports and direct testimonies denouncing the horrors and violence suffered by women, men, and children in Libyan detention centres (see, among others, Amnesty International, 2021a, b).

Alessandra Sciurba has underlined in her work how in both these agreements, as well as in a similar agreement between Italy and Tunisia in 2023, the primary repressive goal of countering irregular migration and containing the mobility and arrival of asylum seekers is pursued by mobilising the humanitarian discourse of ending the pattern where refugees and migrants are paying traffickers and smugglers and 'risking their lives' (Sciurba, 2021a; see also Cuttitta, 2019). Moreover, this happens despite the so-called Libyan Coast Guard frequently operating in close proximity to, or directly alongside, traffickers (Tondo, 2020) whom European governments claim to be combatting. Yet, as a paradox, NGOs that have mobilised to rescue migrant people at sea and protect their rights, also by refusing to cooperate with Libyans, have meantime experienced an unprecedented process of media and judicial criminalisation (Papanicolopulu, 2017), with accusations of facilitating irregular migration and supporting traffickers and smugglers. At the same time—and this is another paradox—repressive actions have focused on punishing migrant people steering boats, deemed as 'presumed smugglers or traffickers', even though they often serve as the final link in an long and systemic chain of exploitation (Ricard-Guay, 2018; Arci Porco Rosso et al., 2023). Indeed, they are often desperate persons operating the boats to financially afford the crossing, victims of trafficking compelled to engage in such activities (Camilli, 2023) or just passengers like the others who have been misidentified by their travel companions during summary interrogations.[18]

The implementation of these EU and national externalisation policies based on a 'militarised humanitarianism'—to use a term from Bernstein (2010)—has occurred through a complete omission of the topic of human rights and the corresponding international legal obligations placed on states. As Enrica Rigo (2022, p. 106) notes in this regard, 'fleeing from sexual and gender-based violence, from the violence of patriarchal exploitation, from trafficking, which can be recognised in a court as a basis for refugee status or a graded form of protection, is used instead, in border and

[18] In recent years, some criminal Courts, such as in Italy, have recognised that these migrant persons have acted 'under a condition of necessity' and, for this reason, cannot be prosecuted (see, for instance, Ricard-Guay, 2018).

"forced" migration containment policies, to justify the closure of borders in the name of combatting traffickers and defending national interests'.[19]

Far from preventing and combatting trafficking and exploitation, it has clearly emerged over these years that externalising border controls and stringent migration policies further increase migrants' vulnerabilities to exploitation and abuse and facilitate the action of abusive actors and traffickers. Thanks also to restrictive migration policies, criminal actors and traffickers effectively hold an exclusive control over the mobility of migrants, directing them towards increasingly perilous routes. Indeed, 'for every border that has been closed through militarisation, another route, usually more dangerous in terms of migrants' security, has been opened'[20] (Sciurba, 2021b, p. 90). This exposes migrants to systematic dynamics of abuse, violence, exploitation, and trafficking during and after the journey, and raises the stakes between life and death (Rigo, 2022, p. 106).

At the same time, as discussed in the chapters examining national contexts, those migrant people who manage to reach countries of arrival, such as Italy, and pass the initial 'selection' in confinement and filtering circuits—hotspots, return detention centres—face long and complex procedures, as well as inadequate accommodation conditions, when submitting their protection requests (Sciurba, 2021a, b; Marchetti & Palumbo, 2021; Carnassale & Marchetti, 2022). All this increases the situational vulnerabilities of migrant people and asylum seekers, further exposing them to dynamics of marginalisation, abuse, and exploitation, especially in low protected and low paid sectors such as agriculture (Corrado & Caruso, 2022).

It is worth noting that, in this context, there has been important European[21] and national case law in the field of international protection recognising fundamental human rights and challenging restrictive asylum, migration, and border control policies and practices (Galicz, 2023; Marchetti & Palumbo, 2021; Saroléa et al., 2021). In particular, in Italy there has been a significant case law granting international protection to victims of trafficking, especially in cases of sexual exploitation, in accordance with the 2006 UNHCR Guidelines n. 7 (UNHCR, 2006; see also Nicodemi, 2020). As discussed in Chap. 6, Italy has also seen noteworthy judicial decisions pertaining to the former humanitarian protection (previously under Article 5(6) of Legislative Decree 286/1998) as well as the current 'special protection' (Art. 19 of Legislative Decree 286/1998) that have focused on the material conditions producing situations of vulnerability, including in cases of labour exploitation (ibid.; Palumbo, 2023).

On the other hand, in several European countries, gaining access to asylum proves challenging for many victims of trafficking, particularly those involved in labour exploitation (Saroléa et al., 2021). Furthermore, outside the asylum procedure, in many European countries including Italy, receiving assistance, support, and

---

[19] My translation in English.

[20] My translation in English.

[21] See, among others, the relevant judgment of the recent ECtHR decision in *J.A. and Others*, (Application No. 21329/18, 30 March 2018) regarding the inhumane conditions of the hotspot centre in Lampedusa suffered by a group of migrant people after being rescued at sea.

a residence permit as a victim of trafficking or other forms of exploitation almost always requires victims' cooperation with law enforcement authorities (Palumbo, 2023). Such an approach, which is contrary to the unconditional assistance of the Anti-Trafficking Directive, primarily focuses on punishing exploiters/traffickers, only granting protection to those migrants who are 'cooperative' in facilitating criminal proceedings. In this framework, what is lost is both the systemic character of exploitation and the interplay of background conditions and factors contributing to the construction of vulnerabilities to exploitation (ibid.). These factors also include the precarity of legal statuses perpetuated by this criminal law approach, which provides victims with temporary residence permits dependent on criminal proceedings, thereby hindering their social and labour inclusion in the long term.

4.2.3 The Issue of Demand and the Neo-Abolitionist Approach to Sex Work

This repressive and migration control-based approach to trafficking and exploitation clearly has consequences on how prevention measures are considered and framed. At the core of this approach is a conceptual shift that leads to viewing exploitation and trafficking, not in their structural and social dimensions, but solely in terms of abusive and pathological relationships between exploiters/traffickers and victims (Marks, 2008; Mantouvalou, 2020). Consequently, the root causes of these issues are found mainly in the profit-seeking practices of exploiters/traffickers and of those who foster demand for the exploitation. Therefore, EU and national measures aimed at preventing trafficking have also focused on targeting the demand. This is evident, for instance, in the last EU Strategy on Trafficking (2021–2025), which prioritises preventive measures and encourages Member States to consider criminalising the knowing use of services exploited from trafficked persons.

While the issue of demand is important, a single focus on it is highly problematic (Anderson & O'Connell-Davidson, 2003). First, this obscures the systemic dimension of exploitation, as well as severe exploitation such as trafficking, and neglects the structural factors that contribute to migrant people's situational vulnerabilities to exploitation and abuse. These factors include stringent migration policies, gender inequalities, and high levels of deregulation and the erosion of labour and social rights in the EU's internal labour market.

Second, it is important to highlight that both the UN Palermo Protocol (Art. 9(5)) and the Council of Europe Convention on Trafficking (Art. 6) emphasise the necessity of taking various actions to address the issue of demand. However, neither document nor the Anti-Trafficking Directive (upon which the EU Strategy relies) provide a definition of demand (Pearson, 2005; Vogel, 2017).

Trying to address the definitional uncertainty concerning this notion, Pearson (2005, p. 4) has identified three levels of demand in the context of trafficking: employer demand (employers, owners, managers, or subcontractors); consumer demand (clients, corporate buyers, household members (domestic work)); third parties involved in the process (including recruiters, agents, transporters and those who participate at any stage of the trafficking process). Within this framework, the meaning of this term varies depending on the context and actors involved. Indeed, as Bridget Anderson and Julia O'Connell-Davidson (2003) note, demand can 'embrace a broad and divergent range of motivations and interests'.

However, in the dominant legal and policy discourses on trafficking, especially at the European level, the term 'demand' is primarily considered in relation to the sex-industry (Calderaro & Giametta, 2019; Rubio Grundell, 2023). Thus policies intended to tackle demand are primarily framed in terms of criminalising clients of sex workers in line with the so-called Swedish/Nordic Model. Such a model has been strongly supported and lobbied at the EU level, especially through the activities of feminist neo-abolitionist groups involved in the European Women's Lobby, promoting it as '*the* solution to the problems of prostitution and gender inequality' (Calderaro & Giametta, 2019).

The neo-abolitionist feminists tend to conflate trafficking with prostitution, always considering both as forms of violence (Chuang, 2010). This approach, on one hand, denies that sex work can be a form of work and, on the other, overlooks that trafficking occurs in other sectors as well. As legal scholar Janie Chuang (2010, p. 1655) has pointed out, the neo-abolitionist paradigm has favoured the development of a reductive narrative of trafficking that 'simplistically depicts trafficking as involving women and girls forced into "sexual slavery" by social deviants'. This narrative tends to conceal the broader structural factors producing trafficking, including states' responsibilities in reducing the possibility of migrating in safe and regular conditions to or within Europe, and in not ensuring that workers, including sex workers, work safely (Andrijasevic, 2010; see also Niina, 2018). At the same time, such a narrative ignores the variety of experiences of sex workers, including migrant sex workers, their agency, and their means of survival and mobility (Garofalo Geymonat & Macioti, 2016).

In her work on the intersection of security and neo-abolitionism in the EU's anti-trafficking policies, Lucrecia Rubio Grundell sheds light on the significant impact feminist neo-abolitionist ideals have had on the development of the EU's anti-trafficking policies, fostering what she calls a 'neoliberalism-vulnerability-security nexus' that has contributed to the depiction of a gendered and culturalised conception of trafficking victims. This frames trafficking as an epiphenomenon of prostitution threatening EU security and thus to be addressed mainly through criminal law strategies. In line with what has been defined a carceral approach to trafficking (Bernstein, 2010), neo-abolitionist discourses on prostitution and trafficking have supported the adoption of repressive measures—such as border enforcement, harsh penalisation (of traffickers and clients), and stronger effective prosecution—as the primary tool to prevent and counter trafficking and 'rescue' victims of trafficking along the 'humanitarian' rhetoric fuelling policies of border controls and containment of 'forced' migration. The relevance of such a form of 'governance feminism' (Halley et al., 2018) in EU anti-trafficking policies has become evident in the current proposal for a revision of the EU Anti-Trafficking Directive (European Commission, 2022a, b).

By providing Member States the possibility to consider criminalising the knowing use of services provided by trafficked persons (Art. 18(4)), the Anti-Trafficking Directive found a sort of compromise, taking into account different, and even opposite, positions among Member States and civil societies, especially with regard to regulation of sex work. By proposing to make this provision binding, the current proposal for revision of the Directive clearly opts for the Swedish/Nordic model, which has also been adopted by other European countries such as France. However, as several studies highlight, although this model is increasingly promoted as means to reduce exploitation and trafficking, it has been proven to have negative effects on the workers, in particular migrant workers in situations of irregularity (Chuang, 2010[22]; Östergren, 2017; Amnesty International, 2016; Calderaro & Giametta, 2019; Vuolajärvi, 2019). For one, it drives prostitution underground, creating more dangerous conditions for people who choose to work in the sex industry or who are forced into it (Calderaro & Giametta, 2019; Vuolajärvi, 2019). This increases sex workers' situational vulnerabilities to abuse and exploitation as they become more exposed to abusers/exploiters and face greater challenges in seeking assistance and help from social workers or organisations or police (Chuang, 2010; Vuolajärvi, 2019). Also, such a model not only stigmatises clients but inevitably also persons who work in the sex industry. Lastly, as has been argued, the criminalisation of clients implies that any consensual exchange of sex for money is illegal, thus rendering the consent of a sex worker always irrelevant. In contrast, according to the definition of trafficking, consent is only irrelevant when illicit means such as violence, fraud, or abuse have been employed (ASGI and EcST, 2023).

In general, as ASGI and EcST (ibid.) emphasise in a statement, the Swedish/Nordic Model supported by the proposed revision of the Anti-Trafficking Directive focuses on punishing clients, whereas policies aimed to prevent trafficking and exploitation in the sex industry should aim at empowering sex workers, considering them primarily as rights holders.

It is worth noting that the proposal for revision of the Anti-Trafficking Directive also provides for adding forced marriage and illegal adoption to the types of exploitation in the definition of trafficking. More importantly, it also proposes expansion of corporate liability through mandatory sanctions for legal entities, including exclusion from public benefits or the closure of facilities. This is a significant provision, especially in the case of labour exploitation. However, it is also essential that there is not just a punitive regime in place but also the possibility for the proceeds to be easily accessible to the workers as compensation for unpaid wages and other remedies. The hope is to 'shift' the focus more towards the possibility of providing greater protections for workers, giving them more 'tools' to negotiate their position

[22] In this regard, Janie Chuang (2010, pp. 1724–1725) argues that 'neither the Swedish nor Dutch prostitution-reform strategy addresses the complex mix of socioeconomic factors, including poverty and discrimination…neither strategy addresses the exploitation of migrants…neither strategy ultimately addresses the demand for trafficked or easily exploited services or labour'.

with their exploiter, employer, or whoever it may be, and incentives to decide to exit exploitation dynamics.

4.3 Concluding Remarks

This chapter analysed the EU's legal and policy instruments and approach to labour exploitation, trafficking, and the protection of exploited and trafficked migrants. In particular, it focused on EU Employer Sanctions Directive 2009/52 and EU Anti-Trafficking Directive 2011/36. The Employer Sanctions Directive primarily aims at addressing irregular migration. Nonetheless, it provides for some important provisions concerning the rights of undocumented migrant workers, such as those on wages owed by employers, facilitating complaints, and the issuance of residence permits. Its protection provisions, however, relied mainly on a repressive-based approach, as is evident in linking the possibility of a residence permit to victims' cooperation in criminal proceedings.

The chapter highlighted how the Employer Sanctions Directive's protection provisions have been inadequately applied at national levels. At the same time, in some contexts, its implementation has contributed to increasing the situational vulnerabilities of irregular migrant workers by not supporting them to escape exploitation but rather pushing them into more exploitative working arrangements. Furthermore, as evident in the case of Italy, the Directive's implementation at the national level fostered changes in the composition of the migrant labour force, especially in sectors such agriculture. This has led many employers to turn to regular migrant workers (such as asylum seekers and EU migrant citizens), who are also in situation of vulnerability due to a combination of factors such as gender, nationality, colour of skin, class, precarious legal status, etc.

The Anti-Trafficking Directive 2011/36 undoubtedly marks a significant turning point in EU legislation in the field by adopting an integrated human rights and gender-based approach. Consistent with this perspective, the Directive contains important provisions such as defining 'position of vulnerability', highlighting the need to consider the structural factors leading people to 'accept' exploitative working conditions. Moreover, it also recognises key principles such as unconditional assistance and non-punishment (non-prosecution or non-application of penalties) for victims.

The Anti-Trafficking Directive reflects a new awareness of the complexities of trafficking and exploitation, and the need to adopt more effective policies that are not focused only on criminal enforcement but also consider the social dimension and the protection of rights of exploited and trafficked persons. However, its innovative elements have been undermined by its inadequate implementation at the national level, especially regarding the unconditional assistance of the victims.

At the same time, the Directive's integrated human rights and gender-based approach has not been reflected and supported in recent EU and national migration and border control policies. Instead, these have invoked the fight against traffickers and the humanitarian rhetoric of 'saving' suffering victims to justify border restrictions and externalisation. As a consequence, detention, abuse, violence, and exploitation have become systematic practices experienced by migrant people moving or attempting to move to Europe.

In this context, the structural and complex dimension of exploitation—including its severe forms such as trafficking—is overlooked and reduced to mere contingent and abusive relationships between exploiters and victims. Such an approach also finds support in feminist neo-abolitionist positions on trafficking, which have recently played a critical role in the ongoing revision of the Anti-Trafficking Directive that advocates criminalising clients.

Such a repressive and migration-control-based approach to exploitation and trafficking creates, in turn, hierarchies of protection that legitimise the protection of some at the expense others. Protection is, indeed, granted to those who merit it by collaborating in criminal proceedings and therefore aid in the prosecution of traffickers and exploiters. In the meantime, the complex interplay of personal and structural factors creating and amplifying migrants' situational vulnerabilities to exploitation and trafficking remains unaddressed.

References

Amnesty International. (2016). *The human cost of 'crushing' the market: Criminalisation of sex work in Norway*. Amnesty International.

Amnesty International. (2017). *EU-Turkey deal: A shameful stain on the collective conscience of Europe*. Press Release, March 17 [online], https://www.amnesty.org/en/latest/press-release/2017/03/eu-turkey-deal-a-shameful-stain-on-the-collective-conscience-of-europe/ (Last Access Apr 2024).

Amnesty International. (2021a). *Greece: Violence, lies, and pushbacks*. Amnesty International (Last Access Apr 2024).

Amnesty International. (2021b). *'No one will look for you': Forcibly returned from sea to abusive detention in Libya*. Amnesty International [online], https://www.amnesty.org/en/documents/mde19/4439/2021/en/ (Last Access Apr 2024).

Anderson, B., & O'Connell-Davidson, J. (2003). *Is trafficking in human beings demand driven? A multi-country pilot study*. Migration Research Series. International Organisation for Migration.

Andrijasevic, R. (2010). *Migration, agency and citizenship in sex trafficking*. Palgrave Macmillan.

Arci Porco Rosso, Borderline Sicilia & Borderline-Europe. (2023). *Finché puoi ascoltare: la criminalizzazione dei cosiddetti scafisti nel 2022*. 10 January 2023 [online], https://arciporcorosso.it/finche-puoi-ascoltare-la-criminalizzazione-dei-cosiddetti-scafistinel-2022/ (Last Access Apr 2024).

ASGI & EcST. (2023). Risarcire e tutelare di più le vittime di tratta, non criminalizzare i clienti, 17 October 2023 [online], https://www.asgi.it/notizie/asgi-e-ecst-risarcire-e-tutelare-di-piu-le-vittime-di-tratta-non-criminalizzare-i-clienti/ (Last Access Apr 2024).

Askola, H. (2007). *Legal responses to trafficking in women for sexual exploitation in the European Union*. Hart Publishing.

Astuti, M., Bove, C., Brambilla, A., Clementi, A., Facchini, D., Giordani, S., Maraone, S., Pignocchi, P., Saccora, D., & Stojanova, I. (2020). *The Balkan route: Migrants without rights in the heart of Europe*. Report. Ri Volti ai Balcani [online], https://www.asgi.it/wp-content/uploads/2020/09/The-Balkan-Route-Report-2020-by-_-Rivolti-ai-Balcani_-italian-network.pdf (Last Access Apr 2024).

Baird, T. (2017). Carrier sanctions in Europe: A comparison of trends in 10 countries. *European Journal of Migration and Law, 19*(3), 307–334.

Bernstein, E. (2010). Militarized humanitarianism meets Carceral feminism: The politics of sex, rights, and freedom in contemporary anti-trafficking campaign. *Signs: Journal of Women in Culture and Society, 36*, 45–71.

Bloch, A., Kumarappan, L., & Mckay, S. (2015). Employer sanctions: The impact of workplace raids and fines on undocumented migrants and ethnic enclave. *Critical Social Policy, 35*(1), 132–151.

Borraccetti, M. (2020). Il contrasto alla tratta di persone a partire dal Consiglio europeo di Tampere 199: attualità e criticità. In M. Giovanetti & N. Zorzella (Eds.), *Ius Migrandi. Trent'anni di politiche e legislazione sull'immigrazione in Italia* (pp. 686–702). Franco Angeli.

Bosma, A., & Rijken, C. (2016). Key challenges in the combat of human trafficking. Evaluating the EU trafficking strategy and EU trafficking directive. *New Journal of European Criminal Law, 7*(3), 315–330.

Calderaro, C., & Giametta, C. (2019). 'The problem of prostitution': Repressive policies in the name of migration control, public order, and women's rights in France. *Anti-Trafficking Review, 12*, 155–171.

Camilli, A. (2023). Why the 'captains' of migrant trafficking boats are often the first victims. *Worldcrunch.com*, 28 March 2023 [online], https://worldcrunch.com/migrant-lives-1/who-are-the-migrant-smugglers (Last Access Apr 2024).

Carnassale, D., & Marchetti, S. (2022). *Vulnerabilities and the Italian protection system*. VULNER Research Report 2.

Chuang, J. (2010). Rescuing trafficking from ideological capture: Prostitution reform and anti-trafficking law and policy. *University of Pennsylvania Law Review, 158*, 1655–1728.

Corrado, A., & Caruso, F. S. (2022). Essential but exploitable: Migrant agri-food workers in Italy and Spain. *European Journal of Migration and Law, 24*(2), 193–216.

Corrado, A., Caruso, F. S., Lo Cascio, M., Nori, M., Palumbo, L., & Triandafyllidou, A. (2018). *Is Italian agriculture a 'pull factor' for irregular migration—And, if so, why?* Open Society European Policy Institute.

Council of Europe. (2005). *Explanatory report to the Council of Europe Convention on action against trafficking in human beings*. Council of Europe Treaty Series, No. 197 [online], https://rm.coe.int/16800d3812 (Last Access Apr 2024).

Cusveller, J., & Kleemans, E. R. (2018). Fair compensation for victims of human trafficking? A case study of the Dutch injured party claim. *International Review of Victimology, 24*(1), 297–311.

Cuttitta, P. (2019). The Central Mediterranean border as a humanitarian space. In L. Nyberg, N. Sørensen, & S. Plambech (Eds.), *Global perspectives on humanitarianism. When human welfare meets the political and security agendas* (pp. 15–39). Danish Institute for International Studies.

De Lange, T. (2011). The privatization of control over labour migration in The Netherlands: In whose interest? *European Journal of Migration and Law, 13*(2), 185–200.

Dewhurst, E. (2011). The right of irregular immigrants to outstanding remuneration under the EU sanctions directive: Rethinking domestic labour policy in a globalised world. *European Journal of Migration and Law, 13*(4), 389–410.

ETUC. (2021). *For Information: ETUC comments on new EU Strategy on combatting trafficking in human beings*. European Trade Union Confederation [online], https://www.etuc.org/en/circular/etuc-comments-new-eu-strategy-combatting-trafficking-human-beings (Last Access Apr 2024).

European Commission. (2002). *Explanatory Memorandum to the proposal for the short-term Residence Permit Directive*. COM (2002), 71 final, par. 7.

European Commission. (2007a). *Proposal for a Directive of the European Parliament and of the Council providing for sanctions against employers of illegally staying third-country nationals*. COM (2007), 249, final.

European Commission. (2007b). *Commission staff working document – Accompanying document to the Proposal for a Directive of the European Parliament and of the Council providing for sanctions against employers of illegally staying third-country nationals*. Summary of the impact assessment, SEC (2007) 604.
European Commission. (2015). *Communication from the Commission to the European Parliament, the Council, the European Economic and Social Committee and the Committee of the Regions. A European Agenda on Migration,* COM (2015) 240 final.
European Commission. (2020). *Third report on the progress made in the fight against trafficking in human beings (2020) as required under Article 20 of Directive 2011/36/EU on preventing and combating trafficking in human beings and protecting its victims*. COM(2020) 661 final.
European Commission. (2021). *Minimum standards on sanctions and measures against employers of illegally staying third-country nationals*. COM(2021) 592 final.
European Commission (2022a). *Proposal for a Directive of the European Parliament and of the Council amending Directive 2011/36/EU on preventing and combating trafficking in human beings and protecting its victims*. COM(2022) 732 final.
European Commission. (2022b). *Report on the progress made in the fight against trafficking in human beings (Fourth Report)*. COM(2022) 736 final.
European Parliament. (2009). *Report on the proposal for a directive of the European Parliament and of the Council providing for sanctions against employers of illegally staying third-country nationals* (Rapporteur Caludio Fava), A6-0026/2009. European Parliament.
European Parliament. (2016). *Preventing and combating trafficking in human beings. European Parliament resolution of 12 May 2016 on implementation of the Directive 2011/36/EU of 5 April 2011 on preventing and combating trafficking in human beings and protecting its victims from a gender perspective* (2015/2118(INI)), P8_TA(2016)0227.
FRA. (2015). *Severe labour exploitation: Workers moving within or into the European Union: States' obligations and victims' rights*. European Union Agency for Fundamental Rights.
FRA. (2021). *Protecting migrants in an irregular situation from labour exploitation. Role of the employer sanctions directive*. European Union Agency for Fundamental Rights.
Friðriksdóttir, B. (2017). *What happened to equality? The construction of the right to equal treatment of third-Country Nationals in European Union Law on labour migration*. Brill | Nijhoff.
Galicz, K. Z. (2023). L'approccio *hotspot* davanti alla Corte Europea dei Diritti dell'Uomo: commento a margine della sentenza nella causa *J.A. e altri contro Italia, Diritti Comparati. Comparare i diritti fondamentali in Europa. Diritti Comparati* [online], https://www.diritticomparati.it/lapproccio-hotspot-davanti-alla-corte-europea-dei-diritti-delluomo-commento-a-margine-della-sentenza-nella-causa-j-a-e-altri-contro-italia-ricorso-n-21329-18/?print-posts=pdf (Last Access Apr 2024).
Garofalo Geymonat, G., & Macioti, P. G. (Eds.). (2016). Sex workers speak. Who listens? *Open Democracy* [online], https://www.opendemocracy.net/en/beyond-trafficking-and-slavery/sex-workers-speak-who-listens/ (Last Access Apr 2024).
Garofalo Geymonat, G., & Selmi, G. (2022). *Prostituzione e lavoro sessuale in Italia. Oltre le semplificazioni, verso i diritti*. Rosenberg & Seller.
Giammarinaro, M. G. (2012). La direttiva 2011/36/UE sulla prevenzione e la repressione della tratta di esseri umani e la protezione delle vittime. *Diritto, immigrazione e cittadinanza, XIV, 1*, 15–33.
Giammarinaro, M. G. (2018). L'individuazione precoce delle vulnerabilità alla tratta nel contesto dei flussi migratori misti. *Questione Giustizia, 2*, 129–134.
Giammarinaro, M. G. (2021). *Revising EU Directive on trafficking? For bad or good reasons?* [online], https://giammarinaro.net/en/revising-eu-directive-on-human-trafficking-for-bad-or-good-reasons/ (Last Access Apr 2024).
Giammarinaro, M. G. (2022). Understanding severe exploitation requires a human rights and gender-sensitive intersectional approach. *Frontiers in Human Dynamics, 4*, 861600. https://doi.org/10.3389/fhumd.2022.861600

Giammarinaro, M. G., & Palumbo, L. (2021). Vulnerabilità situazionale, genere e diritti umani. Analisi della normativa e della giurisprudenza italiana e sovranazionale sullo sfruttamento lavorativo. In G. Gioffredi, V. Lorubbio, & A. Pisanò (Eds.), *Diritti umani in crisi? Emergenze, disuguaglianze, esclusioni* (pp. 45–62). Pacini Giuridica.

Group of Experts on Trafficking in Human Beings of the European Commission. (2009). Opinion No. 4/2009 of the group of experts on trafficking in human beings set up by the European Commission for a possible revision of Council Directive 2004/81/EC of 29 April 2004.

Halley, J., Kotiswaran, P., Rebouché, R., & Shamir, H. (2018). *Governance feminism: An introduction*. University of Minnesota Press.

IOM. (2015). *Report on victims of trafficking in mixed migration flows arriving in Italy by sea: April 2014–October 2015*. Geneva: International Organisation for Migration.

Knockaert, J. (2017). *The employers sanctions directive: A law to address exploitation of undocumented workers? PICUM Blogs* [online], https://picum.org/blog/employers-sanctions-directive-law-address-exploitation-undocumented-workers/ (Last Access Apr 2024).

Krieg, S. H. (2009). Trafficking in human beings: The EU approach between border control, law enforcement and human rights. *European Law Journal, 15*(6), 775–790.

La Strada International. (2020). *New EU Migration Pact increases risks of human trafficking*. La Strada International [online], https://documentation.lastradainternational.org/lsidocs/3374-La%20Strada%20International%20statement%20-%20EU%20Anti-Trafficking%20Day%2018%20October%202020%20-%20def.pdf (Last Access Apr 2024).

La Strada International. (2021). *New EU Strategy on Combatting Trafficking in Human Beings*. International Expert Roundtable: Human Trafficking Reloaded 16 April 2021. YouTube [THB Regional Implementation Initiative, 6:38:35] (Last Access Apr 2024).

La Strada International. (2022). *States should offer trafficked persons access to a residence permit on personal grounds*. Statement [online], https://documentation.lastradainternational.org/lsidocs/3435-La%20Strada%20International%20statement%20Victim%20Rights%20Day%2022%20feb%202022.pdf (Last Access Apr 2024).

Lenaerts, K. (2010). The contribution of the European court of justice to the area of freedom, security, and justice. *International and Comparative Law Quarterly, 59*(2), 255–301.

Lidén, H., Schultz, J., Paasche, E., & Wessmann, H. (2021). *Vulnerable protection seekers in Norway: Regulations, practices, and challenges*. VULNER Research Report 1.

Mantouvalou, V. (2020). Structural injustice and the human rights of workers. *Current Legal Problems, 73*(1), 59–87.

Marchetti, S., & Palumbo, L. (Eds.) (2021) *Vulnerability in the asylum and protection system in Italy: Legal and policy framework and implementing practices*. Vulner Research Report 1.

Marchetti, S., & Palumbo, L. (2022). *10 Years After the Directive 2011/36/EU: Lights and shadows in addressing the vulnerability of trafficked and exploited migrants*. Population and Policy Brief 33. Max Planck Society/Population Europe.

Marks, S. (2008). Exploitation as an international legal concept. In S. Marks (Ed.), *International law on the left: Re-examining Marxist legacies* (pp. 281–307). Cambridge University Press.

Medu. (2015). *Terrainguista. Rapporto sulle condizione di vita e di lavoro dei braccianti stranieri in agricoltura*. Medici per i Diritti Umani.

Minderhoud, P. (2021). Regulation of EU labour migration: At a crossroads after the new pact on migration and asylum? *Utrecht Law Review, 17*(4), 31–44.

Nicodemi, F. (2020). Il sistema anti-tratta italiano compie venti anni. L'evoluzione delle misure legislative e di assistenza per le vittime e le interconnessioni con il sistema della protezione internazionale. In M. Giovannetti & N. Zorzella (Eds.), *Ius Migrandi. Trent'anni di politiche e legislazioni sull'immigrazione in Italia* (pp. 703–728). FrancoAngeli.

Niina, V. (2018). Governing in the name of caring—The Nordic model of prostitution and its punitive consequences for migrants who sell sex. *Sexuality Research and Social Policy, 16*(2), 151–165.

Obokota, T. (2006). *Trafficking of human beings from a human rights perspective: Towards a holistic approach*. Martinus Nijhoff.

Oette, L., & Babiker, M. A. (2017). Migration control à la Khartoum: EU external engagement and human rights protection in the horn of Africa. *Refugee Survey Quarterly, 36*(4), 64–89.

Östergren, P. (2017). *The demand-side in anti-trafficking: Current measures and ways forward*. European Policy Brief.

Paasche, E., Skilbrei, M.-L., & Plambech, S. (2018). Vulnerable here or there? Examining the vulnerability of victims of human trafficking before and after return. *Anti-Trafficking Review, 10*. https://doi.org/10.14197/atr.201218103

Palumbo, L. (2017). Exploiting for care: Trafficking and abuse in domestic work in Italy. *Journal of Immigrant and Refugee Studies, 15*(2), 171–186.

Palumbo, L. (2023). Vulnerability to exploitation through the lens of intersectionality. *European Journal of Migration and Law, 25*, 421–448.

Palumbo, L., & Corrado, A. (Eds.). (2020). *Are agri-food workers only exploited in southern Europe? Case studies on migrant labour in Germany, The Netherlands and Sweden*. Open Society European Policy Institute.

Palumbo, L., & Sciurba, A. (2018). *The vulnerability to exploitation of women migrant workers in agriculture in the EU: The need for a human rights and gender based approach*. European Parliament Study, Policy Department for Citizens' Rights and Constitutional Affairs, European Union.

Papanicolopulu, I. (2017). Immigrazione irregolare via mare, tutela della vita umana e organizzazioni non governative. *Diritto, Immigrazione e Cittadinanza, 3*, 1–29.

Pearson, E. (2005). The Mekong challenge. *Human trafficking: Redefining demand. Destination factors in the trafficking of children and young women in the Mekong sub-region*. International Labour Organisation.

Peers, S. (2016). *EU justice and home affairs law: EU immigration and asylum law*. Oxford University Press.

Peers, S., Guild, E., Acosta-Arcaranzo, D., Groenendijk, K., & Moreno-Lax, V. (2012). *EU immigration and asylum law (text and commentary)*. Brill Nijhoff.

PICUM. (2015). *Employer sanctions: Impacts on undocumented migrant workers' rights in four EU countries*. Platform for International Cooperation on Undocumented Migrants.

PICUM. (2020). *PICUM key messages and recommendations on human trafficking*. Platform for International Cooperation on Undocumented Migrants.

PICUM. (2021). Employers' sanctions: will the EU finally take steps to protect workers? *PICUM Blogs* [online], https://picum.org/blog/employers-sanctions-will-the-eu-finally-take-steps-to-protect-migrant-workers/ (Last Access Apr 2024).

PICUM. (2022). *Unconditional access to services for undocumented victims of crime*. Platform for International Cooperation on Undocumented Migrants.

Ricard-Guay, A. (2018). *Criminalizing migrants who steer the dinghies in the Mediterranean: A collateral effect of migration management?*. EUI working papers, RSCAS 2018/32. Global Governance Programme.

Rigo, E. (2022). *La straniera. Migrazioni, asilo, sfruttamento in una prospettiva di genere*. Carocci Editori.

Rigo, E., & De Masi, F. (2019). Fighting violence across borders: From victimhood to feminist struggles. *The South Atlantic Quarterly, 118*(3), 670–677.

Rijeken, C. (Ed.). (2011). *Combating trafficking in human beings for labour exploitation*. Wolf Legal Publishers.

Rodenhauser, T. (2014). Another brick in the wall: Carrier sanctions and the privatization of immigration control. *International Journal of Refugee Law, 26*(2), 223–247.

Rodotà, S. (2012). *Il Diritto di avere diritti*. Laterza.

Rubio Grundell, L. (2023). *Security meets gender equality in the EU: The politics of trafficking in women for sexual exploitation*. Palgrave Macmillan.

Santoro, E. (2020). Vulnerability between political theory and normative texts: A new language to repeat old things or a new tool to problematize differences in social power? *Revista de Estudos Constitucionais, Hermenêutica e Teoria do Direito, 12*(3), 311–334.

Saroléa, S., Raimondo, F., & Crine, Z. (2021). *Exploring vulnerability's challenges and pitfalls in Belgian Ayslum system. Research report on the legal and policy framework and implementing practices in Belgium*. VULNER Research Report 1.
Sciurba, A. (2017a). Misrecognizing asylum. Causes, modalities and consequences of the crisis of a fundamental human right. *Journal of Legal Philosophy, 1*, 141–164.
Sciurba, A. (2017b). Categorizing migrants by disempowering the right to asylum. A focus on the Sicilian implementation of the 'Hotspot approach'. *Etnografia e Ricerca Qualitativa, 10*(1), 97–120.
Sciurba, A. (2021a). *Le Parole dell'Asilo: Un Diritto di Confine*. Giappichelli.
Sciurba, A. (2021b). Cosi in mare come in terra: cosa resta del diritto d'asilo e dell'orizzonte dei diritti umani. In G. De Marzo & F. Parisi (Eds.), *Diritto e immigrazione. Un quadro aggiornato delle questioni più attuali e rilevanti* (pp. 85–102). Il Foro Italiano - LaTribuna.
Sommarribas, A., Petry, R., & Nienaber, B. (2017). *Illegal employment of third-country nationals in the European Union*. EMN synthesis report. European Commission.
Stoyanova, V. (2017). *Human trafficking and slavery reconsidered*. Cambridge University Press.
Tondo, L. (2020). Senior Libyan coastguard commander arrested for alleged human trafficking. *The Guardian*, 16 October 2020 [online], https://www.theguardian.com/global-development/2020/oct/16/senior-libyan-coastguard-commander-arrested-for-alleged-human-trafficking (Last Access Apr 2024).
UN Special Rapporteur on Trafficking in Persons. (2021). *Implementation of the non-punishment principle. Report of the Special Rapporteur on trafficking in persons, especially women and children, Siobhán Mullally*, A/HRC/47/34.
UNHCR (2006). *Guidelines on International Protection No. 7: The Application of Article 1A(2) of the 1951 Convention and/or 1967 Protocol Relating to the Status of Refugees to Victims of Trafficking and Persons at Risk of Being Trafficked*. HCR/GIP/06/07
Van Liempt, I., Alpes, M.J., Hassan, S., Tunaboylu, S., Ulusoy, O., & Zoomers, A. (2017) *Evidence-based assessment of migration deals: The case of the EU-Turkey Statement*. Final Report. Netherlands Organisation for Scientific Research, Utrecht University.
Verschueren, H. (2016). Employment and social security rights of third-country labour migrants under EU law: An incomplete patchwork of legal protection. *European Journal of Migration and Law, 18*(4), 373–408.
Verschueren, H. (2018). Employment and social security rights of third country nationals under the EU labour migration directives. *European Journal of Social Security, 20*(2), 100–115.
Vogel, D. (2017). The concept of demand in the context of trafficking in human beings. *Psychosociological Issues in Human Resource Management, 5*(1), 193–234.
Vuolajärvi, N. (2019). Governing in the name of caring—the nordic model of prostitution and its punitive consequences for migrants who sell sex. *Sexuality Research and Social Policy, 16*, 151–165.

Chapter 5
Situational Vulnerabilities and Labour Exploitation in Italy: The Case of Agricultural and Domestic Migrant Workers

After drawing on the legal and conceptual framework in Chaps. 1 and 2 and critically discussing, in Chaps. 3 and 4, how EU legal and policy instruments in the ambit of labour migration as well as those aimed at preventing and combatting, exploitation, including trafficking, contribute to creating situations of vulnerability for migrant people, this book now turns to national contexts. The following chapters will respectively focus on Italy (Chaps. 5 and 6) and the UK (Chaps. 7 and 8), critically examining the dynamics of exploitation in these countries, especially in agriculture and domestic and care work, and the commonalities and differences in the legal and policy instruments and approaches aimed at protecting the rights of migrant workers and addressing labour exploitation. By adopting a gender and intersectional perspective, the chapters will focus on the assemblage of factors producing and amplifying situational vulnerabilities to exploitation, taking into account the ambiguities and tensions in relevant national laws and policies.

In particular, building on intensive fieldwork conducted in Italy, especially in Sicily, this chapter critically examines the impact of relevant national migration and asylum policies as well as the exceptional regulatory frameworks of agriculture and domestic work on the living and working conditions of migrant workers. By challenging reductionist and sensationalistic narratives and focusing instead on the systemic dimension of exploitation, the chapter examines how these factors contribute to generating and increasing situational vulnerabilities upon which these sectors rely. The adoption of a gender and intersectional perspective, specifically utilising the conceptual framework of social reproduction, helps shed light on specific forms of exploitation experienced by migrant women and that are based on their situational vulnerabilities, within a socio-economic context marked by the simultaneous functioning of systems of oppression and subordination.

L. Palumbo, *Taking Vulnerabilities to Labour Exploitation Seriously*, IMISCOE Research Series, https://doi.org/10.1007/978-3-031-55424-7_5

5.1 Setting the Scene

5.1.1 Challenges and Changes in Migrant Labour Composition since the 2000s

Characterised by a historical tradition of emigration and a relatively recent history of immigration, Italy is considered part of the 'Mediterranean' model of migration (King et al., 2000). This model is marked by a predominance of family and labour-related migration movements and a high element of 'irregularity' in which employment in sectors such as agriculture and domestic work represents one of the main channels for migrants to access the labour market (ibid.; Pugliese, 2011). Another characteristic is the adoption of increasingly stringent policies as migration becomes more structural and less episodic. As historian Michele Colucci (2018, p. 138) observes, in Italy the 'years of immigration growth run parallel to the gradual tightening of policies'. In particular, since the end of the 1990s, the issue of migration has become highly politicised in the country, leading to the progressive introduction of restrictive migration laws and policies in response to a significant increase in the number of migrant persons – approaching the numbers of Germany, France, and the UK – along with their growing presence in the national labour market (Colucci, 2018; Livi Bacci, 2010). Emblematic, in this regard, was the adoption of Law 189/2002, the so-called Bossi-Fini Law, which strengthened the securitarian approach already characterising existing migration legislation, notably Law No. 40/1998 (the 'Turco Napolitano Law') (Del Lago, 2004). In particular, the Bossi-Fini Law, abolished, among others, the sponsorship entry system established by the 'Turco Napolitano Law' that provided migrant workers with a temporary residence permit to seek a job in Italy. At the same time, the Bossi-Fini Law formally tied the issuance of a work-related residence permit to the existence of a labour contract, the *contratto di soggiorno* or 'residence contract' (Art. 3bis of the Consolidated Act on Immigration, Legislative Decree 286/1998), thereby rendering the presence of migrant workers more precarious and more dependent on employers.

Since the late 2000s, the 'Mediterranean model of migration' has been challenged by several factors, including the European Union enlargement process, the 2008 economic crisis, and the so-called refugee crisis (Chap. 4). The result has been a profound change in migratory movements (Colucci, 2018; Lo Cascio & Perrotta, 2019).

EU enlargement in 2004 and 2007 significantly increased migration, including circular migration, from Member States such as Romania and Poland (Geddes et al., 2020). While this has raised concerns about the risk of 'welfare tourism' (see Chap. 4), less-skilled EU nationals from eastern European countries have gradually joined the ranks of the exploitable labour force in sectors such as domestic work and agriculture, fostering 'social dumping' dynamics (Perrotta, 2011). The feminised character of migration movements from eastern EU countries (especially Romania) – triggered by a complex overlapping of social and economic factors as well as specific gender and familial models and dynamics (Sciurba, 2015) – has resulted in a substantial rise and ongoing presence in the number of migrant women employed in domestic work (Osservatorio Domina sul lavoro domestico, 2022) and, in some regions, agriculture (Palumbo & Sciurba, 2018).

On the other hand, the 2008 global economic crisis made Italy – like many EU countries of arrival – less attractive to migrant workers, leading to a reduction in the number of third-country nationals entering Italy for work (OECD, 2014). At the same time, annual entry quotas for non-EU migrant workers have been considerably reduced since 2008, especially between 2021 and 2020. Recession exacerbated labour market segmentation on the basis of nationality, class, and gender, further confining migrant workers to low-protected and unskilled sectors and consequently exposing them, to dynamics of irregularity and exploitation (ISTAT, 2015; Sacchetto & Vianello, 2013; Sacchetto, 2013). However, agri-food and domestic work have been among the few sectors that did not collapse as a result of the economic downslide.

The spread and intensification of conflicts and wars since 2011 in countries such as Tunisia, Libya, and successively in Syria have led to a significant increase in migrant people reaching Europe, in particular Italy, through unsafe and dangerous routes such the Mediterranean Sea. This peaked in the years of the so-called refugee crisis, notably in 2016 with 181,436 sea arrivals (compared to 13,267 in 2012). Since 2017, following the agreement between Italy and Libya (Chap. 4), there has been a noteworthy decline in sea arrivals (ISMU, 2023). However, starting from 2020, arrivals have resumed an upward trend, reaching 153,071 in 2023 (Ministero dell'Interno, 2023).[1]

As several studies have stressed, the high number of sea arrivals, especially during the 'refugee crisis', must be connected to the closure of nearly all possible legal entry channels for third-country nationals to Italy and Europe, particularly channels related to migration for work reasons (Sciurba, 2021). Moreover, as the data tellingly reveal, since 2011 there has been no 'crisis' in quantitative terms, as the total number of third-country nationals entering Italy has stabilised, if not declined (Colucci, 2018, pp. 184–185). In the same period – and this is significant quantitative data to be considered – especially since 2014, over 20,000 people have lost their lives in the Mediterranean Sea while trying to reach Europe (IOM, 2023).

The fluctuation in the number of sea arrivals must be considered in connection with the stringent EU and national interventions undertaken to curb irregular migration and limit access to the asylum path. As noted in Chap. 4, the EU and Italy have reacted to the so-called refugee crisis by intensifying the externalisation of border controls through a progressive and detailed intervention in transit countries in the Middle East, such as Turkey, and North Africa, such as Libya and more recently in Tunisia[2] (ASGI, 2020; Sciurba, 2021; Giuffré et al., 2022). In this context, as borders are externalised and tightened, the routes chosen by migrant people also

---

[1] Data as of 7 December 2023.

[2] In July 2023, the EU signed a Memorandum of Understanding with the Tunisian government, aligning with a strategy of conditional economic aid and the externalisation of European borders.

change, often becoming more perilous. Thus, for instance, the recent increases in sea arrivals, involving primarily Sub-Saharan migrants departing from Tunisia (ISPI, 2023), should be understood in light of the closure of the Libyan border (due to the 2017 Memorandum between Italy and Libya), at a time when the 2023 agreement between the EU and Tunisia has not yet produced closure effects.

The combined impact of these factors alongside the inadequacies of national systems of recruitment of foreign workers (see Sect. 5.2) reflects a change in migratory movements and, accordingly, in the composition of migrant labour employed in unprotected sectors such as domestic work and agriculture. This involves undocumented migrants, as well as citizens of eastern EU countries – Romanians, Poles, Bulgarians – regular non-EU migrant workers (including seasonal workers), and regular non-EU nationals with a residence permit that is not for work reasons (Palumbo, 2022a, b). These latter have notably included, especially in the agricultural sector, asylum seekers and beneficiaries of international protection mainly from Sub-Saharan Africa and southeast Asian countries (Corrado & Caruso, 2022). This has led to what is referred as a 'refugeesation of the agricultural workforce', particularly in seasonal cultivation (Dines & Rigo, 2015). It is worth noting in this regard that asylum seekers in Italy are allowed to work 60 days after applying for asylum, even if they are not subjected to national legislation concerning the residence permit for work reasons (Martelloni, 2020).

While reliable data are not yet available, recent restrictive asylum reforms such as Law Decree 20 of 10 March 2023,[3] the 'Cutro Decree' (Sect. 5.1.3) and the latest update to the national list of Safe Countries of Origin,[4] including countries such as Nigeria, Gambia, Ivory Coast, and Georgia, likely result in an increase in the number of migrant people in conditions of irregularity. This would significantly impact the legal stratification of the migrant labour force.

However, at time of writing, current official data reveal, as Corrado and Caruso (2022; also Caruso, 2023) have illustrated, that the Covid-19 pandemic further consolidated 'refugeesation of the agricultural workforce' as asylum seekers, whose mobility is extremely limited by their legal status, sought work in the agri-food sector within a highly segregated labour market. Conversely, there has been a drop in the number of EU citizen migrant farmworkers (Caruso, 2023; L'Altro Diritto & FLAI CGIL, 2022). Although still a significant component of the migrant labour force in Italy's agri-food sector (Osservatorio Placido Rizzotto, 2022), many EU citizen migrant workers, especially following the pandemic, have moved to other European countries, such as Germany, to seek better working and living conditions (Corrado & Caruso, 2022).[5] A similar trend can be seen in other 'Mediterranean model' countries such as Spain (ibid.).

---

[3] Law Decree No. 20 of 10 March 2023, *Disposizioni urgenti in materia di flussi di ingresso legale dei lavoratori stranieri e di prevenzione e contrasto all'immigrazione irregolare*.

[4] Decree of 17 March 2023.

[5] As Caruso and Corrado (2022) have shown, the number of Romanian farmworkers in Italy fell by almost 15%, from 98,011 in 2019 to 84,005 in 2020.

Changes in the composition of migrant labour are reflected in new situational vulnerabilities that are particularly utilised and exploited in low-paid and low-protected sectors such agriculture and domestic work. It is, however, noteworthy that irregular migration status is not the predominant factor in situations of vulnerability to exploitation (Corrado et al., 2018). The link between exploitative living and working conditions and irregular migration status has become less obvious, while different factors among migrant workers – including precarious legal status, gender, nationality, class, nationality, ethnicity, and skin colour – contribute to the construction of distinct situations of vulnerability, each susceptible to exploitation in its own way (Palumbo, 2022a, b).

5.1.2 *The National Entry System for Non-EU Migrant Workers: Contradictions, Inadequacies, and Quota Reductions*

Third-country migrant workers' entry is regulated by Law 40 1998, the 'Turco-Napolitano Law' subsequently merged with Legislative Decree No. 286/1998 ('Consolidated Act of provisions governing immigration and rules on the status of foreign nationals', hereafter Consolidated Act on Immigration). The Consolidated Act on Immigration (Article 3) articulates the regulation of the entry routes for work reasons on two levels. The first is a three-year Plan (*Programmazione Triennale*) defining the broad criteria for annual entry flows into national territory (Article 3, paras 1–3). The second involves the Flows Decree (*Decreto Flussi*), which is issued annually to set maximum quotas for workers to be admitted into the national territory based on labour market needs and sector shortages. Considering that the most recent three-year plan (2023–2025)[6] was adopted after a 20-year gap from the previous plan, it can be said that, thus far, the Flows Decree has been the primary instrument regulating admission of third-country migrant workers into the national labour market.

The Flows Decree sets quotas reserved for both dependent (including seasonal and non-seasonal workers) and self-employed work.[7] In line with a restrictive approach aimed at containing migration movements, the Flows Decree can reserve quotas for those states 'with which agreements have been concluded aimed at regulating entry flows and readmission procedures' (Article 21(1) Consolidated Act on Immigration).

The entry system provided by the Flows Decree model is based on an employer-driven mechanism requiring a specific request from resident employers (Italian

[6] Decreto del Presidente del Consiglio dei Ministri del 27 settembre 2023, 'Programmazione dei flussi d'ingresso legale in Italia dei lavoratori stranieri per il triennio 2023–2025'.

[7] This section focuses on the entry route system of migrant workers for dependent employment. It does not address the entry route system of self-employed migrant workers.

nationals or regularly resident foreigner)[8] who must submit an application to the pertinent special office for immigration (*Sportello Unico*) at the local prefecture. The employer must also commit to providing the worker with suitable accommodation upon their arrival and present the proposed 'residence contract' outlining related conditions, guaranteeing to cover the return travel expenses when migrant workers no longer renew their residence permits. In cases of non-seasonal workers, the relevant employment centre must inform the employer if there are available workers in Italy to fill the post.[9] If there are, the employers still have the option to confirm their intention to hire (from abroad) the non-EU worker indicated in the application. The Sportello Unico then proceeds to issue the authorisation to obtain an entry visa (*nulla osta*) for the migrant worker and communicates it to the relevant consular offices in the country of origin, which then issue the entry visa for work reasons.

Therefore, according to this employer-based system, migrant workers can enter the territory only when they have a secured job and the related authorisation, utilising the annual entry window provided each year by the Flows Decree.

From the outset, this system has proven difficult to apply, inadequate in responding to the needs of employers (including private households), and ineffective in preventing irregular migration. First, established quotas have always been set below the effective market needs of the migrant labour force. Furthermore, from 2012 to 2020, quotas – especially for non-seasonal work – were drastically cut, while there has been an increase since 2021 (Corrado et al., 2018; ISMU, 2021; Ambrosini, 2022). In particular, the 2023–2025 three-year Plan provided for a total entry of 136,000 in 2023, 151,000 in 2024, and 165,000 in 2025. This is a substantial increase, considering that, especially between 2015 and 2021, the total number of authorised entries was 30,850. The new Decree significantly contains specific quotas for care and domestic work; the last special quotas for this sector were provided in 2011. However, the overall number of entries (452,000) projected for the three-year period 2023–2025 is still far from the reported labour force demand of 833,000 units as indicated by the government itself.

In addition to limited quotas, the procedure for implementing this entry system is excessively long and complicated, and therefore not effective in responding to labour demand and related needs. It is, in fact, 'impracticable,' especially in sectors like domestic and care work where job requests can be unexpected and urgent (Santoro, 2010, p. 137; Ambrosini, 2022). Moreover, as many studies have demonstrated, this procedure has been open to abusive and illegal practices, including the sale of employment offers for substantial sums of money, with the consequent risk that once the workers arrive in Italy, they may find themselves without a job and consequently fall into irregular status (Ero Straniero, 2023; Amnesty International, 2012; Omizzolo, 2019). Above all, the Flows Decree system relies on the

[8] Art. 22 of Consolidated Act on immigration. See also, in this regard, Court of Cassation, Decision No. 13054, 9 September 2002.

[9] In the latest Flows Decree 2023, a simplification has been introduced in the procedure for the prior verification of the unavailability of the local labour force.

assumption that prospective migrant workers remain in their countries of origin until the entry visa is issued. This condition precludes an effective and transparent matching between job supply and demand (Chiaromonte & Federico, 2021; Giammarinaro, 2023), fostering instead the circumvention of the Flows Decree regulation.

In practice, the interplay of all these factors turns the Flows Decree system into a (legal) device that creates irregularity. Indeed, it has primarily had the effect of pushing many migrants towards irregular channels (Chiaromonte, 2018) and prompting – especially before the implementation of EU Employers Sanction Directive 2009/52/EC – many employers to turn to undocumented migrants already in Italy. In this context, undocumented migrants have sought to regularise their status either through an incorrect use of the Flows Decree system as a 'post-regularisation tool'[10] (Sciarra & Chiaromonte, 2014) or through the periodic government amnesty/regularisation schemes. Since the 1980s, Italian governments have periodically adopted regularisation schemes for undocumented migrant workers to manage (labour) migration (Colucci, 2018). The last such regularisation scheme was adopted in August 2020 to address the impact of the Covid-19 pandemic and resulted in a sort of failure (Corrado & Palumbo, 2022) (see Chap. 6).

The practice of periodically resorting to regularisation schemes has disclosed a system privileging irregular stay – which fosters migrant workers' vulnerabilities to exploitation – as the main path for migrants' social integration rather than making regular migratory channels to Italy more viable and accessible (Palumbo, 2017). This, in turn, has fuelled an undeclared labour market, exploitation, and criminal activities (Palmisano, 2017; Papa, 2018; Amnesty International, 2012).

It is worth highlighting that the Consolidated Act on Immigration (Art. 24) contains specific provisions concerning foreign seasonal work. These aim to simplify the recruitment of seasonal migrant workers, making it faster and more flexible than the procedure for recruiting non-seasonal migrant workers. For instance, in line with the provisions of the Seasonal Workers Directive 2014/36/EU (transposed into national legislation through Legislative Decree 203 of 2016), Article 24 of the Consolidated Act on Immigration provides that local immigration offices may issue a multi-annual authorisation residence permit for seasonal work. Furthermore, the Act provides that a residence permit for seasonal work can be converted into a residence permit for a temporary or permanent dependent (non-seasonal) work permit where there is residual capacity set by annual Flows Decrees (Art. 24 (10). Such a clause is quite innovative with respect to the Seasonal Workers Directive, which lacks a similar one (see Chap. 3). However, this and other noteworthy provisions concerning seasonal migrant workers' admission are weakened by the inefficiencies of the Flows Decree system (Papa, 2020), including the meagre quotas of recent years.

Several studies highlight how the current Flows Decrees system fosters migrant workers' dependence on employers (Sciarra & Chiaromonte, 2014; Corrado et al.,

---

[10] Once in contact with an employer, irregular migrants already in Italy return to their countries of origin and then re-enter Italy within the quotas established by the Flows Decree system.

2018), making the latter 'the arbiters of the only opportunity for migrants to remain on Italian territory' (Giammarinaro, 2022, p. 14). This, consequently, increases and amplifies their situational vulnerability to exploitation and abuse, as it can lead them to accept unfair working and housing conditions to have the possibility to stay (regularly) in Italy.

It is also worth underlining that the link between labour contract and residence permit was bolstered by the 2002 Bossi-Fini Law around the time when Italian labour law was revised,[11] taking on the characteristics derived from labour market deregulation and the fragmentation of typologies of employment contracts (Belluccio, 2020). The proliferation of precarious and flexible contracts has made obtaining and renewing the residence permit more difficult. It has also hampered access social rights and related protection (ibid.), thus fostering social and labour differential inclusion.

Moreover, the rigidity of the rules for renewing a residence permit for work reasons – particularly the constraint closely linked to the income capacity of the migrant worker and the availability of appropriate accommodation – does not seem to take into account the characteristics and the crisis of the national labour market, as well as the enormous difficulties that many migrant people face in finding housing.

Even though the reduction in quotas between 2011 and 2020 involved both non-seasonal and seasonal employment, entries for seasonal workers have been higher than those foreseen for non-seasonal workers (ISMU, 2021). This imbalance – which marks a change with respect to quotas set before 2011 and has been confirmed in the 2023–2025 three-year Plan – is in line with the EU and other European countries' approach and signals a political will to privilege a temporary and precarious migrant workforce essential for the functioning of key and unprotected labour market sectors rather than supporting stable and long-term pathways of labour migration projects.

The recent reform to the Flows Decree, introduced by Legislative Decree 20/2023 ('Cutro Decree'), allows, for example, some entry routes 'outside' the official quotas for those workers participating in professional training courses recognised by the Ministry of Labour following specific agreements with public or private entities operating in migrants' countries of origin. This reform has nonetheless kept the overall structure of the system regulating entries for work intact, with all its contradictions, ambiguities, and inefficiencies (see Paggi, 2023).

In this context, both the deficiencies of the Flows Decree system and the deep-rooted recourse to informal and irregular employment in sectors such as domestic work and agriculture, have meant that labour demand in these key segments has been mainly met by EU citizen migrants from eastern European countries and non-EU asylum seekers and beneficiaries of international protection, alongside undocumented workers (Palumbo & Sciurba, 2018; Corrado et al., 2018; Dines & Rigo, 2015).

[11] In particular, Law 196 of 24 June 1997 (the 'Treu Packet') and Law 30 of 14 February 2003, implemented with Legislative Decree 276 of 10 September 2003 (the 'Biagi Law').

5.1.3 Containing Migration through Progressive Tightening of Access to Asylum

The changes in the migratory movements to Italy – particularly the notable increase in the number of asylum seekers, many of whom are employed in essential sectors in the national labour market – have challenged the prevailing categories in legal and policy discourses on migration. In particular, these have underscored the clear limitations of a rigid distinction between 'economic migration' and 'forced migration' in understanding and addressing the complexity of migratory movements (Mezzadra, 2013; Jubilut & Casagrande, 2019). By overlooking the diversity in subjective conditions of migratory experiences and related economic, social, and environmental factors (Mezzadra, 2013; Recchia, 2020), this distinction also fails to recognise the impact of the Italian entry system's inadequacies for third-country migrant workers (the Flows Decree mechanism). As Recchia (ibid., p. 100) points out, the shortcomings of this system 'have had the effect of pushing the (regular) matching between the demand and supply of work into (different) channels that still allow migrants to work'[12] such as family reunification and the asylum path.

On the other hand, and primarily in response to these changes in migratory patterns, the issue of asylum has taken centre stage in government policies aimed at migration containment. Access to asylum has been subjected to continuous curbs, leading to a progressive erosion of the right to asylum since the 2010s, as Alessandra Sciurba (2021) notes. This peaked with the adoption of Law Decree 13 2017, the 'Minniti Decree', which considerably compressed the right of defence of asylum seekers;[13] the 2017 Memorandum of Understanding between Italy and Libya (renewed in 2020 and 2022); Law Decree No. 113/2018 and Law Decree No. 53/2019, known as the 'Security/Salvini' decrees; and the recent Law Decree 20/2023, known as 'Cutro Decree'.

The 'Security Decree' (No. 113/2018) in particular introduced several restrictive and securitarian measures that have heavily affected legal provisions and protection for migrant people in Italy, especially asylum seekers (Curi, 2019). For instance, it abolished the residence permit for humanitarian reasons, known as 'humanitarian protection' (former Article 5 (6) of the Consolidated Act on Immigration), which aimed to protect people in situations of vulnerability or facing violations of constitutionally protected human rights but who are not eligible for refugee status or subsidiary protection. The 2019 Follow-up Security Decree (No. 53/2019) further closed harbours to NGOs' ships transporting migrants rescued in the Mediterranean Sea by toughening sanctions against them on the grounds that their activities were a 'pull factor' for attracting irregular migrants (Sciurba, 2021).

---

[12] My translation.

[13] The Minniti Decree abolished the second stage of appeal for rejected asylum claims; there are two remaining levels of appeal, the first instance and the Supreme Court. The Decree was converted into Law No. 13 of 18th April 2017.

Such reforms reflect a change in how asylum seekers are viewed and perceived at the political level. Massimo Pastore and Nazarena Zorzella (Pastore & Zorzella, 2020) stress that since the 2010s, the asylum seeker has become a negative figure thanks to dominant public narratives and discourses conveying the notion of an unprecedent 'invasion' – albeit one refuted by official data (Colucci, 2018)[14] – and the suspicion that economic migrants pose as asylum seekers and, therefore, abuse the national protection system (Pastore & Zorzella, 2020). As these scholars argue, this negative image stems from the fact that asylum seekers are 'not subject to the ordinary rules for obtaining the entry visa and residence permit, given the fundamental nature of the right, and… therefore escape the stringent rationale of immigration regulations, becoming the targets of efforts to limit the possibilities of recognizing the right to protection, even to avoid "expanding the net" of immigration'[15] (ibid., p. 129).

The abrogation of humanitarian protection by the 2018 Security Decree should be viewed in this context. By covering a wide spectrum of situations of vulnerability, the former humanitarian protection (former Article 5 (6) Consolidated Act on Immigration) was one of the most widely granted forms of protection for migrants arriving in Italy (Colucci, 2018). While, from a legal perspective, humanitarian protection was used to implement constitutional asylum, as consistently emphasised by the Court of Cassation,[16] in practice it functioned as a form of 'low-intensity regularisation', as observed by Caproglio et al. (2023). Indeed, it provided legal status to many migrant workers engaged in various sectors, including agriculture and domestic labour. Notably, in 2014, humanitarian protection was extensively utilised to confer legal status on Ukrainian women working as domestic helpers in Italy (Lanni, 2016).

In 2020, Law Decree 130/2020, the 'Lamorgese Decree', introduced the residence permit for 'special protection' (Art. 19 of the Consolidated Act on Immigration) to replace the humanitarian protection. However, the broad scope of this special protection's application was significantly impacted by the 2023 'Cutro Decree', which amended Art. 19 of the Consolidated Act on Immigration (Zorzella, 2023). In particular, the Cutro Decree has abrogated the section of Art. 19 that provided for the recognition of special protection based on the migrant person's family ties, as well as their labour and social integration in Italy. This Decree was adopted after the Cutro (Calabria) shipwreck in which at least 90 people, including children, died. In line with previous national restrictive migration and asylum policy and legal reforms, the government's reaction to this tragedy was to increase penalties for facilitating irregular migration and restrict those protection instruments, such as the special protection, that cover a broad spectrum of situations of vulnerability including cases of exploitative working conditions (L'Altro Diritto and FLAI CGIL,

---

[14] As already mentioned, official quantitative data reveal that the total number of migrants entering Italy has stabilised, if not decreased (see Colucci, 2018).

[15] My translation.

[16] See, for instance, Court of Cassation, civil section, decisions no. 4674/1997 and no. 907/1999.

2022). While there is still no data on the impact of this reform, it is likely that the number of individuals in irregular situations will increase.

Those migrant people who manage to arrive in Italy after experiencing violence, abuse, and dangerous travels, and apply for asylum find themselves on a path of uncertainty and limbo (with continuous renewal of the six-month residence permit) that – especially since 2014 – often concludes with a rejection (Sciurba, 2021). This amplifies their situations of vulnerability, exposing asylum seekers to dynamics of abuse and exploitation, especially in those sectors – such as agriculture – particularly prone to irregularity and abusive practices (Corrado & Caruso, 2022).

5.2 Situational Vulnerabilities and Exploitation in the Agricultural Sector

5.2.1 The Migrantisation and Refugeesation of Agricultural Work

For over 30 years, employment in agriculture, especially in Southern Italy, has been one of the main channels to access the informal and undeclared labour market for many migrants (Colloca & Corrado, 2013; Colucci, 2018). Progressively stringent migration and border control policies and the deep-rooted recourse to informal work in agriculture have played a crucial role in the 'respacialisation of migration' (Corrado & Caruso, 2022) towards rural areas and the related occupational segregation of migrant labour in agriculture. Similar to domestic and care work, agricultural work represents one of primary spaces that is 'able to guarantee forms of employment and social reproduction' (ibid, p. 195), albeit in degrading and exploitative conditions.

All this has occurred in a scenario of major transformations and restructuring in Italy's agri-food system within a progressive process of agriculture's defamilisation (Ortiz-Miranda et al., 2013) and capitalist development (Corrado et al., 2016), as also seen in other European countries.

Migrant workers' expanding role in the agricultural sector – described by Molinero-Gerbeau (2020) as the 'migrantisation of agricultural work' – is the result of several factors, including EU enlargement and the 2008 economic crisis that pushed thousands of migrants to turn (and, in many cases, return) to agricultural work (Sacchetto & Vianello, 2013; Colucci, 2018), as well as deficiencies in the entry quota systems and the parallel rise in the number of asylum seekers and refugees from Sub-Saharan Africa and southeast Asia. The latter, as already stressed above, has also shaped a process of agricultural work's 'refugeesation', fostered by the fact that in some regions many asylum reception centres are located in rural areas (Corrado et al., 2018).

Currently, migrant labour in the agri-food sector in Italy entails different nationalities and legal statuses. According to official data of the National Institute for Social

Security (INPS), among EU migrant workers, Romanians continue to be the largest group of farmworkers in Italy, despite the drop in their number especially since the Covid-19 pandemic (Centro studi e ricerche – IDOS, 2023, pp. 291–292; Osservatorio Placido Rizzotto, 2022). The number of non-EU workers has doubled, especially between 2007 and 2020, including Albanians, Moroccans, Indians, Pakistan, Gambians, Nigerians, Senegalese, and Malians (Corrado & Caruso, 2022; see also Centro studi e ricerche – IDOS, 2023). In terms of gender, the elaborations by the Council for Agricultural Research and Economic Analysis (CREA) on official data show that from 2007 to 2017, there was a significant increase in women migrant workers, particularly EU citizens from Romania and Bulgaria (Moschetti & Valentino, 2019; Macrì, 2019). The number has declined since 2019, particularly in the post-pandemic period, as indicated by recent analyses of official data (Di Gregorio & Moffa, 2022). Among non-EU migrant women workers, the main nationalities include Albanians, Moroccans, and Ukrainians (ibid.). In certain rural contexts, like the Ragusa area, Tunisian nationality emerges as another significant component among migrant women working in agriculture (CGIL Ragusa & L'Altro Diritto, 2022).

Although official data provide important indicators of the main trends within the agricultural sector, it cannot accurately depict the reality because of high rates of informality and undeclared work. The estimated rate of irregularity in employment relationships in agriculture is around 39% (Osservatorio Placido Rizzotto FLAI-CGIL, 2022). This particularly involves female migrant labour that tends to be predominantly precarious and grey due to the subordinated roles assigned to women in the family and the social spheres and the consequent conditions of dependence and discrimination (Giammarinaro & Palumbo, 2022).

The presence of migrant women has been significant in Italy's agri-food sector for several decades (Cole, 2007), but their working and living conditions have only recently received attention in the academic sphere and public discourses. In this context, social and legal scholars have sought to bring visibility and complexity to the experiences of women agricultural workers in a male-considered sector, highlighting the systemic nature of exploitation dynamics these women workers often experience (Palumbo & Sciurba, 2018; Giammarinaro, 2022).

5.2.2 Agri-food Restructuring Processes and Value Chain Dynamics

Italy is a top European country for specialised farms, cultivated area, and organic fruit and vegetable production – over one-third of organic fruit orchard farms are found in Italy (34.6%) – and has the second highest number of farms overall, after Romania (Eurostat, 2019).

Since the 1980s, within the dynamics of post-Fordist development and neoliberal globalisation, like other European countries such as Spain, Italy has undergone a major restructuring of its agri-food systems (Corrado et al., 2016). The European Common Agricultural Policy (CAP) supported interventions for modernising agriculture – intensifying production, enlarging scale, adopting chemical inputs, varietal renewal, export orientation, entrepreneurship, and protection from foreign competition, at least until the establishment of the European Single Market in 1993 (Corrado et al., 2018).

Through progressive reforms following World Trade Organisation (WTO) agreements, the CAP has contributed to fostering competitiveness in the EU and global markets. Profit margins and market power in the agricultural sector have been severely weakened by the rapid expansion and concentration of large-scale retail systems. In line with the dynamics of the rearrangement of production processes on a global scale, agri-food supply chains in Italy are buyer-driven, with client companies creating and managing a broad base of selected suppliers on which to build distribution systems.

The process of concentration today is also articulated through the establishment of international super buying centres – that is, alliances between the largest distribution groups aimed at obtaining better contractual conditions through collective negotiation with suppliers. Unlike many other European countries such as the UK, Germany, or Spain national retailers in Italy have survived in a significant manner despite the market's widening penetration by European supermarket chains.[17] The oligopolistic control of prices by these conglomerates through continuous revisions and auctions on the reduction/depreciation of products intensifies pressure on suppliers (Corrado et al., 2018), including through abusive practices,[18] producing an unfair distribution of risks, costs, and profits along supply chains (Oxfam International, 2018).

At the same time, a progressive process of defamilisation of agriculture or family deagrarisation has been matched by the growth of salaried work (Colloca & Corrado, 2013). The recruitment of migrant workers has, on the one hand, helped address these changes, but on the other, has facilitated the capitalist development of the agri-food systems through ongoing intensification, capitalisation, and innovation of production and processing to manage market pressures (Corrado et al., 2016, 2018; see also Lo Cascio & Perrotta, 2022).

With a limited margin to increase prices in wholesale markets, many employers in the agri-food sector tend to squeeze the cost of labour by lowering labourers' working and living conditions, rather than exploring alternative solutions. As Pinto (2019, p. 16) argues, from the farmers' perspective, given a wide availability of a cheap and flexible migrant workforce in situations of vulnerability, an 'alternative strategy for the recovery of productivity, namely the initiation of innovation paths (of product, process or even only in search terms of new markets), it is increasingly complex, more expensive (also in terms of time) and, above all, more risky'.[19] To

[17] It is worth mentioning that, from 1996 to 2001, large food distribution chains doubled their turnover to nearly 100 billion euros, managing to control a 72.4% share of the agri-food market (Federdistribuzione, 2014).

[18] On unfair trading practices by supermarkets, in particular the practice of reverse auction, see Ciconte and Liberti (2019).

[19] My translation.

stay competitive, the recourse to exploitation – long hours, intensified pace, low wages, tax evasion, inadequate accommodations – is for many farmers the more 'convenient' strategy, also facilitated by the specificities of the legal regime regulating this sector.

5.2.3 The Regulation of Seasonal Agricultural Work and Seasonal Migrant Work between Inadequacies, Distortions and Paradoxes

The peculiarities of the Italian legal framework regulating employment and salary conditions in agriculture, which, to some extent, reflect the seasonality and discontinuity of work in this sector, are certainly additional elements that must be considered when analysing the dynamics of exploitation and migrant workers' situational vulnerabilities.

In Italy minimum wage conditions and employment relationships are set out in collective agreements concerning different productive sectors. The structure of collective bargaining in agriculture, which involves trade unions and employers' associations (*associazioni datoriali*), is articulated on national and provincial levels. One of most representative is the 'National Collective agreement for agricultural workers and nursery gardeners' (last reviewed in 2022).[20] Under the national collective agreement (CCNL), workers with a permanent employment contract are paid monthly and for the entire duration of the employment relationship; those in temporary work (including seasonal workers) are paid based on the hours effectively worked during their working days (Art. 45 CCNL). It is then up to the provincial collective agreements to establish contractual wages, delineating tasks and associated professional profiles, as well as their corresponding salaries.

As emerged from my fieldwork and confirmed by official data and other qualitative research (Moschetti & Valentino, 2019; Giammarinaro, 2022; Palumbo, 2022b), the use of temporary employment contracts is widespread in the agricultural sector, especially regarding migrant workers – and in particular migrant women workers (Sect. 5.2.4). This is driven by employers' demand for a labour force in specific geographic and rural areas during particular periods of the year, which, in turn, translates into the need for a temporary, just-in-time, and quick workforce (Corrado et al., 2018). This trend is further supported by 'hyper-flexible regulation' of fixed-term contracts in the agricultural sector (Papa, 2018, p. 247). Under Legislative Decree 375 of 1993 and Law Decree 87 of 2018 – the 'Dignity Decree'[21] – fixed-term, seasonal contracts in agriculture are not subject to legal constraints regarding

[20] *Contratto collettivo nazionale di lavoro per gli operai agricoli e florovivaisti*, 2022–2025.

[21] Legislative Decree No. 375 of 1993 and Law Decree No. 87 of 2018, *Disposizioni urgenti per la dignità dei lavoratori e delle imprese,* the so-called Dignity Decree, was converted into law by Law 96 of 2018.

quantitative limitations on the number of contracts that can be stipulated, maximum duration of extensions, and renewals.[22]

Considering the predominance of short-term contracts in agriculture, this sector is strongly precarious and linked to the 'working day' (Falcone, 2022). This, in turn, clearly has an impact on wages and payment terms. As already underlined, workers with short-term contracts shall be paid for the working hours effectively performed during the working days. In practice, however, many seasonal farmworkers work for around 9–10 hours per day and see only a fraction of the performed working days officially declared by employers, receiving wages significantly below the legal minimum standards. Thus the pay stipulated in the contracts covers only a limited number of hours compared to those actually worked. The real remuneration is often given informally through methods like 'piecework' (*cottimo*) or 'square salary' (*salario di piazza*) – an informal wage lower than what is established by provincial agreements and determined by employers or farmers based on local market conditions (ibid.).

Piecework is used in other European countries, including the UK. Under this practice, workers are paid at a fixed rate for each unit ('piece') they produce or collect. For example, they might be paid based on the number of crates of olives or oranges they fill in a day. In Italy, *cottimo* is regulated by the Civil Code, which obliges employers to pre-emptively communicate information to the employee about constituent elements of the piece rate, the tasks to be performed, and relative payment (Art. 2101, para 3, Civil Code). This provision is limited to imposing an obligation of transparency. The effective regulation of *cottimo* is instead delegated to collective bargaining and, in the case of agriculture, to provincial collective agreements. In many areas, such as Trapani (Sicily) and Nardò (Apulia), a mixture of time-based pay and a piece-rate pay is usually utilised – so-called mixed piecework (*cottimo misto*) (De Martino et al., 2020).

Significantly, the Court of Cassation clarified[23] that, whatever form of piecework is used ('fully piecework' or 'mixed piecework'), remuneration cannot be less than minimum standards in compliance with Art. 36 of the Italian Constitution, according to which workers have the right to a fair remuneration that allows them and their families a free and dignified existence. In practice, however, piecework fosters grey work and exploitative working conditions. It is useful for employers because it incentivises faster work and for longer hours; some workers may also see it as advantageous as they can potentially earn more than an hourly wage as long as they fill a significant number of fruit or vegetable boxes (Lo Cascio & Perrotta, 2019). But this comes at the expense of migrant workers' rights: they toil at an exhausting pace and hours, often without a daily wage and lack adequate labour rights protection, particularly in terms of social security coverage (De Martino et al., 2020).

Such elements – the fixed term seasonal contract, low wages, and related payment modalities – affect workers' situations of vulnerability and their consequent

---

[22] It is worth noting that the last version of the national collective agreement includes some provisions facilitating the conversion from fixed-term contracts to permanent contracts (see Art. 23 of the CCNL) see Falcone (2022).

[23] Court of Cassation, Decision No. 12512/2004, p. 1943.

exposure to dynamics of exploitation. As a trade union member interviewed for this research pointed out: 'the low wages push workers to exceed their contractually stipulated working hours/days, in order to earn what they need to live and support their families. At the same time, the lack of employment stability – tied to the temporary nature of seasonal contracts and, in the case of migrant workers, to the residence permit – makes workers more compliant with employer requests'.[24]

In practice, the ever-present threat of losing permission to stay and work and related difficulty in finding another job within a limited period have a disciplinary effect on migrant workers' behaviour, exacerbating their position of vulnerability.

Furthermore, it is important to consider that, according to the relevant national regulation, seasonal agricultural workers can be hired from 1 January to 31 December of the same year, but employers only officially declare the working days actually performed. In other words, employers officially report employees' working days on a monthly basis after these have been performed.[25] This facilitates undeclared work and extends the temporal dimension of employment relationships indefinitely, resulting in workers being regularly hired for as little as a single day despite having an active employment contract and tasks to complete (Falcone, 2022, p.57).

These dynamics are also linked to the specificities of social security benefits in agriculture. Unemployment benefits in this sector take the form of a sort of compensation for the high seasonality of agricultural production, which necessitates discontinuous work performance. Their purpose is to incentivise workers to stay in the sector (De Martino et al., 2020, pp. 274–275). Unlike other sectors, unemployment benefits in agriculture are not subordinated to any job search obligation. Agricultural workers can access unemployment benefits without regard to their current employment or unemployment status at the time they apply for and receive these benefits. Eligibility criteria for applying include having at least 2 years of insurance coverage in the sector and a minimum of 102 effective working days (in a 2-year period).

The relative accessibility of unemployment benefits in agriculture makes these benefits particularly exposed to abusive and illegal practices such as 'fake farmworkers' (*finti braccianti*). Under this practice, which often involves criminal actors and organisations, 'fake workers' (primarily nationals) pay employers/farms to be registered as employees, thereby gaining access to unemployment benefits. In reality, the working days of these 'fake workers' are performed mainly by non-EU migrant workers who, due to various status-related reasons, often find themselves ineligible for unemployment benefits. These include migrant workers without a residence permit but also, for instance, regular non-EU migrant seasonal workers.

In this regard, it is worth noting that aside from not having access to family reunification in accordance with Seasonal Workers Directive 2014/36/EU, non-EU migrant seasonal workers in Italy are also excluded from family and unemployment

[24] Interview with R. Falcone, Flai-CGIL, June 2020.

[25] Until January 2019, employers were required to submit a form to the National Institute for Social Security (INPS) every 3 months, declaring the working days performed by workers. This has changed, and employers must now declare monthly the working days performed by the farmworkers.

benefits (Art. 25 Consolidated Act on Immigration). As highlighted from several testimonies collected during the fieldwork, this exclusion is not only critical in terms of protection of the principle of equal treatment (McBritton, 2017) but also plays a distorting role, as seasonal migrant workers lack motivation to avoid forms of irregularity. Indeed, apart from the requirement of working a minimum number of days (i.e., 34 working days) to be eligible for a residence permit for seasonal work, workers have no real incentive to encourage employers to accurately report the actual number of working days they have performed. As a result, the exclusion from unemployment benefits encourages the involvement of seasonal migrant workers in grey conditions (with a regular contract but in which the number of working days does not correspond to that of the working days effectively performed), undeclared wage payments, and in abusive practices such 'fake farmworkers'.

This differs for asylum seekers. Although the National Institute for Social Security (INPS) argued that asylum seekers employed in agriculture with a fixed-term contract cannot access unemployment benefits, this was rejected by two recent decisions of the Tribunal of Foggia (Labour Section) in Southen Italy.[26] The Tribunal censured the erroneous overlap made by the INPS between seasonal work permits and 'permits with a duration of less than nine months' (including asylum seeker residence permits, also considered 'short permits'). It clarified that, regardless of the duration and supposed 'shortness' of the residence permits, only seasonal work permits are not covered by unemployment and family benefits (according to Article 25 (1 and 2), Consolidated Act on Immigration). Therefore, residence permits for asylum requests (regulated by Legislative Decree 142/2015) allow access to such forms of income support. Both decisions significantly challenge discriminatory practices (even indirect) by institutions such as the INPS that amplify situations of vulnerability. By recognising asylum seekers' right to access to welfare measures and, consequently, protecting asylum seekers' social reproductive dimension, these decisions have strengthened migrants' bargaining power.

It is important here to underline that, as already mentioned in Chap. 3, asylum seekers hosted in reception centres cannot have an income higher than the annual social allowance (currently around 6,947.33 euros), otherwise they are denied admission to reception measures (such as accommodation, meals, and pocket money of roughly 2.50 euros per day). However, this provision induces many asylum seekers to accept situations of contractual irregularity, especially when there is a pressing need to financially support their families and, in many cases, to send remittances to their family in the country of origin (L'Altro Diritto & FlaiCGIL, 2022). On the other hand, the employment of asylum seekers hosted in reception centres allows employers to reduce the reproduction costs of the labour force as the costs of workers' accommodation are covered by the asylum reception system. This encourages irregularities and, at the same time, an outsourcing of labour force reproduction costs, which, by shifting from the employers/businesses to the reception system do not burden the production chain, for instance, of the agricultural sector (Palumbo, 2022b).

[26] See Tribunal of Foggia, Decision No. 754/2022, 23 February 2022 and Decision of 8 September 2021.

5.2.4 Migrant Women Employed in the Agricultural Sector: The Case of Ragusa

As underlined in the earlier sections, continuous intensification, capitalisation, and innovation of agri-food production and processing has shaped a low-wage, flexible, and exploitable migrant labour force to cope with market and price pressures from large retail groups (Corrado et al., 2016). This system has been facilitated by agricultural work's features such as seasonality and the sector's historical characterisation by weak labour regulations and high rates of irregularity. At the same time, this system takes advantage of the different situations of vulnerability of migrant workers and related weak bargaining power, which are also produced by the inconsistencies of relevant national legislation, policies, and related practices in the field of migration, labour, and social rights. By adopting a gender and intersectional perspective, this section delves into migrant farmworkers situational vulnerabilities to exploitation, centring on the living and working conditions of women migrant farmworkers, with a particular focus on migrant women employed in the greenhouses of Ragusa.

5.2.4.1 Living and Working Conditions in Greenhouses

The case of farmworkers employed in the greenhouses of Ragusa typifies the dynamics of processes characterising both the agri-food sector and the migration composition in Italy over the last 30 years as well as the dynamics of exploitation experienced by migrant farmworkers.

Beginning in the late 1960s, the agricultural area in Ragusa has been marked by a conversion from seasonal production to a permanent cultivation, primarily through the greenhouse system (Aiello, 1987; Bellassai & Scillieri, 2000). Hence, it is referred to as the 'Transformed Area' of Ragusa.[27] This transformation has led, particularly since the mid-1980s, to the recruitment of a migrant labour force recognised for its permanence. This is in contrast to other Italian agricultural contexts where many migrant laborers – especially before the significant employment of asylum seekers residing in reception centres – typically stay temporarily in the work areas and then relocate to other regions according to the requirements of seasonal production (Corrado et al., 2018).

The permanency dimension of migrant farm labour in Ragusa has shaped a systemic organisation of employment relationships, with many employers/companies providing migrant workers and their families with accommodation. However, living conditions are often left inadequate and degrading so as to contain workers' reproduction costs (Palumbo, 2022a, b). Such a systemic organisation of labour relations

[27] The 'Transformed Area' encompasses the rural area in the Province of Ragusa, including the municipalities of Acate, Vittoria, Santa Croce Camerina, Comiso, and Scoglitti.

has taken place especially with 'the massive arrival of Romanian workers'.[28] Indeed, while in the past the migrant workers employed in the greenhouses of Ragusa were mainly Tunisians (Cole, 2007), since the early 2000s, and especially after 2007 with Romania's accession to the EU, there has been a significant increase in both men and women Romanian farmworkers, peaking around 2016–2017 (Palumbo & Sciurba, 2018; Sanò, 2018).[29]

From the outset, Romanian workers have been paid less than Tunisians, who are more skilled in the sector, more unionised, and have been in the area longer, creating solid relationships with local people. Furthermore, having the opportunity to move freely within the EU, most Romanians tend to see their migration project as a temporary experience, thus becoming competitive in terms of wages and contractual conditions. This leads them to 'accept' substandard and even abusive working conditions as their aim is to collect money to be sent back home and return there soon. Additionally, the irregular employment of EU migrant workers is less risky for employers as it is not in itself subject to criminal sanctions unlike the employment of undocumented non-EU workers, which is prohibited by Art. 22 of the Consolidated Act of Immigration, in accordance with the Employer Sanctions Directive.

Another distinctive feature of Ragusa is the significant presence of women migrant workers, primarily Romanians employed in agriculture (Pitti & D'Amanti, 2010; Palumbo & Sciurba, 2018). Historically women workers have been present in some segments of the agricultural sector in the area, in particular vegetable, plant, or flower cultivation in nurseries or fruit and vegetable packaging. However, it is mainly with the arrival of Romanian migrants that women began working as farmworkers in greenhouses.

The increase in Romanian farmworkers has also seen more workers from the Roma Romanian community. Within the racialised and gendered hierarchy of exploitation, they most often endure the harshest conditions due to prejudice and practices of stigmatisation that continue to significantly impact this ethnic minority (D'Agostino, 2018; Mantovan, 2021; Palumbo, 2022b).

According to the latest INPS data, the approximately 5200 agricultural companies within the 'Transformed Area' employ 28,778 male and female workers: 14,772 are Italian and 14,006 are migrants (CGIL Ragusa & L'Altro Diritto, 2022). Given the significant prevalence of temporary and irregular/grey employment in this sector, these figures would be considerably higher if undeclared work was included. Among migrant workers Tunisians (5307) rank first, followed by Romanians (2632) and Albanians (2558). In line with data cited above, these estimates also reveal that in recent years, especially after the Covid-19 pandemic, there has been a roughly 40% drop in the number of EU workers, particularly Romanians (ibid.). As already noted, a key reason is that many EU migrant workers opt to seek better living and working conditions in other European countries such as Germany.

---

[28] Interview with Giuseppe Scifo, General Secretary of the Ragusa Trade Union CGIL, October 2019, Ragusa.

[29] For instance, official data for 2107 revealed that in the Vittoria area there were 1791 Romanian workers while the number of Tunisians was 1586 (EBAT-Ragusa, 2017).

These data highlight the significant presence of Albanian, Algerian, and Moroccan workers, as well as workers from Sub-Saharan (Senegal, Gambia, Nigeria) and Asian countries (Bangladesh and India) (CGIL Ragusa and L'Altro Diritto, 2022). The presence of workers from Sub-Saharan and Asian countries – a novelty for the region – is linked to the 'widespread network of reception accommodation for asylum seekers in the province of Ragusa, largely connected to the hotspot in Pozzallo (Ragusa)' (ibid.). The data confirms the 'refugeesation' (Dines & Rigo, 2015) and widespread employment of asylum seekers in Italian agriculture. As a recent study emphasised, asylum seekers represent the 'perfect victims of labour exploitation: they are people with regular residence status in the territory, with whom contracts can be made, but at the same time, they have a fragile legal and social status' (L'Altro Diritto & FlaiCGIL, 2022).

Despite these changes in the composition of the migrant workforce employed in the greenhouses of the 'Transformed Area', the presence of migrant women workers, especially Romanian, remains significant. Indeed, the data reveals that in 2021 there were 2081 migrant women agricultural workers in the Ragusa area; the largest group were Romanians, followed by Tunisians and Albanians (CGIL Ragusa and L'Altro Diritto, 2022).

5.2.4.2 Salary Disparities, Irregularities, and Denied Rights

Specific elements characterise the working and living conditions of women agricultural workers and, consequently, the dynamics of exploitation to which they are subjected. Foremost is the issue of wages. Women agricultural workers, especially women migrant workers, are often paid less. As emerged from the fieldwork, women farmworkers may earn 30–35 euros per day while men farmworkers are paid 40–45 euros.

As Giammarinaro (2022) underlines, gender salary disparity is an element emerging in many rural areas of the country. Stereotypical conceptions of women's skills, physical strength, and attitudes are used to justify such gender wage inequalities. As a social worker told me: 'women farmworkers often earn less than men, also because it is assumed that, given the physically demanding nature of agricultural work, women may have more difficulty in performing it, and, as a result, they are paid lower wages'.[30] But a migrant female farmworker employed in a local agricultural company emphasised that 'the women work as hard as the men'[31] in the greenhouses, usually for 9–10 hours a day, enduring high temperatures in the summer and low temperatures in the winter, inhaling pesticides for very low wages, and living in run-down housing (Palumbo & Sciurba, 2018; Piro, 2020).

The prevalence of temporary and irregular work in the agricultural sector is especially evident in the case of migrant female labour which, also due to the roles

[30] Interview with Michele Mililli, Proxima Association, February 2023, Ragusa.

[31] Interview with a woman migrant farmworker, June 2018, Ragusa.

assigned to women in the family and social spheres and the resulting conditions of dependence and discrimination, tends to be particularly precarious and informal (Palumbo, 2022a, b). According to official INPS data, the predominant contract type in agriculture is fixed term, especially among women agricultural workers. In 2019, for example, this type of contract applied to 90.2% of men and 95.8% of women (Giammarinaro, 2022). Furthermore, as seen in the same data and confirmed by the collected testimonies, it is not uncommon for migrant women agricultural workers to have a fixed-term contract with fewer than 51 annual recorded workdays or 102 recorded workdays over two years (Moschetti & Valentino, 2019). It follows that many women migrant workers are excluded from accessing various welfare measures such as agricultural unemployment benefits[32] and maternity allowances that are guaranteed only to those workers with contracts exceeding 51 working days per year.

It is worth also noting that according to the national Consolidated Act on maternity and paternity (Legislative Decree 151/2001), seasonal agricultural workers can obtain a maternity benefit when, in either the year of the request or in the previous year, they have officially worked at least 51 working days. This benefit provided by the INPS is equal to 80% of the last salary received by the worker and therefore depends on the number of working days declared in that month. Considering that the practice of under-declaring working days is widespread and that in contexts such as the Ragusa greenhouses there is a tendency to declare an average of 10 days per month, it is clear how significantly this impacts maternity benefit levels, compressing the reproductive rights of women workers and their protection. From my fieldwork in Ragusa, cases have emerged of women farmworkers who, driven by the need to earn money to support their families, work at exhausting paces until the day before giving birth. Similar situations have emerged in other rural areas of Italy (ActionAid Italia, 2022; Omizzolo, 2021).

Certainly, these difficulties are exacerbated in the case of women who work in conditions of totally irregularity, including those EU migrant women who have not registered their residence within three months of their arrival in Italy as required by Legislative Decree 30/2007, transposing Directive 38/2004/EU. This is illustrated by one of the cases that I became aware of during my fieldwork, involving an 18-year-old Romanian girl working in the Ragusa greenhouses without an employment contract throughout her pregnancy. As a social worker from an anti-trafficking centre who assisted this girl and her baby pointed out, ‘in addition to not having a contract, the girl did not have a residence, and therefore, she did not have a doctor. Thus, in nine months, she never had any medical check-ups or visits. She only went to the hospital when she gave birth’.[33]

[32] It’s worth noting that here we are discussing migrant women workers in regular conditions, either as EU citizens or non-EU migrant workers with a residence permit, excluding those who have a residence permit for seasonal work. As mentioned earlier, migrant workers with a seasonal work permit do not have access to unemployment benefits.

[33] Interview with Michele Mililli, Proxima Association, April 2022, Ragusa.

Migrant women farmworkers' difficulties in accessing gynaecological services and assistance are a crucial issue that emerged clearly during the fieldwork. These include limited reception hours at the few (public) gynaecological clinics in rural areas. As a social worker stressed during the interview, 'migrant farmworkers are often unaware of their rights and the limited available services. Additionally, they face challenges in accessing these services because they reside in areas not served by public transportation, and, in many cases, they do not have their own vehicles'.[34]

Among doctors there is also a high number of 'conscientious objectors' who refuse – for personal or religious reasons – to perform voluntary abortion.[35] This forces many women to turn to private doctors, paying large sums of money. Those who rely instead on the public health service often face long waiting times, with the risk of exceeding the limit of 90-days of gestation established by Law 194/1978 for voluntary termination of pregnancy. Some women return to their home countries, such as Romania, to have an abortion in a hospital; others resort to unsafe methods for clandestine abortions, endangering their own health and that of the unborn (Giammarinaro & Palumbo, 2022; ActionAid Italia, 2022).

5.2.4.3 Worker Mothers, Reproductive Work, and the Presence of Minors in Rural Areas

The burden of reproductive work, in particular of family and care responsibilities, significantly affects living and working conditions of women workers, both locals and migrants, employed in the agricultural sector. For migrant women (both EU and non-EU citizen migrants), this burden is exacerbated by the lower wages, poor accommodation, and lack of solid social and family networks.

In some cases, women agricultural workers migrate with their husband or partner, leaving their children with family in their country of origin, or travel alone while the whole family stays at home. In other situations – for example many Romanian, Bulgarian, or Albanian women – female workers move with the entire family nucleus, which includes their children, and often 'choose' to work in agriculture rather than the domestic sector to keep the children with them (Palumbo & Sciurba, 2018). When they emigrate alone, female workers often have an urgent need to send their wages to the country of origin to support their children or dependent family members. On the other hand, when they bring their children with them, they face difficulties associated with reconciling work and care. In both cases, the burden of these responsibilities places women under significant pressure, creating or exacerbating their situations of vulnerability to discrimination, exploitation, and

[34] Interview with a social worker, January 2023, Ragusa.

[35] It is worth underlining that, according to Law 194 of 1978, abortion is available for free in the first 90 days of pregnancy. After the first trimester, abortion is only allowed if there's a risk to the mother's health or if there are fetal anomalies. However, while it is legal, actually getting the procedure can be difficult because there are few doctors who perform it. See Mattalucci and De Zordo (2022).

gender-based violence and abuse by employers and illegal labour intermediaries, often referred to as '*caporali*' (Palumbo, 2022a, b; ActionAid Italia, 2022).

For migrant women who arrived in Italy with their entire family, the burden of reproductive and care work is intertwined with housing and transportation. In Ragusa many migrant farmworkers live in sub-standard accommodation – sometimes lacking basic services such as electricity and water – near the greenhouses in isolated areas far from urban centres. These degrading living conditions are part of a production system based on the reduction of the reproduction costs of workers (Rigo, 2022). This, in turn, enables abusive employers and illegal intermediaries to profit from expenses related to transportation or water and to use access to essential goods and services as a tool to blackmail workers (Palumbo & Sciurba, 2018). It should be emphasised that this system is facilitated by the absence – in Ragusa as well as many other rural regions – of effective institutional interventions aimed at ensuring and supporting access to suitable housing and transportation for migrant workers (Corrado et al., 2018). This is aggravated by the rise of racist attitudes and discrimination that make it difficult, and in some contexts impossible, for migrant individuals to access decent housing (Caruso & Corrado, 2022; ANSA, 2022).

In some cases, especially in the case of Romanian and Bulgarian women, the lack of welfare services, including childcare and adolescent support, is offset by the care activities provided by elderly migrant women within the family unit (mothers, mothers-in-law, aunts) who come to Italy to assist with the children while the mothers work late in the countryside. Sometimes more closed family care chains come into play, where brothers, and more frequently older sisters, do not attend school and instead stay at home to care for younger siblings while the parents are working in the fields. In other cases, as one of the migrant women interviewed said, 'women workers pay other migrant women, some without adequate training, to take care of their children'.[36] Some bring their children to their workplaces and are 'forced to keep them in the car while they work',[37] while others, out of desperation, lock the door and leave their children alone until the end of the day. The criteria often used by relevant institutions to assess the parenting capabilities of migrant women do not take into account the situations of vulnerability in which these workers find themselves, the constraints they face, and the burden of family responsibilities they must bear.

All these factors expose women to anxiety and stress, as well as cause significant school absenteeism in rural areas (Giammarinaro & Palumbo, 2022); thousands of minors in the Ragusa area do not attend school because their parents lack the means to take them or there is no public transport (Palumbo & Sciurba, 2018). Many of these minors (aged 13–17), when not taking care of younger siblings, also work as farmworkers to contribute to the family income. Emblematic in this regard is the story collected during the fieldwork regarding a young woman who grew up living

[36] Interview with a woman migrant farmworker, March 2021, Ragusa.

[37] Interview with Michele Mililli from the anti-trafficking organisation Proxima Association, based in Ragusa, April 2022.

in degrading conditions in the greenhouses of Ragusa taking care of her younger siblings instead of going to school. At the age of 15 she too began to work in the fields to contribute to the family's subsistence. As one of the social workers interviewed underlined, 'minors are often used to apply pesticides or chemical products to the plants because they have small hands and don't damage the leaves. However, these products are highly aggressive and harmful, and the minors have never used any type of protection, such as masks or gloves'.[38]

In a context of degradation and exploitation structurally permeated by patriarchal values and discrimination mechanisms, the burden of reproductive work and family responsibilities thus creates and amplifies the situations of vulnerability of migrant women farmworkers, also exposing minors to living conditions marked by isolation, invisibility, abuses, and violence, including gender violence, as discussed in Sect. 5.4.

On the other hand, the presence of minors and consequent family and care responsibilities are also a factor contributing to the resilience of many women, prompting them to oppose abuse and abandon situations of exploitation. Moreover, the care and protection of the psychophysical well-being of the minor can constitute, when certain conditions exist, an element that allows non-EU migrant women to undertake a regularisation path pursuant to Art. 31 of the Consolidated Act on Immigration. This residence permit, which provides for the possibility to carry out a work activity, can be issued to a parent or relative of a child, when it is demonstrated, for example, that the minor is monitored by a paediatrician, is enrolled in school, and has an emotional bond with a parent or family member such as to believe that the presence and closeness of this parent/family member responds to the child's best interest. In the 'Transformed Area' of Ragusa, there have been several cases of Albanian women farmworkers who have obtained a residence permit under Art. 31. That minors' school education is one of the conditions for obtaining the permit means that mothers and children must live in urban centres, therefore in less isolated and marginalised contexts (Giammarinaro & Palumbo, 2022).

As discussed in the next sections, similar dynamics concerning the intertwining of work and living spaces – and the consequent compression of the reproductive dimension of female workers along with the related pressures on family responsibilities – occur in the domestic and care sector, playing a fundamental role in amplifying the situational vulnerabilities of these workers.

[38] Interview with Michele Mililli from the anti-trafficking organization Proxima Association, based in Ragusa, April 2022.

5.3 Situational Vulnerabilities and Exploitation in the Care and Domestic Work Sector

In a labour market highly segmented by gender, nationality, and class axes, the agricultural sector serves as one of the main available sectors for 'low-skilled' migrant workers, including migrant women, with different legal statuses. Similar observations apply to the domestic and care work sector, particularly concerning women migrant workers employed in this field.

By examining immigration trends in Italy, historian Michele Colucci (2018, p. 198) revealed Italian households as representing the primary 'place where we can observe the deep relationship between social transformation and immigration'. After the Second World War, domestic and care work, especially with regard to childcare, began to be carried out by migrant women workers (Gissi, 2018). This presence progressively changed in size and composition, especially since the 1980s, with migrant workers also performing care activities for elderly and dependent people and becoming an essential component of the Italian 'familistic' welfare system (Sarti, 2013; Gissi, 2018).

Regularly-employed domestic workers almost quintupled in the last 30 years (ISMU, 2021), with some 961,358 people officially registered in 2021 as employed in domestic and care work according to recent INPS data (Osservatorio Domina sul lavoro domestico, 2022).

Domestic and care work is a highly feminised and migrantised sector: 84.9% of workers are women and 70% are migrant workers, chiefly from eastern Europe (Romania, Ukraine, Moldova, and Albania), Asia (Philippines, Sri Lanka, and India), and Latin America (such as Peru, Ecuador). Despite the significance of these estimates, accurate data are however difficult to obtain due to the high degree of undeclared work in this sector. Recent official figures show that the share of irregular work in domestic/care work is around 52.3% (Osservatorio Domina sul lavoro domestico, 2022).

The extensive employment of migrant workers in the domestic and care work sector, often in substandard and exploitative conditions, needs to be read in a broad frame that takes into account the loopholes in welfare policies, the general undervaluation of care-giving work, the related specific regulatory regime on domestic/care work, and the inconsistencies of national policies on migration and labour mobility.

5.3.1 The Familistic- and Migrant Worker-Based Model of Care

Feminist critical theories have highlighted how reproductive work, including domestic and care work, has traditionally been undervalued as a public and political issue and also as labour (Picchio, 1992; Saraceno, 2007). In particular, Italian materialist feminist scholars have stressed the essential role of devaluation of reproductive work, traditionally performed by women, in the development of the capitalist system as it allows for the containment of the costs of labour (Picchio, 1992; Fortunati, 1981; Del Re, 2020).

The devaluation of reproductive work has found support, and is simultaneously reflected, in the familistic organisation of the Italian welfare regime. As Silvia Borelli (2021, p. 287) writes, 'capital has then achieved a second victory: by shifting the burden of care from the state to individual families, public spending, and consequently, the tax burden are effectively contained'.[39]

Indeed, the Italian welfare model typically delegates to families, especially to women, the main role of providing care to family members who need assistance (Saraceno, 2007; Da Roit & Sabatinelli, 2005; Sarti, 2013). The state provides households with modest monetary transfers rather than efficient childcare and care in-kind services. Care is viewed, indeed, as a family issue, whose burden, according to a male breadwinner model, is mainly on women's shoulders. As Busi (2020) argues, this welfare model developed on the principle of 'conciliation' between family and work time, without ever questioning its strong gender connotation. Moreover, state supports in the form of cash benefits and exiguous care allowances provided at the local level do not cover the costs of private care. In addition to being insufficient, these monetised measures have been introduced without also providing structured and long-term care services (Casalini, 2017).

These social and economic factors have intersected with the increase in feminised migratory movements to and within Europe (especially since the first decade of 2000), resulting in a particularly intense form of commodification of care through a cheap and flexible female migrant labour force (Vianello, 2009; Sciurba, 2015). As feminist scholars have pointed out, this has led to a transition from a 'family model of care' to a 'migrant in the family model of care' in which (women) migrant workers have 'met unsatisfied needs for care while ensuring the continuity of a family-based long term care model' (Bettio et al., 2006, p. 278). The migrant-in-the-family model is a 'cost-effective solution' leading to significant savings in public spending while allowing households to maintain 'a gendered division of tasks, as well as to save money' (Farris & Marchetti, 2017, p. 121; Sarti, 2022). This all comes at the expense of migrant workers in terms of working conditions and protection of rights where gender asymmetries intertwine with class-, nationality-, race- and ethnicity-related inequalities, perpetuating the devaluation of domestic and care work (Sciurba, 2015).

The process of commodification of care work and employment of migrant domestic workers has occurred in many European countries with diverse welfare regimes, including the UK liberal welfare regime (Van Hooren, 2012). The peculiarity of the Italian case is the widespread delegation of elderly care to migrant workers, resulting in the common use of the derogatory term '*badante*' to refer to migrant workers assisting elderly or dependent people in private houses. Indeed, the Italian model entails an unusual recourse to low-paid and flexible domestic and care work by households with different economic, social, and cultural backgrounds, including

[39] My translation.

many families that in the past could not have afforded to be employers. As legal scholar Silvia Borelli (2021, p. 286) notes, in this do-it-yourself model of welfare 'the degree of satisfaction with care work depends mainly on the cost of care work. The lower the cost of labour, the more families will be able to access it'.[40]

Italian migration policies have played a crucial role, not without contradictions, in sustaining the growing presence of migrant workers in the domestic and care sector and, consequently, in making migrant domestic workers (especially migrant women) a fundamental resource for the Italian 'familistic' welfare system (Colucci, 2018; Sarti, 2013). In particular, from 2005 to 2011 and then again in 2023, the Flows Decree system has paid special attention to domestic work, setting specific quotas for domestic workers (Castagnone et al., 2013).

However, the inadequacies and limits of the Flows Decree system – particularly with regard to the mechanism of long-distance matching between job demand and supply – have clearly emerged in the case of care/domestic work. In addition to the difficulties associated with lengthy and complex bureaucratic procedures, many employers of care and domestic workers are not willing to hire a person whom they have not met, especially when they would be sharing their home with them (Ambrosini, 2013). Many thus opt to employ migrant workers already in Italy, including irregular migrants trying to regularise their status afterwards, for instance, through regularisation/amnesty for undocumented workers (see Sect. 5.1.2). Moreover, the reduction, especially from 2012 to 2022, in annual quotas for non-seasonal workers, has particularly hit the domestic and care sector, limiting possibilities – apart from a few exceptions – to regularly migrate to Italy to work in this sector.

On the other hand, given the extent of irregular migrant employment in domestic work and the essential roles played by migrant workers in this sector, domestic and care workers have been among the main beneficiaries of the regularisation schemes adopted by the Italian government over the last decades (in particular, in 2002, 2009, 2012, and lastly in 2020 in connection to the pandemic crisis), disclosing the significant dependence of Italian families on migrant labour. As discussed in Chap. 7, this emerged clearly during the 2020 regularisation scheme applying to care/domestic work and agri-food sectors during the pandemic (Corrado & Palumbo, 2022; Caprioglio & Rigo, 2020).

5.3.2 The Regulatory Framework of Domestic and Care Work: Exceptions and Limited Protection

In a relevant essay on housework and family law exceptionalism,[41] legal scholar Maria Rosaria Marella (2008, 2018) underlined that in both civil law and common law systems housework is dominated by the principle of solidarity – gratuitousness (in both legitimate family and in the context of unmarried couples). As Marella

[40] My translation.

[41] On the concept of family exceptionalism see also Halley and Rittich (2010).

(2018, p. 298) pointed out: 'housework has a legal – albeit limited – significance, but only within the logic of family law exceptionalism. This means that the rationale of market is rejected in this case, in the name of solidarity, which is conceived as the ultimate foundation of family relations'. Such a framing of housework as a bulwark of family law exceptionalism, according to Marella, is a tolerated residuum of a patriarchal model relying on a gendered division between productive and reproductive work.

In line with Marella's analysis, influences of a family law exceptionalism (Halley & Rittich, 2010) can also be found in the Italian legal regime covering paid domestic and care work. Indeed, as social political scholar Alisa Del Re (2020, p. 39) argues, the fact that care and domestic work has entered the market, is paid, and often contracted does not save it from 'the breadth and the quality of the tasks that are required, often indefinite and linked to forms of implied affectivities that are impossible to regulated in a contract'.[42] The persistent hierarchical separation between productive work – socially associated with men and governed by market logics – and reproductive work – socially assigned to women and excluded from market relations – is reflected in the weak status of domestic and care work. This has contributed to an exceptional regulatory framework for (paid) domestic and care work, 'where the "workers' rights", shaped by the political and union culture around the factory worker during the Fordist era, have found limited application'[43] (Busi, 2020, p. 14).

More specifically, in Italy domestic and care work is regulated by the provisions contained in Articles 2240 and 2246 of 1942 Civil Code and Law 339/1958 on the protection of domestic work.[44] The choice of including the provisions concerning domestic work under the section of the Civil Code entitled 'subordinated work in particular relationships' has consecrated domestic work relationships as different with respect to other employment relationships (Suardi, 2016, p. 247). Such a conception of domestic work can also be found in Law 339/1958. This law introduced a regulation of employment relationships in paid domestic and care work, establishing the rights and duties of workers and employers and defining labour standards and conditions. It applies to workers who perform domestic and care work for at least 4 hours per day for the same employer. However, although it marked a fundamental step forward in the recognition and protection of the rights of domestic and care workers, Law 339/1958 relies on a conception of domestic work as differing from other employment: it excludes domestic workers from enjoying many rights with respect to important issues such as maternity leave, illness, and occupational safety and health and does not establish the maximum duration of the working day (Borelli, 2021; Sarti, 2022).

The First National Collective Agreement for domestic workers was signed in 1974 after an important ruling by the Constitutional Court of 1969 No. 98

[42] My translation.

[43] My translation.

[44] Law 339 of 2 April 1958, *Per la tutela del rapporto di lavoro domestico*.

abolishing the ban on collective bargaining in this sector as provided by Art. 2068 of the Civil Code. Since then, collective bargaining has integrated relevant national legislation, providing a framework of rights and protections within the domestic work relationship and representing the main source of the sector's regulation. The main national collective agreement for domestic workers, Contratto Collettivo Nazionale del Lavoro Domestico CCNL, has been renewed several times, most recently in 2023.

In 2013, Italy ratified ILO Convention No. 189 on decent working conditions for domestic workers. By doing so, the country committed itself to guaranteeing domestic and care workers decent work and to equating their protections with those enjoyed by the workers in other sectors (Marchetti et al., 2021). Yet, despite this important normative development, there are several aspects that limit full protection of the rights for this category of workers (Basenghi, 2010; Borelli, 2021). For example, domestic and care workers have limited social security protections and have no sickness allowance, which is covered by the employer only for a limited period (Art. 27 CCNL).[45] Furthermore, maternity is partially protected, as it is limited to prohibiting women from working during the mandatory leave period. It also prohibits their dismissal from the beginning of pregnancy until the end of the mandatory leave, provided that conception occurred during the work relationship (Art. 25 CCNL). Furthermore, domestic and care workers can be dismissed without just cause or justified reasons.[46]

The legal regime on paid domestic/care sector is a 'sort of "world in itself" where many of the normal rules governing the dynamics of the [employment] relationship are weakened if not, even, sterilised'[47] (Basenghi, 2010, p. 208). Such an exceptional legal regime relies on a 'subtractive logic' (Basenghi, 2010; Borelli, 2021) that prevents domestic and care workers from some protection and rights, determining an inequality of treatment compared to other types of workers and an infringement of fundamental rights, such as for example health protection (Maioni & Zucca, 2016).

A subtractive logic also influences the national regulation regarding seasonal workers whose protection, as discussed in Sect. 5.2, is weakened compared to those of workers in other sectors. While the special legal regime governing agricultural/seasonal work is tied to its seasonal and related temporary nature – which is accentuated when it involves migrant seasonal workers – the special legal regime in the case of care and domestic work is primarily connected to the distinctive nature of

---

[45] Sick pay is covered by the employer, not the INPS (National Social Security Institute). To improve social and health protection for domestic workers, the 'Cassa Colf' (Domestic Workers Fund) was established. This fund is the instrument created by the National Collective Labour Agreement for Domestic Work to provide benefits and services for registered workers and employers.

[46] In the contract of domestic workers, dismissal *ad nutum* is allowed, i.e., a just cause for dismissal is not necessary. The employers must give a notice of dismissal; if not, there is provision for compensation.

[47] My translation.

the domestic and care work relationship. This occurs in the homes of employers and, therefore, within the private sphere of a family – an 'environment' typically considered outside the standard business and market logic (Marella, 2018).

In both cases, especially when involving migrant workers, the specific regulations governing domestic/care work and agricultural work contribute to a process that, as Rigo (2022, p. 81) argues, assigns migrants to hierarchical regimes, not only of labour relations but of the reproduction of life itself. This, in turn, generates and amplifies migrant workers' situational vulnerabilities, exposing them to dynamics of abuse and exploitation that also rely on the compression of workers' costs of reproduction.

The shortcomings in the legal regimes of sectors such as domestic work and seasonal agricultural work came to the fore during the Covid-19 health emergency. In practice, the 'weak' legal status of these workers obstructed them from accessing social and labour rights protection and participating in social welfare programmes, including income support measures (Giammarinaro & Palumbo, 2020; Sarti, 2022). However, the first pandemic Decree adopted by the Italian government in March 2020, known as '*Cura Italia*' (Care for Italy),[48] containing the financial support package for crisis-affected workers did not cover, paradoxically, domestic and care workers. A subsequent Decree, No. 34/2020 converted into Law No. 77 of 17 July 2020, provided for some protections covering also domestic and care workers (Article 85) and for a regularisation scheme for migrant workers in conditions of irregularity in the agriculture and domestic and care work sectors (Article 103).

5.3.3 Being a Worker in a Private Family Setting

Domestic and care work is a low-paying and demanding occupation (Borelli, 2021) in which most migrants engage in the absence of better job opportunities. In this context, the features of domestic/care work, in particular the peculiar interpersonal relationship between employers and domestic/care workers, play a significant role. On the one hand, employers can be an important resource for domestic and care workers (Ambrosini, 2013) as they may provide them food, accommodation – even if often substandard – as well as help and a place to hide, especially in the case of undocumented workers. In this sense, domestic and care work – similarly to the agricultural sector – constitutes a sector where migrants in situations of vulnerability can seek 'refuge'.

On the other hand, the devaluation of this work and some inherent aspects of this sector, especially in the case of live-in work, may foster the violation of labour rights, and various forms of exploitation (Sciurba, 2015; Palumbo, 2017; Maioni, 2022). These aspects include the overlap between employment and family relations and the high levels of intimacy and proximity.

[48] Law-Decree No. 18 of 17 March 2020.

Testimonies collected during fieldwork are confirmed by the literature (Nare, 2013; Sarti, 2010): employers of domestic/care workers seldom perceive themselves as such. Unlike entrepreneurs or company owners, employers of domestic/care workers do not make any profit. They often do not know their rights and duties and are not familiar with managerial issues of hiring and supervising (Triandafyllidou & Marchetti, 2015). This also leads many households to turn to organisations or agencies, including informal and illegal ones, to hire domestic and care workers 'escaping in this way the management of employment relationships'.[49] These intermediaries, as underlined in Sect. 5.4, play a crucial role in dynamics of exploitation.

In her study exploring the demand for migrant workers in domestic work, migration scholar Bridget Anderson (2007, p. 254) pointed out that the 'foreignness' of migrant workers can help 'employers and host families manage their deep discomfort around the introduction of market relations into the home'. The perception of migrants as inherently different helps families set boundaries and manage power within the domestic sphere as they do not identify with migrant workers who are seen as 'naturally' inclined toward these jobs (Nare, 2013). However, for many employers 'foreignness' has to fit into categories considered culturally 'acceptable'; for instance, as emerged from the fieldwork, there is a preference for White Christian workers and more reluctance to employ Black Africans. Social stereotypes and prejudices significantly affect employers' preference for a particular nationality (Anderson, 2007).

Therefore, only those migrants who have particular characteristics can make their way into the Italian household. By dressing up their power with paternalistic/maternalistic attitudes, many employers refer to the worker as 'one of the family' (Nare, 2013). As Lena Näre pointed out, in domestic/care work, there is a 'tendency to perceive the labour relationships, not as a contractual in an economic sense, but as family like' (ibid., p. 407). Yet, the perception of the worker as 'one of the family', which also reflects the devaluation of domestic and care work, often carries the risk that employers may use it to justify the violation of rules (Parreñas, 2001; Borelli, 2021). The idea of a family relationship, in fact, may be used to make the worker more respectful and available to work longer hours, undertaking more tasks to please the employers. Where family and employment dimensions overlap, employers often use the language of 'helping' and 'supporting' to neutralise exploitative treatments and foster forms of subjection through a pretence of gratitude (Palumbo, 2017). As a member of a trade union interviewed for this research pointed out, such a discourse is then supported by the rhetoric that migrants 'ought to be "grateful" for the job opportunities given to them, the possibility to have a place to stay and make do with what they have'.[50] As discussed below, restrictions on the reproduction costs of domestic and care workers, including accommodation, play a functional role in the dynamics of containment of labour costs and exploitation.

[49] Interview with Cristina Falaschi from an organisation for victims of exploitation and trafficking based in Cesena, March 2016.

[50] Interview a member of a Domestic Workers' Trade Union, February 2015, Rome.

5.3.4 Invisibility, Denied Rights, and Dynamics of Exploitation

The constant blurring between family and employment relationships, along with the limited protection and rights of domestic and care workers, leads to a 'house-by-house' basis deregulation and compression of workers' living and working conditions (Maioni, 2022, p. 72). Such situations can even include cases in which domestic and care workers are deprived of fundamental rights and occur in particular in live-in migrant domestic work, where living and working spaces overlap, working hours often become extended thus increasing workloads, and tasks are heterogeneous and challenging to categorise (Maioni & Zucca, 2016; Sciurba, 2015).

Indeed, migrant domestic and care workers, especially live-in workers, often work for more than 10 hours a day and with night vigils that are not considered overtime, while according to the collective agreement the maximum working time for live-in domestic workers is 54 hours per week. In live-in situations the boundaries between free time and working hours are not clearly demarcated, consequently workers tend to be seen as being at the constant disposal of the employers. As a migrant domestic worker told me: 'in theory I should work until 7 pm but actually I also work in the nights as the old lady constantly needs help'.[51]

The most common solution adopted by employers is to regularly employ a domestic/care worker, even in cases of co-habitation, for a 'fictitious' time of 25 hours per week. This solution is the result of a 'downward convergence' of interests between employers and workers: employers pay social security contributions for a number of hours they consider 'adequate', at the lowest possible cost, while the threshold of 25 hours is sufficient for migrant workers to have the minimum income (equal to the amount of the social allowance) to obtain a residence permit (Marchetti, 2016).

Wages are on average considerably lower than those provided for in collective bargaining and vary considerably from northern to southern Italy, where the salary for live-in care can drop to 600 euros per month (Palumbo, 2017). In addition to reflecting different socio-economic contexts, this disparity between regions is also due to the presence or absence of local or regional initiatives aimed at supporting households, for example through economic subsidies (Maioni & Zucca, 2016).

On the other hand, it is worth underlining – without justifying any forms of irregularity and exploitation – that, in the absence of adequate state support and a tax regime offering significant reliefs, and considering that in Italy the average value of household incomes as well as of pensions is low (around 1,300 euros per month), few people can afford the cost of regularly employing a live-in domestic and care worker to which the cost of a second domestic worker for replacement during leave periods and holidays should also often be added along with the cost of coverage during the nights. As one of the social workers interviewed argued, 'the recourse to migrant workers, willing to accept poor working conditions and protection, represents the only way in which many families can meet their care needs for dependent

[51] Interview with a migrant domestic worker, March 2016, Cesena.

family members'.[52] As a consequence, most live-in domestic workers perform work that should be done by at least two people (Santoro, 2010).

Exploitative working conditions (in terms of wages and working hours) constitute, therefore, an indispensable component for the functioning of such a model. As a former Senator pointed out during an interview for this research, the Italian system of care 'relies on a "collective hypocrisy": families are not effectively supported by the state in dealing with domestic and care work issues – for instance, there is no structured plan for non-self-sufficient people – but, at the same time, there is a sort of tolerance for the "people's do-it yourself answer," which mainly consists in the employment of a *badante* and involves forms of irregularity and exploitation'.[53]

As with agricultural workers, the social reproduction dimension of domestic and care workers is the main ambit affected by the compression of labour costs (Rigo, 2022). Indeed, limited and inadequate accommodation for live-in domestic and care workers function to contain of the costs of labour. Furthermore, in the live-in situation, where the boundaries in terms of tasks and distinction between free time and working time tend to blur, the worker's privacy may be highly restricted (Palumbo, 2017; Maioni, 2022). As one of the live-in domestic/care workers interviewed told me, 'actually, I don't really have a space where I feel that I'm alone and can rest…I constantly feel that, even when I can rest, I cannot truly do it, as she constantly needs my help'.[54]

All this contributes to making live-in domestic/care work an all-embracing work situation that distorts employment relations, exacerbating dependency and power relationships.

The compression of the social reproduction sphere of domestic and care workers can reach extreme cases in which workers are deprived of a salary as it is substituted with payment in kind – that is, room and board. As emphasised by a social worker interviewed during the fieldwork, people accept such situations because they need a place to sleep or because the employers allow them to stay in the house with their children: 'a woman that we assisted accepted having not salary because with a little baby it was difficult for her to find a job'.[55]

Isolation and invisibility are factors that, similar to the conditions of migrant farmworkers living and working in the rural areas, amplify the situational vulnerability of migrant domestic workers to exploitation. Moreover, in the invisibility of the private context protected by household walls and escaping labour inspections, the specific situation of imbalance of power between employer and employee characterising domestic/care work can produce an escalation of exploitation, abuse, and violence (sometimes mutual[56]) (Palumbo, 2017).

[52] Interview with a social worker from a support service for care and domestic work in Cesena, March 2017.

[53] Interview with a former Senator, Bologna, March 2015.

[54] Interview with a migrant domestic worker, Cesena, March 2017.

[55] Interview with a social worker from the organisation for victims of exploitation and trafficking, Proxima Association, based in Ragusa, March 2019.

[56] Interview with an expert on domestic work, Bologna, March 2015.

One of most severe cases collected during the fieldwork regarded a young Indonesian woman brought to Italy by a couple – a Libyan man and an Italian woman – to work as a domestic worker, cleaning and taking care of their house. The young woman had inadequate accommodation, was deprived of her passport, and for around 16 months, worked every day from 5.30 a.m. to 1.00 a.m., without time off, for a monthly salary of 200 USD, which was not consistently paid. She was also verbally and physically abused by her employer (Palumbo, 2017). Although there have been no convictions in this case, as recounted by the social worker who assisted this exploited woman, 'she obtained a significant compensation that allowed her to return home to her son as she desired and to arrange her living conditions'.[57] Such a case highlights the extreme manifestation of certain trends commonly observed in domestic and care work: the complete availability of the worker, bordering on situations of trafficking and slavery, while invisibility is exacerbated by the confiscation of documents.

As in the case of migrant farmworkers, the burden of family and care responsibilities plays a meaningful role in contributing to the situational vulnerabilities of migrant domestic workers. Many domestic and care workers (especially those who work as live-in workers) often migrate alone and are mothers who have left their countries precisely to build a different and better future opportunity for their children. As the relevant literature has pointed out, many of these women have to leave their children behind, within a system that has been well-documented as a specific aspect of many female migrations on a global scale (see, for instance, Vianello, 2009; Sciurba, 2015).

As Alessandra Sciurba (2015, p. 89) has argued, these migrant women mothers and their children are separated because even the *badanti* model of care typically prevents them from living together: 'the cohabiting with the care recipient, the relatively low wages earned (which are worth more in their home country than in Italy), and the long continuous working hours make are all prohibitive factors'. The weight of family and care responsibilities places women domestic and care workers under significant pressure, related to the need to earn and support their own families, leading them to accept exploitative working conditions, given the absence of non-exploitable employment alternatives.

5.4 The Role of Intermediaries and Agencies in the Agricultural and Domestic Work Sectors

In the absence of effective institutional recruitment and job services, the recourse to informal and illegal intermediaries is widespread in sectors characterised by the employment of a significant migrant labour force such as agriculture and domestic

[57] Interview with Cristina Falaschi from an organisation for victims of exploitation and trafficking, Cesena, September 2023.

and care work (Corrado et al., 2018; Amorosi, 2022). In the agricultural sector, the illegal gang-mastering, or '*caporalato*', in some regions has become *de facto* the main intermediation and recruiting system capable of guaranteeing in an efficient way the availability of a significant share of just-in-time and flexible labour force, allowing for a substantial reduction in labour costs (Corrado & Caruso, 2022). As further discussed in Chap. 6, in the last 10 years more institutional and media attention has been paid to the phenomenon of *caporalato*. Often expressed in sensationalistic tones, this has driven the focus away from the root causes of labour exploitation in the agricultural sector, overlooking the role of other abusive actors (including employers) in the dynamics of exploitation as well as the complexity of *caporalato* and the different modalities through which it operates.

As several studies have highlighted, far from being and acting in a homogenous way, the *caporalato* covers a plurality of mechanisms and practices (Avallone, 2016; Corrado et al., 2018; Perrotta, 2015). Some *caporali* are simple team leaders who 'select' workers and recommend them to the employer as reliable workers; others also organise shifts and control the volumes of product collected, for instance in the cases of piecework, retaining for themselves a share for this logistic work of intermediation or coordination. In some cases, the *caporali* strictly control and manage workers' daily lives, including recruitment, accommodation (usually in ghettos or abandoned houses in the countryside), transport, meals, work time and wages, and social contacts. Often these situations involve blackmail, abuse, and violence, including cases of serious exploitation and trafficking (Omizzolo, 2019), as the recent case, discussed in Chap. 6, involving Romanian women and men workers, recruited by compatriots in their home country and then subjected to labour and sexual exploitation and degrading living conditions in the rural area of Ragusa (Palumbo, 2020).

The different roles and practices performed by *caporali* are also strongly related to the living and social reproduction conditions of workers. Indeed, as discussed in the section on the working and living conditions in Ragusa, the greater the compression of workers' social reproduction capacities, the more relevant and necessary the function of *caporali*, and in general of informal and abusive intermediaries/actors in relation to employment, accommodation, and mobility, and more generally access to basic services. In these dynamics, as further underlined in the next section, gendered power relationships and norms play a crucial role.

Informal and illegal intermediaries and groups are also a critical factor in the domestic and care sector (Palumbo, 2017; Amorosi, 2022). As emerged during the fieldwork, and was confirmed in some investigations,[58] there have been many cases of illegal actors recruiting migrant women in Italy or from the countries of origin (especially from eastern European countries, including Romania and Moldova) for employment in the domestic/care sectors under exploitative conditions. Poor salary, exhausting working hours, and inadequate accommodation characterise the working and living conditions experienced by the women involved in these exploitation

[58] See, in this regard, Redazione Salerno Today (2021) and Ferrara (2022),

dynamics, which in some cases amount to trafficking. As a social worker interviewed for this research pointed out, these dynamics often also involve abuse and gender-based violence: 'we intercepted some situations where abusive intermediaries make women understand (or tell them explicitly) that if they are willing to provide sexual services they can obtain a better working conditions and payment'.[59] As highlighted below, the intersection of labour exploitation and forms of gender-based violence, including harassment and sexual coercion, is a recurring element in the work experiences of many women employed in the agricultural and domestic/care sectors (Palumbo & Sciurba, 2018; Sciurba, 2015).

In recent years, there has also been increased involvement of employment and temporary work agencies in the recruitment of workers in sectors such as domestic and care work and agri-food systems. As Marchetti (2022, p. 48) argues, resorting to intermediaries and agencies 'has become a pragmatic necessity for employers in order to overcome the practical and bureaucratic difficulties involved in the international recruitment of private care workers'. In line with these considerations, several testimonies collected in the fieldwork have underlined that, for instance, in the domestic and care work, families contact intermediaries or agencies because they urgently need a live-in domestic worker and because this helps them manage the relationship with domestic workers. As a social worker significantly argued in this regard, 'it is a way to free families from an employer-worker relationship. In this context, family considers that the employment relationship is managed by the agencies, and therefore, they delegate to them the matters related to the management of this relationship'.[60]

While some agencies respect applicable legislation and the rights of workers, others act without the necessary authorisation or move in a 'grey area', profiting from the gaps and shortcomings in relevant regulations. These latter include, for instance, irregular social cooperatives that are particularly active both in the domestic/care and agricultural sectors, as several criminal investigations have revealed (Giammarinaro, 2022, p. 18; Franciosi, 2022).[61] These 'fake' cooperatives do not fit the cooperative model, but instrumentally use the legal form of a cooperative to act instead as illegal intermediaries, circumventing relevant legislation and national collective agreements.

There have also been several cases of abusive subcontracting in the agri-food sector (Franciosi, 2022). Under national law (Art. 1655 of the Civil Code) entrepreneurs can outsource their production cycle to a third-party enterprise if they do not interfere in the contractor's organisation of the workers or means necessary to carry out the work. The entrepreneur is jointly and severally liable, together with the contractor, for workers' wages and social security contributions (Art. 29 Legislative Decree No. 276/2003). However, what often happens in practice is that the

[59] Interview with Cristina Falaschi from an organisation for victims of exploitation and trafficking, Cesena, March 2015.

[60] Interview with a social worker, March 2015, Cesena.

[61] See also Bartelli (2021)

contractor is limited to supplying the workers who are *de facto* managed and organised by the entrepreneur/employer, in violation of the law.

Cases of abusive subcontracting also involve posted work in agriculture. Although posting has had less impact compared to other European countries since Italian companies can benefit from a set of regulatory tools that offer advantages similar to those offered by posting, posted workers are concentrated mainly in northern regions, reflecting the productive structure of the Italian labour market (Iannuzzi & Sacchetto, 2020, p. 111).

The use of subcontracting chains makes monitoring and enforcement of workers' rights more difficult (Franciosi, 2022). The result is a system that dilutes responsibility for workers' exploitation and fosters tax and contribution evasion, producing, in turn, unfair competition between companies and social dumping dynamics. It is in this sense that scholars have referred to a new form of *caporalato* facilitated by labour market liberalisation and deregularisation processes that shape a 'dark grey' labour market, with the 'transposition of exploitation within legal apparatus/systems that ensure its formal regularity, while keeping intact its essence in terms of unjust profit and violations of the rights of workers and people'[62] (Olivieri, 2016, p. 49).

5.5 Labour Exploitation, Gender Violence, and the Transit between Sectors and Practices of Exploitation

The arduous conditions faced by many women in the agricultural and domestic and care work sectors, especially migrant women workers, are often accompanied by various forms of harassment, extortion, and gender-based violence – psychological, verbal, physical, economic, and sexual (ActionAid Italia, 2022; Rizzi, 2022; Giammarinaro, 2022) – from employers, *caporali*, and other intermediaries to keep these women in a state of oppression and subjugation.

In the agricultural sector, forms of gender-based discrimination, abuse, and violence occur in various places: in the vehicles transporting women to the fields, in the greenhouses and warehouses, or in the employer-supplied accommodations (Giammarinaro & Palumbo, 2022; ActionAid Italia, 2022). For example, in some packaging companies in the Ragusa area where the workforce is predominantly composed of women, specific practices are put in place with the explicit aim of controlling and disciplining the women workers. Access to the toilet, for instance, is constantly monitored in some warehouses and bathroom breaks are restricted to avoid disrupting work rhythms. As the General Secretary of the Trade Union CGIL in Ragusa pointed out, 'women workers are forced to swipe their badge every time they go to the restroom, and this means that the two/three minutes it takes them to go to the bathroom are deducted from their pay. These control mechanisms, in

[62] My translation in English.

addition to having an economic impact, create a form of psychological conditioning on these workers who are constantly monitored'.[63] Such practices have a significant impact on the health of women with menstrual cycles, those who are pregnant, or those with chronic illnesses.

Verbal and sexual abuse, blackmail and harassment are part of the daily lives of many women agricultural workers employed in the greenhouses of Ragusa (Palumbo & Sciurba, 2018). These cases have also been documented through judicial investigations.[64] Similar dynamics of exploitation and gender violence have emerged in many other rural areas of Italy (ActionAid Italia, 2022). In these contexts, women workers live in fear of being harassed and abused – and in fear of retaliation if they refuse. Retaliation can take various forms, from threats of being fired and not being paid or having fewer declared working days to more violent reactions. One of the stories collected during the fieldwork in Ragusa concerned a Romanian woman worker who experienced labour exploitation and sexual abuse by her employer for 9 years (Giammarinaro & Palumbo, 2020). As a social worker of the local anti-trafficking NGO that assisted this woman explained to me, 'this woman was undergoing this situation because she was afraid of that man, but also because she needed to work, in order to guarantee a dignified life for her six children left in the Romania'.[65] In 2015, the woman decided to escape and report the employer to the police.

In some cases, the threats and abuse involve the women's children, who, besides being witnesses to abuse, including sexual abuse, sometimes become an additional tool for blackmailing by employers, intermediaries, or other exploiters on whom women depend for housing, transportation, and access to basic services. Family responsibilities and social reproduction conditions thus become central aspects around which forms of labour exploitation and sexual abuses develop. One of the stories collected in Ragusa involved a Romanian woman who worked in the greenhouses and lived with her children in housing provided by the employer. She had asked the employer to help her by accompanying her children to school. However, in exchange, she was forced to comply with his sexual requests. As a social worker of an anti-trafficking NGO pointed out, 'this woman accepted in order to protect her children and not lose her job and housing. It was the absence of concrete and fair work alternative that led this woman to "consent" to these forms of exploitation and abuse'.[66] She decided to leave only when she understood that her children's safety was at risk.

The overlap and intersection between labour exploitation and forms of gender violence, including sexual harassment and blackmail, is also a recurring element in the domestic and care work sector (Sciurba, 2015; Palumbo, 2017; Degani, 2022).

---

[63] Interview with Giuseppe Scifo, General Secretary of the Trade Union CGIL, May 2022, Ragusa.

[64] See, for instance, the Tribunale di Catania, Sez. GIP/GUP, Decision No. 1397/2019, concerning the so-called case of Boschetari (Palumbo, 2020).

[65] Interview with Ausilia Cosentini from the anti-trafficking organisation, Proxima Association, based in Ragusa, March 2019.

[66] Interview with an anti-trafficking social worker, March 2014, Ragusa.

Even here, commitment to their family and care responsibilities, and the related need to support their families financially, increase women's situational vulnerabilities to exploitation, making their resistance to exploitation and abuse even more difficult. This occurs both when children are left behind or when they stay with the mothers-workers. Indicative is the case of a Ukrainian woman who left exploitative conditions in the agricultural sector for a job in domestic work. She was employed in the house of an elderly man who allowed her to stay there with her children. However, this situation soon resulted in dynamics of control, with the employer even resorting to sexual blackmail: 'he agreed [to welcome] my child into his home thinking that he has finally found what he was looking for and now we have reached the condition that...he doesn't provide me with food and controls everything...he tried to get all the satisfaction, now he has lost hope'.[67] She strategically tried to fend off the employer's demands by suggesting marriage, knowing he would never accept: 'Now he thinks that he has to send me away...but if he does so, it is not easy to find a job as a domestic worker with a child...If he closes the door and throws me out, I call the police...I don't have a contract'.[68]

Certainly, the invisible nature of domestic and care work renders identifying and tackling cases of exploitation and abuse even more difficult. Being isolated in the employer's household with limited or no access to information and assistance measures exacerbates domestic and care workers' situations of vulnerability to exploitation and abuse.[69] Further, when cases of exploitation in domestic work are reported, it is not easy to prove the elements of exploitation because of the lack of documents regarding employment relations, working hours, pay, and so on as well as difficulty in obtaining verbal evidence. For instance, the Court of Cassation has already had an opportunity to state that 'the proven permanence of the worker at the employers' domicile is not sufficient to also confirm the performance of working activity for the entire aforementioned period of permanence' (Civil Court of Cassation, labour section, No. 22399/2013).[70] Consequently, it is up to the worker to offer proof, which in the absence of any documentation, can only be done via testimonials. As Paggi (2022, p. 59), a lawyer, has pointed out, if there are already obstacles in proving work performance, 'one can easily imagine what the concrete difficulties are in demonstrating deprivation of personal freedom, as well as vexatious or extortionate conduct, or sexual abuse and harassment'.

As the Ukrainian woman's story illustrates, in their limited labour mobility between limited sectors – including domestic and care work, agriculture, and sex work – migrant women workers often transit from one type of exploitation to another, experiencing a multiplicity of discrimination and violence. This shows how the boundaries between care, sex, and agricultural work can be blurred in practice,

[67] Interviewed conducted on 28 March 2014. Sabine was still in this working relationship when she was interviewed.

[68] Interviewed conducted on 28 March 2014.

[69] Labour inspectors can intervene in this sector only if there is a request for intervention from a domestic worker or from the trade union or NGOs providing support to the victim.

[70] See also in this regard, Civil Court of Cassation, Labour Section, No. 28703/2020.

often involving dynamics of exploitation and abuse (Garofalo Geymonat et al., 2022). For example, my research on women farmworkers in Calabria reveals that many women seeking asylum and beneficiaries of international protection (mostly of Nigerian nationality) who work as farmworkers, often in irregular and exploitative conditions, have experienced human trafficking for sexual exploitation in their past (Palumbo, 2023). In Ragusa it emerged that many Romanian women who found employment in the greenhouses – albeit in most cases under irregular and exploitative conditions – were previously employed as domestic and care workers, receiving low wages and often experiencing abuse from their employers (Sciurba, 2015). Other studies have highlighted cases of women transiting from domestic and care work to sex work and vice versa, often in exploitative conditions (Amorosi, 2022). There are also cases in which women work simultaneously as sex workers, waitresses, or cooks, for example, in the informal settlements, often in conditions of exploitation and abuse (Peano, 2017; Giammarinaro, 2022).

This cycle of abuse, violence, and exploitation frequently includes forms of domestic violence by partners or husbands, who in certain situations are also work colleagues. The intersections between different forms of gender violence and dynamics of labour exploitation, which are mutually reinforcing, reveal the limits of strict taxonomies – especially 'taxonomies of violence' (Kleinman, 2000, p. 227) and taxonomies of exploitation. As scholars from different fields emphasise (see for instance Pinelli, 2019; Mantouvalou, 2020; Rigo, 2022), strict taxonomies concerning violence and exploitation rely on binaries such as public vs private, productive vs reproductive, ordinary vs extreme violence or exploitation, physical vs structural, that are inadequate for understanding the complexities of dynamics of exploitation and violence and the multiplicity of their effects in the experiences of people, in particular of women.

The harsh, violent, and degrading life and work contexts that many migrant women farmworkers experience can seriously compromise their psychophysical health and self-esteem. At times, they employ solidarity strategies to help each other and to protect the younger workers (Giammarinaro & Palumbo, 2020). In some extreme cases, as a social worker of the anti-trafficking centre in Ragusa explained, 'they bear all this with the use of alcohol and, as happened in a tragic case, there are those who, sucked into this context of degradation, arrived to force their daughters into prostitution'.[71]

Many women's reluctance to talk about and report the exploitation and violence they have suffered can be traced back to the multiple intersectional factors that produce their situations of vulnerability. These include, for instance, low negotiation power, fear of retaliation, social stigma associated with poverty, and above all the absence of concrete alternatives of life – in particular, possibilities to find a job in decent and non-exploitative conditions.

When not facing particularly serious forms of exploitation but receiving a salary that, albeit low, allows them to live – the workers sometimes still consider their

[71] Interview with Michele Mililli, Proxima Association, April 2022, Ragusa.

working conditions an opportunity for autonomy in the context of their migration project or more generally of the life project. From the various testimonies collected, it emerges that the agency of these women workers is never completely annulled by exploitation, even if in extreme situations the range of choices is so severely limited they are led to accept exploitation itself as a lesser evil. Typical in this regard is the case of some Romanian women workers who – after having suffered labour exploitation and sexual blackmail by employers and intermediaries – have 'chosen' to work as sex workers in greenhouses because this, even in exploitative conditions, allows them to earn more than working in the fields.

On the other hand, migrant women workers have often seized the opportunity to escape from exploitation when a real and practicable alternative of unexploited work has been presented to them. In many cases, the decision to abandon an exploitative situation often takes place when the (very high) tolerance threshold is exceeded, the spaces for autonomy and choice are drastically reduced or the health and well-being of the children are at risk, as in the case of the mothers with children mentioned above (Palumbo & Sciurba, 2018). These manifestations of what can be called 'agency in tension', to paraphrase an expression introduced by Camille Schmoll (Schmoll, 2022, pp. 177–180), reveal how migrant women act or try to act and negotiate in a context marked by gendered and racialiacised power relationships and structural injustices. In doing so, they implement a variety of strategies to regain some power over their paths and projects of life and family responsibilities.

5.6 Concluding Remarks

As underlined in this chapter, within a context marked by restrictive migration policies and a labour market strongly stratified along gender, class, and nationality lines, employment in sectors such as agriculture and domestic and care work stands out as one of the limited job alternatives for 'low skilled' migrant workers in Italy, with different legal status.

The national entry route system for non-EU migrant workers based on the so-called Flows Decree (Law No. 40/1998) has proven to be inefficient. Annual quotas for both seasonal and non-seasonal migrant workers have been limited, especially between 2012 and 2020. In addition, the Flows Decree entry system relies on a long and complicated employer-driven mechanism, fostering irregularities and abusive practices.

Migrant seasonal workers have access to limited rights and protection. Indeed, in line with the approach of the Seasonal Workers Directive, the Italian legal regime on migrant seasonal workers maintains their temporary status by restricting their access to social benefits, such as unemployment benefits for agricultural workers. Additionally, it denies them access to their right to family reunification, thereby managing and controlling migrants' social reproduction sphere. All these elements contribute to the creation and amplification of the migrant seasonal workers' situational vulnerabilities to exploitation and abuse.

Due to the lack of an effective national entry system for third-country national migrants, labour demand in the agriculture and domestic work sectors, has been mainly offset by undocumented migrants, eastern EU nationals (especially Romanians, Poles and Bulgarians), and refugees and asylum seekers. The different situations of vulnerability in which migrant persons find themselves – for instance, with respect to legal migration status, gender, nationality, or class – seem to translate into a variety of possibilities for their exploitation in the agricultural and domestic work sectors.

By paying specific attention to the working and living conditions of women migrant workers, this chapter has shed light on how wage disparities, irregularities, and denied rights (including reproductive rights) are a constant in the working and living conditions in the domestic and agricultural sectors in Italy. For these women, irregular working conditions (such as employment contracts with fewer hours than those effectively performed by the workers) result in a lack of protections related to pregnancy and maternity, making it even more challenging to balance work and reproductive and family related activities and responsibilities. All of this, in turn, is closely connected to housing and transportation issues in a context characterised by isolation, invisibility, and dependence on employers, *caporali* and other intermediary actors. As argued in this chapter, in both the agriculture and domestic work sectors, inadequate housing conditions are not only the direct result of a relationship of subjugation but are more generally part of a production model based on exploitative practices, which also entail the compression of the reproduction costs of migrant workers.

The daily life of many women migrant workers employed in these sectors is also marked by gender-based harassment and violence within a system that relies on the specific vulnerabilities of these women and their need to have employment. In this context, family and reproductive responsibilities play a crucial role in increasing women's situational vulnerabilities to exploitation and abuse.

For many migrant women, employment in agriculture represents one of the few job alternatives, along with domestic and sexual work. This translates into a sort of circularity between these sectors and, therefore, often a dynamic transition from one form of exploitation to another. From the various stories and testimonies collected, it emerges that the agency of migrant women involved in these dynamics is never completely annulled by exploitation, even if in extreme situations the range of choices is enormously limited. On the other hand, escape from exploitation occurs only when a tangible and feasible alternative of non-exploitative work is presented to them.

References

ActionAid Italia. (2022). *Cambia Terra - Dall'invisibilità al protagonismo delle donne in agricoltura*. ActionAid.

Aiello, F. (1987). Momenti ed aspetti della serricoltura: l'esperienza del Ragusano. In AA. VV., *Cinquant'anni diagricoltura in Sicilia dagli anni '30 agli anni '80. atti del convegno regionale*. Centro Studi Feliciano.

Ambrosini, M. (2013). *Irregular migration and invisible welfare*. Palgrave Macmillan.
Ambrosini, M. (2022). *Le politiche sugli ingressi di lavoratori migranti in Italia e in altri paesi dell'Unione europea. Nota tematica*. Organizzazione Internazionale del Lavoro.
Amnesty International. (2012). *Italy: Exploited labour: Migrant workers in Italy's agricultural sector.* Amnesty International [online], www.amnesty.org/en/documents/eur30/020/2012/en/ (Last Access Apr 2024).
Amorosi, L. (2022). Sfruttamento lavorativo nel lavoro domestico: un approccio empirico. In Slaves No More (Ed.), *Donne gravemente sfruttate. Il diritto di essere protagoniste* (pp. 78–98). Edizioni Gruppo Abele.
Anderson, B. (2007). A very private business: Exploring the demand for migrant domestic workers. *European Journal of Women's Studies, 14*(3), 247–264.
ANSA. (2022). Razzismo: 'Italiana nata in Africa, nessuno mi affitta casa', *Ansa.it*, 19 February 2020 [online], https://www.ansa.it/emiliaromagna/notizie/2022/02/19/razzismo-italiana-nata-in-africa-nessuno-mi-affitta-casa_86333d21-a19a-4871-9274-7cdfc1d28ae7.html (Last Access Apr 2024).
ASGI. (2020). *ASGI, L'esternalizzazione delle frontiere e della gestione dei migranti: politiche migratorie dell'unione europea ed effetti giuridici*. Associazione per gli Studi Giuridici sull'Immigrazione.
Avallone, G. (2016). The land of informal intermediation. The social regulation of migrant agricultural labour in the Piana del Sele, Italy. In A. Corrado, C. De Castro, & D. Perrotta (Eds.), *Migration and agriculture. Mobility and change in the Mediterranean area* (pp. 59–74). Routledge.
Bartelli, C. (2021). Stretta sulle false cooperative. *ItaliaOggi.it*, 17 August 2021 [online], https://www.italiaoggi.it/news/stretta-sulle-false-cooperative-2530271 (Last Access Apr 2024).
Basenghi, F. (2010). La legge 339/1958: continuità e innovazione. In R. Sarti (Ed.), *Lavoro domestico e di cura: Quali diritti?* (pp. 207–222). Ediesse.
Bellassai, E., & Scillieri, B. (2000). Immigrazione e internazionalizzazione nella provincia di Ragusa. In CeSPI (Centro Studi di Politica Internazionale), *Immigrazione e processi di internazionalizzazione dei sistemi produttivi italiani* (pp. 65–80). Working Paper n. 9, CeSPI.
Belluccio, D. (2020). Lavoro, welfare e immigrazione: reddito universale di residenza vs limitazioni all'accesso alla miseria del presente. In M. Giovannetti & N. Zorzella (2020) (eds), *Ius Migrandi: la pubblicazione per i 20 anni di "Diritto, immigrazione e cittadinanza"* (pp. 410–429). FrancoAngeli.
Bettio, F., Simonazzi, A., & Villa, P. (2006). Change in care regimes and female migration: The 'care drain' in the Mediterranean. *Journal of European Social Policy, 16*(3), 271–285.
Borelli, S. (2021). Le diverse forme dello sfruttamento nel lavoro domestico di cura. *Lavoro e diritto, 2*, 281–301.
Busi, B. (2020). Genere, "razza" e composizione di classe nel lavoro domestico e di cura. In B. Busi (Ed.), *Separate in casa. Lavoratrici domestiche, femministe e sindacaliste: una mancata alleanza* (pp. 11–35). Ediesse.
Caprioglio, C., & Rigo, E. (2020). Lavoro, politiche migratorie e sfruttamento: la condizione dei braccianti migranti in agricoltura. *Diritto, Immigrazione e Cittadinanza*, 3, 33–56.
Caproglio, C., Montella, T., & Rigo, E. (2023). La strage che diventa legge. *Jacobin Italia*, 28 April 2023 [online], https://jacobinitalia.it/la-strage-che-diventa-legge/ (Last Access Apr 2024).
Caruso, F. S. (2023). Agricoltura, lavoro e migrazioni nella Piana di Lamezia. In A. Corrado, L. Leone, & R. Liotti (Eds.), *Le dannate delle terra* (pp. 45–64). Rubbetino.
Caruso, F., & Corrado, A. (Eds.). (2022). *Essenziali ma invisibili. Analisi delle politiche e delle iniziative di contrasto allo sfruttamento e per l'inclusione dei lavoratori migranti in agricoltura nel sud Italia*. Rosenberg & Sellier.
Casalini, B. (2009). Schiavitù domestica e mercificazione del lavoro di cura. In T. Casadei & S. Mattarelli (Eds.), *Schiavitù* (pp. 195–214). FrancoAngeli.
Casalini, B. (2017). The market, social justice and elderly care. A reflection starting from the Italian case. *Politey News, XXXIII*, 123–137.

Castagnone, E., Salis, E., & Premazzi, V. (2013). *Promoting integration for migrant domestic workers in Italy*. FIERI.
Centro studi e ricerche – IDOS. (2023). *Dossier statistico immigrazione*. Inprinting srl.
CGIL Ragusa & L'Altro Diritto. (2022). *La nazionalità delle lavoratrici e dei lavoratori stagionali agricoli stranieri nella fascia trasformata della provincia di Ragusa* [online], www.adir.unifi.it/laboratorio/quartorapporto-sfruttamento-lavorativo.pdf (Last Access Apr 2024).
Chiaromonte, W. (2018). Cercavamo braccia, sono arrivati uomini. Il lavoro dei migranti in agricoltura fra sfruttamento e istanze di tutela. *Giornale di diritto del lavoro e di relazioni industriali, 158*, 321–356.
Chiaromonte, W., & Federico, V. (2021). The labour market needs them, but we don't want them to stay for good: The conundrum of migrants, refugees and asylum seekers' integration in Italy. In V. Federico & S. Baglioni (Eds.), *Migrants, refugees and asylum seekers' integration in European labour markets* (pp. 193–212). (IMISCOE research series). Springer.
Ciconte, F., & Liberti, S. (2019). *Il grande carrello. Chi decide cosa mangiamo*. Laterza.
Cole, J. E. (2007). In pursuit of 'green gold': Immigration and the fortunes of a Sicilian greenhouse. *Journal of Modern Italian Studies, 12*(4), 387–396.
Colloca, C., & Corrado, A. (2013). *La globalizzazione delle campagne. Migranti e società rurali nel Sud dell'Italia*. Franco Angeli.
Colucci, M. (2018). *Storia dell'immigrazione straniera in Italia. Dal 1945 ai nostri giorni*. Carocci Editore.
Corrado, A., & Caruso, F. S. (2022). Essential but exploitable: Migrant agri-food workers in Italy and Spain. *European Journal of Migration and Law, 24*(2), 193–216.
Corrado, A., & Palumbo, L. (2022). Essential farmworkers and the pandemic crisis: Migrant labour conditions, and legal and political responses in Italy and Spain. In A. Triandafyllidou (Ed.), *Migration and pandemics* (pp. 145–166). (IMISCOE research series). Springer.
Corrado, A., De Castro, C., & Perrotta, D. (Eds.). (2016). *Migration and agriculture. Mobility and change in the Mediterranean area*. Routledge.
Corrado, A., Caruso, F. S., Lo Cascio, M., Nori, M., Palumbo, L., & Triandafyllidou, A. (2018). *Is Italian agriculture a 'Pull Factor' for irregular migration – And, if so, why?* Open Society European Policy Institute.
Curi, F. (Ed.). (2019). *Il decreto Salvini. Immigrazione e sicurezza. Commento al d.l. 4 ottobre 2008, n. 113, conv. con modif. in legge 1 dicembre 2018, n. 132*. Pacini Giuridica.
D'Agostino, M. (2018). La cittadinanza europea di fronte alla migrazione dei rom: l'europeizzazione della governance e le politiche locali di riterritorializzazione dell'etnicità. In L. D'Alessandro & A. Montanari (Eds.), *Diseguaglianze e crisi della fiducia. Diritto, politica e democrazia nella società contemporanea* (pp. 170–187). Franco Angeli.
Da Roit, B., & Sabatinelli, S. (2005). Il modello mediterraneo di welfare tra famiglia e mercato. *Stato e mercato, 2*, 267–290.
De Martino, C., D'Onghia, M., & Schiuma, D. (2020). Condizioni salariali e previdenziali. In P. Campanella (Ed.), *Vite sottocosto* (pp. 259–288). Aracne editrice.
Degani, P. (2022). Domestic/care work and severe exploitation. The limits of Italian migrant regularization schemes. *Frontiers in Human Dynamics: Refugees and Conflict, 4*. https://doi.org/10.3389/fhumd.2022.818351
Del Lago, A. (2004). *Non persone. L'esclusione dei migranti in una società globale*. Feltrinelli.
Del Re, A. (2020). Il lavoro di riproduzione e il mercato. In B. Busi (Ed.), *Separate in casa. Lavoratrici domestiche, femministe e sindacaliste: una mancata alleanza* (pp. 37–62). Ediesse.
Di Gregorio, M., & Moffa, G. (2022). Le lavoratrici straniere in agricoltura: storie di vulnerabilità. In Slaves No More (Ed.), *Donne gravemente sfruttate. Il diritto di essere protagoniste* (pp. 124–135). Edizioni Gruppo Abele.
Dines, N., & Rigo, E. (2015). Postcolonial citizenships and the 'refugeeization' of the workforce: Migrant agricultural labor in the Italian Mezzogiorno. In S. Ponzanesi & G. Colpani (Eds.), *Postcolonial transitions in Europe: Contexts, practices and politics* (pp. 151–172). Rowman and Littlefield.

EBAT-Ragusa. (2017). *Rapporto Iscritti elenchi Anagrafici anno 2017*. EBAT.

Ero Straniero. (2023). *La lotteria dell'ingresso per lavoro in Italia: i veri numeri del decreto flussi* [online], https://erostraniero.it/wp-content/uploads/2023/12/Dossier-decreto-flussi-dicembre-2023.pdf (Last Access Apr 2024).

Eurostat. (2019). *The fruit and vegetable sector in the EU – A statistical overview*. European Union.

Falcone, R. (2022). Agricoltura e sfruttamento: ritorno al futuro. *L'Altro Diritto Rivista, 6*, 36–64.

Farris, S. R., & Marchetti, S. (2017). From the commodification to the corporatization of care: European perspectives and debates. *Social Politics, 2*, 109–131.

Federdistribuzione. (2014). *La mappa del sistema distributivo in Italia 2014* [online], www.federdistribuzione.it (Last Access Apr 2024).

Ferrara, C. (2022). La tratta delle badanti moldave per far risparmiare gli italiani. *Domani*, 19 June 2022 [online], https://www.editorialedomani.it/economia/disuguaglianze/la-tratta-delle-badanti-moldave-per-far-risparmiare-gli-italiani-eju5o96t (Last Access Apr 2024).

Fortunati, L. (1981). *L' arcano della riproduzione. Casalinghe, prostitute, operai e capitale*. Marsilio Editori.

Franciosi, U. (2022). Lo sfruttamento nell'appalto e subappalto di manodopera. In Osservatorio Placido Rizzotto & FLAI-CGIL (Eds.), *Agromafie e caporalato—VI Rapporto* (pp. 51–60). Ediesse.

Garofalo Geymonat, G., Marchetti, S., & Palumbo, L. (2022). Migrant women workers in Europe: Forms of irregularity and conditions of vulnerability. In I. va Liempt, J. Schapendonk, & A. Campos-Delgado (Eds.), *Research handbook on irregular migration* (pp. 215–226). Edward Elgar Publishing.

Geddes, A., Hadj-Abdou, L., & Brumat, L. (2020). *Migration and mobility in the European Union* (2nd ed.). Red Globe Press.

Giammarinaro, M. G. (2022). *Analisi di genere delle politiche di prevenzione e di contrasto dello sfruttamento lavorativo in agricoltura*. International Labour Organisation (ILO).

Giammarinaro, M. G. (2023). *La migrazione per lavoro: Legislazione e prassi applicative in Italia*. International Labour Organisation (ILO).

Giammarinaro, M. G., & Palumbo, L. (2020). Le donne migranti in agricoltura sfruttamento, vulnerabilità, dignità e autonomia. In Osservatorio Placido Rizzotto & FLAI-CGIL (Eds.), *Agromafie e caporalato—V Rapporto* (pp. 81–114). Ediesse.

Giammarinaro, M. G., & Palumbo, L. (2022). Le condizioni di lavoro e di vita delle lavoratrici agricole tra sfruttamento, violenza, diritti negati e forme di agency. In Osservatorio Placido Rizzotto & FLAI-CGIL (Eds.), *Agromafie e caporalato—VI Rapporto* (pp. 63–82). Ediesse.

Gissi, A. (2018). Le estere : immigrazione femminile e lavoro domestico in Italia (1960-80). *Meridiana: rivista di storia e scienze sociali, 91*(1), 37–56.

Giuffré, M., Denaro, C., & Raach, F. (2022). On 'safety' and EU externalization of borders: Questioning the role of Tunisia as a 'safe country of origin' and a 'safe third country'. *European Journal of Migration and Law, 24*(4), 570–599.

Halley, J., & Rittich, K. (2010). Critical directions in comparative family law: Genealogies and contemporary studies of family law exceptionalism. *The American Journal of Comparative Law, 58*(4), 753–775.

Iannuzzi, F., & Sacchetto, D. (2020). Italian labour inspectors facing posted workers phenomena. In J. Arnholtz & N. Lillie (Eds.), *Posted work in the European Union: The political economy of free movement* (pp. 109–127). Routledge.

IOM. (2023). *Deaths during migration recorded since 2014, by region of incident. Missing migrants project: Data*. International Organization for Migration [online], https://missingmigrants.iom.int/data (Last Access Apr 2024).

ISMU. (2021). *Libro verde sul governo delle migrazioni economiche*. Report. Fondazione ISMU (Initiatives and Studies on Multi-ethnicity).

ISMU. (2023). *Sbarchi e accoglienza: 10 anni tra alti e bassi*. Comunicato Stampa. Fondazione ISMU (Initiatives and Studies on Multi-ethnicity). www.ismu.org/sbarchi-e-accoglienza-i-dati-degli-ultimi-10-anni-tra-alti-e-bassi/

ISPI. (2023). *Migranti e migrazioni in Italia: la dashboard con tutti i numeri*. Istituto per gli Studi di Politica Internationale [online], www.ispionline.it/it/pubblicazione/migranti-e-migrazioni-in-italia-la-dashboard-con-tutti-i-numeri-126051 (Last Access Apr 2024).

ISTAT. (2015). *Rapporto annuale 2015. La situazione del Paese*. Istituto Nationale di Statistica. www.istat.it/it/files/2015/05/Rapporto-Annuale-2015.pdf (Last Access Apr 2024).

Jubilut, L. L., & Casagrande, M. M. (2019). Shortcomings and/or missed opportunities of the global compacts for the protection of forced migrants. *International Migration, 57*(6), 139–157.

King, R., Lazaridis, G., & Tsardanidis, C. (Eds.). (2000). *Eldorado or fortress? Migration in Southern Europe*. Palgrave Macmillan.

Kleinman, A. (2000). The violences of everyday life: The multiple forms and dynamics of social violence. In D. Veena, A. Kleinman, P. Ramphele, & P. Reynolds (Eds.), *Violence and subjectivity* (pp. 226–241). California Press.

L'Altro Diritto and FLAI CGIL. (2022) *Quarto rapporto del laboratorio sullo sfruttamento lavorativo e sulla protezione delle sue vittime* [online], www.flai.it/wp-content/uploads/2022/05/IV-Rapporto_low.pdf (Last Access Apr 2024).

Lanni, A. (2016). *Piu i no dei si, le risposte dell'italia alle richiese d'asilo*. Open Migration [online], https://openmigration.org/analisi/piu-i-no-dei-si-le-risposte-dellitalia-alle-richieste-dasilo/ (Last Access Apr 2024).

Livi Bacci, M. (2010). *In cammino. Breve storia delle migrazioni*. Il Mulino.

Lo Cascio, M., & Perrotta, D. (2019). The intertwinement of symbolic and structural violence: Migrant agricultural labourers in two regions of Southern Italy. In J, Vassilopoulou, J, Brabet, & V. Showunmi (Eds.), *Race discrimination and management of ethnic diversity and migration at work (International perspectives on equality, diversity and inclusion, 6)* (pp. 175–200). Emerald Publishing Limited.

Lo Cascio, M., & Perrotta, D. (2022). Subcontracted migrant labour and just-in-time retail chain requirements: A qualitative research on the bagged salad commodity system in Northern Italy. *Revue Européenne des Migrations Internationales, 38*(3–4), 115–137.

Macrì, M. C. (Ed.). (2019). *Il contributo dei lavoratori stranieri all'agricoltura italiana*. CREA.

Maioni, R. (2022). Lavoro domestico e di cura tra sfruttamento, potenzialità e prospettive. In Slaves No More (Ed.), *Donne gravemente sfruttate. Il diritto di essere protagoniste* (pp. 69–77). Edizioni Gruppo Abele.

Maioni, R., & Zucca, G. (Eds.). (2016). *Viaggio nel lavoro di cura. Chi sono, cosa fanno e come vivono le badanti che lavorano nelle famiglie italiane*. Ediesse.

Mantouvalou, V. (2020). Structural injustice and the human rights of workers. *Current Legal Problems, 73*(1), 59–87.

Mantovan, C. (2021). Donne e rom: segregazione razziale, oppressione di genere e resistenze. *Sociologia urbana e rurale, 125*(2), 62–79.

Marchetti, S. (2016). Domestic work is work? Condizioni lavorative delle assistenti familiari in Italia, tra finzioni e realtà. In R. Maioni & G. Zucca (Eds.), *Viaggio nel lavoro di cura. Chi sono, cosa fanno e come vivono le badanti che lavorano nelle famiglie italiane* (pp. 101–123). Ediesse.

Marchetti, S. (2022). *Migration and domestic work*. IMISCOE Short Reader. Springer.

Marchetti, S., Cherubini, D., & Garofalo Geymonat, G. (2021). *Global domestic workers: Intersectional inequalities and struggles for rights*. Bristol University Press.

Marella, M. R. (2008). Radicalism, resistance, and the structures of family law. *Unbound: Harvard Journal of the Legal Left, IV*, 70–81.

Marella, M. R. (2018). Family-relations law between 'stratification' and 'resistance'. In R. Sarti, A. Bellavitis, & M. Martini (Eds.), *What is work? Gender at the crossroads of home, family, and business from the early modern era to the present* (pp. 295–325). Berghahn Books.

Martelloni, F. (2020). L'accesso al lavoro dei richiedenti e dei titolari di protezione internazionale, tra diritto e prassi. In W. Chiaromonte, M. D. Ferrara, & M. Ranieri (Eds.), *Migranti e lavoro* (pp. 111–132). Il Mulino.

Mattalucci, C., & De Zordo, S. (2022). Demographic anxiety and abortion: Italian pro-life volunteers' and gynecologists' perspectives. *Medical Anthropology, 41*(6–7), 674–688.

McBritton, M. (2017). *Migrazioni economiche e ordinamento italiano. Una prospettiva giuslavoristica*. Cacucci.

Mezzadra, S. (2013). Moltiplicazione dei confini e pratiche di mobilità, *Ragion pratica. Rivista semestrale, 2*, 413–432.

Ministero dell'Interno. (2023). *Cruscotto statistico del 7 dicembre 2023. Sbarchi e accoglienza dei migranti*. Dipartimento per le Libertà civili e l'Immigrazione [online], https://www.interno.gov.it/sites/default/files/2023-12/cruscotto_statistico_giornaliero_07-12-2023.pdf (Last access Dec 2023).

Molinero-Gerbeau, Y. (2020). La creciente dependencia de mano de obra migrante para tareas agrícolas en el centro global. Una perspectiva comparada. *Estudios Geográficos, 81*(288), 1–27.

Moschetti, G., & Valentino, G. (2019) L'impiego delle straniere in agricoltura: i dati inps e i risultati di un'indagine diretta in puglia, nelle aree di Cerignola (FG) e Ginosa (TA). In CREA (Ed.), *Il contributo dei lavoratori stranieri all'agricoltura italiana* (pp. 45–70). CREA

Nare, L. (2013). Migrancy, gender and social class in domestic labour and social care in Italy – An intersectional analysis of demand. *Journal of Ethnic and Migration Studies, 39*(4), 601–623.

OECD. (2014). *Is migration really increasing? Migration policy debates*. Organisation for Economic Cooperation and Development.

Olivieri, F. (2016). Giuridificare ed esternalizzare lo sfruttamento. Il caso dei lavoratori immigrati nella vitivinicoltura senese. In E. Rigo (Ed.), *Leggi, migranti, caporali. Prospettive critiche di ricerca sullo sfruttamento del lavoro in agricoltura* (pp. 47–67). Pacini Editore.

Omizzolo, M. (2019). *Sotto padrone. Uomini, donne e caporali nell'agromafia italiana*. Feltrinelli.

Omizzolo, M. (2021). *Lo sfruttamento lavorativo delle donne migranti nella filiera agro alimentare: il caso dell'Agro Pontino*. Our Food, Our Future Report [online], https://back.weworld.it/uploads/2021/10/Ricerca-AgroPontino.pdf (Last Access Apr 2024).

Ortiz-Miranda, D., Moragues-Faus, A., & Arnalte-Alegre, E. (Eds.). (2013). *Agriculture in mediterranean Europe: Between old and new paradigms* (Research in rural sociology and development) (Vol. 19). Emerald Publishing Limited.

Osservatorio domina sul lavoro domestico. (2022). *Quarto rapporto annuale sul lavoro domestico*. Osservatorio domina sul lavoro domestico [online], www.osservatoriolavorodomestico.it/documenti/rapporto_annuale_2022.pdf (Last Access Apr 2024).

Osservatorio Placido Rizzotto & FLAI-CGIL. (2022). *Agromafie e caporalato—VI Rapporto*. Futura-Ediesse.

Oxfam. (2018). *Al giusto prezzo. I diritti umani nelle filiere dei supermercati italiani*. Oxfam Italia.

Paggi, M. (2022). Lo sfruttamento nel lavoro domestico di cura: dall'invisibilità sociale all'invisibilità giuridica. In A. Brambilla, P. P. Degani, & N. Zorzella (Eds.), *Donne straniere, diritti umani, questioni di genere*, (pp. 51–66). Centro di Ateneo per i Diritti Umani 'Antonio Papisca'. Università degli Studi Padova.

Paggi, M. (2023). Le "nuove" disposizioni in materia di flussi di ingresso legale dei lavoratori stranieri: il vecchio che avanza. *Questione Giustizia*, 6 April 2023 [online], https://www.questionegiustizia.it/articolo/flussi-paggi (Last Access Apr 2024).

Palmisano, L. (2017). *Mafia caporale. Racconti di egemonia criminale sui lavoratori in Italia*. Fandango Libri.

Palumbo, L. (2017). Exploiting for care: Trafficking and abuse in domestic work in Italy. *Journal of Immigrant & Refugee Studies, 15*(2), 171–186.

Palumbo, L. (2020). Tratta di esseri umani e sfruttamento lavorativo in agricoltura: Il caso dei 'boschetari' nelle serre del Ragusano. In S. Greco & G. Tumminelli (Eds.), *Migrazioni in Sicilia 2019* (pp. 261–272). Mimesis Edizioni.

Palumbo, L. (2022a). Exploitation in the agri-food sector in Europe. A comparative analysis of the impact of migration and labour regimes in producing migrants' vulnerabilities. *European Journal of Migration and Law, 24*, 287–312.

Palumbo, L. (2022b). Sfruttamento lavorativo e vulnerabilità in un'ottica di genere. Le condizioni di vita e di lavoro delle lavoratrici migranti nelle serre del Ragusano. *L'Altro Diritto Rivista, 6*, 194–229.

Palumbo, L. (2023). Le donne migrant nel settore agricolo. Vulnerabilità intersezionali, sfruttamento e agency. In: A. Corrado, L. Leone e R. Liotti, *Le dannate della terra. Donne e migrazioni nell'agricoltura della piana di Lamezia* (pp. 169–204). Rubbettino.

Palumbo, L., & Sciurba, A. (2018). *The vulnerability to exploitation of women migrant workers in agriculture in the EU: The need for a human rights and gender based approach.* European Parliament Study. Policy Department for Citizens' Rights and Constitutional Affairs, European Union

Papa, V. (2018). Paradossi regolativi e patologie occupazionali nel lavoro agricolo degli stranieri. In P. Campanella (Ed.), *Vite sottocosto* (pp. 243–258). Aracne editrice.

Papa, V. (2020). Il lavoro stagionale dei migranti. In W. Chiaromonte, M. D. Ferrara, & M. Ranieri (Eds.), *Migranti e lavoro* (pp. 279–294). Il Mulino.

Parreñas, R. S. (2001). *Servants of globalization: Women, migration and domestic work.* Stanford University Press.

Pastore, M., & Zorzella, N. (2020). 30 anni di legislazione italiana in materia di condizione giuridica della persona straniera. Alcune chiave di lettura. In M. Giovannetti & N. Zorzella (Eds.), *Ius Migrandi: la pubblicazione per i 20 anni di 'Diritto, immigrazione e cittadinanza'* (pp. 104–132). Franco Angeli.

Peano, I. (2017). Global care-commodity chains: Labour re/production and agribusiness in the district of Foggia. *Sociologia del Lavoro, 146*, 24–39.

Perrotta, D. (2011). *Vite in cantiere. Migrazioni e lavoro dei rumeni in Italia.* Il Mulino.

Perrotta, D. (2015). Il caporalato come sistema: un contributo sociologico. In E. Rigo (Ed.), *Leggi, migranti e caporali. Prospettive critiche e di ricerca sullo sfruttamento del lavoro in agricoltura* (pp. 15–30). Pacini Giuridica.

Picchio, A. (1992). *Social reproduction. The political economy of the labour market.* Cambridge University Press.

Pinelli, B. (2019). *Migranti e rifugiate. Antropologia, genere e political.* Raffaelo Cortina Editions.

Pinto, V. (2019). Rapporti lavorativi e legalità in agricoltura. Analisi e proposte. *Giornale di diritto del lavoro e di relazioni industriali, 1*, 7–36.

Piro, V. (2020). Politiche migratorie e disfunzioni funzionali. Il caso della legge Martelli. *Meridiana, 97*, 245–260.

Pitti, C., & D'Amanti, S. (2010). *Storie di donne immigrate. Indagine sulle difficoltà e disagi affrontati dalle donne che approdano nella nostra terra. Quali limiti della nostra accoglienza, quali ostacoli.* Ministero dell' Interno [online], www1.interno.gov.it/mi (Last Access Apr 2024).

Pugliese, E. (2011). The Mediterranean model of immigration. *Academicus International Scientific Journal, Entrepreneurship Training Center Albania, 3*, 96–107.

Recchia, G. A. (2020). L'accesso al lavoro dei migranti economici. In W. Chiaromonte, M. D. Ferrara, & M. Ranieri (Eds.), *Migranti e lavoro* (pp. 93–110). Il Mulino.

Redazione Salerno Today. (2021). Reclutavano straniere per schiavizzarle in agricoltura e come badanti: smantellata la rete in Cilento, in 9 nei guai. *Salernotoday.it* [online], 19 June 2021 [online], www.salernotoday.it/cronaca/immigrazione-clandestina-sfruttamento-moldave-rumene-cilento-9-arresti-19-giugno-2021.html (Last Access Apr 2024).

Rigo, E. (2022). *La straniera. Migrazioni, asilo, sfruttametno in una prospettiva di genere.* Carocci Editori.

Rizzi, E. S. (2022). Le donne straniere negli insediamenti informali tra discriminazioni intersezionali, grave sfruttamento e violenza. In A. Brambilla, P. Degani, M. Paggi, & N. Zorzella (Eds.), *Donne straniere, diritti umani, questioni di genere* (pp. 231–250). Centro di Ateneo per i Diritti Umani 'Antonio Papisca'. Università degli Studi Padova.

Sacchetto, D. (2013). Migrazioni e lavoro nella sociologia italiana. In S. Mezzadra & M. Riccardi (Eds.), *Movimenti indisciplinati. Migrazioni, migranti e discipline scientifiche* (pp. 50–67). Ombre Corte Edizioni.

Sacchetto, D., & Vianello, F. A. (2013). Crisi economica e migranti: il ritorno del lavoratore povero. *Mondi Migranti, 1*, 79–100.

Sanò, G. (2018). *Fabbriche di plastica: il lavoro nell'agricoltura industriale*. Ombre Corte Edizioni.

Santoro, E. (2010). La regolamentazione dell'immigrazione come questione sociale: dalla cittadinanza inclusiva al neoschiavismo. In E. Santoro (Ed.), *Diritto come questione sociale* (pp. 129–180). Giappichelli.

Saraceno, C. (2007). *Mutamenti della Famiglia e Politiche Sociali in Italia*. Il Mulino.

Sarti, R. (Ed.). (2010). *Lavoro domestico e di cura: Quali diritti?* Ediesse.

Sarti, R. (2013). Italia domestica. Breve storia del personale di servizio. In S. Pasquinelli & G. Rusmini (Eds.), *Badare non basta. Il lavoro di cura: attori, progetti, politiche* (pp. 19–40). Ediesse.

Sarti, R. (2022). Passato che non passa o futuro che avanza? Il lavoro domestico tra sfruttamento legale e illegal. In Slaves No More (Ed.), *Donne gravemente sfruttate. Il diritto di essere protagoniste* (pp. 57–68). Edizioni Gruppo Abele.

Schmoll, C. (2022). *Le dannate del mare. Donne e frontiere nel mediterraneo*. Astarte Edizioni.

Sciarra, S., & Chiaromonte, W. (2014). Migration status in labour law and social security law. In C. Costello & M. Freedland (Eds.), *Migrants at work* (pp. 121–133). Oxford University Press.

Sciurba, A. (2015). *La cura servile, la cura che serve*. Pacini Editore.

Sciurba, A. (2021). *Le parole dell'asilo: un diritto di confine*. Giappichelli Editore.

Suardi, F. (2016). Il rapporto di lavoro domestico. In R. Maioni & G. Zucca (Eds.), *Viaggio nel lavoro di cura. Chi sono, cosa fanno e come vivono le badanti che lavorano nelle famiglie italiane*. Ediesse.

Triandafyllidou, A., & Marchetti, S. (2015). *Employers, agencies, and immigration: Paying for care* (1st ed.). Routledge.

Van Hooren, F. J. (2012). Varieties of migrant care work: Comparing patterns of migrant labour in social care. *Journal of European Social Policy, 22*(2), 133–147.

Vianello, F. A. (2009). *Migrando Sole. Legami transnazionali tra Ucraina e Italia*. FrancoAngeli.

Zorzella, N. (2023). La riforma 2023 della protezione speciale: eterogenesi dei fini? *Questione Giustizia*, 14 September 2024 [online], www.asgi.it/wpcontent/uploads/2023/09/Questione-Giustizia_Zorzella.pdf (Last Access Apr 2024).

Chapter 6
The Italian Approach to Addressing Exploitation and (Not) Protecting Exploited Migrant Workers

In recent years in Italy, parallel to tightening and externalising border policies and placing restrictions on the right to asylum, there has been a growing institutional focus on the exploitative working conditions of migrant workers, especially migrant farmworkers. This has led, among other things, to the adoption of Law No. 199 of 2016 addressing labour exploitation and illegal gang-mastering.[1] This Law, which resulted from the work of many experts and activists in the field, is an important milestone. Since its adoption, investigations against exploitation (even in sectors other than agriculture) have increased (L'Altro Diritto and FLAI CGIL, 2022). Also, there have been noteworthy case law developments that have shown an attempt to frame migrants' related vulnerabilities to exploitation from a contextual perspective in line with a situational approach (Giammarinaro & Palumbo, 2022). However, as discussed in this chapter, the social provisions of this Law are still inadequately implemented.

At the international level, Italy is considered a model with respect to legislation concerning assistance and protection of victims of exploitation and trafficking, particularly through Art. 18 of the Consolidated Act on Immigration, D.lgs 268/1998. Even so, several elements, including inadequate implementation of this provision, have undermined its innovative character (Giammarinaro & Nicodemi, 2022; Palumbo & Romano, 2022). Also, Article 18 and related practices rely on a model of victim (mainly linked to trafficking for sexual exploitation) that no longer reflects the dynamics of exploitation and trafficking, especially in cases of labour exploitation.

By drawing on these issues, tensions, and contradictions, and adopting a gender and intersectional perspective, Chap. 6 critically examines Italian legislation,

[1] Law No. 199 of 29 October 2016, *Disposizioni in materia di contrasto ai fenomeni del lavoro nero, dello sfruttamento del lavoro in agricoltura e di riallineamento retributivo nel settore agricolo.*

L. Palumbo, *Taking Vulnerabilities to Labour Exploitation Seriously*, IMISCOE Research Series, https://doi.org/10.1007/978-3-031-55424-7_6

policies, and related practices aimed at preventing and addressing labour exploitation and protecting the rights of migrant workers. More specifically, it delves into whether and to what extent these laws and policies help produce and exacerbate situations of vulnerability rather than address them.

6.1 Trafficking, *Caporali*, and Exploitation in Laws and Policies Before Law 199/2016

Even before the adoption of the UN Convention against Transnational Organised Crime in 2000 and related Protocols (see Chap. 1), Italy was one of the first countries in Europe to establish a system for protecting victims of exploitation and trafficking, paying special attention to issues related to their assistance and support (Nicodemi, 2020). As discussed below, this system—based on Article 18 of the Consolidated Act on Immigration—has centred on the rights of the victims rather than considering them as a mere means for criminal law action (Giammarinaro, 2012).

The system was adopted in the late 1990s when the trafficking processes mainly concerned women coming from Eastern Europe involved in dynamics of exploitation in the sex industry (UNODC, 2009; Giammarinaro, 2014). Since then, while the development of a national anti-trafficking system has focused on protecting the victims, national migration policies—in line with those of other European countries and the EU—have become progressively more stringent, and the issue of trafficking has been framed only in terms of irregular migration and organised crime. All this, as already stressed in previous chapters, has led to a convergence between restrictive migration and anti-trafficking policies whose aim primarily is to prevent irregular migration and combat traffickers rather than protect those migrants involved in situations of exploitation and trafficking (Andrijasevic, 2010).

As it has become even more evident in recent years, strengthening border controls, denying entry, detention, and deportation do not operate solely as mechanisms of exclusion as they do not necessarily stop or prevent migratory movements. Rather they have channelled and forced migrants towards dangerous routes such as the Mediterranean Sea. This has produced and amplified migrants' situations of vulnerability, further exposing them to dynamics of exploitation and trafficking (Sciurba, 2021; Kuschminder & Triandafyllidou, 2019). This, in turn, has fostered a vicious cycle between stringent migration policies and anti-trafficking interventions.

In the framework of expanding national policies of border externalisation and increasingly tight access to asylum (Cuttitta, 2019; Sciurba, 2021), asylum policies have also intertwined with anti-trafficking and restrictive migration policies. The rhetoric of the fight against traffickers has become the conceptual framework for promoting emergency interventions and restrictive migration and asylum policies (Chap. 4). This has led to progressive compression of the right to asylum (Sciurba, 2021), further amplifying migrants' situations of vulnerabilities to exploitation. Emblematic in this regard, as mentioned above, are the 2017 Memorandum of

Understanding between Italy and Libya (renewed in 2020 and 2022), 2018–2019 Security Decrees (Law Decree No. 113/2018 and Law Decree No. 53/2019) and the recent so called Cutro Decree (Law Decree 20/2023)((Chap. 5). By preventing migrants from reaching Italy and supporting the so-called Libyan coastguards (frequently operating in close proximity to, or directly alongside, traffickers (Tondo, 2020)), these measures have strengthened the role of abusive actors, exposing migrants to recurrent dynamics of debts, violence, exploitation, and trafficking during their journey (see, among others, Amnesty International, 2021; Kuschminder & Triandafyllidou, 2019). At the same time, by narrowing migrant people's access to protection and regularisation, they have further increased the conditions of insecurity and precarity for those migrants who have been able to reach Italy, exposing them again to dynamics of irregularity, exploitation, and abuse (Corrado et al., 2018; Della Puppa & Sanò, 2021; L'Altro Diritto and FLAI CGIL, 2022).

In such a context marked by increasingly restrictive migration and asylum policies, national institutional attention to the issue of labour exploitation has, however, also grown since the second half of the 2010s. With Law 199/2016, which amended Article 603-bis of the national Criminal Code (CC) regarding labour exploitation and illegal intermediation, the concept of labour exploitation itself has started to become part of the vocabulary in dominant political and legal discourses (Sect. 6.2). Prior to its passage, the primary institutional focus was on illegal gangmasters known as *caporali*. The earlier provision contained in the Criminal Code's Article 603-bis mainly addressed illegal gangmasters (not labour exploitation itself) and, in practice, did not touch abusive employers. Indeed, the conduct of the *caporali* was subject to criminal sanctions, while, although not excluded, the employer's liability effectively took the form of complicity. This provision was adopted in 2011 (with Legislative Decree 148/2011), following the 'riots' of migrant farmworkers in Rosarno (Calabria) in January 2010 (Corrado, 2011) and the two-week strike of migrant farmworkers in Nardò (Apulia) in August 2011 (Perrotta & Sacchetto, 2014).

By focusing on *caporali*, the former version of Article 603-bis had driven attention away from the complex dynamics of exploitation. At the same time, it revealed that, in line with the EU policies of that period (specifically the Employer Sanctions Directive), Italian national legislation chose to address labour exploitation primarily through criminal law instruments rather than addressing it within immigration and labour law through measures for regularisation and protection.

As one of the lawyers interviewed for this study argued, 'the rhetoric surrounding *caporalato*, which accompanied the adoption of [former] Article 603bis, similar to the rhetoric of traffickers and smugglers (*scafisti*), often presented in sensationalistic tones, has diverted the attention away from the root causes of exploitation and trafficking and their complexity'.[2] Indeed, rather than being accompanied by labour and social rights policies to address structural factors related to exploitation, especially in sectors such agriculture and domestic work, a criminal law response to exploitation mobilised humanitarian infrastructures relying on an emergency-based

[2] Interview with a migration lawyer, Florence, March 2015.

approach (Dines & Rigo, 2015). As discussed below, this emergency-based approach still characterises policies for preventing and combatting exploitation adopted under Law 199/2016.

On the other hand, both the new law's limited scope and inadequacies in formulating the provision, made previous versions of Article 603-bis hard to apply in practice (Di Martino, 2015; Ferranti, 2016). In particular, it contained certain indicators of labour exploitation that referred mainly to the conduct of employers rather than intermediaries, creating difficulties in its practical application. As Caprioglio and Rigo (2020, p. 51) note, 'it would be naïve to attribute this inconsistency to good-faith errors in legislative technique, without taking into account the political compromise choices that led to the adoption of this provision'.[3]

Such a compromise was also confirmed when transposing the Employer Sanctions Directive with Legislative Decree 109/2012 into national legislation. In line with the EU Directive, this Legislative Decree introduced a residence permit (issued on the proposal of the chief of police and with the favourable opinion of the public prosecutor) to undocumented workers who were victims of 'particular labour exploitation' and who report employers and collaborate in criminal proceedings against them, as per (Art. 22 (12-quarter) of Consolidated Act on Immigration). But the Decree referred to a definition of 'particular labour exploitation' that did not conform to the definition of labour exploitation offered by the Employer Sanctions Directive (see Chap. 2) and that was limited it to aggravating circumstances. These included cases where employed workers are more than three, cases involving the employment of minors, or situations exposing workers to danger. As Caprioglio and Rigo (2020) have underlined, apart from the last circumstance, the other cases have a rationale as aggravating factors in criminal law but have little to do with the material conditions that determine labour exploitation from a workers' protection perspective.

Moreover, the choice of identifying situations in which the number of recruited workers exceeds three as aggravating circumstances was primarily aimed at avoiding severe penalties for the numerous Italian households employing undocumented migrant domestic workers. As a former Senator interviewed pointed out: 'If we had embraced Directive 2009/52/EC [Employer Sanctions Directive] in an extreme way, there would have been the risk of sending many Italian families to prison whom, however, the state had not helped to face the issue of caring for non-self-reliant people. I am not happy about this choice but it was obligatory. Yet, I know that this makes it very difficult to address cases of exploitation and trafficking'.[4] Therefore, in line with that 'tolerant' approach described in Chap. 5, the legislator decided to 'accept' to a certain degree the employment of irregular migrant domestic workers, acknowledging their necessity to the functioning of the national welfare system.

As mentioned in Chap. 4, the Employer Sanctions Directive includes other provisions on the protection of undocumented workers. However, in Italy, as in other

---

[3] My translation.

[4] Interview with a former Senator, Bologna, March 2015.

European countries (Berntsen & de Lange, 2018; Rijken & de Lange, 2018), protection provisions of the Employer Sanctions Directive have been inadequately transposed into national legislation. For instance, Legislative Decree 109/2012 did not introduce measures to systematically and objectively inform migrant workers about their rights. Moreover, it did not establish efficacious mechanisms through which workers can recover outstanding or differential wages, including in cases where third-country migrants have returned or have been returned (Paggi, 2012; ASGI, 2015; see also Pittaluga & Momi, 2020).

In general, with the Employer Sanctions Directive's transposition into national legislation in 2012, labour exploitation was, once again, primarily conceived as a criminal law phenomenon rather than as a systemic issue that required addressing the interplay of structural factors creating inequalities and injustices and, therefore, helping produce situations of vulnerability to exploitation and abuses.

On the other hand, as underlined in previous chapters, since the 2010s, there has been an increase in both EU citizen migrants and non-EU asylum seekers and refugees experiencing exploitation and trafficking for labour exploitation in sectors such as agriculture and domestic work. This has made evident the need to adopt adequate measures addressing contemporary forms of exploitation and protect the rights of victims, regardless of workers' migration status (Palumbo, 2016; Santoro, 2021) as Article 22 of Consolidated Act on Immigration applies only to undocumented workers.

In 2014, EU Directive 2011/36 on trafficking was transposed into national legislation with Legislative Decree 24/2014 on 'Prevention and Suppression of Trafficking in Human Beings and Protection of Victims'. This presented a significant opportunity to improve the Italian legal framework for protecting migrant workers and the rights of victims of exploitation and trafficking, irrespective of the regularity of their residence permit. While it resulted in the introduction of some important provisions, it did not, however, effectively develop an integrated, comprehensive approach to trafficking, as outlined in the EU Directive on trafficking (Nicodemi, 2015; Trucco, 2020).

Legislative Decree 24/2014 amended those provisions of the Italian Criminal Code regarding the crimes of 'slavery' (Art. 600) and trafficking in persons (Article 601).[5] In particular, Article 601 concerning the crime of trafficking was amended to adopt a more extensive and structured definition of this offence in line with the Anti-Trafficking Directive 2011/36/EU. Incorporating this definition contributed to a broader understanding of trafficking (Giammarinaro, 2012) even by judicial authorities as it encompasses various forms of exploitation (not limited to sexual exploitation) and considers not only cross-border movements but also internal movements within the same country.[6]

[5] Italy ratified the 2000 UN Convention against transnational organised crime and its Protocol (including the Palermo Protocol) with Law 146/2006.

[6] This understanding of trafficking has since been supported by relevant case law of the ECtHR, including for example by the decision in *S.M. v. Croatia* of 25 June 2020 recognising that trafficking can occur within the same country. However, as noted in Chap. 1, this decision has not clarified the relationship between the concept of trafficking and the concepts included in Article 4 of ECHR (slavery, servitude and forced labour). See also Stoyanova (2020).

However, there are some inadequacies in how the definition of trafficking provided in Directive 2011/36/EU was transposed into Italian law. As mentioned in Chap. 4, to strengthen the protection of those in situations of vulnerability, the European legislation—in line with the international provisions on trafficking (2000 Palermo Protocol and 2005 Council of Europe Convention)—established the principle of the irrelevance of the consent of the victim of trafficking to exploitation. Diverging from the international and supranational approach, the Italian legislator did not include this principle in implementing the Anti-trafficking Directive 2011/36 (Trucco, 2020).[7] However, the Court of Cassation has had the opportunity to clarify that the victims' conditions of vulnerability make their consent to exploitation legally invalid (Court of Cassation, No. 49148/2019.)

Nor did Legislative Decree 24/2014 incorporate the important definition of 'position of vulnerability' offered by Anti-trafficking Directive 2011/36. Instead, it only refers to specific situations of 'vulnerable persons' such as 'minors, unaccompanied minors, the elderly, disabled persons, women (especially when pregnant), single parents with minor children, people with mental illness, persons who have undergone torture, rape, and other serious forms of psychological, physical, sexual or gender violence' (Art. 1). This categorisation of vulnerable people into distinct groups viewed as ontologically vulnerable seems to overlook the situational dimension of vulnerability reflected in the definition of a 'position of vulnerability' provided by Anti-trafficking Directive (see Chaps. 2 and 4). In other words, it seems to overlook the intersection of different personal and structural factors that simultaneously interact to contribute to a person's situations of vulnerability to exploitation (Palumbo, 2022; Giammarinaro & Palumbo, 2021). Furthermore, Legislative Decree 24/2014 downplays gender dimensions and dismisses the need for a gender approach in addressing trafficking, as provided by the Anti-trafficking Directive; the Decree's sole reference to a gender perspective consists of a brief reference to gender violence in Article 1.

In addition to these gaps in transposing the definition of trafficking provided by the Anti-trafficking Directive, Legislative Decree 24/2014 failed to introduce some of the Directive's important provisions including, among others, those concerning non-prosecution or non-application of penalties to the victims (Art. 8) and adequate and unconditional assistance (Art. 11) (see Sect. 6.5). Furthermore, the Decree established compensation of €1500.00 for victims who have been ascertained with a final Court judgment. The exiguity of the amount, combined with the long time it takes to obtain it—in the current legal system, many years can pass for a judgment to become definitive—and the constraint of the availability of resources,

---

[7]As legal scholar Lorenzo Trucco (2020) argues, while this element can be inferred from other provisions of national criminal legislation, explicitly establishing the principle of the irrelevance of the victim's consent in cases of trafficking could make it easier for investigators, prosecutors, and judges to apply it when dealing with human trafficking cases and facilitate a more consistent approach (GRETA, 2019, p. 57).

expressively provided by Legislative Decree 24/2014, makes this compensation more a symbolic instrument than an effective tool for victims' support and empowerment (Nicodemi, 2020, 2022; Palumbo & Romano, 2022).

6.2 Law 199/2016 and Defining Labour Exploitation through Indicators

Law 199, 'Provisions to counter undeclared employment, exploitative labour in agriculture, and wage realignment in the agricultural sector' was passed in October 2016. Its adoption followed a series of tragic incidents related to the gruelling and exploitative working and living conditions of agricultural workers—including cases involving local women farmworkers[8] to address the shortcomings of Article 603-bis of the national Criminal Code (on crime of 'illegal gang-mastering and labour exploitation'). Law 199/2016 resulted from the work of many experts and activists in the field (Osservatorio Placido Rizzotto & FLAI-CGIL, 2018). Although it focuses primarily on criminal measures, it also introduced provisions aimed at enhancing transparency in supply chains and addressing workers' placement, transportation, and accommodation (Laforgia, 2020).

The first significant change introduced by Law 199 was to revise the restrictive approach and inadequacies of the former formulation of Art. 603-bis regarding he crime of 'illegal gang-mastering and labour exploitation'. In doing so, it also addressed what clearly emerged as a disparity in the treatment of non-EU undocumented workers—who were protected by national provisions (Art. 22 (12) of the Consolidated Act on Immigration) implementing the Employer Sanctions Directive—and local, EU, and non-EU regular workers who were not adequately protected in cases of labour exploitation that did not meet the thresholds of severe cases, such as slavery (Art. 600 of the CC) or trafficking (Art. 601 of the CC) (Ferranti, 2016).[9]

Law 199/2016 approached labour exploitation as a stand-alone offence. More specifically, it amended Art. 603-bis, targeting both illegal intermediaries/gangmasters—i.e., 'whoever recruits a workforce for the purpose of assigning it to work for third parties in conditions of exploitation, taking advantage of the workers' state of

[8] Among the tragic cases was the death of an Italian woman farmworker, Paola Clemente, from exhaustion in the fields of Andria (Apulia) in July 2015.

[9] Given these inadequacies of the legal framework and consequent difficulties in addressing cases of labour exploitation, especially in the case concerning regular non-EU migrants or EU citizens, most prosecutors—especially before the adoption of Act 199/2016—preferred to charge the accused persons with the offence not directly related to labour exploitation, such as 'private violence', 'kidnapping', 'abuse in family', or 'extortion' to obtain a successful conviction (Palumbo, 2016, p. 15). See, for instance, Cass. pen. Sez II, decision No. 656 del 4.11.2009; Cass. pen. Decision No. 32525 del 1.7.2010.

need'[10] (para. 1)—and abusive employers—i.e., 'whoever uses, hires, or employs a workforce, including through intermediation activities referred to para 1, exploiting workers and taking advantage of their state of need' (para. 2).[11]

Unlike the previous formulation, the new Art. 603-bis no longer refers to the existence of organised criminal activity. Furthermore, violence or threats of violence are no longer essential elements of the offence, but comprise aggravating circumstances.[12] This allows for addressing exploitation cases that do not reach severe levels and were at risk of escaping sanctions before the changes introduced by Law 199/2016, as emphasised by the case law.[13] Law 199/2016 also provided for mandatory confiscation in the case of conviction, the possibility of judicial control of the company and, in cases aggravated by violence, mandatory arrest.

For the offense to be established, two conditions are required: the exploitation of the worker and the taking advantage of their state of need. Regarding the concept of labour exploitation, the new provision, in line with the former formulation, provides for four indicators. The first listed in the new Article 603bis concerns the 'repeated payment of wages excessively below the level fixed by national or local collective agreements or anyway disproportionate to the quantity and quality of performed work'. The choice of use the term 'repeated'—in the place of 'systematic'—highlights that it is sufficient that this conduct be repeated more than once, but still be persistent over time (Di Martino, 2019).

The second category of indicators concerns 'the repeated violation of the regulations concerning working hours, weekly-off, compulsory leave and holidays'. Even in this case, the violation should be persistent over time.

The third category of indicators addresses the important issue of the workers' health and, in particular, the 'violations of safety and hygiene regulations in the workplace'. Unlike the previous formulation, it is no longer necessary, for the purpose of integrating the offense, that the exposure of the worker to 'health, safety, or personal well-being danger' is found; the violation of relevant legislation is sufficient, but repetition is not necessary.

Lastly, the fourth category of indicators concerns degrading working conditions, methods of surveillance, and accommodation conditions, which—unlike the previous provision—should no longer be 'particularly' degrading. This indicator significantly addresses the issue of living conditions, as labour exploitation also involves degrading housing conditions due to the overlap between working and living/reproductive spaces and times. This is evident in the cases of exploitation in agriculture

---

[10] My translation.

[11] My translation in English. According to the amended version of Art. 603bis of CC, labour exploitation is punishable with between one and 6 years in prison and a fine of 500 to 1000 euros for each worker concerned.

[12] In addition to violence or threats, other aggravating circumstances of the crime leading to a higher penalty are where 'the number of the employed persons is higher than three, or at least one of the workers concerned is less than 16 years old, or the person is exposed to serious dangers related to the characteristics of work or the working conditions' (Art. 603 bis. Para. 3).

[13] See Court of Cassation, Penal Sect. IV, Decision No. 5081/2019, December 2018.

and domestic work, as highlighted in Chap. 5. The new provision, therefore, pays attention to the pervasive aspects of exploitation, which also relies on the compression of workers' social reproductive sphere. Furthermore, the use of the term 'degrading' recalls an expression found in Art. 4 of EU Charter of Fundamental Rights, under Sect. 6.1, 'Human Dignity', and is also part of the lexicon concerning the crime of torture established by Art. 3 of the ECHR.

As Article 603bis expressively affirms—and the orientation of relevant case law of Court of Cassation pointed out[14]—for the existence of the offence it is sufficient that only one of these indicators occurs.

The importance and innovative aspect of these indicators relies on their orientation function. They should not be viewed as exhaustive in covering all possible conditions of exploitation, but rather serve as interpretative aids in determining the presence of exploitation (Di Martino, 2019, p. 93). They serve as 'hints' to guide relevant authorities in the evidentiary evaluation on a case-by-case basis (Ferranti, 2016). The contextual relevance of indicators allows for adapting the definition of labour exploitation to diversified situations (Di Martino, 2019).

The new formulation of Article 603-bis—and, in particular, the indicators—has fostered an intense debate, especially among criminal law scholars, regarding the interpretation of such indicators and their application (Piva, 2017; Di Martino, 2019; Torre, 2020). The same debate focuses on the limits of criminal law in addressing socially structural issues, such as labour exploitation (Di Martino, 2015; Torre, 2020; Rigo, 2022; Giammarinaro, 2022). This point will be addressed later in this chapter.

It is worth underlining that the definition of labour exploitation in Art. 603-bis as amended by Law 199 substantially reflects the definition in the Employer Sanctions Directive (see Chap. 2). More specifically, the indicators encompass all aspects of work protected by the Italian Constitution (particularly under Art. 36), and therefore are part of a broader framework concerning the protection of human dignity in labour activity. In this sense, in a significant way, through the indicators Art. 603-bis provides a definition of labour exploitation that recognises the dignity of working and living conditions as a criterion for establishing limits on contractual freedom, especially on the freedom of private economic initiative. As discussed in Chap. 2, this entails a conception of human dignity that, far from being an abstract and moral value, refers to its social dimension and, consequently, requires that individuals are in situations that secure decent working and living conditions (Rodotà, 2012).

However, unlike the definition provided by the Employer Sanctions Directive, the definition of labour exploitation contained in Art. 603-bis does not integrate a gender perspective, confirming the 'false' gender neutrality that, as noted by Maria Virgilio (2022, p. 41), is 'taken for granted in criminal law legislation' and that feminist legal scholars have always contested (Mackinnon, 1989). Indeed, the indicators do not consider the forms characterising the conditions of exploitation experienced by women workers. These, as underlined in Chap. 5, include sexual blackmail, harassment, violence, and specific forms of control and dependence,

---

[14] See, for instance, Court of Cassation, Penal Sect. IV, Decision No. 17939/2018, 12 December 2018.

especially when women workers live where they work, as in the case of domestic or agricultural work. These dynamics of exploitation and violence are often marked by the burden of family and reproductive work responsibilities that lead many women to accept abusive and degrading working and living conditions. In this sense, the absence of a gender perspective certainly represents a critical element of Art. 603-bis.

6.3 'State of Need' and Vulnerability in Recent Case Law on Exploitation and Trafficking: A Situational Perspective

As recent studies have underscored, the complexity of situations of vulnerability, in its situational dimension, is still inadequately addressed in relevant case law on exploitation and trafficking (Giammarinaro & Palumbo, 2021). Nevertheless, there have been some significant developments in national case law on this matter (Di Martino, 2022; Giammarinaro & Palumbo, 2022).

While most decisions concerning trafficking cases focused on situations of sexual exploitation, in recent years there have been some interesting rulings regarding situations of trafficking for labour exploitation that consider vulnerability from a situational perspective. One judicial decision that deserves mention is the ruling of the Preliminary Investigating Judge (GUP) of the Tribunal of Catania in the '*boschetari*' case.[15] This involved a situation of trafficking for labour exploitation in which Romanian farmworkers were employed under conditions of exploitation and severe abuse in the greenhouses in Ragusa. Among the farmworkers, there were also young women, some of them minors, who in addition to being victims of trafficking for labour exploitation were also sexually abused.

In line with the approach of the request for precautionary measures, the decision of the GUP of the Tribunal of Catania focused on the situations of vulnerability of the persons involved, recognising the abuse of this position as one of the main 'coercive' methods used by the exploiters. More specifically, the judge highlighted how the claimants' situation of vulnerability was determined by the interplay of personal (for instance, age) and structural factors, such as the degrading and poor social and living conditions in the country of origin, as well as the situation of isolation and degradation in the Ragusa greenhouses. In this sense—in a significant and correct way—the Tribunal did not consider it relevant that the victims were EU citizens, underlining how the status of EU citizens does not preclude situations of vulnerability to exploitation, even severe forms such as trafficking (Palumbo, 2020). Therefore, by challenging an abstract concept of vulnerability as referring to individuals or groups perceived as inherently vulnerable, and focusing instead on its situational

[15] Tribunale di Catania, Sezione del Giudice per le indagini preliminari, Decision No. 1397/2019, N.R.G. 2151/2018, N.R.G.G.I.P. 3889/2019.

dimension, the Catania judge focused on the multiplicity and intertwinement of personal and material elements that contribute to creating a situation in which a person has no other option than to accept exploitation and abuse, as mentioned by the Anti-Trafficking Directive 2011/36.

As previously emphasised, for cases of labour exploitation that do not amount to trafficking but fall under Art. 603-bis of the Criminal Code, two conditions are required: the worker's exploitation according to the indicators and the taking advantage of their state of need. With regard to the notion of 'state of need', certain case law has embarked on an interesting path by moving away from an orientation supporting a purely patrimonial conception of the state of necessity as a mere lack of economic means of subsistence[16] and emphasising a meaning that—in our opinion—is consistent with a situational conception of vulnerability. In particular, a few years ago, a decision by the Judge for Preliminary Investigation (GUP) of the Tribunal of Prato paved the way for a different approach in a case of labour exploitation in the textile sector (GUP, Tribunal of Prato, Decision 4/11/2019). The GUP affirmed that the notion of a 'state of necessity' has a broader, personalistic significance, affecting all aspects of a person's life and not limited solely to the financial or economic aspect. Therefore, according to the GUP, the notion of 'state of need' must be clearly distinguished from both the 'more binding' 'state of necessity' referred to in Art. 54 of the Italian Criminal Code[17] and from the different and more stringent 'situation of poverty', which could be faced through social assistance institutions (ibid., p. 25).

Drawing from this broad conception of 'state of need' and taking into account the international and supranational instruments on trafficking and related doctrine, the judge has underlined the need to distinguish between taking advantage of a state of need in labour exploitation (Article 603-bis) and taking advantage of a situation of vulnerability in the contiguous cases of trafficking and slavery (respectively, Articles 601 and 600 of the Criminal Code). More precisely, the judge interpreted the state of need as a situation that can be 'temporary and contingent', involving 'psychological, health, and various other issues' (ibid., p. 50). However, it has an impact 'even if limited and without absolute compulsion' on the capacity for autonomy and free determination, including contractual, of the victim who is in such a state of need (ibid., p. 46).

In an innovative way, therefore, the Prato judge made a distinction between the 'less pressing and compelling' nature of the state of need in cases of labour exploitation and the 'position of vulnerability' in cases of trafficking, which carries a more severe connotation. Such an interpretative approach has been confirmed by the

---

[16] See, in particular, Court of Cassation, Penal section, Decision No. 18778, 25 March 2014; and Decision No. 27427/2020, 20 October 2020.

[17] Art. 54 of the Italian Criminal Code exempts from sanctions acts that have been necessary to avert the risk of serious danger. Article 54 also requires that the agent person had not intentionally caused the dangerous situation, and the latter could not have otherwise been avoided. Furthermore, Art. 54 (para. 3) provides that the state of necessity caused by a threat from others does not hold the person threatened responsible; rather, it holds accountable the one who issued the threat

Court of Cassation,[18] which ruled that the state of need should not be understood as a state of necessity that completely annihilates any freedom of choice. Instead, it should be seen as a situation of severe difficulty, even if temporary, which limits the victim's will and leads them to accept particularly disadvantageous conditions.

The interpretative perspective proposed by the Prato judge and followed by the above-mentioned rulings of Court of Cassation highlights the complexity of vulnerabilities to exploitation and their situational dimension. The focus is indeed on the multiple and variable factual circumstances that can impact the worker's will and the extent to which their contractual self-determination is compromised. In this sense, the distinction between the less compelling nature of the state of need in cases of labour exploitation and the more serious nature of the vulnerability in cases of trafficking is in line with a situational conception of vulnerability that varies in form and intensity depending on the individuals and contexts in which they are situated (Giammarinaro & Palumbo, 2021). Thus, a worker's situation (of vulnerability) can be characterised as a state of need when it constitutes an 'urgent distress' that impacts the freedom of choice of the person involved without taking on the characteristics of compulsion; in other cases, it may be a situation characterised by greater severity, corresponding to the absence of effective alternatives, in line with the definition of a position of vulnerability provided by Directive 2011/36/EU on trafficking and relevant international instruments (see Chap. 4).

Such an approach, in turn, is in line with a conception of exploitation as a continuum ranging from less severe forms to situations of trafficking or slavery and characterised by varying degrees of submission or acceptance or both to certain exploitative situations. Along this continuum, as the dynamics of exploitation in agriculture and domestic work reveal (Chap. 5), various forms of exploitation are linked to different situational vulnerabilities, which vary in forms and degrees.

6.4 Preventive Interventions: Small Changes and Big Continuities

Through Article 603-bis of the Criminal Code, as amended by Law 199/2016, Italy is one of the few European countries that criminalises labour exploitation as such, regardless of whether it can be classified as slavery, trafficking, or forced labour. Art. 603-bis is, in this sense, certainly notable for its significance, especially with regard to the above-mentioned indicators, as it provides one of the few legal definitions of labour exploitation. Since its revision in 2016, investigations and proceedings for cases of labour exploitation and illegal gang-mastering have increased (Santoro & Stoppiani, 2022), not only in agriculture but in other sectors as well, including domestic work—even though the individuals who are accused and convicted are still mostly the intermediaries, especially in domestic work (Borelli, 2021).

[18] Court of Cassation, Penal section, Decision No. 45615/2021; Court of Cassation, Penal section, Decision No. 24441/2021.

However, as substantial international and national scholarship, especially feminist scholarship, has highlighted (Shamir, 2012; Kotiswaran, 2017; Rigo, 2016; Mantouvalou, 2020; Giammarinaro, 2022), social phenomena with systemic characteristics such as labour exploitation cannot be defined, understood, and addressed solely through the use of criminal law. From a criminal law perspective, exploitation tends to be primarily regarded as a contingent event and, in any case, only attributable to the level of abusive and pathological interpersonal relationships between exploiters and victims. Such representations may make sense within the confines of a repressive view of criminal phenomena but are not well-suited to capture and thus address the socially pervasive dimension of a phenomenon like exploitation.

It is worth noting that while Law 199/2016 focuses on criminal law measures and tools, it also introduces some provisions of a 'social' nature designed to enhance labourers' working and living conditions and promote transparency in supply chains, particularly within the agri-food sector. To fully implement these provisions, Law-Decree 199/2018, 'Operational Table for the definition of a new strategy to combat the illegal gang mastering and the exploitation of labour In agriculture'[19]—the so-called *Caporalato* table—was introduced.

This Table was established in October 2019. It is chaired by the Minister of Labour and Social Policies and comprises all relevant governmental bodies at the national and local levels, as well as the primary third sector organisations. Due to the complexity and cross-cutting nature of interventions aimed at preventing and addressing exploitation in the agricultural sector, its work has been organised into thematic groups on different topics, including fair agri-food chains, workers' accommodation and transportation, protection, and assistance measures for victims.

In February 2020, the Table approved a three-year Plan (*Piano Triennale di contrasto allo sfruttamento lavorativo in agricoltura e al caporalato*) to combat labour exploitation in agriculture and illegal gang mastering; approval was extended for another 3 years in 2022. In line with a comprehensive and holistic approach, the plan provides for interventions in the fields of prevention, assistance, protection, and the labour and social inclusion of persons who have been victims of exploitation. It involves the active participation of relevant regional and local institutions and authorities for each of the administrative regions.

This section offers a critical analysis of measures and interventions related to protection of workers' rights, accommodation, and mobility implemented under the three-year plan to combat labour exploitation and illegal gang-mastering. These initiatives concern the agricultural sector. Indeed, while there has been greater focus on labour exploitation since 2016, this attention has been primarily, if not exclusively, trained on the working and living conditions of migrant workers in agriculture. Other sectors such as domestic/care work have not received adequate institutional attention.

---

[19] *Tavolo operative per la definizione di una nuova strategia di contrasto al caporalato e allo sfruttamento lavorativo in agricoltura.*

6.4.1 The Network of Quality Agrarian Labour

Regarding supply chains, Law 199/2016 strengthened the national Network of Quality Agrarian Labour (*Rete del Lavoro Agricolo di Qualità*) established by Legislative Decree 91/2014 to register companies that respect fair labour and employment conditions. Law 199/2016 focuses on the Network as a tool to combat exploitation, going beyond a purely repressive approach and introducing incentives for agricultural companies to comply with regulations.

The requirements that companies must meet to be part of the Network include: no criminal convictions; no administrative sanctions, even if not definitive, for violation with regard to labour law, social legislation, and the obligations concerning the payment of taxes and fees in the 3 years prior to applying; being current with the payment of social security contributions and insurance premiums; and applying collective agreements.

However, these requirements do not include respect for the rights of workers by upholding collective agreements along the entire supply chain. In addition, according to Legislative Decree 91/2014, once enrolled in the Network enterprises are subjected to fewer controls. This last provision has been contested by trade unions as it may facilitate companies' ability to violate the law and the rights of workers (Palumbo, 2016).

Despite these incentives, at the time of writing, only some 6,700 of 200,000 potentially eligible agricultural companies are registered.[20] This exiguous participation is due to an interplay of factors that includes strict requirements for enrolling; companies' concerns about being 'burdened' by additional bureaucracy; and, above all, the lack of mechanisms to encourage companies to join (Palumbo & Sciurba, 2018; De Angelis, 2022). It is worth noting that Emilia Romagna and Apulia, the two regions with the highest participation of companies in the network, offer incentives to businesses. In Emilia Romagna there are regional public economic incentives related to the Programme for the Rural Development, while in Apulia there are private incentives promoted by the large-scale retail trade (De Angelis, 2022). However, as has been argued, the latter strategy involving large retailers risks nurturing a system that relies on unequal distribution of power along value chains, resulting in the compression of worker rights (ibid.).

Although the number of labour inspectors and the quality of their activities has been bolstered—with the support of cultural mediators provided by IOM[21] since the adoption of the three-year National Plan against *caporalato* and labour exploitation—labour inspections are still inadequate. This is due mainly to insufficient financial and human resources. For instance, in the Ragusa area (Sicily), there are only 63 labour inspectors for around 6000 farms. The shortfall in labour inspections

[20] For the list, see https://www.inps.it/prestazioni-servizi/la-rete-del-lavoro-agricolo-di-qualita

[21] The 'Su.Pre.Me' and 'A.L.T. Caporalato' projects promoted by the Ministry of Labour and Social Policy under the three-year National Plan against *caporalato* and labour exploitation have provided for the participation of intercultural mediators from IOM in the activities conducted by the National Labour Inspectorate.

acts a factor fostering businesses to stay in irregularity and deters them from participating in compliance and transparency initiatives.

Low participation in the Network of Quality Agrarian Labour is also linked to the difficulties related to the activation and operation of the Territorial Sections (*sezioni territoriali*) as provided under Law 199/2016. These sections play the role of decentralised structures responsible for facilitating local-level collaboration for implementing the three-year Plan against *caporalato* and labour exploitation. They also provide support to local authorities in drafting multisectoral plans and help direct them to the Regions, the Table, and the Network's Steering Committee, according to their specific responsibilities and competencies. The Territorial Sections are composed of entities such as immigration services, local institutions, employment centres, and bilateral bodies formed by employers' and workers' organisations in agriculture. They aim to promote initiatives at the local level regarding active labour policies, addressing undeclared work and contribution evasion, organising a seasonal labour migrant force, and assisting migrant workers. From this perspective, the *sezioni territoriali* could serve as important instruments for developing and implementing local policies designed to offer services to companies, enhance protection of farmworkers' rights, and address farmworkers' living and mobility conditions. However, at the time of writing, only 32 local sections have been established—a figure disproportionate to the number of Italian provinces (Osservatorio Placido Rizzotto & FLAI-CGIL, 2022). As emerged during the fieldwork for this research, the work of many of these sections progresses slowly and inconsistently. The difficulties regarding both the activation of Territorial Sections and the operations of those already established are largely due to uncertainties stemming from legislative provisions on their nature and functions, the characteristics of the context in which they are established, and their composition (De Angelis, 2022).

The inadequate functioning of these Territorial Sections has undoubtedly undermined those innovative aspects of Law 199/2016 that extend beyond a purely repressive dimension. As a result, this Law is often seen as valuable primarily from a criminal law perspective, with the risk of being used to fuel dominant rhetoric and discourse sensationalising labour exploitation when law enforcement authorities apprehend abusive intermediaries and employers.

An important aspect in which the Territorial Sections could play a crucial role that will have a significant impact on the protection of farmworkers' rights and the fair functioning of the agri-food supply chain is the national-level implementation of the non-conditionality clause provided by the European Common Agricultural Policy (CAP). As discussed in Chap. 3, this clause linking CAP payments to compliance with labour and employment conditions for agricultural workers is an important tool for protecting agricultural workers' rights (Canfora, 2022; Palumbo & Corrado, 2020).

In March 2023, the National Monitoring Committee for the implementation of the Strategic Plan for the CAP 2023–2027 was established (DM n° 0137910, 03/03/2023). This committee will regulate and monitor the social conditionality among various measures. Approximately 80 representatives from institutions, organisations, agricultural cooperatives, environmental groups, and food-related entities participate in this committee, with many also being part of the *Caporalato* Table. However, the space allocated to workers' representatives appears insufficient. As trade unions have pointed out, the Decree establishing the Monitoring Committee for the CAP grants one seat to each of the employer associations within the Table but a single seat for all workers' unions, both confederal and autonomous, disregarding any criteria of representation and representativeness.[22] The limited presence of labour organisations is certainly a critical factor that can significantly affect how social conditionality is regulated and implemented. Another crucial issue concerns the lack of participation of migrant rights and women's rights associations. In particular, the gender dimension appears to be lacking in defining the regulation of social conditionality. While experts and NGOs such as ActionAid Italy have emphasised the importance and necessity of taking the gender dimension into account in all policies aimed at addressing and preventing labour exploitation (ActionAid Italia, 2022; Giammarinaro, 2022), this aspect remains largely neglected, including in the context of the regulation and implementation of social conditionality.

Lastly, with regard to the interventions concerning the agri-food chain and value distribution, it is worth underlining that in 2021 Italy transposed into national law EU Directive 2019/633/EU on unfair trading practices in business-to-business relationships in the agricultural and food supply chain (the so-called Directive on unfair trading practices) through Legislative Decree 198/2021. As mentioned in Chap. 3, beyond some critical aspects, this Directive is an important instrument for addressing irregularity and supporting both a more equitable value distribution along the supply chain and transparency in commercial relationships. Its implementation into national legislation had led to the ban of 'double auctions',[23] a practice used by large retailers to purchase products that creates pressure on the lowest levels of the supply chain system, namely producers and workers (Corrado et al., 2018; Ciconte & Liberti, 2019). Legislative Decree 198/2021 also introduced specific regulations for the below-cost selling of agricultural and food products, limiting the scope of admissibility of below-cost selling—unplanned and agreed in writing between the parties—to only the hypotheses of unsold products at risk of perishability. Furthermore, the Decree has included, amongst unfair trading practices, the 'imposition of contractual conditions excessively burdensome for the seller, including that of selling agricultural and food products at prices below production costs' (Art. 5). As Canfora and Leccese (2022) argue, the legislator has thus focused attention on the basic issue that concerns the functioning of the supply chains, i.e., the fair remuneration of supplies linked to the methods of definition of the sale price.

[22] See for instance FLAI-CGIL (2023)

[23] The auctions are used by some large retailers to purchase products like tomatoes, oil, coffee, legumes, or milk. Retailers make an offer to sell their produce, then a second auction takes place, starting from the lowest price offered in the first round (see Corrado et al., 2018).

6.4.2 *Accommodation and Mobility Measures: The Persistence of a Reparative and Emergency-Based Approach even after Covid-19*

As highlighted in Chap. 5, labour exploitation in sectors such as agriculture and domestic and care work encompasses not only wage reduction and excessive working hours but also pertains to the organisation of the labour force, its reproduction (Rigo, 2022), and, therefore, the conditions related to the accommodation and mobility of workers. Indeed, as shown regarding the living conditions of domestic workers or women laborers in the greenhouses of Ragusa or even asylum seekers in reception centres, exploitation occurs through a continuous cost squeeze related to the reproduction of this workforce, resulting in many of these workers living in degrading and inadequate conditions.

As emphasised in the previous chapters, these inadequate and degrading conditions of migrant workers, especially those employed in 'key sectors' such as agriculture and domestic work, came into clear focus during the Covid-19 pandemic. While the global health emergency could have been an opportunity for adopting structural interventions, nothing has actually been done in this sense. The main national intervention concerned a regularisation scheme for undocumented workers in agriculture and domestic/care work sectors, which were recognised as essential sectors (Article 103 of the so-called 'Relaunch Decree'- Law-Decree 34/2020, converted into Law No.77 of July 2020). However, it was clear from the outset that significant shortcomings would affect its impact, resulting in a limited number of regularised migrants, especially in agriculture (Palumbo, 2020). Indeed, as numerous reports and studies have pointed out, the 2020 regularisation scheme essentially failed, with a low number of residence permits issued, especially in the agricultural sector (Schiavone, 2020; Corrado & Palumbo, 2022).

It is worth noting that in line with the previous regularisation schemes, the 2020 plan relied mainly on an employer-driven approach, providing a limited space of action for the workers. The limitations of this approach are particularly evident for cases characterising the domestic and agricultural sectors, where irregular recruitment of workers is connected to exploitation of workers in situations of vulnerability (Palumbo, 2020). The regularisation plan also included a pathway, referred to as the second channel, for obtaining a temporary residence permit to seek employment (ibid.).[24] The temporary residence permit to search for work, established in this second channel of the plan, is a relative novelty for the Italian legal system, which

[24] The 2020 regularisation scheme established two channels. The first channel allowed employers to apply to conclude a fixed-term employment contract for foreign nationals or to declare the existence of a relationship of irregular employment with Italian/EU citizens or foreign nationals present in Italy before 8 March 2020, who had also not left the country since that date. The second channel allowed foreign citizens (with a residence permit that had expired since 31 October 2019, who were able to prove they worked in one of the eligible sectors before that date and who had been present in Italy before 8 March 2020) to apply for a six-month temporary residence permit to look for a job in these sectors.

since the adoption of the 2002 Bossi-Fini Law has closely linked residence permits for work reasons to the existence of a work contract. However, prerequisites for this second path significantly narrowed its scope, leaving out numerous migrant people in situations of irregularity and precariousness, including many of those who were affected by the above-mentioned Security Decrees (Chap. 5). Lastly, by applying only to the agricultural and domestic/care sectors, the plan overlooked sectors such as logistics, construction, tourism, and food services that have high rates of undeclared work, including by migrant workers in irregular and exploitative conditions.

Building on a utilitarian and emergency logic similarly to previous regularisation programmes, the 2020 scheme clearly revealed the limits of temporary, selective, emergency-based, and excessively bureaucratic measures. This is especially true when it comes to addressing migrant workers' situations of vulnerability and exploitation.

The Relaunch Decree (Article 103) also provided that competent national and regional authorities adopt—including through the implementation of the measures established by the three-year national Plan against exploitation—interventions and actions to guarantee adequate and safe accommodation and services, as well as to combat undeclared work and exploitation, in accordance with with the actions provided by Law N. 199/2016. However, while there have been no interventions concerning the protection of rights of workers in sectors such as domestic work, the initiatives developed to implement Law 199/2016 have de facto left the legal and policy framework concerning the rights of farmworkers and their living conditions unchanged.

More specifically, especially since 2020 with the adoption of the three-year national Plan on labour exploitation and illegal gang mastering, several initiatives and projects have been funded to full implement Law 199/2016, particularly with regard to the provisions concerning workers' recruitment, transportation, and accommodation (Caruso & Corrado, 2021).These projects are intended to develop interventions for workers' social and labour integration to prevent and combat labour exploitation in the agricultural sectors and strengthen networks for assisting and supporting the victims.

Many of these numerous projects contributed to creating and strengthening mechanisms of collaboration and consultation among various institutions and civil society actors and developing multi-agency and multi-disciplinary intervention practices. However, in a context where substantial financial resources have been mobilised on the issue of exploitation in agriculture—and consequently numerous interventions have been initiated in this field—several interviewees for this research highlighted the risk overlapping projects and practices, even within the same territories. Furthermore, none of these projects entailed structural interventions, especially regarding issues such as workers' accommodation and transportation (ibid.). In line with initiatives adopted before Law 199/2016 (Dines & Rigo, 2015), these projects mobilised humanitarian infrastructures relying on an emergency-based approach.

The housing model promoted in many of these interventions in various contexts—for example, in the rural areas of Calabria (San Ferdinando and Tauranova),

Apulia (Foggia), and Sicily (Cassibile-Siracusa)—is to utilise cargo containers as 'guest quarters' remote from the surrounding urban areas. Such a model reintroduces a separation between migrant workers and the local population, with the risk of reproducing dynamics of marginalisation, isolation, and invisibility (Caruso & Corrado, 2021). This, in turn, amplifies situations of vulnerability, reinforcing farmworkers' dependence on abusive actors (intermediaries, employers, etc.) for mobility and for accessing basic services for their reproduction such as health services. More generally, this model perpetuates and fosters the compression of the reproduction sphere of migrant labour force and related costs that is crucial element of a system of production relying on exploitation (Caprioglio & Rigo, 2020), as illustrated in Chap. 5. These containers thus become a source for an exploitable labour force.

Moreover—and strictly related to the issue of social reproduction of migrant workers—most of the projects funded under the three-year National Plan on labour exploitation and *caporalato* have not integrated a gender perspective. This means that, with exception of few initiatives, no attention has been given to the complexity of migrant women workers' situations of vulnerability or their needs. Therefore, the issues discussed in Chap. 5 related to women workers' access to social and reproductive rights, gender pay disparities, the weight of family and care responsibilities in amplifying situations of vulnerability to exploitation, and the connection between labour exploitation and gender violence so far have not been addressed in many of the initiatives promoted under the National Plan.

It is thus not surprising that a recent report by the National Association of Italian Municipalities (ANCI) revealed that there are at least 10,000 migrant people living in informal settlements or unauthorised accommodations (dilapidated farmhouses, squatted buildings, etc.). All these are zones of deprivation of rights without essential services and open to dynamics of exploitation and abuse (Giovannetti et al., 2022). The data also show that in more than one out of five settlements there are households with women workers and children (23.3% of cases). Here, children live in a context of complete invisibility and segregation and in unhealthy conditions, while the burden of family and, more generally, reproductive work responsibilities further expose migrant women to dynamics of exploitation and abuse.

6.5 Protection of Exploited Persons: Limits of Current Legal Instruments and Their Inadequate Implementation

With regard to assistance and protection measures, the Italian system is considered a good model in the international and European scenario as, since the 1990s, it has provided specific measures to protect and support victims of exploitation and trafficking.[25] The main legal instrument is Article 18 of the Consolidated Act on Immigration, which provides victims of violence or severe exploitation with assistance and a residence permit. Article 18 applies in cases of violence or exploitation and when there is a 'concrete danger' to the personal safety of the victim as a consequence of escaping exploitation or reporting it or both.

The situation of exploitation or violence can be ascertained in two ways: by police and investigating authorities in the ambit of a criminal proceedings for the crime of aiding, abetting, or exploitation for prostitution or for the other crimes for which mandatory arrest in *flagrante delicto* as envisaged by Article 380 of Criminal Procedural Code (these crimes include slavery (Art. 600 of the CC), trafficking (Art. 601 of CC) and labour exploitation (Art. 603bis of CC) when committed through violence or threats); or by the social services in the context of social-assistance interventions by public or private social workers (these services include anti-trafficking organisations, anti-violence services[26]).

The most innovative aspect of Article 18 is that it foresees two paths through which the residence permit can be issued. One is the 'judicial path' requiring victims to report to police or cooperate with relevant authorities in the framework of criminal proceedings. In this case, the residence permit is issued by the Questore (police headquarters) also upon proposal of the public prosecutor or with their favourable opinion.

The other is the 'social path', which is not dependent on victims' reports or participation in the criminal proceedings. Here, the residence permit is issued by the Questore upon the proposal of social assistance organisation, such as the anti-trafficking NGOs, that have ascertained the condition of exploitation or violence.[27] This path is unique in the international and European scenario as most EU countries and non-EU countries provide protection and a residence permit to victims of exploitation and trafficking only when they report or cooperate with relevant authorities in the scope of criminal investigation and proceedings.

It is worth highlighting that in both the social and judicial paths the residence permit is not dependent on the existence or outcomes of criminal proceedings. This is another innovative feature of Article 18 as in most of countries there is a strong link between the criminal-juridical qualification of the offence of slavery, trafficking, or forced labour and the possibility of giving assistance and issuing a residence permit to a victim of slavery, trafficking, or forced labour (Giammarinaro, 2014). Thus in these countries, if the offence is not qualified as slavery, trafficking, or

[25] It is worth mentioning that in 2003, Italy adopted Act No. 228/2003, *Misure contro la Tratta di Persone* (Measures against trafficking in human beings) amending the Italian Criminal Code in line with the 2000 UN Palermo Protocol on trafficking.

[26] According to Art. 27 of D.p.r. 349/99, these must be social services provided by institutions and NGOs enrolled in the official register of organisations conducting activities in favour of migrant persons. These include anti-violence centres, voluntary associations, third-sector bodies, street units, and anti-trafficking toll-free numbers.

[27] It is worth highlighting that the procedure envisaged by the 'social path' is only mentioned in the text of Art. 18, being regulated in detail by Art. 27 of the implementing regulation (D.p.r 349/99).

forced labour the victim does not receive any help. By contrast, in Italy the fact that the residence permit is disentangled from the criminal-juridical qualification facilitates providing assistance and protection to victims of a broader area of exploitation.

Therefore, in a somewhat visionary way—especially with regard to its social path—Article 18 of Consolidated Act on Immigration introduced, at a very early stage of international actions against trafficking (for instance, before the adoption of the 2005 Council of Europe Anti-Trafficking Convention), an approach based on the principle of unconditional assistance for the victims of exploitation that considers the safeguarding of their rights as a priority that cannot be subordinated to criminal actions.

The residence permit provided under Article 18—now entitled 'residence permit for special cases' following the amendments of so-called Security Decree (Law Decree 113/2018 converted into Law 132/2018) –[28] is valid for 6 months and can be renewed for 1 year or longer if necessary for the purposes of justice. The residence permit can be converted into a residence permit for work or study purposes, giving persons the opportunity to regularise their position in Italy.

Significantly, the residence permit provided by Art. 18 is conditional on the person's participation in the assistance and social integration programme. This is carried out by officially registered anti-trafficking NGOs and associations and is aimed at supporting the victims' social and labour inclusion by providing them with accommodation and support, including access to education and training services. The residence permit can be revoked in the event the concerned person interrupts the programme or adopts conduct considered incompatible with the programme's purpose.

As a 2007 Government Circular clarifies, Article 18 applies to both non-EU and EU citizens. This extension to EU citizens relied on the awareness of the increasing presence of EU migrant workers in situations of exploitation and abuse, especially following the EU enlargement process. In the case of EU citizens, as they do not need a residence permit, the application of Article 18 results in practice in the person's participation into the programme of assistance (including accommodation) and social integration carried out by anti-trafficking NGOs and associations.

However, despite its broad and innovative provision, Article 18 has been inadequately and arbitrarily implemented across the country from the start (Nicodemi, 2015, 2020). Moreover, in recent years it has emerged clearly that Article18 is based on and refers to forms and dynamics of exploitation that have changed today (Giammarinaro & Nicodemi, 2022).

There are many salient points concerning Article 18 and its implementation. First, the 'social path' has rarely been applied, especially in cases of labour exploitation[29] and victims are often required to report or cooperate or both with competent

[28] Before the amendments introduced by 2018 Security Decree, the residence permit provided under Article 18 of D.lgs 286/1998 was entitled 'residence permit for humanitarian reasons'.

[29] For instance, according to official data, in October 2019 there were 462 residence permits issued under Article 18, most to women victims of sex trafficking coming from Nigeria (250), Albania (66), and Morocco (54) (Ministero dell'Interno, 2019).

authorities to obtain a residence permit (GRETA, 2019; Nicodemi, 2015). While the Ministry of Interior has clarified, with specific circulars,[30] that the residence permit is not conditional on the presentation of a complaint or collaboration with the police, in practice the 'judicial path' remains the privileged one (Nicodemi, 2020; Palumbo & Romano, 2022). This has affected the application of Article 18 as many undocumented migrants might be reluctant to report abuses and cooperate with authorities, especially in the absence of an effective complaint mechanism, adequate compensation, concrete alternative employment opportunities and long-term prospects for social and labour inclusion.

Second, the competent authorities have an appreciable margin of discretion in assessing the requirement of 'concrete and current danger' and they often do not take into account the specific needs and condition of the victims, and the interplay of different factors creating and amplifying their situations of vulnerability (Palumbo & Romano, 2022). It should be noted that, especially in the case of labour exploitation, a person's subjugation is rarely exercised with violence or threat, and in any case, does not expose the person to an immediate danger to their safety. However, this does not mean that workers do not need assistance and protection. As discussed earlier, most migrant domestic workers and farmworkers accept exploitative conditions because of their situational vulnerabilities. Many do not face immediate safety risks after deciding to leave exploitative working conditions. Nonetheless, as international reports note, these workers can face a danger related to the eventual risk of 're-exploitation'—that is, the risk of being involved again in dynamics of exploitation, for instance to pay debts incurred with abusers or traffickers for the trip to Italy (UNODC, 2020; Santoro, 2021). Furthermore, many of these workers may suffer the consequences of exploitation, which could have lasted for months or even years, with prejudicial consequences in terms of the person's psycho-physical well-being. On the basis of these considerations, many legal experts and scholars have underlined the need to revise the text of Article 18, removing the requirement of 'danger' (Giammarinaro & Nicodemi, 2022) and enabling a broad application of this instrument.

Another critical point concerning Article 18 concerns the fact that it often takes a long time to issue the residence permit granted under this provision. Furthermore, the permit is for only 6 months with the possibility of renewal for 1 year. This limited period appears to be inadequate to guarantee an effective process of the victims' social integration and is totally disconnected from the real times of inclusion in the national labour market. Moreover, there are often also problems and delays with its renewal (GRETA, 2019; Nicodemi, 2020), with the consequence of increasing migrants' situations of vulnerability.

Additionally, the requirement of participation in programmes of assistance and social integration is often experienced by victims as a period of isolation and deprivation of their personal freedom and autonomy. Not infrequently, they materialise into projects that (re)affirm subordinate positions (Palumbo & Romano, 2022). It is

[30] For instance, the Circular of the Ministry of Interior No. 11050 of 28 May 2007.

worth noting that these programmes under Article 18 were originally developed to address victims of exploitation in the sex industry who experience specific trauma and need specific security protection. Today, while there are still victims of exploitation and trafficking who require specific structured assistance and rehabilitation programmes, the primary need for most people, especially victims of labour exploitation, is to receive support and assistance in finding alternative job opportunities. In order words, what they need is to have a non-exploitative job.

It is also important to note that the effectiveness of Article 18 social and integration programmes is hampered by the lack of practical and promptly available job alternatives for migrant workers. This is especially true in areas or regions like Sicily with high levels of unemployment and poverty. In the absence of effective social and labour pathways, many people decide to abandon Article 18 programmes to undertake alternative routes, often preferring to return to degrading and exploitative working conditions. Typical in this regard is the case of many Romanian women farmworkers who managed to escape from exploitation in the greenhouses of Ragusa. However, because they could not find a stable alternative job quickly through the Article 18 programme, they chose to return to work in the greenhouses in conditions of exploitation, violence, and isolation. Among these cases is the one discussed in Chap. 5 of the working woman with children who experienced labour exploitation and sexual abuses by the employer (Palumbo & Sciurba, 2018; Sciurba, 2015).

In general, it might be argued that the path offered by Article 18 is characterised by an aura of precariousness and uncertainty that over time has led more and more people to opt for alternative forms of protection that ensure greater possibilities for long-term regularisation, such as international protection. Furthermore, national funds for anti-trafficking organisations are insufficient and discontinuous, and victims do not receive adequate reimbursement and compensation (Giammarinaro, 2022; Nicodemi, 2020; GRETA, 2019).

It is not, therefore, surprising that the number of residence permits issued under Article 18 has fallen in recent years (Nicodemi, 2020). This datum must be viewed in relation with the rise in the number of migrants, including exploited and trafficked migrant workers, who have applied for international protection (ibid.). I will return to this point later in this section.

Here, it is also important to mention that Italian legislation contains another instrument providing a residence permit for victims of labour exploitation. This is Article 22 (para. 12-quater) of the Consolidated Act on Immigration. As mentioned above, it was introduced through Legislative Decree 109/2012 implementing the Employer Sanctions Directive 2009/52/CE and provides a residence permit to undocumented migrant workers who are victims of labour exploitation and report and cooperate with relevant authorities. This residence permit has a duration of 6 months and may be renewed for 1 year or longer depending on the length of the criminal proceedings. Such a residence permit allows the person to work and can be converted into a work-residence permit.

Although in the last couple of years the number of Article 22 residence permit issued has increased—especially thanks to the aforementioned joint intervention of

IOM and the national labour inspectorate (OIM, 2023)—these figures continue to be low, as also emerged from the testimonies collected during the fieldwork (see also Caprioglio & Rigo 2020; Giammarinaro & Nicodemi, 2022). This low number can be read as a lack of awareness among the relevant local authorities, especially police and prosecutors (GRETA, 2019, p. 50). It should also be seen in relation to two main elements. The first concerns this residence permit's 'conditional' nature. Unlike the Article 18 residence permit, the residence permit under Article 22 is issued by the *Questore* on proposal or with the approval of a public prosecutor on the condition that the victim reports and co-operates in criminal proceedings against the employer. This requirement, as already stressed, significantly prevents many exploited migrants from applying as they are reluctant to report abuses and cooperate with authorities, especially in the absence of adequate compensation mechanisms and an effective alternative pathway for social and labour inclusion. Moreover, contrary to Article 18, Article 22 does not provide victims with the possibility to participate in a programme of social and labour inclusion.

The second factor affecting the limited issue of Article 22 residence permit is that it applies only to undocumented third-country migrant workers and omits all cases of exploitation involving regular migrants, including migrant workers with a residence permit for seasonal work and asylum seekers that today constitute a significant share of exploited workers.

Given the limits of legal protection instruments such as Article 18 and Article 22 and, more specifically, the fact that they do not offer a protection that is particularly convenient for migrant people, it is not surprising that in recent years many non-EU migrant workers victims of exploitation have undertaken other regularisation channels—first and foremost the asylum channel. In particular, former humanitarian protection (previous Art. 5, para. 6 of the Consolidated Act on Immigration) and now special protection (Art. 19 Consolidated Act on Immigration[31]) have provided many migrants, including victims of exploitation and trafficking, with the possibility to be regularised. Indeed, the relatively broad grounds for obtaining this protection and the related attention to the elements of applicants' social and labour integration have made this form of protection an important instrument covering a broad spectrum of situations of vulnerability, taking into account the working experiences of the concerned person and also applying in cases of labour exploitation and trafficking (Caprioglio & Rigo, 2020; Marchetti & Palumbo, 2021). As already highlighted in Chap. 5, some legal scholars have pointed out that humanitarian protection first, and special protection now, resulted in a sort of 'low-intensity regularisation' that allows migrant workers to obtain a residence permit intersecting the dynamics of gendered and racialised labour market (Caprioglio et al., 2023).

Given the extensive nature of this form of protection, it is not surprising that, in accordance with increasingly restrictive migration policies aimed at combatting traffickers and limiting access to asylum, the Cutro Decree (Decree 20/2023) has

[31] 'Social protection' under Art. 19 D.lgs 286/1998 was introduced by Law Decree 130/2020 (converted into Law on 18 December 2020, no. 173), replacing 'humanitarian protection', which—as already mentioned in Chap. 5—was abrogated in 2018 by Security Decree (Decree Law 113/2018).

addressed special protection under Article 19. Among other things, the Decree has narrowed the scope of application of special protection by removing the provision that allowed for it to be granted based on the migrant's family ties and their social and labour inclusion in Italy. As has been argued, this reform is in contrast with Article10 of the Italian Constitution obliging Italy to conform to international treaties thus giving rise to the duty to protect the right to private and family life of migrant persons (Zorzella, 2023). While it should be emphasised that respect for the state's constitutional and international obligations remains in the national legal framework, including respect for Article 8 of the ECHR, the new regulatory framework will both make the procedures more complex and also lead to an increase in judicial appeals.Furthermore, the Decree eliminated the possibility of converting a residence permit for special protection into a work permit. This means that migrants who had obtained this protection are no longer supported in a process of labour inclusion and so are further exposed to the risks of irregularity and abuse.

6.6 Referral Mechanisms Between the Anti-Trafficking and Asylum Systems and Attention to Situational Vulnerabilities in Case Law on Asylum

As pointed out above, in the current context of restrictive and selective migration and asylum policies and legislation, there has been in an increase in the number of migrants—including victims of exploitation and trafficking—applying for international protection, in accordance with the 2006 UNHCR Guidelines n.7 regarding the possibility of granting refugee status to victims—or potential victims—of trafficking. In this scenario, Italy has adopted specific coordination mechanisms to facilitate the identification of victims of exploitation, and in particular of trafficking, among asylum seekers and refer them to specialised and appropriate support and assistance services.

This coordination mechanism was developed in 2017 through the Guidelines for identifying trafficking victims among applicants for international protection and referral procedures (UNHCR, 2017). These were outlined by UNHCR Italy in association with the National Commission for the Right of Asylum (CNDA) to improve the convergence between asylum and anti-trafficking systems in accordance with relevant provisions contained in Legislative Decree 24/2014 (Art.10) transposing Anti-Trafficking Directive 2011/36. These UNHCR Guidelines are intended for the Territorial Commissions (TCs)—the bodies appointed to examine applications for international protection—and provide some standard operating procedures (including indicators) to support the early identification of victims. While originally focused only on trafficking sexual exploitation, these guidelines were updated in 2021 to give more attention to victims of labour exploitation.

In practice, the referral procedure introduced by the UNHCR Guidelines provides that when the TCs identify the presence of exploitation or trafficking indicators during the asylum seeker's hearing, they may report the case to an anti-trafficking organisation and, if necessary, can suspend asylum proceedings while waiting for a 'feedback note'.[32] This referral mechanism allows victims to benefit from adequate forms of assistance. It also helps the TCs acquire a more complete picture of elements necessary for evaluating an application for international protection. However, as the 2017 UNHCR Guidelines have clarified, the main function of such a referral mechanism is not to support TCs in making their own decision with respect to the recognition of international protection, but to 'allow the applicant, who is believed to be a victim of trafficking, to get in touch with the services specifically designed for their protection and assistance'[33] (UNHCR, 2017, p. 58). The aim is therefore to provide applicants with adequate assistance and support, addressing their specific needs and situations of vulnerability.

These referral procedures have been initiated by all TCs and, in most cases, formalised through Memoranda of Understanding (Protocols) with anti-trafficking organisations. Furthermore, such referral mechanisms have also been applied in other contexts, including reception centres and local civil tribunals (Nicodemi, 2020).

In updating the guidelines (UNHCR, 2021), one of the main changes is the greater attention to labour exploitation by developing specific indicators. These have been shaped around recurrent elements identified by Territorial Commissions and other key actors, including anti-trafficking organisations, with respect to cases of labour exploitation involving asylum seekers. The specific attention to labour exploitation has helped support Territorial Commissions in identifying cases of exploitation and trafficking. However, the lack of a provision for direct involvement of trade unions in the referral system is a shortcoming in terms of addressing different forms of labour exploitation and situations of vulnerability of exploited migrants.

In general, it might be argued that since implementing this system, there has been a significant increase in international protection granted to victims of trafficking and exploitation, especially victims of exploitation in the sex industry (Nicodemi 2020; Palumbo and Romano 2022). In its report on Italy, GRETA (2019) noted that a referral system is a sort of good practice in the European scenario, considering that many countries have not adopted any coordination mechanism between anti-trafficking and the asylum system. Indeed, this mechanism contains innovative elements, creating the space for a careful and thorough assessment of victims' vulnerabilities and the development of appropriate responses to their specific protection needs (Nicodemi 2020). However, there are also significant limitations that need to be highlighted.

First, as emerged from the data collected and interviews with relevant stakeholders, including members of the TCs, a crucial point is the temporal dimension.

---

[32] The 2021 version of the Guidelines offers two options: (1) the suspension of asylum proceedings when potential indicators of trafficking or exploitation are identified and the TCs decide to report the case to anti-trafficking organisations, awaiting feedback before resuming the procedure; (2) the alternative possibility that, if the TC already possesses all the necessary information to make a decision on international protection, they can refer the case to anti-trafficking organisations without suspending asylum proceedings (Giammarinaro & Nicodemi, 2021).

[33] My translation.

Indeed, the hearing in front of the TCs usually takes place when the person has already been in Italy for a long time, i.e., at least a few months. Therefore, at best he or she has already been exploited for a significant period or has escaped from a situation of exploitation. Moreover, the time related to referral and coordination mechanisms between asylum and anti-trafficking systems is often too long for exploited persons, who just need to find a job to make money, mainly to send to their families or pay debts incurred for their migration project (Marchetti & Palumbo, 2021; Carnassale and Marchetti 2022).

While the referral mechanisms between asylum and anti-trafficking systems have increased the granting of international protection to victims of trafficking—in particular to victims of trafficking for sexual exploitation—analysis of several decisions of TCs, especially concerning migrant women victims of trafficking in the sex industry, reveals a worrying tendency to deny protection when applicants do not self-identify as victims, fail to provide detailed accounts of the exploitation they endured, or do not show that they want to escape exploitative situations (Palumbo 2023). According to such a model, victims are expected to display their vulnerability and be deemed 'worthy' of protection, without revealing ambiguities and nuances; they must demonstrate a willingness to be 'collaborative'. Such a stereotypical approach, based on the perfect victim model (Pinelli 2019), affects the recognition of the situations of vulnerability of the exploited persons, overlooking the interplay of factors creating vulnerabilities to exploitation (Boiano and Cecchini 2020). Furthermore, requiring applicants to be 'collaborative' in providing detailed information about the context and dynamics of exploitation they experienced significantly weakens the referral system, which should instead aim to sustain a more appropriate assessment of the victim's personal conditions and protection needs. As Giovannetti and Zorzella (2022) argue, this approach distorts the asylum system because what should be prerequisites for the concrete recognition of situations of vulnerability (such as, for example, the reticence to talk about exploitation) according to the same UNHCR-identified indicators of exploitation and trafficking, instead becomes a reason for denying protection.

As the analysis of relevant documents reveals, there is a tendency, especially in the case of victims of trafficking, to subordinate the recognition of the right to international protection to the applicant's participation in the assistance and social integration programme provided by the anti-trafficking system (Art. 18 of Consolidated Act on Immigration). This is, again, a distortion of the asylum system. Indeed, as underscored by Maria Grazia Giammarinaro (2018), a former UN Special Rapporteur on Trafficking, the referral mechanism between anti-trafficking and asylum systems cannot be used to 'channel' victims towards the trafficking system.

One of the main concerns behind this restrictive approach is that recognising refugee status or some other form of protection to victims who have not freed themselves from the criminal network favours traffickers/abusers who could, hypothetically, exploit them by taking advantage of their condition of regularity (Nicodemi 2020). However, this fails to consider some central issues. One, that behind these asylum applications is a real need for protection and that recognition of a residence permit can be a driver for the exploited person to escape the context of exploitation.

The condition of irregularity, on the contrary, exposes the victims to dynamics of blackmail and dependence on the exploiters. Two, with regard to the dimension of self-identification as a victim of exploitation and trafficking, it is worth underscoring that many people are well aware of the forms of exploitation they experience but in most cases have accepted exploitative conditions because of their limited options. This is especially true when persons must financially support their families or repay a debt or both (Santoro 2021).

However, in contrast to these limited and reductive approaches, in recent years there has been a significant Italian case-law orientation, both by the Court of Cassation and local Civil Tribunals, in the field of international protection. Such case law has paid attention to the difficulties applicants may have in reconstructing their past and traumatic experiences.[34] It has also taken into consideration the interplay of personal and structural factors—including gendered and racialised injustices, social and family contexts, and institutional aspects—combining to create and exacerbate vulnerabilities.[35] Furthermore, in some decisions, judges have further underlined the importance of considering the indicators of trafficking and exploitation defined by the UNCHR Guidelines to recognise the applicant's situation of vulnerability, irrespective of the fact that the person does not clearly refer to conditions of exploitation or self-identify as a victim.

Difficulties in the mechanisms of coordination/referral between anti-trafficking and asylum systems emerge also in relation to cases of labour exploitation in Italy, especially in cases that do not amount to trafficking. TCs often struggle to identify cases of labour exploitation because they do not have competencies in this field and because asylum seekers often are not inclined during the asylum interview to talk about their work experiences in Italy. Further, asylum seekers do not see it as the main focus of their application for protection because they fear losing their reception due to their undeclared salaries.[36] Recent research by the Centre l'Altro Diritto and Flai-CGIL (2022) has shown that in many cases the path of protection, developed under a referral procedure between asylum and anti-trafficking systems, does not start or is interrupted as exploited migrants have not made contact with the anti-trafficking organisation or have broken off contact. In this context, the element of the timing of procedures plays a crucial role as many migrants are not willing to wait long periods without guarantee that this path will provide them with an opportunity in terms of social and labour inclusion.

On the other hand, in recent years greater attention to the various factors contributing to vulnerability to exploitation in Italy has been observed in the context of proceedings for the recognition of international protection, especially by some Civil

[34] See Tribunal of Bologna, Decree of 17.7.2019, no. 3272; Tribunal of Trento, Decree of 17.1.2019.

[35] See Court of Cassation, Civ., Decision of 24.11.2017, no. 28152; Court of Cassation, Civ., Decision of 17.5.2017, no. 12333; Tribunal of Bologna, Decree of 17.7. 2019, no. 3272. See Marchetti and Palumbo (2021).

[36] As noted in Chap. 5, asylum seekers hosted in reception centres cannot have an income higher than the annual amount of the national social allowance (that is around 6,500 euros per year) otherwise they are denied admission to reception measures.

Tribunals (Marchetti & Palumbo, 2021). There has been significant case law concerning former humanitarian protection and, subsequently, the current special protection under Article 19 of Consolidated Act on Immigration. This case law has focused on the vulnerabilities of applicants, including their vulnerability to exploitation, as well as their social and labour integration in Italy. This has paved the way for granting protection to asylum seekers in exploitative working conditions.

Two decisions of the Tribunal of Milan[37] (2021) recognising former humanitarian protection for two asylum seekers victims of labour exploitation in the rural areas deserve mention. The decision of 12 May 2021 (RG 57114/2018) concerns a young Gambian who fled his country because his stepmother repeatedly threatened and mistreated him. The TC rejected his application for international or subsidiary protection on grounds that the story behind the expatriation was not credible as it was supported by elements that were 'vague, generic and not attributable to a real experience' (p. 5). The Commission did not even recognise the presence of the necessary requirements for humanitarian protection. By overturning this decision, the Tribunal of Milan recognised the requirements of humanitarian protection in line with the principles affirmed by the Court of Cassation in its consolidated case law in the field (in particular, decision n. 4555 of 23 February 2018). Specifically, the Tribunal underlined that the applicant had an 'experience characterised by serious violence, family abuse, and a long and tortuous migratory path, evidently resulting in a profound vulnerability'.[38] The judge also pointed out that during the judicial hearing, it emerged that the applicant laboured as a farmworker in the rural area of Foggia (Apulia) in 'inhuman' and degrading working and living conditions:

> without a regular employment contract, for about six to seven hours per day [he worked] hunched over the fields to harvest vegetables, seven days a week, without the possibility of being able to take holidays or rest days, or being able to protect his health by taking advantage of sick days...the applicant live[d] in a house with a tin roof, consisting of a single room in which are placed four beds, together with three other workers...while the shared bathroom is in one separate structure; for this accommodation the applicant pay[ed] the employer the sum of 150 euros per month, thus further reducing the already meagre salary.[39]

On the basis of these considerations, the Milan judge argued that the condition of labour exploitation—not reported to competent authorities—'integrates an element of the already wide vulnerability in the present case. A vulnerability that has its roots in the total absence of concrete alternative solutions, given the impossibility to find a regular job combined with the fear of losing the one found which – although irregular and without the minimum guarantees of protection – allows [him] to survive in an extremely inhuman and degrading context' (ibid., p. 21).

The Tribunal of Milan decisions marked an important step in the understanding of the situational dimension of the vulnerability to exploitation, especially labour exploitation, drawing attention to both the different material elements (such as

[37] Tribunale di Milano, decreto del 12.5.2021, RG. 42,440/2019; decreto del 12.5.2021, RG. 57,114/2018.

[38] My translation.

[39] My translation.

precarious status of asylum seekers) that determine and accentuate the situation of vulnerability of the applicants and the different shades of vulnerability. From this perspective, labour exploitation not only relies on the situation of vulnerability of the concerned person but, at the same time, exacerbates such a situation, further entrapping the person in exploitative dynamics.

6.7 Concluding Remarks

In a context characterised by increasingly restrictive and selective national migration and asylum policies that contribute to the production and amplification of vulnerabilities, Law 199/2016 brought institutional attention to the issue of labour exploitation, primarily in the agricultural sector. Importantly, Law 199/2016 approached labour exploitation as a stand-alone offence, amending Article 603-bis of the Italian Criminal Code. More precisely, Article 603-bis contains the crime of 'illegal gang-mastering and labour exploitation' and defines exploitation by referring to indicators in relation to pay, working hours and rest, safety, working conditions, methods of surveillance and 'degrading' housing situations. This represented an important change introduced by Law 199/2016 as most of EU countries do not include a definition of labour exploitation per se.

However, the impact of Law 199/2016 has been predominantly in the repressive dimension to exploitation. In fact, despite several initiatives being launched (e.g., the Network of Quality Agricultural Labour) and numerous projects being funded under the National Plan implementing Law 199/2016, almost nothing has been done to strengthen the rights of workers and improve their housing and mobility conditions. Interventions on accommodation (i.e., cargo containers) have instead resulted in models that rely on the compression of migrants' reproductive spheres supporting a production system in which exploitation is also based on the reduction of workers' reproductive costs. Furthermore, most of these projects and initiatives have neglected to consider the complexity of migrant women's situations of vulnerability and the factors that contribute to exposing them to dynamics of exploitation and abuse.

In this context, even the protection measures for victims of exploitation and trafficking, such as Article 18 of the Consolidation Act on Immigration and related practices, have displayed shortcomings. They have demonstrated difficulties in recognising and addressing changes and complexities in the dynamics of exploitation and related situational vulnerabilities. This, in turn, has resulted in many exploited migrant people not receiving adequate assistance and support.

On the other hand, a greater focus on the various factors contributing to vulnerabilities to exploitation on a situational perspective has been observed in the context of decisions for the recognition of international protection by some Territorial Commissions as well as by some Civil Tribunals. However, the Cutro Decree's abolition of that part of Article 19 of the Consolidation Act on Immigration that provided for the recognition of special protection based on relational affective ties and labour and social integration of migrant persons in Italy will have a significant impact. It will probably push tens of thousands of people into irregular status, most of whom are workers, partly due to the simultaneous tightening of the possibilities for converting residence permits.

Therefore, while it is true that in Italy, with Law 199/2016, attention has been refocused on forms of exploitation that do not necessarily reach extreme cases like trafficking, the institutional response continues to be focused on criminal aspects. Structural factors that contribute to vulnerabilities and undermine the protection of migrant workers' rights are still being overlooked, and little attention is paid to exploitation in other sectors, such as domestic work. Meanwhile, channels for the protection and regularisation of migrants are becoming increasingly restricted.

In this scenario, it clearly emerges that the issue of exploitation cannot be addressed solely through a repressive approach but requires the adoption of a series of measures that prioritise the social dignity of persons, viewed (as discussed in Chap. 2) in its material/social dimension and therefore as a guarantee that nobody lives and works in exploitative and degrading conditions (Rodotà, 2012).

References

ActionAid Italia. (2022). *Cambia Terra - Dall'invisibilità al protagonismo delle donne in agricoltura*. ActionAid.

Amnesty International. (2021). *'No one will look for you': Forcibly returned from sea to abusive detention in Libya*. Amnesty International [online], https://www.amnesty.org/en/documents/mde19/4439/2021/en/ (Last Access Apr 2024).

Andrijasevic, R. (2010). *Migration, agency and citizenship in sex trafficking*. Palgrave Macmillan.

ASGI. (2015). *La tutela delle vittime della tratta e del grave sfruttamento: il punto della situazione oggi in Italia*. Associazione per gli Studi Giuridici sull'Immigrazione.

Berntsen, L., & de Lange, T. (2018). Employer sanctions instrument of labour market regulation, migration control, and worker protection? In C. Rijken & T. de Lange (Eds.), *Towards a decent labour market for low waged migrant workers*. Amsterdam University Press.

Boiano, I., & Cecchini, C. L. (2020). Le frontiere del diritto: gli artt. 18 e 18bis TU 286/98 in una prospettiva di genere e femminista. In M. Giovanetti & A. Zorzella (Eds.), *Ius Migrandi. Trent'anni di politiche e legislazioni sull'immigrazione in Italia* (pp. 662–685). FrancoAngeli.

Borelli, S. (2021). Le diverse forme dello sfruttamento nel lavoro domestico di cura. *Lavoro e diritto, 2*, 281–301.

Canfora, I. (2022). La regolazione delle filiere agroalimentari. Quali criticità? In Osservatorio Placido Rizzotto & FLAI-CGIL (Eds.), *Agromafie e caporalato—VI Rapporto* (pp. 103–112). Futura Editrice.

Canfora, I., & Leccese, V. (2022). *La condizionalità sociale nella nuova PAC (nel quadro dello sviluppo sostenibile dell'agricoltura)*. Massimo D'Antona Centre for the Study of Labour Law, Working Paper 460. University of Catania.

Caprioglio, C., & Rigo, E. (2020). Lavoro, politiche migratorie e sfruttamento: la condizione dei braccianti migranti in agricoltura. *Diritto, Immigrazione e Cittadinanza, 3*, 33–56.

Caprioglio, C., Montella T., & Rigo, E. (2023). La strage che diventa legge. *Jacobin Italia*, 28 April 2022 [online], https://jacobinitalia.it/la-strage-che-diventa-legge/ (Last Access Apr 2024).

Carnassale, D., & Marchetti, S. (2022). *Vulnerabilities and the Italian protection system: An ethnographic exploration of the perspectives of protection seekers*. VULNER Research Report 2.

Caruso, F., & Corrado, A. (Eds.). (2021). *Essenziali ma invisibili. Analisi delle politiche e delle iniziative di contrasto allo sfruttamento e per l'inclusione dei lavoratori migranti in agricoltura nel sud Italia*. Rosenberg and Sellier.

Ciconte, F., & Liberti, S. (2019). *Il grande carrello. Chi decide cosa mangiamo*. Laterza.

Corrado, A. (2011). Clandestini in the Orange towns: Migrations and racisms in Calabria's agriculture. *Race/Ethnicity Multidisciplinary Contexts, 4*(2), 191–201.

Corrado, A., & Palumbo, L. (2022). Essential farmworkers and the pandemic crisis: Migrant labour conditions, and legal and political responses in Italy and Spain. In A. Triandafyllidou (Ed.), *Migration and pandemics* (pp. 145–166). IMISCOE Research Series. Springer.

Corrado, A., Caruso, F. S., Lo Cascio, M., Nori, M., Palumbo, L., & Triandafyllidou, A. (2018). *Is Italian agriculture a 'pull factor' for irregular migration—And, if so, why?* Open Society European Policy Institute.

Cuttitta, P. (2019). The Central Mediterranean border as a humanitarian space. In N. Nyberg Sørensen & S. Plambech (Eds.), *Global perspectives on humanitarianism. When human welfare meets the political and security agendas* (pp. 15–39). Danish Institute for International Studies.

De Angelis, G. (2022). *La rete del Rete del Lavoro Agricolo di Qualità nel contrasto al caporalato: tra interesse pubblico e privato*. Istituto Ricerche Economiche Sociali.

Della Puppa, F., & Sanò, G. (Eds.). (2021). *Stuck and exploited. Refugees and asylum seekers between exclusion, discrimination and struggles*. Edizioni Ca' Foscari.

Di Martino, A. (2015). 'Caporalato' e repressione penale: una correlazione (troppo) scontata? In E. Rigo (Ed.), *Leggi, migranti e caporali. Prospettive critiche e di ricerca sullo sfruttamento del lavoro in agricoltura* (pp. 69–100). Pacini Editore.

Di Martino, A. (2019). *Sfruttamento del lavoro. Il valore del contesto nella definizione del reato*. Il Mulino.

Di Martino, A. (2022). Questioni di legittimità costituzionale sul reato di sfruttamento lavorativo: punti e contrappunti. *L'Altro Diritto Rivista, 6*, 1–35.

Dines, N., & Rigo, E. (2015). Postcolonial citizenships and the 'Refugeeization' of the workforce: Migrant agricultural labor in the Italian Mezzogiorno. In S. Ponzanesi & G. Colpani (Eds.), *Postcolonial transitions in Europe: Contexts, practices and politics* (pp. 151–172). Rowman and Littlefield.

Ferranti, D. (2016). La legge n. 199/2016: Disposizioni penali in materia di caporalato e sfruttamento del lavoro nell'ottica del legislatore. *Diritto Penale Contemporaneo* [online], https://www.dirittopenalecontemporaneo.it/ (Last Access Apr 2024).

FLAI-CGIL. (2023). *Comitato di monitoraggio piano strategico Pac, Fai, Flai e Uila: 'Ingiustificata discriminazione verso il sindacato'* [online], https://www.flai.it/primo-piano/comitato-di-monitoraggio-piano-strategico-pac-fai-flai-e-uila-ingiustificata-discriminazione-verso-il-sindacato/ (Last Access Apr 2024).

Giammarinaro, M. G. (2012). La direttiva 2011/36/EU sulla prevenzione e la repressione della tratta di esseri umani e la protezione delle vittime. *Diritto, immigrazione e cittadinanza, XIV*(1), 15–33.

Giammarinaro, M. G. (2014). Verso una strategia contro la tratta e lo sfruttamento. In E. Nocifora (Ed.), *Quasi schiavi. Paraschiavismo e super-sfruttamento nel mercato del lavoro del XXI secolo* (pp. 123–140). Maggioli Editore.

Giammarinaro, M. G. (2018). L'individuazione precoce delle vulnerabilità alla tratta nel contesto dei flussi migratori misti. *Questione Giustizia, 2*, 129–134.

Giammarinaro, M. G. (2022). Understanding severe exploitation requires a human rights and gender-sensitive intersectional approach. *Frontiers in Human Dynamics, 4*, 861600. https://doi.org/10.3389/fhumd.2022.861600.

Giammarinaro, M. G., & Nicodemi, F. (2021). L'edizione aggiornata delle linee guida su L'identificazione delle vittime di tratta tra i richiedenti protezione internazionale e procedure di referral. *Questione Giustizia*, 18 May 2021 [online], https://www.questionegiustizia.it/articolo/l-edizione-aggiornata-delle-linee-guida-su-l-identificazione-delle-vittime-di-tratta-tra-i-richiedenti-protezione-internazionale-e-procedure-di-referral (Last Access Apr 2024).

Giammarinaro, M. G., & Nicodemi, F. (2022). Un'ottica sociale e di diritti per contrastare lo sfruttamento. In Slaves no More (Ed.), *Donne gravemente sfruttate. Il diritto di essere protagoniste* (pp. 219–231). Edizioni Gruppo Abele.

Giammarinaro, M. G., & Palumbo, L. (2021). Vulnerabilità situazionale, genere e diritti umani. Analisi della normativa e della giurisprudenza italiana e sovranazionale sullo sfruttamento lavorativo. In G. Gioffredi, V. Lorubbio, & A. Pisanò (Eds.), *Diritti umani in crisi? Emergenze, disuguaglianze, esclusioni* (pp. 45–62). Pacini Giuridica.

Giammarinaro, M. G., & Palumbo, L. (2022). Vulnerabilità attraverso la lente dell'intersezionalità, nella normativa e nella giurisprudenza europee e italiane. In Slaves no More (Ed.), *Donne gravemente sfruttate. Il diritto di essere protagoniste* (pp. 19–33). Edizioni Gruppo Abele.

Giovannetti, M., & Zorzella, N. (2022). Donne, straniere e vulnerabilità. In A. Brambilla, P. Degani, M. Paggi, & N. Zorzella (Eds.), *Donne straniere, diritti umani, questioni di genere* (pp. 25–50). Università degli Studi Padova.

Giovannetti, M., Miscioscia, S., & Somai, A. (2022). *Le condizioni abitative dei migranti che lavorano nel settore agro-alimentare*, Progretto InCas, Anci [online], (Last Access Apr 2024).

GRETA. (2019). *Report concerning the implementation of the Council of Europe Convention on Action against Trafficking in Human Beings by Italy.* Council of Europe.

Kotiswaran, P. (Ed.). (2017). *Revisiting the law and governance of trafficking, forced labor, and modern slavery.* Cambridge University Press.

Kuschminder, K., & Triandafyllidou, A. (2019). Smuggling, trafficking, and extortion: New conceptual and policy challenges on the Libyan route to Europe. *Antipode, 52*(1), 206–226.

L'Altro Diritto & FLAI CGIL. (2022). Quarto rapporto del laboratorio sullo sfruttamento lavorativo e sulla protezione delle sue vittime, Centro ADIR [online], https://www.adir.unifi.it/laboratorio/quartorapporto (Last Access Apr 2024).

Laforgia, S. (2020). Il contrasto allo sfruttamento lavorativo dei migranti. In W. Chiaromonte, M. D. Ferrara, & M. Ranieri (Eds.), *Migranti e lavoro* (pp. 173–192). Il Mulino.

Mackinnon, C. (1989). Feminism in legal education. *Legal Education Review, 85* [online], https://www.austlii.edu.au/au/journals/LegEdRev/1989/7.html (Last Access Apr 2024).

Mantouvalou, V. (2020). Structural injustice and the human rights of workers. *Current Legal Problems, 73*(1), 59–87.

Marchetti, S., & Palumbo, L. (Eds.) (2021). *Vulnerability in the Asylum and protection system in Italy: Legal and policy framework and implementing practices.* Vulner Research Report 1.

Ministero dell'Interno – Dipartimento della Pubblica Sicurezza (2019). *1 Commissione (Affari costituzionali) del Senato della Repubblica. Indagine conoscitiva sul fenomeno della prostituzione* [online], https://www.senato.it/application/xmanager/projects/leg18/attachments/documento_evento_procedura_commissione/files/000/036/201/DIREZIONE_CENTRALE_ANTICRIMINE.pdf (Last Access Apr 2024).

Nicodemi, F. (2015). *La tutela delle vittime di tratta e del grave sfruttamento: Il punto della situazione oggi in Italia* [online], https://www.asgi.it/notizia/look-out-report-sfruttamento-lavorativo-tratta-italia (Last Access Apr 2024).

Nicodemi, F. (2020). Il sistema anti-tratta italiano compie venti anni. L'evoluzione delle misure legislative e di assistenza per le vittime e le interconnessioni con il sistema della protezione internazionale. In M. Giovanetti & N. Zorzella (Eds.), *Ius Migrandi. Trent'anni di politiche e legislazioni sull'immigrazione in Italia* (pp. 703–728). FrancoAngeli.

Nicodemi, F. (2022). L'emersione tardiva della vicenda di tratta nel procedimento giurisdizionale per il riconoscimento della protezione internazionale. *Questione Giustizia*, 5 May 2020 [online], https://www.questionegiustizia.it/articolo/emersione-tardiva-tratta (Last Access Apr 2024).

OIM. (2023). *OIM e INL rinnovano la collaborazione nel contrasto allo sfruttamento lavorativo*, 15 June 2023 [online], https://italy.iom.int/it/news/oim-e-inl-rinnovano-la-collaborazione-nel-contrasto-allo-sfruttamento-lavorativo (Last Access Apr 2024).

Osservatorio Placido Rizzotto & FLAI-CGIL (Eds.). (2018). *Agromafie e caporalato—IV Rapporto.* Eddiesse.

Osservatorio Placido Rizzotto & FLAI-CGIL (Eds.). (2022). *Agromafie e caporalato— VI Rapporto*. Futura Editrice.

Paggi, M. (2012). La tutela degli immigrati irregolari vittime di grave sfruttamento in ambito lavorativo: un percorso ad ostacoli per l'effettivo recepimento della direttiva 52/2009. *Diritto, Immigrazione e Cittadinanza, 4*, 87–104.

Palumbo, L. (2016). *Trafficking and labour exploitation in domestic work and the agricultural sector in Italy*. RSCAS Research project report, European University Institute.

Palumbo, L. (2020). Tratta di esseri umani e sfruttamento lavorativo in agricoltura: Il caso dei 'boschetari' nelle serre del Ragusano. In S. Greco & G. Tumminelli (Eds.), *Migrazioni in Sicilia* (pp. 261–272). Mimesis.

Palumbo, L. (2023). Vulnerability to exploitation through the lens of intersectionality. *European Journal of Migration and Law, 25*, 421–448.

Palumbo, L., & Corrado, A. (2020). *Are agri-food workers only exploited in Southern Europe. Case studies on migrant labor in Germany, Netherlands, and Sweden*. Open Society Foundations.

Palumbo, L., & Romano, S. (2022). Evoluzione e limiti del sistema anti-tratta italiano e le connessioni con il sistema della protezione internazionale. In G. Garofalo Geymonat & G. Selmi (Eds.), *Prostituzione e lavoro sessuale in Italia* (pp. 64–84). Rosenberg and Sellier.

Palumbo, L., & Sciurba, A. (2018). *The vulnerability to exploitation of women migrant workers in agriculture in the EU: The need for a human rights and gender based approach*. European Parliament Study. Policy Department for Citizens' Rights and Constitutional Affairs, European Union.

Perrotta, D., & Sacchetto, D. (2014). Migrant farmworkers in Southern Italy: Ghettoes, caporalato and collective action. *Workers of the World, 1*(5), 75–98.

Pinelli, B. (2019). *Migranti e rifugiate. Antropologia, genere e politica*. Edizioni libreria.

Pittaluga, C., & Momi, C. (2020). L'impatto della direttiva 52/2009/CE sul fenomeno dello sfruttamento lavorativo tra i braccianti agricoli. In Rigo, E. (Ed.). (2016). *Leggi, migranti e caporali. Prospettive critiche e di ricerca sullo sfruttamento del lavoro in agricoltura*. Pacini Giuridica.

Piva, D. (2017). I limiti dell'intervento penale sul caporalato come sistema (e non condotta) di produzione: brevi note a margine della L. 199/2016. *Archivo Penale, 1*, 184–196.

Rigo, E. (Ed.). (2016). *Leggi, migranti e caporali. Prospettive critiche e di ricerca sullo sfruttamento del lavoro in agricoltura*. Pacini Giuridica.

Rigo, E. (2022). *La straniera. Migrazioni, asilo, sfruttametno in una prospettiva di genere*. Carocci Editori.

Rijken, C., & de Lange, T. (Eds.). (2018). *Towards a decent labour market for low waged migrant workers*. Amsterdam University Press.

Rodotà, S. (2012). *Il diritto di avere diritti*. Editori Laterza.

Santoro, E. (2021). La protezione delle vittime di sfruttamento lavorativo: Una pratica sovversiva di alcuni capisaldi della nostra cultura giuridico-politica. *Sociologia del diritto, 3*, 164–189.

Santoro, E., & Stoppiani, C. (2022). Lo sfruttamento lavorativo e la protezione delle sue vittime. In Centro studi e ricerche – IDOS. *Dossier statistico immigrazione 2022"* (pp. 131–136). Edizioni IDOS.

Schiavone, G. (2020). La regolarizzazione nell'anno della pandemia: prime riflessioni. In Centro studi e ricerche – IDOS. *Dossier statistico immigrazione 2020* (pp. 131–136). Edizioni IDOS.

Sciurba, A. (2015). *La cura servile, la cura che serve*. Pacini Editore.

Sciurba, A. (2021). *Le parole dell'asilo: un diritto di confine*. Giappichelli Editore.

Shamir, H. (2012). A labor paradigm for human trafficking. *UCLA Law Review, 60*(1), 76–136.

Stoyanova, V. (2020). The Grand Chamber Judgment in *S.M. v Croatia*: Human trafficking, prostitution, and the definitional scope of Article 4 ECHR. *StrasbourgObservers*, 3 July 2020, https://strasbourgobservers.com/2020/07/03/the-grand-chamber-judgment-in-s-m-v-croatia-human-trafficking-prostitution-and-the-definitional-scope-of-article-4-echr/ (Last Access Apr 2024).

Tondo, L. (2020). Senior Libyan coastguard commander arrested for alleged human trafficking. *The Guardian*, 16 October 2020 [online], https://www.theguardian.com/global-development/2020/oct/16/senior-libyan-coastguard-commander-arrested-for-alleged-human-trafficking (Last Access Apr 2024).

Torre, V. (2020). L'obsolescenza dell'art. 603-bis c.p. e le nuove forme di sfruttamento lavorativo. *Labour and Law, 6*(2), 73–97.
Trucco, L. (2020). L'evoluzione della normativa relativa allo sfruttamento lavorativo dei migranti/caporalato e fattispecie correlate. In M. Giovannetti & N. Zorzella (Eds.), *Ius Migrandi: la pubblicazione per i 20 anni di 'Diritto, immigrazione e cittadinanza'* (pp. 639–662). Francoangeli.
UNHCR. (2017). *L'identificazione delle vittime di tratta tra i richiedenti protezione internazionale e procedure di referral. Linee guida per le Commissioni Territoriali per il riconoscimento della protezione internazionale*. United Nations Refugee Agency.
UNHCR. (2021). L'identificazione delle vittime di tratta tra i richiedenti protezione internazionale e procedure di referral. Linee guida per le Commissioni Territoriali per il riconoscimento della protezione internazionale. Versione Aggiornata. United Nations Refugee Agency.
UNODC. (2009). *Global Report on trafficking*. United Nations Office on Drugs and Crime.
UNODC. (2020). *Legislative guide on the trafficking in persons protocol only, 2020 update*. United Nations Office on Drugs and Crime.
Virgilio, M. (2022). Sfruttamento e violenza contro le donne. Gli strumenti giuridici tra normativa ed effettività. In Slaves No More (Ed.), *Donne gravemente sfruttate. Il diritto di essere protagoniste* (pp. 41–53). Edizioni Gruppo Abele.
Zorzella, N. (2023). La riforma 2023 della protezione speciale: eterogenesi dei fini? *Questione Giustizia* [online], https://www.asgi.it/wp-content/uploads/2023/09/Questione-Giustizia_Zorzella.pdf (Last Access Apr 2024).

Chapter 7
Situational Vulnerabilities and Labour Exploitation in the UK: The Case of the Agricultural and Domestic Migrant Workers

This chapter's critical focus is on the legal and regulatory framework concerning migrant workers in the UK, with special attention paid to migrant seasonal workers and domestic workers. The UK was selected for study as a country with a distinct migration history, legal framework, and economic model. Unlike Italy, which has a historical tradition of emigration and with only a recent history of immigration, the UK is among European countries, including Germany and France, traditionally receiving migrants (King et al., 2000). Another difference is that the UK has been traditionally characterised by a liberal market economy, displaying low state intervention and encouraging deregulation and flexibility (Hall & Soskice, 2001). Furthermore, and partly related to its liberal market economy model, the UK opted out of various EU Directives on labour migration before its exit from the EU. These included the Employer Sanctions Directive and the Seasonal Workers Directive. On the other hand, like Italy, since the 2000s the UK has progressively embraced selective and stringent migration and asylum policies. These policies have encouraged the sectoral concentration of migrant labour and led to a stratification of migrant workers with varied legal statuses, and consequently, varying rights and levels of protection.

As in Italy and other European countries, agriculture and domestic work in the UK are sectors especially reliant on the labour of migrant workers, many of whom hold temporary legal status or are in conditions of irregularity and often experience abuse and exploitation, including severe exploitation (Kalayaan, 2019; FLEX, 2021; GRETA, 2021). Adopting a gender and intersectional perspective, this chapter critically analyses relevant labour and migration regulatory and legal regimes. In this light, it examines the interplay of factors that contribute to creating and exacerbating migrant workers' situational vulnerabilities to exploitation and pays attention to similar patterns and dynamics across these sectors.

L. Palumbo, *Taking Vulnerabilities to Labour Exploitation Seriously*, IMISCOE Research Series, https://doi.org/10.1007/978-3-031-55424-7_7

7.1 Setting the Scene

7.1.1 Major Milestones in UK Migration Policies between 2000 and 2023

Similar to Germany, since the early 2000s, the UK has adopted 'a neo-liberal modernising agenda to loosen rules as part of a broader economic strategy of meeting skills shortages and attracting highly qualified migrants' (Geddes et al., 2020, p. 71). It shaped policy tools for selecting and attracting third-country migrants, including through the development of a skills-based programme for migrant workers with 'exceptional skills' and a fast-track work permit system for skilled migrant workers for sectors experiencing 'severe skill shortages' (ibid.). In particular, between 2002 and 2008, the High Skilled Migrant Programme (later replaced by the Tier 1 visa) was implemented allowing migrants' entry on the basis of their level of education and earnings, without introducing any limits on their numbers. Also, work permit regulations (later replaced by the Tier 2 visa) were weakened to better respond to the needs of employers (Calò et al., 2021).

At the same time, the UK was one of the first European countries (together with Ireland and Sweden) to grant immediate labour market access to nationals of the eight central and east European countries that joined the EU in May 2004: Czech Republic, Estonia, Hungary, Latvia, Lithuania, Poland, Slovakia, and Slovenia (Wright, 2017). In addition to shortages in key economic sectors, one reason for this openness was that Britain 'had long been advocate of a "wider" EU, which it was hoped would diminish federal impulses and therefore sought to build bridges to new member states' (Geddes & Scholten, 2016, p. 36). Furthermore, as Geddes and Scholten also highlighted, this decision fitted with a more 'general ideological commitment to ensuring competitiveness in the global economy' (ibid.). Given the sufficient supply of labour in so called low-skilled jobs following the 2004 and 2007 EU enlargements, a route for 'low-skilled' labour migration had never been made operational (Sumption & Fernandez-Reino, 2018) and, as discussed below (Sect. 7.1.2), in practice still remains closed, with only a few exceptions for certain occupations, such as care and health workers.

The main consequence of these liberalisation policies for both EU and non-EU migrant workers was the highest inflow of migrants in the UK's history (Dennison & Geddes, 2018). More specifically, the number of EU national migrant workers was much larger than expected. As Dennison and Geddes (2018) have highlighted, in 2014 the number of EU nationals moving into the UK outnumbered, for the first time, third-country migrant workers. The UK government's initial reaction was to try to reduce migration into lower-skilled employment. But given that much of such migration concerned EU citizens, it was impossible to control and limit it.

The global economic crisis in 2008 led the UK to change its migration policies. In 2010, the UK government defined and introduced a 'net migration target'—that is a sort of balance between immigration and emigration—with the aim of reducing immigration to the UK to the tens of thousands annually. This target also included free movement of EU citizens, even if they could not be subject to immigration controls, as the only restriction adopted with respect to EU citizens can be on grounds of public policy, public security, or public health, according to the Citizen's Rights Directive 2004/38/EC. However, this restrictive UK migration policy was unsuccessful as the identified 'net migration target' never even came close to being reached (ibid.).

In general, since the 2000s, especially following the 2008 economic crisis, policies and legislation prioritising migration control over integration have gained support, leading to progressively stringent migration and border controls, as well as restrictive asylum policies (Geddes & Scholten, 2016). As a consequence, the number of migrant persons ultimately granted leave to stay has remained low when compared to other European countries such as Germany and Italy (Calò et al., 2021).

Calò and colleagues see a new phase in UK migration policies emerging in 2015. The election of a new Conservative government committed to renegotiating the UK-EU relationship, the rise of populist movements, and the implementation of austerity measures following the 2008 economic crisis 'have, alongside aspects of the campaign to leave the European Union, contributed to the development of a dominant narrative in UK policymaking that emphasises the securing of borders and a more restrictive disposition towards migration more generally' (Calo et al., 2021, p. 237).

In the context of the 'hostile environment' against migration (Åhlberg & Granada, 2022), the implementation of the Immigration Acts in 2014 and 2016 introduced more stringent migration and asylum policies. For instance, the 2014 Act aimed at facilitating the removal of migrants without leave to remain, limiting access to housing and health services, in particular the National Health Service or NHS (Wallace, 2018), and overhauling the appeals process. This latter provision of the Act was found unlawful by the Supreme Court in June 2017, in the case of *R (Kiarie) v Secretary of State for the Home Department*; *R (Byndloss) v Secretary of State for the Home Department* [2017] UKSC 42. In this decision, the Supreme Court highlighted that 'deport first, appeal later' was a breach of the procedural requirements of Article 8 of the ECHR regarding the right to a private and family life. As a result of this ruling, asylum seekers as well as refugees and migrants are allowed to stay in the UK while their appeals are being processed.

The 2016 Immigration Act introduced further restrictive interventions to control migrants' mobility and combat irregular migration. It established penalties (a monetary fine, six-month custodial sentence, and the confiscation of any income earned during the relevant working period) for employers who hire undocumented migrants and landlords who rent properties to migrants in irregular conditions. At the same time, it prevented undocumented migrants from accessing everyday necessities, such as a bank account (Calò et al., 2021, p. 23). As Judy Fudge (2018, p. 28) significantly argued, 'the new crime of illegal working was inextricably linked by the government to both the distinct problem of enforcing labour standards in a neoliberal labour market and the perceived crisis of sovereignty caused by illegal migration'.

According to Lucila Granada from the organisation Focus on Labour Exploitation (FLEX), 'as a result of these repressive provisions migrants facing exploitation are less likely to be identified and supported due to fear of punishment, and abusive employers are seldom brought to justice'.[1] In practice, therefore, irregular workers have no right to be paid for their work, including compensation and remedies. It is worth noting, in this regard, that the UK opted out of the 2009 Employer Sanctions Directive, which, as highlighted in Chap. 4, established some important provisions protecting the rights of undocumented migrants, such as wage recovery and facilitation in complaint mechanisms.

The main narrative underpinning the UK's restrictive policies on migration and asylum, especially since the second decade of the 2000s, was that migration has a negative impact on public services and leads to a downwards pressure on wages.[2] In this scenario, debates about free movement and immigration became progressively entwined, while migration (including intra-EU mobility) became a highly contested issue in British politics. Indeed, the 'politicisation of EU migration' played a key role in the Brexit campaign (Dennison & Geddes, 2018). As highlighted in Chap. 3, the idea of welfare tourism/shopping by intra-EU migrants coming from countries with less developed welfare systems generated strong concern. In this context, as Dennison and Geddes (2018) underlined, the 'Leave campaign' ahead of the Brexit referendum in 2016 intertwined EU migration, the so-called refugee crisis, and the possibility of Turkey's accession to the EU to fuel and amplify concerns about migration-related issues. The Leave campaign's main message 'to take control of national borders and thus reduce immigration'—as Geddes et al. (2020, p. 139) noted—'resonated because control had actually been the main objective of migration policy in the UK for a long time and people were very receptive to the claim that it had been lost'.

The result of the 2016 referendum and subsequent implementation of Brexit revealed deep divisions in British society based on social class, nationality, age, and geography (Baglioni et al., 2019). And it cast a shadow of uncertainty and invisibility over all those European workers who, until that moment, had enjoyed free movement for work-related reasons, playing a crucial role in 'essential' sectors with low wages and limited protection, such as agriculture (Alberti and Cutter 2022; see also Zambelli et al., 2022).

On the other hand, in the last few years, particularly since 2019, there has been an increase in net migration, especially of non-EU nationals reaching some 662,000 in 2022 (Sumption et al., 2023), therefore exceeding the pre-Brexit average of net migration of between 200,000 and 250,000 people a year. This rise was due to an increase in the number of non-EU citizens entering the UK to study, work, or escape conflicts and wars, including the arrival of refugees from Ukraine (ibid.). In

---

[1] Interview conducted June 2021

[2] 'In the last decade or so, we have seen record levels of long-term net migration in the UK, and that sheer volume has given rise to public concern about pressure on public services…as well as placing downward pressure on wages for people on the lowest incomes. The public must have confidence in our ability to control migration' (Department for Exiting the European Union, 2017).

response to such record high numbers, the current British government has declared its intention to reduce net migration.

In line with this approach, increasingly stringent migration and asylum policies have been adopted. These policies included the adoption of the 2022 Nationality and Borders Act and culminated with the 2023 Illegal Migration Act. This latter establishes that those who arrive in the UK irregularly, including asylum seekers and potential victims of trafficking and modern slavery, will not be able to stay in the national territory. Instead, they will be detained and promptly removed, either to their home country or to a safe third country. While it is too early to assess the impact of this very recent act, it is possible to argue that, given its dire implications for the human rights of the affected migrant individuals and for international human rights obligations, it will likely exacerbate the situations of vulnerability for migrant people, further exposing them to dynamics and cycles of abuse, exploitation, and trafficking (Antislavery International 2023).

7.1.2 UK Policies on Labour Migration and the Post-Brexit Regulation: The Points-Based System

As highlighted above, the UK regulation of migrants' entry and stay for work reasons has progressively tightened over the decades, with the goal of prioritising specific categories of workers, especially those highly skilled, and restricting access for the other categories of workers (Sumption and Fernandez-Reino 2018; Baraggia and Celoria 2022; Green & Hogarth, 2017). In particular, in 2008, a 'points-based' system was introduced through the implementation of progressive amendments to the Immigration Rules. Such a system is based on the sponsorship and points-based assessment, which essentially functions as a checklist of requirements (measured in points) that migrants must fulfil to be eligible for employment (McBritton 2022). In January 2021, with the end of free movement for EU citizens in the UK, a new points-based system for immigration was implemented that maintains the basic structure of the former system, based on points and sponsorship (UK Government, 2022; see also Walsh 2021).

More specifically, before the changes resulting from the Brexit process, the points-based system provided for a five-tier structure for non-EU nationals' work and study: highly skilled workers (Tier 1), medium skilled workers (Tier 2), low skilled workers (Tier 3—never opened), students (Tier 4), and temporary workers (Tier 5). Each tier had different eligibility rules, but most visas under this scheme required a sponsorship from a list of licensed companies. For instance, the Tier 2 visa required a skilled job offer by one of the recognised and licensed sponsors. Points were assigned based on the type of employment contract offered by the sponsor and on the salary that the person would earn in the United Kingdom, which should be at least £30,000 (Baraggia and Celoria 2022). Other visas, such as the

Youth Mobility scheme (Tier 5) did not require a sponsorship but applied to a limited number of eligible countries.

The combination of stringent requirements and conditions has created obstacles and barriers, making it notably arduous for non-EU migrants to access the UK labour market (Calò et al. 2021). Furthermore, significantly, Tier 3—the route for low-skilled labour migration—was never made operational because 'there has been sufficient supply of labour in low-skilled jobs following the 2004 and 2007 EU enlargements' (Sumption and Fernandez-Reino 2018, p. 5). Moreover, from 2010 to 2012, skill requirements for non-EU migrants to be admitted to the UK were raised, with the exclusion of many middle-skilled jobs from Tier 2 work permits. As a result, the UK work visa system for non-EU citizens was primarily designed for graduate jobs, leading to a significant proportion of migrants employed in non-graduate, low-skilled jobs being from EU countries (Vargas-Silva, 2018). For example, in 2017, an estimated 500,000 EU citizens were employed in low-wage jobs such as cleaning, waiting tables, warehousing, and food processing (Sumption & Fernandez-Reino, 2018, p. 3).

In January 2021, with the end of free movement for EU citizens in the UK, the new points-based system replacing the previous 'Tier System' brought both EU and non-EU nationals under the same regulatory framework for migration (Alberti et al., 2020). Indeed, the new element is the application of this system to EU citizens, essentially treating them on par with non-EU migrants regarding entry and work. This alignment, as has been emphasised, clearly underscores the UK government's specific intent to contain migration, particularly from eastern EU countries (Sumption & Kieranas, 2021; Baraggia & Celoria, 2022),[3] and 'select migrants who will contribute the most to the UK's economy' (Walsh, 2021, p. 2).

The new points-based system provides for different types of work visa on a short- or long-term basis, depending on skills and qualifications. In particular, the main long-term route is the Skilled Worker visa.[4] To get this, workers must meet a specific set of requirements totalling 70 points. Some of the requirements are mandatory. These include: a job offer from a Home Office-licensed sponsor before moving to the UK, a job that is on the list of eligible occupations, and ability to speak English to the required standard. The first two mandatory elements carry 20 points each, while the English language level carries 10 points. These 50 points are not 'tradable'. They, therefore, operate more like checkboxes: if an individual does not

[3] It is worth underlining that EU citizens and their families who started living in the UK before 1 January 2021 were able to apply to the free EU settlement scheme before 30 June 2021. If they applied to the EU Settlement Scheme successfully, they could continue living and working in the UK after 30 June 2021. They have been given either settled status or pre-settled status. These different statuses have different rights and depend on how long the persons have been living in the UK when they apply. However, both settled and pre-settled status allow people to work in the UK, use the NHS for free, enroll in education or study in the UK, access public funds such as benefits and pensions, and travel in and out the UK.

[4] The Skilled Work Visa is for 5 years; after 5 years, it is possible to apply to settle permanently in the UK.

meet all criteria, they do not qualify for the Skilled Worker visa. The other 20 points are awarded for meeting a salary threshold for the future job.

A new significant element introduced by the new system is a lower minimum salary threshold.[5] This is the highest of the following options: £26,200, £10.75 per hour, or the 'going rate' for that specific occupation that the migrant worker will do. However, the salary can be lowered (not below £20,960) if the applicant is a new entrant to the labour market; the job is on the Shortage Occupation List; or the applicant has a PhD in a subject that is relevant to the job. Applicants with skills on the shortage occupation list benefit from a lower application fee. However, these fees constitute only a small part of the total cost that migrants must pay when applying for the Skilled Worker visa, which also includes the healthcare surcharge (that is usually £624 per year) (Walsh, 2021).[6]

Defining the salary threshold in the new system has been one of the most controversial aspects in drafting the new immigration rules (Alberti et al., 2020, p. 10). The government's decision to establish a lower salary threshold for jobs on the Shortage Occupation List was not aligned with the recommendations of the Migration Advisory Committee (MAC). The committee had underscored the risks associated with making exceptions to the salary threshold based on the Shortage Occupation List (MAC, 2020). In their recommendation they stressed that instead of solving skills shortages, this would have the effect of fostering shortage: 'a shortage is generally an indication that wages are below market-clearing levels so that allowing these jobs to pay lower salaries could have the effect of perpetuating shortage' (MAC, 2020, p. 8). In other words, this could have distorting effects on the labour market, where certain sectors may be discouraged from improving pay conditions to make them more attractive (Alberti & Cutter, 2022).

In December 2021 care work was added to the Shortage Occupation list to address the shortage of care workers, thus allowing these workers to use the Health and Care Worker visa (another long-term visa with lower costs compared to visas under the Skilled Work route and previously aimed at higher-paid workers). Since then there has been a significant increase in the number of Health and Care Worker Visas granted, rising from 47,194 in the year ending 2022 to 121,290 in the year ending June 2023 (Home Office, 2023). As care work is included in the Shortage Occupation list, care workers typically need to be paid at least £20,960 to qualify for this visa. As a recent document by various organisations and academics noted, this low minimum salary requirement fosters a precarious condition for care workers who 'may struggle to meet essential living costs together with the (legal or illegal) costs related to accessing this employment in the first instance' (Joint Submission, 2023, p. 13). In addition, factors such as the strong dependency of care workers on individual sponsors under the Health and Care Worker Visa contribute to exacerbating care workers' situations of vulnerability to exploitation in a sector that is already

[5] Under the previous points-based system, non-EU citizens were only permitted to come to the UK for employment in graduate-level positions that had a salary of at least £30,000 (MAC, 2020).

[6] Migrants applying for this visa must also prove they have enough personal savings.

characterised by poor working conditions and abusive treatment (ibid.; see also Unison, 2023).

Scholars such as Jonathan Portes (2022) have noted that the new points system is in a way more 'liberal' than the previous scheme as it is significantly less restrictive for migrants from outside the EU. More precisely, this new system includes elements of de-regulation, such as removing the resident labour market test, lowering the skills threshold, and eliminating the cap on the number of people who can come on the skilled worker channel (Alberti et al., 2020, p. 11). However, these elements are accompanied by the establishment of a more stringent migration regime for all the categories of migrants, requiring a sponsored job offer for all 'tiers' and demonstrating specific skills assessed by the MAC (Portes, 2022; Alberti et al., 2020, p. 11). In general, as labour scholar Gabriella Alberti highlighted, elements of liberalisation and de-regulation sneak behind a restrictive and selective system.[7] In this regard, it is important to the stress two important critical aspects of this system.

First, of course, the new points-based system significantly restricts the rights of EU citizens who previously enjoyed freedom of movement, and accordingly could move freely to the UK to live, study, or work, with the ability to switch employers easily, access welfare benefits, and bring family members to the UK. Work visas under the points-based system impose numerous restrictions on workers' rights—such as limited possibility to change employers and access to public funds—increasing their vulnerability to abusive practices, especially in the case of low-protected sectors such as care work (Åhlberg et al., 2022). As discussed below, rights restrictions become even more pronounced in the case of temporary migrant workers.

Second, apart from care workers and seasonal workers, the new points-based system does not provide channels for 'low-skilled' and 'low-paid' workers. In particular, with regard to seasonal workers, migrant workers can apply for a Temporary Worker visa (which has replaced the former Tier 5 visa) under several categories,[8] including a Seasonal Worker visa (T5) for migrants who want to go to the UK for up to 6 months to do farm work. To apply for this visa, migrants must have a sponsor and meet other eligibility requirements: be 18 years or older when they apply; have a certificate of sponsorship reference number from their UK sponsor[9]; and have enough money to support themselves in the UK (at least £1270 available in their bank account). There is no English language requirement. Migrant workers who have been granted the Seasonal Worker Visa are allowed to study. However, they cannot take a permanent job, work a second job, get public funds, or bring their family members with them.

Being therefore trapped in a temporary condition, workers with short-term work visas have limited access to rights. Similarly, as seen in the EU and Italian legal

[7] Interview with Gabriella Alberti, University of Leeds, June 2021.

[8] Government Authorised Exchange Visa (Temporary Work); Seasonal Worker Visa (Temporary Work); Creative Worker Visa (Temporary Work); Religious Worker Visa (Temporary Work); Charity Worker Visa (Temporary Work); International Agreement Visa (Temporary Work)

[9] A certificate of sponsorship is a reference number that holds information about the job and the applicant's personal details.

frameworks for seasonal migrant workers, the restrictions on the reproductive conditions of seasonal workers, particularly the lack of family reunification, play a crucial role in controlling their mobility and maintaining their temporary status. This, in turn, as discussed below, contributes to creating situations of vulnerability to exploitation.

In general, in line with the enduring UK trend of restrictive and selective labour migration policies that prioritise productive skilled workers (Dias-Abey, 2022), the new points-based system does not, in practice, offer a migration path for low-skilled and low-wage workers, except for care workers, while providing seasonal workers with temporary and limited residence permits. This has particularly affected those sectors, such as hospitality, where before Brexit employers heavily relied on EU citizens who now are ineligible for work visas (Sumption et al., 2022). For instance, the hospitality industry experienced a significant decline of just over 98,000 EU citizen jobs between 2019 and 2021 (ibid.) In this regard, a recent study by Sumption et al. (2022) has highlighted that the UK's post-Brexit migration policy, along with factors such as the impact of the Covid-19 pandemic, constitutes one of the main contributors to labour shortages in certain sectors.[10]

According to several testimonies collected for this research, the new points-based system is likely to contribute to the creation of more situations of exploitation, including severe forms. In this line, for instance, David Camp (2020, p. 6) emphasises that the rules on charging recruitment fees and associated costs to applicants under the new immigration system are inadequate and put workers at great risk of debt bondage. The case of care workers is emblematic in this regard. While the fees for the Health and Care Worker Visa are lower than those for the Skilled Worker Visa, they are still relatively high. As Kate Roberts from the organisation Focus on Labour Exploitation (FLEX) has argued, this 'may push many migrant care workers into debt, amplifying their vulnerabilities to exploitation'.[11] This debt condition, in turn, is further exacerbated by the fact that care workers often pay illegal fees to recruitment agencies in their countries of origin (Åhlberg et al., 2022).

As Camp (2020, p. 6) observes, the practical absence of a migration route for lower skilled workers drives recruitment channels 'underground and facilitates dynamics of exploitation, including of trafficking'. Camp pays special attention to people coming as visitors who may overstay in grey status condition with the risk of being involved in dynamics of abuse and exploitation. In line with these analyses, recent research highlights that Brexit has contributed to expanding irregularity thus increasing migrants' situational vulnerabilities to abuse and exploitation. As Åhlberg and Granada (2022, p. 129) argue, 'the risk is that some employers, unable to recruit from abroad and unable to attract workers from the domestic labour force, will turn to irregular workers'. This, in turn, may lead to cases of people overstaying or

[10] Interestingly, Sumption et al. (2022) have highlighted that several occupations eligible for skilled work visas, such as construction, have experienced relatively low take-up, possibly due to administrative costs and the challenges of adapting to a new system.

[11] Interview conducted in November 2022.

holding other visas, such as student visas, being exploited, for instance, in the hospitality sectors (GLAA, 2021).

On the other hand, as discussed below, those workers such as seasonal migrant workers employed under Temporary Work Schemes, such as the Seasonal Worker Visa, also find themselves in situations of exploitation and abuse.

7.2 (Lack of) Access to the Labour Market for Asylum Seekers

Similar to what has happened in Italy and other European countries, in the UK the right to asylum has been subject to increasingly stringent measures aimed at reducing the number of asylum seekers and preventing their social and labour inclusion (Geddes & Scholten, 2016). This trend has been further intensified by recent sets of policies, such as the 2022 Nationality and Borders Act and 2023 Illegal Migration Act that seek to deter people from claiming asylum by providing easier removal to 'safe third countries' without assessing their asylum claims and by limiting rights that have been traditionally crucial for the integration of refugees (Walsh & Sumption, 2023).

Whereas in Italy this process of tightening asylum significantly started in the second decade of the 2000s, restrictive asylum policies have been applied since the early 2000s in the UK, supported by the idea that many asylum seekers were 'bogus' and, accordingly, did not deserve welfare state support or facilitation in accessing the labour market (Geddes, 2003). For instance, in 2002, asylum seekers' right to work was significantly limited, preventing asylum seekers from being integrated into the national job market (Mayblin, 2016).

Indeed, until mid-2002, asylum seekers could apply for permission to work after waiting 5 months for an initial decision on their asylum claim. In 2002, this waiting period was extended to 12 months for an initial decision or a response to a further submission for asylum (Par 11b of the Immigration Rules). Furthermore, according to the rule, to obtain permission to work, the 12-month waiting period should not be attributed to mistakes made by the asylum seekers in the application; in practice, asylum seekers should not be held responsible for delays in decision-making. If they are, they are not allowed to work. It is worth noting that the provision establishing a 12-month waiting period for access to the labour market conflicts with the recast EU Reception Conditions Directive, which, as mentioned in Chap. 3, allows labour market restrictions for asylum seekers for no more than 9 months (Article 15(1)). However, at that time, the UK government decided to opt out of the amendments to the EU Reception Conditions Directive.

Moreover, those asylum seekers who are given permission to work can only take up jobs specified under the Shortage Occupation List. This was decided in September 2010 following the case of *R (ZO (Somalia) and others) v Secretary of State for the Home Department* [2010] UKSC 36. In this judgment, the Supreme Court decided that restricting employment for refused asylum seekers who had made further applications on their claim was against the Reception Conditions Directive. Given that such a judgment would have allowed asylum seekers access to the UK labour market after 12 months from their application or appeals, the UK Government defined jobs on the Shortage Occupation List as the only employment options available to asylum seekers. This permission to work expires once the asylum claim has been finally determined (i.e., when there is no more opportunity to appeal).

To date the UK's Shortage Occupation List primarily covers skilled jobs requiring specific competencies. Given that it is extremely difficult for many asylum seekers to meet the conditions required for these jobs, accessing the UK labour market after the 12-month period is very challenging for them (Mayblin, 2016). For this reason, the current UK policy on asylum has been described as, in practice, providing an 'illusory' right to work for most asylum seekers (Free Movement, 2020).

Two recent judgments have found the Home Office's policy guidance on granting asylum seekers permission to work unlawful, especially regarding the restriction from the Shortage Occupation List jobs. One challenge was brought by an identified victim of trafficking who had been waiting for over a year for a decision concerning her asylum claim (*R (oao IJ (Kosovo)) v. Secretary of State for the Home Department* [2020] EWHC 3487). The other concerned the challenge brought by an asylum seeker with a complex immigration experience and whose asylum claims dated from 2016 (*R(C6) v Secretary of State for the Home Department (asylum seekers' permission to work)* [2021] UKUT 94). In both cases the Courts argued that the Home Office's policy guidance for caseworkers is unlawful as it fails to recognise the possibility of making exceptions to the general policy to restrict permission to work to Shortage Occupation List jobs. In particular, in the first case, Mr. Justice Charles Bourne pointed out that 'the limitation makes it much harder and in many cases impossible for an individual to obtain paid work. It may prevent them from working at all, thereby exposing them to a risk of isolation and affecting their self-esteem' (*R(oao IJ (Kosovo)) v Secretary of State for the Home Department* [2020] EWHC 3487, para. 92). As a consequence of these judgments, the Home Office must review its guidance. Yet, this does not imply a broader change of policy on restricting asylum seekers' permission to work is required.

According to Section 95 of the Immigration and Asylum Act 1999, asylum seekers are also excluded from mainstream national welfare benefits, such as child benefit and disability living allowance. They are entitled to weekly support for housing and pocket money (£39.63, with an additional £3–5 if pregnant or the mother of a child under the age of three) to cover the costs of essential living needs and to prevent destitution.

Under Section 95 of the 1999 Immigration and Asylum Act, destitution consists of lacking access to adequate accommodation or the inability to meet essential living needs. *R (Refugee Action) v Secretary of State for the Home Department*, [2014] EWHC 1033, provided further clarification of the definition of essential living needs. This case concerned the claim by Refugee Action (a charity in England and Wales) for a judicial review of the decision of the Secretary of State in 2013 freezing the income support to asylum seekers (equivalent at that time to £36.62 per week for a single person). The judge argued that the rate was not enough to guarantee an adequate standard of living as stipulated by the European Reception Conditions Directive and did not cover items such as household goods, nappies, and medical goods considered to be fundamental (Bales, 2015). However, following the reconsideration by the Secretary of State, it was decided to keep the same cash amount, which was raised to £37.75 in 2018 according to the 2018 Asylum Support Amendment Regulations No. 30.

Yet this judgement is particularly relevant because it questioned the asylum system's restrictions and—as the ECtHR pointed out in *M.S.S. v. Greece and Belgium* (see Chap. 3)—highlighted how the lack of adequate support for essential living needs affects the situations of vulnerability of asylum seekers, increasing the risk for them to be exposed to dynamics of exploitation and abuse.

In the same vein, the Lift the Ban coalition of NGOs, trade unions, think tanks, and other groups have stressed that the exclusion of asylum seekers from the labour market and therefore from employment makes them fully dependent on the state for their means of subsistence (Refugee Action/Lift the Ban Coalition, 2020; see also Bales, 2013, 2015). This condition of dependence creates, fosters, and exacerbates asylum seekers' situations of vulnerability. This, in turn, increases their risk of being involved in situations of undeclared work and therefore their exposure to exploitation and abuse (Lewis & Waite, 2015).

Far from preventing situations of abuse and exploitation, the UK asylum policy 'contributes to rendering asylum seekers susceptible to forced labour by systematically denying basic rights, especially the right to work, and by offering property-level support within the asylum system, or through operating an intentional policy of destitution for those refused asylum' (ibid., p. 67). All this produces what Lewis and Waite call a 'precarity track' or what could be called a 'situational vulnerability track' for asylum seekers who continue to be at risk of entering severely exploitative forms of work. The use of threats of denunciation to immigration authorities and intimidation is a 'predominant tool of coercion used to discipline workers' (ibid., p. 60).

It is worth mentioning that migrants granted refugee status or humanitarian protection are entitled to work in any profession and at any skill level without any restrictions, either as employees or self-employed. Thus, they have the same right to work as British citizens. However, as several studies demonstrate and interviews with key stakeholders confirm, they face bureaucratic delays and significant barriers to decent employment. Consequently, many end up in low-paid, low-skilled, or informal labour, and are often involved in situations of exploitation (Calò et al., 2021; Lewis & Waite, 2015).

In this context, the 2023 Illegal Immigration Act, which prevents individuals arriving in the UK via irregular routes, whether by land, air, or sea, from accessing asylum or modern slavery support, will likely exacerbate the vulnerabilities of migrant people, including asylum seekers. This may further expose them to irregularities, exploitation, and abuse (Anti-Slavery International, 2023).

7.3 Situational Vulnerabilities and Exploitation in the Agricultural Sector

As in other European countries, in the UK too migrant workers are an essential component of the national agri-food system. However, official statistics do not capture the true scale of migrant labour in the agricultural sector because 'seasonal workers and those living on farms in communal accommodation are excluded from the sampling frameworks of government employment surveys' (Milbourne & Coulson, 2021, p. 431). Some significant data on seasonal workers in Scotland have been collected in a recent report by the UK organisation FLEX. This report highlights that the 'horticultural sector accounts for a large percentage of all migrant labour in Scottish agriculture, placed at 84% of all migrant agricultural labour in 2018' (FLEX, 2021, p. 24). Furthermore, the report emphasises how before the introduction of the scheme on seasonal workers—the Seasonal Workers Pilot (SWP)—the majority of seasonal migrant workers employed in the Scottish agricultural sector were European citizens, in particular from Romania and Bulgaria (ibid.).

Indeed, with the EU enlargements, in addition to a rapid increase in the number of EU nationals in the UK, the geography of this migration 'has been different from traditional patterns of immigration in that significant numbers of migrants have bypassed large cities and moved directly to towns and rural areas' (Milbourne & Coulson, 2021, p. 431). This trend was primarily attributed to the employment opportunities sought by many migrants from eastern or central EU countries in the agri-food sector.

Brexit has significantly threatened this continued supply of migrant workers from EU countries to UK agriculture. Since Britain exited the EU, the UK government has clearly affirmed the aim to break the dependence on low-paid migrants. But according to many agri-food employers, the chances of attracting Britons to work in this sector are very low (Pro-Force Ltd, 2021). Most British workers are indeed reluctant to accept hard, low-paid, precarious, and low-status work (Potter & Hamilton, 2014; Milbourne & Coulson, 2021). This emerged visibly during the 'Pick for Britain' campaign launched in summer 2020 in an effort to recruit local workers—especially those hit by or made unemployed by the pandemic—into the fields and food packaging depots: of 450 UK-based workers (including British workers) placed with employment agencies, fewer than 4% remained on the assignment at the end of the season (Pro-Force Ltd, 2021). As Milbourne and Coulson (2021, p. 436) correctly argued, 'Pick for Britain not only failed to recruit many UK workers but also highlighted some of the conditions under which agri-food pickers and packagers were expected to work'.

Over recent years many reports and studies have denounced the poor and exploitative working and living conditions of agri-food workers, especially migrant workers, in the UK: long working hours, low wages, and substandard and unsafe accommodations (Geddes & Scott, 2010; Allain et al., 2013; Davies, 2019). Frequently, there are situations that amount to forced labour and trafficking (FLEX, 2021). One of the most notable cases is *Antuzis & Ors v. DJ Houghton Catching*

Services Ltd & Ors (2019), involving six Lithuanian men who were sent by DJ Houghton Chicken Catching Services Company to various farms around the country to catch chickens. These workers were subjected to physical and verbal abuse, underpayment, unsanitary and over-crowed accommodations, and long, intense working hours. The High Court ruled in favour of this group of workers, arguing that they were subject to a gruelling and exploitative work regime, and awarded them financial compensation (*Antuzis & Ors v DJ Houghton Catching Services Ltd & Ors* [2019] EWHC 843 (QB)).

7.3.1 Supply Chain Dynamics and the Reliance on Migrant Labour

Exploitative and abusive working conditions in the UK agricultural sector also need to be read taking into account supply chain dynamics. Indeed, market power and profit margins in the agri-food systems have been significantly weakened by the concentration process in the food industry and the expansion and centralisation of power in large-scale retailing systems (Corrado et al., 2016). In line with the dynamics of the reorganisation of production processes on a global scale, agri-food chains in the UK are buyer-driven, with retail companies playing a central role in selecting and managing suppliers on which to build distribution systems.

In this scenario characterised by long supply chains, the oligopolistic control of prices by a small number of large retailer and supplier companies through continuous reduction/depreciation of products imposes an increasingly intense pressure on the different supply actors (growers, processors, labour providers) below them (Craig et al., 2012). For example, government data suggest that the prices paid to farms for strawberries barely rose between 2008 and 2018 (UK Government, 2018). As recent data reveal, the UK has some of the lowest food prices in Western Europe (O'Connor & Evans, 2021). The pressure from retailers up the supply chain—as the FLEX report underlined—has 'led to declining margins for growers, meaning some have gone out of business and others have been forced to increase their supply' (FLEX, 2021, p. 25) by intensifying production and becoming involved in the packing and processing also of imports (Rogaly, 2008, p. 5). As Rogaly highlighted in his important work on this issue, manifestations of an intensification of workplace regimes in UK agriculture since the 1990s can be found in three areas: the increased demand for migrant workers by agricultural employers; a change in the kind of gang-master companies operating in the subsector; and the use of piece rates (i.e., paying agri-food workers according to unit output) so as to increase the work required to earn the agricultural minimum wage and its daily equivalent.

As emphasised in the case of Italy (Chap. 5), the workforce is a crucial domain where employers shift the pressures of the market. In fact, labour represents 'one of the few, arguably only, means by which firms can exercise a degree of control over their ever-tightening profit margins' (Scott, 2017, p. 25). In this regard, migrant workers have been preferred by agri-food employers as they are seen as 'reliable, flexible, and compliant' (Rogaly, 2008, p. 500), and accordingly able to respond to the needs and requirements of retailers and supply chain dynamics (MAC, 2013; Geddes & Scott, 2010). The recruitment of a migrant labour force and the replacement of local workers in the agricultural sector have also been fostered by the introduction of the UK National Minimum Wage in 1999. Indeed, as FLEX (2021, p. 25) has underlined in this regard, 'whilst farms previously employed young and casual local workers at peak production periods, these roles became less viable after the introduction of the UK national minimum wage', thus fuelling a shift to migrant workers.

By noting the complex nature of seasonality as framed in supply chain relationships, the UK Migration Advisory Committee (MAC) has highlighted that demand for workers varies throughout the year due to supply chain demands and the nature of agri-food crops. As the MAC (2013, p. 129) noted, the 'seasonal and varied high to low intensity nature of horticultural work means worker demand in high season can grow to four and a half times the demand at low season'. The intensity of the periods is then affected by the 'just-in-time ordering by the supermarkets' (ibid.), responding to sudden fluctuations in consumer demand (see also Geddes, 2003).

At the same time, these work patterns affect the reproduction conditions of the workers as they are required 'to live on site in order to respond to the varying demands imposed by external factors including weather, crop ripening rates, and retailer requirements' (FLEX, 2021, p. 25). This, in turn, makes workers more tied to and dependent on employers, increasing their vulnerabilities to exploitation and abuse.

In this scenario, labour market intermediaries such as gangmasters or employment agencies play a crucial role, by providing flexible labour at short notice. These actors have become a key component of 'labour supply chains' and, as discussed below, play a crucial role in the seasonal workers scheme. Their presence complicates the employment relationships, especially when there are numerous intermediaries involved (Davies, 2019; Mantouvalou, 2023). This, in turn, increases the possibility of abuse and exploitative practices occurring, concealing responsibilities (FLEX, 2021).

7.3.2 The Regulatory Framework in the Agricultural Sector and Spaces of Irregularity

Rules on employment terms and conditions for agricultural workers differ in England, Wales, Scotland, and Northern Ireland. For example, since October 2013, following the abolition of the Agricultural Wages Board for England and Wales, the terms and conditions have changed for agricultural workers starting new jobs in England (including workers supplied by a licensed gang master), as the Agricultural Minimum Wage also ceased to exist in this country. More specifically, workers who started on or after 1 October 2013 must receive the National Minimum Wage and other statutory minimum terms of employment. With regard to workers employed before 1 October 2013 (including those supplied by a licensed gangmaster), they are still entitled to the terms and conditions of their contract according to the Agricultural Wages (England and Wales) Order 2012. They still have the right to the Agricultural Minimum Wage if stipulated in their contract. In other words, the entitlements and any other terms and conditions already agreed will continue to apply unless the contract is changed by mutual agreement or expires. As another example, agricultural workers in Wales must be paid at least the Agricultural Minimum Wage or the National Minimum Wage if that is higher. The Agricultural Minimum Wage depends on the workers' job grade and category. However, in general, agricultural workers must always be paid at least the appropriate National Minimum Wage.

In the UK, agricultural workers may be paid per task they perform or piece of work they do, for example, for each box of fruit packed. This is known as 'piece work'. In this case, they must be paid either at least the minimum wage for every hour worked or a 'fair rate' for each task or piece of work (HMRC, 2016).

As already highlighted, the introduction of the National Minimum Wage in 1999 and the subsequent use of the piece rate system have in some way contributed to the replacement of local and casual workers with migrant workers from EU and non-EU countries. Indeed, as research on Scottish agriculture has shown, this has resulted 'in a gradual reduction of the casual (e.g. teenaged) workforce on fruit farms as the piece rate had facilitated a less regimented/casual working day where workers controlled their own output' (Thomson et al., 2018, p. 22).

While the piece rate system offers the possibility of paying workers above the minimum wage, in practice it is used 'to increase productivity for those at or around the minimum wage threshold' (Scott, 2017, p. 10). Indeed, in the context of greater deregulation and flexibility in recent years, there has been growing use of piece rate payments along with 'zero hours' contracts—which require workers to be on call at all times—to raise productivity levels (FLEX, 2021). While these kinds of contract may provide workers with more flexibility, their nature raises the level of insecurity and means that employers 'are in a far stronger position to dictate terms than workers, which could result in exploitation and harm' (Davies, 2019). However, following intensive advocacy work by organisations supporting seasonal workers, since April 2023 workers on the agricultural Seasonal Worker Visa must be provided with a minimum of 32 paid hours of work per week (Department for Environment, Food and Rural Affairs, 2023).

Overall, the piece rate system is inadequately regulated, providing room for irregularities and undermining the minimum wage (Thomson et al., 2018, p. 63). For instance, FLEX (2021, p. 34) noted that many seasonal workers in Scotland are paid a 'fluctuating piece rate with regular period of worklessness in penalty for not meeting their work quota'. At the same time, the lack of clarity in how rates are calculated, coupled with the non-disclosure of pertinent information to workers, significantly impacts their working conditions (ibid., p. 51).

Similar to Italy, where piece rate payments are employed in some rural areas (Chap. 4), the use of this payment method, often coupled with flexible temporary contracts like zero-hours contracts, places migrant workers in a state of uncertainty and precarity, heightening their situational vulnerabilities. As one stakeholder interviewed for this research argued, 'given the very limited alternative employment options available to seasonal workers, this form of payment and treatment at work poses a very high risk to workers'.[12]

In this scenario, the precarity of legal status characterising non-EU seasonal migrant workers involved in the Seasonal Worker Visa Scheme is a further element that intensifies migrants' situational vulnerability to dynamics of exploitation and abuse.

7.3.3 *The Seasonal Worker Scheme: Between Temporariness, Exploitative Practices, and Limitations in Workers' Social Reproduction Sphere*

In 1945, a Seasonal Agricultural Worker Scheme (SAWS) was introduced in the UK aimed at ensuring there were enough farmworkers during the harvest seasons. This scheme defined a quota of about 3000 workers per year, which remained constant until 2004. That year, in the context of a review of the agri-food system, the annual quota was raised to 25,000 workers. Successively, about 4 years later, the eligibility for the SAWS was limited to workers from A2 countries (Bulgaria and Romania). However, in 2013 the UK government abolished the SAWS in line with the adoption of a more restrictive approach to migration policies and on the basis that there would be an adequate number of workers coming under free movement rules, especially from Romania and Bulgaria (Scott, 2017).

In 2019, responding to intensive lobbying from major agri-food stakeholders, especially prominent farming unions, and recognising the sector's specific labour needs, the UK Government introduced the Seasonal Workers Pilot—which involved establishing the Seasonal Worker Visa (former Tier 5). Renamed the Seasonal Worker Visa (SWV) in 2020, this temporary immigration route facilitates the recruitment of migrant workers from outside the EU to work on UK farms, providing them with strict temporary visas. Notably, the SWV scheme is the sole work visa explicitly created to enable licensed scheme operators to sponsor migrant workers in low-wage sectors. This scheme has been implemented to address labour shortages in the UK agricultural sector, particularly during the peak harvest period. As stressed above, this became a pressing concern, especially after the end of free movement for EU citizens, who constituted a significant component of migrant farmworkers in the UK.

This model enables the recruitment of a limited number of temporary migrant workers for specific roles in the agricultural sector and for the limited duration of 6 months. Migrant workers are recruited through a small number of recruitment

---

[12] Interview conducted in September 2021.

companies, known as 'scheme/pilot operators', authorised by the government to arrange Seasonal Work visas. These recruiters are endorsed by the Department for Environment, Food and Rural Affairs (DEFRA) and licensed by the Gangmasters and Labour Abuse Authority (GLAA) that oversees labour providers in the food and food processing sectors. Therefore, farmers must hire migrant seasonal workers through these scheme operators; they cannot sponsor Seasonal Worker visas directly. It is worth noting that workers are often required to pay for the visa and travel prior to coming to the UK.[13]

In order to become scheme operators under the SWV, companies are required to respect a number of minimum standards, including: compliance with GLAA regulations; capability to provide sponsored workers to growers and employers across the UK; and adequate systems, processes, and polices to deliver the scheme to the standard required by the Home Office. Scheme Operators must ensure certain conditions are met for the workers they sponsor: a safe work environment; fair treatment by their employer; compliance with national minimum wage and holiday pay; time off and breaks; provision of equipment to do their job safely; hygienic and safe accommodations; safe vehicles for transport; no threats or violence; no withholding of ID documents; and provision for reporting concerns and changing employer, where possible (Home Office, 2022a).

Scheme Operators are also required to implement mechanisms to monitor their workers' employment conditions during their stay in the UK and to provide relevant information and data to the Home Office. Assessing labour providers' success also depends on migration outcomes, such as that migrants are granted entry authorisation and return home at the end of the six-month visa.

In view of the end of free movement of EU workers, since 2021 the UK government has progressively extended quotas under the SWV. In 2023 this was around 55,000 (plus 2,000 for the poultry route) while in 2020, 7,236 visas were issued to seasonal workers. Most recent immigration status data suggest not all visas may be used. The SWV also applies to EU migrant workers. When the Seasonal Worker Scheme was launched, workers mostly came from Ukraine (McKinney et al. 2023). The number of visas issued to workers coming from Ukraine has now dropped significantly as a result of the Russian invasion in 2022 (Roberts, 2022); today, a much wider range of nationalities is represented in the scheme that includes workers from central Asian countries such as Kyrgyzstan, Uzbekistan, and Taijkistan (Home Office, 2023).

The adoption of the SWV and the increases in its quotas might be considered a significant step forward addressing the labour shortages caused by the end of free movement for EU citizens in the UK and sustaining regular employment of seasonal migrant workers. In the absence of other specific channels for the medium and low skilled sector in the UK, the SWV in agriculture is an attractive path because it provides for low admission requirements and offers workers some

[13] The visa cost is currently set at £244, but since 2021 there has been a £55 reduction for workers from a range of specified countries.

accommodations. However, similar to other temporary migration programmes adopted in European countries like Italy or Spain (Corrado & Palumbo, 2022; Palumbo & Sciurba, 2018), the SWV scheme is associated with high risks of labour abuse and exploitation.

First, as emerged from several reports and data collected for this study, migrant seasonal workers recruited under the SWV often find themselves working and living in conditions different from those described before arriving in the UK. This is amplified by difficulties related to language barriers and lack of translation of relevant documents. Therefore, when arriving in the UK, migrants often experience degrading, unsafe, and exploitative treatment, including low salary through piece rate payments, long working hours, lack of safety measures, and threats (FLEX, 2021; Mantouvalou, 2023; Mellino & Chapman, 2023).

Many migrant seasonal workers incur debts to travel to the UK to work (FLEX, 2021). The Bureau of Investigative Journalism revealed that it very common for migrant seasonal workers to pay fees to recruiters, which is illegal in the UK (Mellino & Chapman, 2023). Migrant workers' condition of indebtedness further increases their situational vulnerabilities, leading them to 'accept' conditions that they otherwise would not have. As a member of a London-based charity stressed during an interview, 'many workers report incurring debts to come to the UK as seasonal workers, which placed them in a more vulnerable position to abuse and exploitation'.[14] Such situations of vulnerability are differently amplified according to the worker's gender, class, age, and family responsibilities.

Furthermore, in line with the temporary migration programme model, the SWV links the workers to employers, making migrants extremely dependent on them for their working and living conditions. The sphere of workers' social reproduction conditions is again extremely important to consider. As emphasised by the MAC (2013), employers prefer workers who are tied, i.e., living on the farm or nearby. This—similar to what occurs in rural areas in Italy, such as Ragusa—makes the workers more isolated and dependent on the employers or other actors with regard to transportation and access to other services. As a trade union representative interviewed for this research pointed out, 'a lot of these places where migrant seasonal workers work are away from towns and villages, so they then have to rely on their employer, who will often say to them that they are going to go into the local town and go shopping and they would then give them a list of food that they want, and that would also be deducted out of their salaries'.[15]

Moreover, accommodation provided by employers is often inadequate, lacking appropriate furniture and facilities. Once again, these are methods for wage theft. Indeed, as the trade unionist above pointed out, 'they put seasonal workers in living accommodation, so out of their wages they will take some money for what it costs to get them to come over; they will then take what's classed as their rent from them, and a lot of the time the accommodation that they're living in is a dormitory, sharing

[14] Interview conducted in June 2021.

[15] Interview conducted in September 2021.

with up to twenty other people, or they're put in caravans where they're sharing caravans with another four or five people'.[16] Such conditions reveal, once again, how dynamics of exploitation also rely on the compression of workers' reproduction costs.

While migrant seasonal workers have the theoretical ability to change employers, in practice, they often face significant barriers that make it impossible to do so. Indeed, the fact they are allowed to change employers only through the scheme operator who sponsored their visa plus the fact their stay is temporary, even for just a couple of weeks, make it very difficult for the workers to find another employer (FLEX, 2021). While the operator is required by the scheme to make sure that workers are permitted to move to another employer[17] and workers' requests for transfer should be approved whenever possible, there are no clear criteria about the process for considering transfer requests. This, in turn, means that the operators have broad discretionary power to approve or reject those requests. In this context, if workers decide to change employers, they risk losing their jobs, which may result in being without accommodation or facing deportation or both (Work Rights Centre, 2022). Therefore, this system can discipline and effectively 'punish' migrants who contest violations and want to change employers by leading them to leave the scheme and become irregular. This situation is further exacerbated by the fact that many have incurred high debts to support their journey. As Kate Roberts from FLEX pointed out during an interview, 'all these significant financial risks considerably reduce workers' freedom to terminate their employment contracts'.[18] Moreover, like other temporary migrant workers, migrant seasonal workers do not have access to public funds (Immigration Rules Appendix Temporary Work – Seasonal Worker). This means they are excluded from many social benefits, including, for instance, housing and homelessness assistance, housing benefit, income-based jobseeker's allowance, income-related employment, and support allowances.

All these factors are interconnected with, and, simultaneously, intensified by the temporary nature of the conditions in which these workers find themselves, making it difficult to contest exploitative working and living conditions. In line with the approach of other policy and legal instruments (such as the Seasonal Workers Directive) based on temporary migration programmes, the SWV scheme ensures the temporary status of migrant seasonal workers by limiting their social reproduction conditions, denying them, for instance, the right to family reunification.

The lack of family reunification can, in turn, be considered a factor that also affects the gender composition of migrant seasonal labour force. Official data for seasonal migrant workers disaggregated by gender are difficult to find. However, seasonal migrant women are often fewer than men (FLEX, 2021). This can be due to several factors. For instance, as a member of a charity pointed out during the

[16] Interview conducted in September 2021.

[17] See, in this regard, Home Office (2022b).

[18] Interview conducted in November 2022.

interview,[19] women often face greater difficulties in affording costs such as those related to the visa. Additionally, according to dominant traditional and patriarchal models, most women still have the primary responsibility for reproductive and family-related commitments. In this sense, as already underlined in Chap. 3 with regard to the EU Seasonal Workers Directive, the fact that seasonal workers are not allowed to bring their family with them is disadvantageous for women, preventing many of them from leaving their countries and taking up seasonal work in the UK.

As emerged from the data collected, as in the Italian context, in the UK cases of abuse and exploitation also involve sexual harassment. Additionally, the high level of uncertainty, stressful, harsh, and intense working conditions have significant consequences on workers' health, both physical and mental. The need to earn money to support family in the countries of origin is one of the main aspects that create stress for migrant seasonal workers (FLEX, 2021; Davies, 2019). 'The combination of hazardous conditions, intense work and a lack of due diligence towards workers can result in workplace injuries as a form of harm' (Davies, 2019, p. 305). Reproductive health is notably affected. Episodes of miscarriages among women workers, especially during the earlier stages of pregnancy, are not uncommon (Davies, 2019).

7.4 Situational Vulnerabilities and Exploitation in the Domestic Work Sector

In addition to the Seasonal Worker Visa scheme for agricultural workers, another migration route for low-skill and low-wage occupation is the Overseas Domestic Worker Visa (included in the Immigration Rules in 2002, with significant changes taking place in 2012 and again in 2016), which can be granted to domestic workers visiting the UK with their employers. Therefore, this scheme does not create a real independent route of entry for domestic workers to address labour market shortages in the UK as workers enter along with their employers (Fudge & Strauss, 2014).

As mentioned above, in 2022 care work was added to the national Shortage Occupation List and care workers were allowed to use the Health and Care Worker Visa. Between June 2022 and June 2023, this visa represented 57% of all work visas granted (Home Office, 2023). As recent research has underlined, migrant care workers, especially live-in workers, often experience low-pay, substandard and exploitative working and living conditions (Åhlberg et al., 2022). The conditions and requirements of the Health and Care Worker Visa have further exacerbated these dynamics, increasing the situational vulnerabilities of care workers (Joint Submission, 2023). Indeed, similar to the case of seasonal migrant workers under the SWV, although the Health and Care Worker Visa is a long-term visa, factors such as dependence on employers under the sponsorship system and incurring debts to pay visa fees and recruitment agencies play a crucial role in reducing care

[19] Interview conducted in June 2021.

workers' bargaining power vis-a-vis employers, exposing them to exploitative and abusive practices (Åhlberg et al., 2022; Mantouvalou, 2023).

Similar yet distinct dynamics are encountered by migrant domestic workers employed under the Overseas Domestic Worker Visa. This section delves into the working and living conditions of these workers, as this visa is emblematic of temporary migration policies that significantly restrict the mobility and social reproductive conditions of migrant workers. According to Home Office data, each year the UK government issues around 20,000 Overseas Domestic Workers visas to migrant workers coming mainly from the Philippines, India, and Indonesia; most are to women (Kalayaan, 2019). In 2017–2018, the Kalayaan organisation, which has been assisting domestic workers in the UK for more than 30 years, found that 72% of workers who registered for advice and support have encountered exploitation and trafficking (ibid.).

7.4.1 The Exceptional Regulatory Framework of Domestic Work: Exclusion, Exemptions, and Undervaluation of Domestic Labour

Before looking at the specificities of the ODW Visa and the related rights granted (or, better to say, not granted) to domestic workers, it is worth saying a few words on the UK regulatory framework concerning domestic work.

As already emphasised in the Italian case, in the family and private sphere employment relationships tend to be concealed (Anderson, 2007). Skills, indeed, tend to become invisible in this context (Lutz, 2008). 'The end-result product from this gendered labour, and its remuneration, depend on the interpersonal relationship developed between worker and employer' (Maroukis, 2017, p. 158), perceived as family like relationships. This context, which escapes labour inspectorate controls, facilitates the compression of domestic workers' rights up to cases of severe exploitation and abuse.

It is worth noting that similar to what happens in other national contexts such as Italy, in the UK too, domestic workers' rights are weakened compared to other workers and, to some extent, are even more restricted than in other countries, including Italy. Indeed, domestic workers in the UK are excluded from a number of basic labour protections (Mantouvalou, 2012) such as a maximum weekly working time of 48 hours, length of night work, and night work by young workers (Regulation 19 of the 1998 Working Time Regulations; Mundlak, 2005). Domestic workers thus often experience extremely long working hours (Kalayaan, 2019), which as Mantouvalou (2012) rightly argued may violate their right to private and family life under Article 8 of the ECHR.

Furthermore, domestic workers are excluded from health and safety provisions, including those on workplace inspections that apply in other sectors (Section 51 of the 1974 Health and Safety at Work Act 1974). This implies that exploitation and abuse frequently persist, concealed within the domestic sphere, leaving workers in lack of protection. As significantly reported by legal scholars Virginia Mantouvalou and Natalie Sedacca (2020), during the drafting of the 2011 ILO Convention, the UK Government representative argued 'we do not consider it appropriate, or practical, to extend criminal health and safety legislation, including inspections, to cover private households employing domestic workers. It would be difficult, for instance, to hold elderly individuals, who employ carers, to the same standards as large companies' (see UK Parliament, 2011). Therefore, protection of the rights for domestic workers is weakened, if not excluded, in order to safeguard employers' right to privacy, while neglecting the issues of irregularity and abuse characterising this sector.

Moreover, although this exemption was removed in April 2024, the National Minimum Wage had previously been disapplied in relation to 'work relating to the family household'. Indeed, according to former Regulation 57(3) of National Minimum Wage (NMW) Regulations 2015/621, the national minimum wage did not apply when 'the worker resides in the family home of the worker's employer' and 'is not a member of the family, but is treated as such, in particular as regards to the provision of accommodation and meals and sharing of tasks and leisure activities' (former Regulation 57(3)). This exemption was originally introduced to apply to au pairs, broadly defined as being on a fixed-term linguistic or cultural exchange and performing limited work. However, in practice, it had been frequently applied in the case of live-in domestic workers. As legal scholars Siobhán Mullally and Clíodhna Murphy underlined, the family worker exemption, more than any other 'reinforces the public private divide that limit the enforcement of decent work standards for domestic workers…It is a line that is, of course, deeply gendered and reflects continuing categorisation of domestic work as work like no other' (Mullally & Murphy 2014, p. 417). This provision reproduced a devaluation of domestic work and, more broadly, reproductive work. The narrative of being 'treated as a member of the family', and the related assumption that domestic work is not work, was incorporated into the Regulation to justify the denial of minimum wage payment.

As emerged from the analysis of case law, over the years, the employers of domestic workers have sometimes been successful in supporting this exemption as a defence to national minimum wage claims brought against them, such as in the Court of Appeal Case *Nambalat v Taher & Anor.: Udin v. Pasha & Ors. [2012] EWCA Civ 1249*. In other cases, such exemption has been successfully challenged by the Courts' decisions, such as *Akwiwu & Anor v Onu* [2013] UKEAT 0283_12_0105 and *Ayayi v Abu & Anor (Rev 1)* [2017] EWHC 3098, establishing domestic workers' entitlement to the minimum wage. However, as Sedacca (2022) illustrates, it is only the recent *Puthenveettil v. Alexander & George, & Others* No. 2361118/2013, judgment of 15 December 2020, that has posed a 'general challenge' to the family worker exemption itself. Indeed, the London South Employment Tribunal accepted the claimant's argument that this exemption was unlawful and indirectly discriminatory based on sex. Accordingly, the exemption was disapplied and the claimant was entitled to the national minimum wage. More specifically, the claimant argued that the provision indirectly discriminates on the grounds of sex as most family workers in the private household are women, resulting in a higher number of women being precluded from earning the National Minimum Wage. In this regard, the claimant provided substantial evidence about the significant presence of women in domestic work and about women trafficked for domestic servitude in the UK.

Respondents tried to deny the disproportionate presence of women in the domestic work sector and also disputed that women are put at a particular disadvantage by the family work exemption, underlining that the National Referral Mechanisms (NRM) statistic that, per annum, 2.1% of women in domestic work were victims of domestic servitude, implied that 'overall around 98% of female and male workers must be happy with Reg 2(2) [formerly Reg. 57], were in good relationships with their employers and never had any issues' (para. 51 of the judgment). However, the London South Employment Tribunal significantly contested this point made by the respondents, underlining that the prevalence of underpaid and exploited domestic workers is not covered by the formally identified victims of trafficking. Significantly, in its argumentation, the Tribunal paid special attention to the situations of vulnerability of overseas domestic workers that expose them to dynamics of abuse and exploitation and create difficulties in accessing support (para. 53).

At the same time, by referring to relevant ILO documents, including Article 12(2) of the ILO Convention 189 on domestic work, the Employment Tribunal argued that the family worker exemption applied to more women than men and places women at particular disadvantage compared to men (para 55–59). Regarding its aim, the Tribunal argued that this exemption to support working families—as claimed by the respondents—can be legitimate since it 'underpins as a social policy enabling mothers to return to the workplace and fulfil their career ambitions' (para 86). In particular, the Tribunal crucially noted that the aim is to encourage 'the return to employment of one category of workers by denying to another category of workers the statutory right to be paid' (para. 97). However, according to the judges, there was no cogent evidence provided on proportionality and the balance of competing interests between these two categories of workers. As the Tribunal argued, the government could have adopted a less discriminatory way to meet these social policy objectives (paras 99–100). The Tribunal, therefore, found that this exemption was indirectly discriminatory against women and was not a proportionate means of achieving a legitimate aim.

It is interesting to note that the claim was brought under both domestic legislation (the Equality Act 2010) and EU equal pay law. The Employment Tribunal noted that Article 157 TFEU is directly effective. The judges ruled that despite the UK's withdrawal from the EU, the legislation that was in operation immediately before the 'exit day' would continue to be relevant with respect to 'interpretation, disapplication and quashing' of rules made beforehand (para. 111). Given that there was no way of reading the family worker exemption as compatible with relevant EU law provisions, the Tribunal was bound to dis-apply it (paras 110–114).

In April 2023, the Employment Appeal Tribunal dismissed Ms. Puthenveettil's appeal and confirmed that the exemption as applied in this case was indeed unlawful (*Thukalil and anor v Puthenveettil and anor* [2023] EAT 47). As Sedacca (2021) contends, the *Puthenveettil* judgment represents a critique and substantial challenge of the extreme devaluation of domestic work in the implementation of the family worker exemption. In particular, this decision powerfully calls into question the application of the family worker exemption as a way to undervalue domestic/care work and exploit the vulnerabilities of domestic workers, especially overseas domestic workers. Interestingly, in this regard, the *Puthenveettil* decision emphasised that the needs of working families or other groups of women cannot be used to diminish or deny the essential rights and protection of (women) domestic workers (Sedacca, 2022). This reasoning echoes feminist analyses of social reproduction, stressing that with the devaluation of reproductive work the entry of women into the labour market often comes at the cost of the work and social subordination of other women, namely, migrant women who take their place in care and social reproduction tasks (see, for instance, Farris, 2019).

Following this judgment, in October 2021 the Low Pay Commission (2021) argued that the exemption was 'not fit for purpose' and recommended that the government remove it. In 2022, the government announced that exemption would be removed. However, it was not until October 2023, following a sustained campaign by workers' rights organisations (Joint Response to the Low Pay Commission Consultation, 2023), that the government eventually took steps to eliminate the Family Worker exemption. This was accomplished through the drafting of the National Minimum Wage (Amendment) (No. 2) Regulations 2023, which came into force in April 2024.

This reform represents a significant accomplishment challenging the devaluation of domestic work perpetuated and reinforced by legal rules. However, numerous issues persist, including the regulation of working hours for domestic workers, revealing the need to address and challenge the forms of devaluation of this work embedded in legal norms.

It is worth noting that the UK has not yet ratified ILO Convention 189 of 2011 on domestic workers. This is a significant limitation in terms of protecting the rights of domestic workers. As Staiano (2017, p. 94) observes, 'the refusal to sign the Convention may be inscribed within a general reclaiming of state sovereignty with respect to the choice of the best strategies to prevent and suppress trafficking and labour exploitation'. This choice, together with the restrictive approach of the Overseas Domestic Workers Visa scheme, reveals a tendency of circumventing human rights standards and resorting to 'sovereigntist, territorially-based prerogatives' (Mullally & Murphy, 2014, p. 408).

7.4.2 *Overseas Domestic Worker Visa: Invisibility, Isolation, and Limited Rights*

The Overseas Domestic Workers (ODW) Visa is granted to domestic workers visiting the UK with their employers,[20] and therefore does not create an independent route of entry for domestic workers to fill labour market shortages in the UK. Under this scheme, migrant domestic workers' entry is completely dependent upon that of their employers (Mantouvalou, 2023).

The statute includes cleaners, chauffeurs, cooks, nannies, and those providing personal care for the employer and their family. To apply for this type of visa, workers must live outside the UK, be a domestic worker in a private household, have worked for their employer for at least 1 year, and meet other eligibility requirements. These latter include being at least 19 years old, working in the same household as their employer or one they use regularly, being able to support themselves in the UK without the need for public funds, and planning to leave the UK at the end of 6 months. Holders must return home at the end of the 6 months; they cannot extend an ODW visa.[21]

Domestic workers with the ODW Visa can travel abroad and return to the UK to complete their stay. They can change employers to another job as a domestic worker in a private household, provided their stay does not exceed 6 months.[22] Their employment options are limited to domestic work, and they are prevented from engaging in alternative occupations. They cannot live in the UK for long periods of time through frequent visits. Furthermore, similar to migrant seasonal workers, overseas domestic workers are precluded from receiving public funds, resulting in the denial of various social benefits. Additionally, they do not have access to the right to family reunification.

It is worth mentioning that prior to 2012 domestic workers holding this visa were allowed to change employers, apply to renew their visa annually based on full time employment as a domestic worker in a private household, and, after 5 years, apply for indefinite leave to remain, and eventually for UK citizenship. In practice, this legal framework allowed migrant domestic workers access to the UK labour market with a long-term perspective and supported their social and labour integration in the country. However, in 2012 the government introduced restrictions preventing overseas domestic workers from switching employers and renewing the visa. The government invoked 'controls on immigration as essential to curbing abuse by

[20] The employer must be either a: (a) British citizen who usually lives outside the UK and who does not intend to remain in the UK for more than 6 months; (b) foreign citizen who is coming to the UK on a visit and who does not intend to remain for more than 6 months.

[21] As highlighted below if they enter the NRM system while their visa is still valid it may be extended until they receive a decision. If they receive a positive decision they may apply for a 2 year ODW Visa (Kalayaan, 2019)

[22] As underlined below, this change was introduced only in 2016 following the government's commissioned review of the ODW Visa promised during the passage of the Modern Slavery Act and carried out by James Ewins QC.

unscrupulous employers' (Mullally & Murphy, 2014, p. 412). However, far from preventing abuse, the motivation behind the change was to reduce net migration to the UK and select migrant workers for admission. In particular, as argued by Mullally and Murphy, this restrictive reform must be read in the context of the introduction of the points-based immigration system that sought to restrict access for low-skilled and economically less valuable workers, thus denying them opportunities for long-term residence (ibid.). In this framework, the government allowed for temporary admission of domestic workers, ensuring that 'productive', 'highly skilled' migrants could come to the UK and bring domestic workers with them. Overseas domestic workers were (and still are) then seen as (unproductive) adjuncts to 'higher-earning' employers (Sedacca, 2022, p. 783).

In practice, this reform to the visa system has established a tie between the visa and the employer, making the worker's right to work and remain in the UK dependent on the contract with their specific employer. This link established by the ODW Visa has faced substantial criticism by domestic workers' organisations and academic scholars. They have underlined how this significantly exposes migrant workers to situations of exploitation, creating substantial challenges for them in enforcing their rights at work in cases of abuses (Mullally & Murphy, 2014; Kalayaan, 2019; Mantouvalou, 2023). As a Parliamentary briefing written by some organisations in 2015 highlighted, 'the hidden and unregulated nature of domestic work in a private household, combined by the workers' status as a migrant and dependence on their employer for work, immigration status, accommodation and information about the UK means that workers on this visa are especially vulnerable to abuse'. An independent review by James Ewins (2015) revealed how working conditions of migrant domestic workers worsened as a consequence of the 2012 ODW Visa reform, including physical verbal or sexual abuse, inadequate food and accommodation, and salary below the National Minimum Wage. The review demonstrated how the ODW Visa regime has played a role in creating and exacerbating the situations of vulnerability of migrant domestic workers, resulting in holders' diminished bargaining power and a sense of feeling 'trapped' and 'owned' by their employer (Sedacca, 2019).

In 2016, following Ewins's report and NGOs' and other associations' requests that the legislation be revised—especially with regard the right to change employer—the UK government slightly amended the rules on the ODW Visa. Under this reform, introduced by the Immigration Act 2016, overseas domestic workers holding visas were permitted to change employers for any reason during the six-month period of their stay in the UK but cannot extend their stay beyond this period. ODW visa holders who receive a positive conclusive grounds decision under the National Referral Mechanism for victims of trafficking are entitled to apply for additional leave to remain as a domestic worker, allowing them to stay up to two more years in this capacity.

As emerged from the relevant literature (Kalayaan, 2019) as well as from data collected for this research, the 2016 reform has had a very limited impact, especially with respect to domestic workers' situation of dependence on employers. Firstly, *t*he right to change employers within a six-month visa period has been deemed relatively ineffective (Mantouvalou, 2018, p. 15): 'domestic labour is a work sector that requires special relationships of trust between the worker and the employer, which it takes time to build'. Furthermore, the conditions of isolation and dependence on employers make it difficult for workers to seek advice and assistance. As the Kalayaan (2019, p. 6) organisation underscored, many ODW visa holders 'had no or limited control over when they were able to flee their abusive employer and escaped with only a few months or weeks remaining on their visa'. This challenge is exacerbated by the limited access to information that workers have, coupled with the fear that often prevents them from approaching authorities for assistance.

It is worth noting that, as underscored above, the 2016 Immigration Act (section 34) introduced measures that target undocumented migrant workers by criminalising illegal work and has made being an irregular migrant worker a criminal offence (Davies, 2016). Accordingly, if undocumented workers report to the authorities that they have been victims of exploitation they may risk ending up in immigration detention for deportation. In light of this, many domestic workers would opt to stay with unscrupulous employers rather than risk being deported (Mantouvalou, 2018).

Futhermore, as is evident from the collected data and is confirmed by relevant reports. There is extensive evidence that many domestic workers experience various violations of labour rights, including severe exploitation such as situations of trafficking and slavery. However, the 2016 revised ODW scheme lacks specific provisions regarding visa extensions for domestic workers who experience exploitation but may not qualify as victims of severe exploitation (ibid.). This represents a significant limitation, as highlighted in Chap. 8, leaving a significant number of exploited migrant workers without protection. Indeed, those migrant domestic workers who escape abusive employers but who are not recognised as victims of trafficking become undocumented. This, in turn, exposes them to further forms of exploitation and abuse (Mantouvalou, 2023).

The Kalayaan report (2019, p. 6) significantly highlights that 'despite suffering abuse at the hands of their initial employer, workers tell us they want to find another employer who will offer decent work and a workplace free from violence and harassment. For many, their focus remains on being able to provide for their families and remit money home'. The crucial issue for workers is to find alternative (not exploitative) employment and to send remittances to their families. In the absence of a viable alternative, they often choose to endure exploitative conditions.

It is also worth noting that migrant domestic workers cannot seek recourse to public funds. That means that they cannot claim most social benefits, such as for instance housing programmes. As a consequence, domestic workers have no option but to accept live-in arrangements provided by the employers. As with migrant seasonal workers, this was particularly detrimental during the Covid-19 pandemic when many domestic workers were unable to access basic financial support and relied on an emergency hardship fund (Mantouvalou & Sedecca, 2020).

Therefore, far from really addressing the situation of vulnerability of domestic workers, the ODW Visa regime has negative ramifications for migrant domestic workers (rather than for abusive employers) as in cases of exploitation they have no other option than to accept exploitative working conditions or leave and become undocumented. In this sense, Mantouvalou (2023) observes that this visa traps migrant domestic workers 'in ongoing cycles of exploitation'.

It is important to note that the impact of legal exclusions and restrictive visas on migrant domestic workers was highlighted by the ECtHR in *Rantsev v Cyprus and Russia* (Application No. 25965/04, 7 January 2010), where the Court pointed out that a very restrictive visa regime was incompatible with Article 4 of ECHR prohibiting slavery, servitude, forced and compulsory labour. However, despite the stark implications of the visa's restrictive regime (especially the ODW Visa) on migrants' rights, the UK courts have often been reluctant to recognise and address the situations of vulnerability brought about by migration status. The above-mentioned *Ajayi v Abu case* is a sort of exception in this regard as the High Court recognised that the claimant domestic worker was in a situation of vulnerability because she believed that her visa tied her to work for the employers/defendants (see para. 82). But as Mantouvalou and Sedecca (2020) stressed, in *Taiwo & Anor v Olaigbe & Ors* [2016] UKSC 31, the Supreme Court highlighted Parliament's decision not to read the immigration status (as opposed to nationality) in the list of protected characteristics in the 2010 Equality Act and did not accept the claimant's argument that this attribute was closely associated to nationality (para. 26). Therefore, the Court declined to find discrimination on the grounds of migration status.[23]

7.5 Concluding Remarks

This chapter has critically examined the UK legal and policy framework concerning migrant workers, especially migrant seasonal workers and domestic workers. Similarly to the case of Italy, albeit characterised by different migration histories and patterns, in the UK, migration policies have increasingly tightened, restricting access channels for low-skilled migrant workers, while limiting asylum seekers' access to the national labour market. Such a restrictive and selective approach was reaffirmed in 2021 with the revised points-based system implemented after the end of free movement for EU citizens in the UK and, accordingly, applying also to EU citizens.

In addition to the recent changes to the Health and Social Care Visa, the other only migration channels for so-called 'low-skilled' workers are the Seasonal Workers Visa and the Overseas Domestic Worker Visa. These two schemes grant temporary residence permits to migrant workers, resulting in limited rights and protection. Both seasonal migrant workers and overseas domestic workers are allowed to change employers, yet in practice, factors like the duration of their stay hinder the effectiveness of this right. Additionally, these schemes maintain the temporary

[23] Goodman has pointed out on the impossibility of the Court to read immigration status into nationality provisions. The government could have considered amending the Modern Slavery Act 2012 to 'rectify Tribunals' inability to compensate mistreated migrant workers' but it did not (Goodman, 2020).

status of these workers by denying them access to the right of family reunification, thus managing and restricting migrants' social reproduction sphere. Consistent with this restrictive approach, both seasonal migrant workers and domestic workers are barred from accessing most social benefits, including social assistance and housing programmes, for instance. This exacerbates their dependence on employers, particularly concerning living conditions.

This, in turn, facilitates dynamics of exploitation that rely on the compression of the costs related to the living and reproduction conditions of workers. Indeed, like what occurs in these sectors in Italy, in both sectors employers provide migrant workers with substandard living conditions and accommodation, as this is functional to reduce and contain the labour costs.

All these factors, coupled with the unique nature of the agriculture and domestic work sectors, the exceptional regulatory regime governing these labour market segments, and gender-related dynamics, contribute to create specific situational vulnerabilities for migrant workers that are used and exploited by employers and which benefit the national economy. Even in this case, pressure related to the need to pay debts or to send money to support families in the countries of origin further amplifies migrants' situations of vulnerability, making it even more difficult for them to escape exploitative dynamics.

Chapter 8 will explore whether and how UK policies designed to combat and prevent labour exploitation while protecting victims address these situational vulnerabilities or if they instead contribute to their exacerbation.

References

Åhlberg, M., & Granada, L. (2022). The making of irregular migration: Post-Brexit immigration policy and risk of labour exploitation. *Journal of Poverty and Social Justice, 30*(2), 120–140.

Åhlberg, M., Emberson, C., Granada, L., Hussein, S., & Turnpenny, A. (2022). *The vulnerability of paid, migrant, live-in care workers in London to modern slavery*. Rights Lab University of Nottingham.

Alberti, G., & Cutter, J. (2022). Labour migration policy post-Brexit: The contested meaning of regulation by old and new actors. *Industrial Relations Journal, 53*(5), 430–445.

Alberti G., Bessa I., Ciupijus Z., Cutter J., Forde C., & Roberts M. (2020). *The coronavirus pandemic and the post-Brexit regulation of migration*. CERIC Briefing Paper. Centre for Employment Relations Change and Innovation Leeds University Business School.

Allain, J., Crane, A., LeBaron, G., & Behbahani, L. (2013). *Forced labour's business models and supply chains*. Joseph Rowntree Foundation.

Anderson, B. (2007). A very private business: Exploring the demand for migrant domestic workers. *European Journal of Women's Studies, 14*(3), 247–264.

Anti-Slavery International. (2023). *Anti-slavery day: The "Illegal Migration" Act 2023 and its implications for survivors in the UK*. Blog Post 12 October 2023 [online], https://www.antislavery.org/latest/illegal-migration-act-2023-implications-anti-slavery-day/ (Last Access Apr 2024).

Baglioni, S., Biosca, O., & Montgomery, T. (2019). Brexit, division, and individual solidarity: What future for Europe? Evidence from eight European countries. *American Behavioral Scientist, 63*(4), 538–550.

Bales, K. (2013). Universal credit: Not so universal? Deconstructing the impact of the asylum support system. *Journal of Social Welfare and Family Law, 35*(4), 427–443.

Bales, K. (2015). The 'essential living needs' of asylum seekers: Lessons learned from R (refugee action) v secretary of state for the home department [2014] EWHC 1033. *Journal of Social Welfare and Family Law, 37*(2), 247–249.

Baraggia, A., & Celoria, E. (2022). Regno Unito. In P. Bonetti, M. D'Onghia, P. Morozzo della Rocca, & M. Savino (Eds.), *Immigrazione e lavoro: quali regole? Modelli, problemi e tendenze* (pp. 132–166). Editoriale Scientifica.

Calò, F., Baglioni, S., Montgomery, T., & Biosca, O. (2021). Regulating Fortress Britain: Migrants, Refugees and Asylum Applicants in the British Labour Market. In V. Federico, & S. Baglioni (Eds.), *Migrants, refugees and Asylum seekers' integration in European labour markets* (pp. 235–258). IMISCOE Research Series. Springer.

Camp, D. (2020). The Impact of the new UK Immigration system on human trafficking into the UK. *Alliance HR* [online], https://www.ihrb.org/uploads/member-uploads/The_impact_on_Human_Trafficking_of_the_new_UK_Immigration_System_-_October_2020.pdf (Last Access Apr 2024).

Corrado, A., & Palumbo, L. (2022). Essential farmworkers and the pandemic crisis: Migrant labour conditions, and legal and political responses in Italy and Spain. In A. Triandafyllidou (Ed.), *Migration and pandemics* (pp. 145–166). IMISCOE Research Series. Springer.

Craig, G., Geddes, A., & Scott, S. (2012). *Experiences of forced labour in the UK food industry*. Joseph Rowntree Foundation.

Davies, A. C. L. (2016). The Immigration Act 2016. *Industrial Law Journal, 45*(3), 431–442.

Davies, J. (2019). From severe to routine labour exploitation: The case of migrant workers in the UK food industry. *Criminology & Criminal Justice, 19*(3), 294–310.

De Corrado, A., Castro, C., & Perrotta, D. (Eds.). (2016). *Migration and agriculture. Mobility and change in the Mediterranean area*. Routledge.

Dennison, J., & Geddes, A. (2018). Brexit and the perils of 'Europeanised' migration. *Journal of European Public Policy, 25*(8), 1137–1153.

Department for Environment, Food and Rural Affairs. (2023). *Agriculture: Pay question for department for environment, food and rural affairs* [online], https://questions-statements.parliament.uk/written-questions/detail/2023-06-27/191419 (Last Access Apr 2024).

Department for Exiting the European Union. (2017). *The United Kingdom's exit from and new partnership with the European Union White Paper* (Policy Paper). Department for Exiting the European Union [online], https://www.gov.uk/government/publications/the-united-kingdoms-exit-from-and-new-partnership-with-the-european-union-white-paper (Last Access Apr 2024).

Dias-Abey, M. (2022). Path dependent policymaking in the post-Brexit United Kingdom: What's new about the 'points-based' labour migration system? *European Law Open, 1*(3), 720–732.

Ewins, J. (2015). *Overseas domestic workers visa: Independent review* [online], https://www.gov.uk/government/publications/overseas-domestic-workers-visa-independent-review (Last Access Apr 2024).

Farris, S. (2019). Social reproduction and racialised surplus populations. In P. Osborne, É. Alliez, & E. Russell (Eds.), *Capitalism: Concept, idea, image—Aspects of Marx's capital today* (pp. 121–134). CRMEP Books.

FLEX - Focus on Labour Exploitation. (2021). Focus on Labour Exploitation (2021), *New report highlights risks of human trafficking on UK Seasonal Workers Pilot* [online], https://labourexploitation.org/news/new-report-highlights-risks-of-human-trafficking-on-uk-seasonal-workers-pilot/ (Last Access Apr 2024).

Free Movement. (2020). *Asylum seeker set to challenge "illusory" right to work rules*. Free Movement Blog [online], https://freemovement.org.uk/asylum-seeker-set-to-challenge-to-illusory-right-to-work-rules/ (Last Access Apr 2024).

Fudge, J. (2018). Illegal working, migrants and labour exploitation in the UK: Liminal legality and the Immigration Act 2016. *Oxford Journal of Legal Studies, 38*(3), 557–584.

Fudge, J., & Strauss, K. (2014). Migrants, unfree labour, and the legal construction of domestic servitude. In P. Kotiswaran (Ed.), *Revisiting the law and governance of trafficking, forced labor and modern slavery* (pp. 524–555). Cambridge University Press.

Geddes, A. (2003). Migration and the welfare state in Europe. *The Political Quarterly, 74*(s1), 150–162.

Geddes, A., & Scott, S. (2010). UK food businesses' reliance on low-wage migrant labour: a case of choice or constraint? In A. Anderson & M. Ruhs (Eds.), *Who needs migrant labour?* (pp. 194–215). Oxford University Press.

Geddes, A., & Scholthen, P. (2016). *The politics of migration & immigration in Europe* (2nd end ed.). SAGE Publications.

Geddes, A., Hadj Adbou, L., & Brumat, L. (2020). *Migration and mobility in the European Union*. Red Globe Press.

GLAA. (2021). *Couple arrested after GLAA discovers care workers sleeping on floor mattresses*. Gangmasters and Labour Abuse Authority [online], https://www.gla.gov.uk/whats-new/latest-press-releases/21122021-couple-arrested-after-glaa-discovers-care-workers-sleeping-on-floor-mattresses/ (Last Access Apr 2024).

Goodman, C. (2020). *Domestic workers' rights and the Equality Act: Tribunal finds "au pair" exemption unlawful in minimum wage claim by migrant domestic worker* [online], https://www.cloisters.com/insights/domestic-workers-rights-and-the-equality-act-tribunal-finds-au-pair-exemption-unlawful-in-minimum-wage-claim-by-migrant-domestic-worker (Last Access Apr 2024).

Green, A. E., & Hogarth, T. (2017). Attracting the best talent in the context of migration policy changes: The case of the UK. *Journal of Ethnic and Migration Studies, 43*(16), 2806–2824.

GRETA. (2021). *Evaluation report. United Kingdom.* Third Evaluation Round, Council of Europe.

Hall, P. A., & Soskice, D. (2001). *Varieties of capitalism: The institutional foundations of comparative advantage*. Oxford University Press.

HMRC. (2016). *HMRC Internal Manual: National Minimum Wage Manual.* [online], https://www.gov.uk/hmrc-internalmanuals/national-minimum-wage-manual (Last Access Apr 2024)

Home Office. (2022a). *Seasonal worker visa route request for information (RFI)* [online], https://www.gov.uk/government/publications/seasonal-workers-pilot-request-for-information/seasonal-workers-pilot-request-forinformation (Last Access Feb 2021).

Home Office. (2022b). *Workers and temporary workers: Guidance for sponsors* [online], https://assets.publishing.service.gov.uk/media/62ffc211d3bf7f20e2f41de4/sponsor-guidance_part-1-apply-for-licence_08-22.pdf (Last Access Sept 2023).

Home Office. (2023). *National statistics. Why people come to the UK? To work* [online], https://www.gov.uk/government/statistics/immigration-system-statistics-year-ending-march-2023/why-do-people-come-to-the-uk-to-work (Last Access Apr 2024).

Joint Response to the Low Pay Commission Consultation. (2023). *The 'family worker exemption': Regulation 57 of the national minimum wage regulations 2015*, 9 June 2023 [online], https://drive.google.com/file/d/1z6u7jfG2VnuQbqGBn_ijot9UAo4V3duC/view (Last Accesss Apr 2024).

Joint Submission. (2023). *Joint submission to the independent chief inspector of borders and immigration (ICIBI) call for evidence submission for the inspection of the immigration system as it relates to the social care sector*, 25 September 2023 [online], https://labourexploitation.org/app/uploads/2023/09/ICIBI-Submission-social-care-sector.pdf (Last Access Apr 2024).

Kalayaan. (2019). *Dignity, not destitution. The impact of differential rights of work for migrant domestic workers referred to the national referral mechanism.* Kalayaan – Justice for Migrant Domestic Workers.

King, R., Lazaridis, G., & Tsardanidis, C. (Eds.). (2000). *Eldorado or fortress? Migration in southern Europe*. Macmillan.

Lewis, H., & Waite, L. (2015). Asylum, immigration restrictions and exploitation: Hyper-precarity as a lens for understanding and tackling forced labour. *Anti-Trafficking Review, 5*, 49–67.

Lutz, H. (2008). *Migration and domestic work: A European perspective on a global theme.* Ashgate.

MAC. (2013). *Migrant seasonal workers: The impact on the horticulture and food processing sectors of closing the seasonal agricultural workers scheme and the sectors based scheme.* Migration Advisory Committee.

MAC. (2020). *Annual report, 2020.* Migration Advisory Committee.

Mantouvalou, V. (2012). Human rights for precarious workers: The legislative precariousness of domestic labour. *Comparative Labor Law and Policy Journal, 34*, 133.

Mantouvalou, V. (2018). The UK Modern Slavery Act 2015 three years on. *The Modern Law Review, 81*(6), 1017–1045.

Mantouvalou, V. (2023). *Structural injustice and workers' rights.* Oxford University Press.

Mantouvalou, V., & Sedacca, N. (2020). The human rights of domestic workers: Mahlangu v. Ministry of Labour and the Transformative Nature of the South African Constitution. *UK Labour Law* [online], https://uklabourlawblog.com/2020/12/11/the-human-rights-of-domestic-workers-mahlungu-v-ministry-of-labour-and-the-transformative-nature-of-the-south-african-constitution-by-virginia-mantouvalou-and-natalie-sedacca/#comments (Last Access Apr 2024).

Maroukis, T. (2017). Keeping up appearances: The British public policy response to the trafficking of domestic workers in a changing regime of social protection. *Journal of Immigrant & Refugee Studies, 15*(2), 155–170.

Mayblin, L. (2016). Complexity reduction and policy consensus: Asylum seekers, the right to work, and the 'pull factor' thesis in the UK context. *The British Journal of Politics, 18*(4), 812–828.

McBritton, M. (2022). Le migrazioni economiche: Accesso al territorio e accesso al mercato del lavoro. In P. Bonetti, M. D'Onghia, P. Morozzo della Rocca, & M. Savino (Eds.), *Immigrazione e lavoro: quali regole? Modelli, problemi e tendenze* (pp. 542–554). Editoriale Scientifica.

McKinney, C. J., Coe, S., & Stewart, I. (2023). *Seasonal worker visas and UK agriculture.* House of Commons Library Briefing Paper, 9665, 4, 23 June [online], https://commonslibrary.parliament.uk/research-briefings/cbp-9665/ (Last Access Apr 2024)

Mellino, E., & Chapman, M. (2023). All that is missing is a whip': Home Office ignored migrant worker abuses on farms. *The Bureau of Investigative Journalism*, 22 October 2023, [online], https://www.thebureauinvestigates.com/stories/2023-10-22/all-that-ismissing-is-a-whip-home-office-ignored-migrant-worker-abuses-on-farms/ (Last Access Apr 2024).

Milbourne, P., & Coulson, H. (2021). Migrant labour in the UK's post-Brexit agri-food system: Ambiguities, contradictions and precarities. *Journal of Rural Studies, 86*, 430–439.

Mullally, S., & Murphy, C. (2014). Migrant domestic workers in the UK: Enacting exclusions, exemptions, and rights. *Human Rights Quarterly, 36*(2), 397–427.

Mundlak, G. (2005). Recommodifying time: Working hours of 'live-in' domestic workers. In J. Conaghan & K. Rittich (Eds.), *Labour law, work, and family* (pp. 125–151). Oxford University Press.

O'Connor, S., & Evans, J. (2021). Brexit: The low-paid migrant workers 'trapped' on Britain's farms. *Financial Times*, 15 March 2021 [online], https://www.ft.com/content/11e49a14-5b89-4f23-ba47-2cde24dcd1ef (Last Access Apr 2024).

Palumbo, L., & Sciurba, A. (2018). *The vulnerability to exploitation of women migrant workers in agriculture in the EU: The need for a human rights and gender based approach.* European Parliament Study. Policy Department for Citizens' Rights and Constitutional Affairs, European Union.

Pro-Force Ltd. (2021). *Written evidence. Submitted by James Mallick, Director of Compliance*, Pro-Force Ltd. [online], https://committees.parliament.uk/writtenevidence/12847/default/ (Last Access Apr 2024).

Portes, J. (2022). The economics of the UK's post-Brexit immigration system. In J. Portes (Ed.), *The economics of Brexit: What have we learned?* (pp. 71–80). Report, Centre for Economic Policy Research. CEPR Press.

Potter, M., & Hamilton, J. (2014). Picking on vulnerable migrants: Precarity and the mushroom industry in Northern Ireland. *Work, Employment and Society, 28*(3), 390–406.

Refugee Action/Lift the Ban Coalition. (2020). *Lift the Ban: Why giving people seeking asylum the right to work is common sense* [online], https://www.refugee-action.org.uk/lift-the-ban/ (Last Access Apr 2024).

Roberts, K. (2022). *The UK needs migrant workers. This means it also needs visa options which offer workers a fair deal.* FLEX, Blog [online], https://labourexploitation.org/news/the-uk-needs-migrant-workers-this-means-it-also-needs-visa-options-whichoffer-workers-a-fair-deal/ (Last Access Apr 2024).

Rogaly, B. (2008). Intensification of workplace regimes in British horticulture: The role of migrant workers. *Population, Space and Place, 14*(6), 497–510.

Scott, S. (2017). Informalisation in low-wage labour markets: A case study of the UK food industry. *Population, Space and Place, 23*(7), 10.

Sedacca, N. (2019). Migrant domestic workers and the right to a private and family life. *Netherlands Quarterly of Human Rights, 37*(4), 288–310.

Sedacca, N. (2021). A crucial and long-needed step against the devaluation of domestic work: 'Family worker' exemption dis-applied in Puthenveettil v Alexander & ors. *UK Labour Law* [online], https://uklabourlawblog.com/2021/03/01/a-crucial-and-long-needed-step-against-the-devaluation-of-domestic-work-family-worker-exemption-dis-applied-in-puthenveettil-v-alexander-ors-by-natalie-sedecca/ (Last Access Apr 2024).

Sedacca, N. (2022). Domestic workers, the 'family worker' exemption from minimum wage, and gendered devaluation of women's work. *Industrial Law Journal, 51*(4), 771–801.

Staiano, F. (2017). *The human rights of migrant women in international and European law.* Giappichelli Editore – Eleven International Publishing.

Sumption, M., & Fernández-Reino, M. (2018). *Exploiting the opportunity? Low-skilled work migration after Brexit.* University of Oxford: The Migration Observatory [online], https://migrationobservatory.ox.ac.uk/resources/reports/exploiting-the-opportunity-low-skilled-work-migration-after-brexit/ (Last Access Apr 2024).

Sumption, M., & Kierans, D. (2021). *Integration in the UK and the post-Brexit immigration system.* University of Oxford: The Migration Observatory [online], https://migrationobservatory.ox.ac.uk/resources/commentaries/integration-in-theuk-and-the-post-brexit-immigration-system/

Sumption, M., Forde, C., Alberti, G., & Walsh, P. W. (2022). *How is the end of free movement affecting the low-wage labour force in the UK?* University of Oxford: The Migration Observatory. [online], https://migrationobservatory.ox.ac.uk/resources/reports/how-is-the-end-of-free-movement-affecting-the-low-wage-labour-force-in-the-uk/ (Last Access Apr 2024).

Sumption, M., Walsh, P. W., & Brindle, B. (2023). *Briefing: Net migration to the UK.* University of Oxford: The Migration Observatory.

Thomson, S. G., McMorran, R., Bird, J. B., Atterton, J., Pate, L. P., Meador, J. E., DeLima, P., & Milbourne, P. (2018). *Farm workers in Scottish agriculture: Case studies in the international seasonal labour market.* The Scottish Government.

UK Government. (2018). *Latest horticulture statistics.* Department for Environment, Food & Rural Affairs, 31 May 2018 [online], https://www.gov.uk/government/statistics/latest-horticulture-statistics (Last Access Apr 2024)

UK Government. (2022). *The UK's points-based immigration system: an introduction for employers (accessible version)* [online], https://www.gov.uk/government/publications/uk-points-based-immigration-system-employer-information/the-uks-pointsbased-immigration-system-an-introduction-for-employers (Last Access Apr 2024).

UK Parliament. (2011). *Convention on domestic workers.* Volume 530: debated on Wednesday 29 June 2011 [online], https://hansard.parliament.uk/commons/2011-06-29/debates/11062959000001/ConventionOnDomesticWorkers (Last Access Apr 2024).

Unison. (2023). *Migrant care staff in UK 'exploited and harassed' by employers, says Unison.* News Release. 10 July 2023 [online], https://www.unison.org.uk/news/press-release/2023/07/migrant-care-staff-in-uk-exploited-and-harassed-by-employers-says-

unison/#:~:text=Migrant%20staff%20coming%20to%20the,says%20UNISON%20today%20(Monday) (Last Access Apr 2024).
Vargas-Silva, C. (2018). *The fiscal impact of immigration in the UK*. University of Oxford: The Migration Observatory.
Wallace, T. (2018). Policy-driven evidence: Evaluating the UK government's approach to immigration policy making. *Critical Social Policy, 38*(2), 283–301.
Walsh, P. W. (2021). *The UK's 2021 points-based immigration system*. University of Oxford: The Migration Observatory [online], https://migrationobservatory.ox.ac.uk/resources/primers/policy-primer-the-uks-2021-points-based-immigration-system/ (Last Access Apr 2024).
Walsh, P. W., & Sumption, M. (2023). *Why the government's economic impact assessment of the illegal migration act tells us little about the act's economic impact. Commentary*. University of Oxford: The Migration Observatory [online], https://migrationobservatory.ox.ac.uk/resources/commentaries/why-the-governments-economic-impact-assessment-of-the-illegal-migration-act-tells-us-little-about-the-acts-economic-impact/ (Last Access Apr 2024).
Work Rights Centre. (2022). *Weed out exploitation*. Work Rights Centre, 2 March 2022.
Wright, C. F. (2017). Employer organisations and labour immigration policy in Australia and the United Kingdom: The power of political salience and social institutional legacies. *British Journal of Industrial Relations, 55*(2), 347–371.
Zambelli, E., Benson, M., & Sigona, N. (2022). 'British-European families after Brexit'. Research Brief, 3 [online], https://doi.org/10.5281/zenodo.6834639 (Last Access Apr 2024).

Chapter 8
The UK Approach to Addressing Exploitation and (Not) Protecting Exploited Migrant Workers

By critically analysing UK labour migration policies and focusing on the policy and legal regimes concerning seasonal migrant workers and migrant domestic workers—in particular the Seasonal Workers Visa and the Overseas Domestic Worker visa—Chap. 7 pinpointed the assemblage of factors creating and exacerbating migrant workers' situational vulnerabilities to exploitation, highlighting similar patterns and dynamics across these sectors. Chapter 8 critically explores the UK legal and policy instruments adopted to address exploitation, in particular severe exploitation and trafficking, behind the country's reputation as being in the vanguard of the fight against modern slavery.

Already in 2004, the UK was one of the first countries to establish a non-departmental public body to regulate labour activity, the Gangmasters Licensing Authority (GLA)—renamed the Gangmasters and Labour Abuse Authority (GLAA) in 2017—through a licensing scheme aimed at protecting workers and upholding labour standards in agriculture, horticulture, shellfish gathering, and related processing and packaging industries in the UK. Above all, in 2015 the UK adopted the Modern Slavery Act (c 30) aimed at preventing and prosecuting modern slavery and protecting the victims, which has been hailed as a 'landmark' piece of legislation (Home Office, 2015). Nonetheless, the primary focus of this Act on severe exploitation is not without problems. Also, more than nine years after the Act's passage, there are numerous critical issues concerning the identification mechanism and the support and protection measures for victims, particularly in terms of achieving effective social and labour integration and making a new life. These deficiencies and challenges are expected to worsen, due to the progressively more stringent migration and asylum policies adopted by the UK, particularly since 2022 (Haynes, 2023; Anti-Slavery International, 2023; Sumption et al., 2022).

Building on these issues and tensions—and considering the specificities of the UK context especially in terms of the migration system and labour market conditions—this chapter critically examines if and how legal and policy interventions in

L. Palumbo, *Taking Vulnerabilities to Labour Exploitation Seriously*, IMISCOE Research Series, https://doi.org/10.1007/978-3-031-55424-7_8

the UK address labour exploitation as a continuum. Consequently, it also explores whether these interventions respond to the vulnerabilities of exploited individuals or, conversely, contribute to amplifying them.

8.1 The Strengthening of a Punitive and Repressive Approach to Irregular Migrants and a 'Hostile Environment' for Modern Slavery Victims

Since the end of the 1990s, the UK has increasingly adopted repressive legal instruments to address irregular migration. Especially since the 2000s, the UK government has significantly increased sanctions against employers hiring irregular migrants, leading up to the enactment of the 2014 and 2016 Immigration Acts. This latter, in particular, provided for the criminalisation of both those who employ irregular migrants and the act of working with irregular migration status (Chap. 7).

It is worth noting in this regard that the UK opted out of the EU Employer Sanctions Directive 2009/52 penalising employers of irregular third-country migrants. As explained by the UK Government, this decision was influenced by various factors, including concerns about 'the creation of additional administrative burdens on both employers and the public sector' and guaranteeing 'additional rights to illegally-staying employees, including provision of back payments where an employee has earned less than the minimum national wage, which would be difficult to administer and would send the wrong message by rewarding breaches of immigration legislation' (Home Office, 2011). According to the government, 'existing domestic provisions achieve similar outcomes without the additional burdens and costs the directive would impose on both business and the public sectors' (ibid.). This approach has once again confirmed the national government's concern that granting rights and protection to 'irregular migrants' might encourage migration. Simultaneously, it has underscored how the provisions establishing sanctions against employers of third-country migrants primarily aim to address irregular migration rather than prevent exploitation and protect the rights of the migrants involved.

As highlighted in relevant literature (Dwyer et al., 2016; Calò et al., 2021) and further underscored by the testimonies collected during this research, the impact of these repressive migration policies has been geared more towards increasing barriers to migrants' legal and social inclusion in the labour market rather than towards deterring irregular migration or addressing employers and irregular employment practices. In particular, the introduction of the offence of illegal working with the 2016 Immigration Act has contributed to pushing migrants into precarious employment conditions in the labour market's least protected and regulated sectors such as agriculture and domestic work. This has further exposed migrants to dynamics of exploitation and abuse as employers seek to manage risks by lowering wages or increasing working hours or both (Dwyer et al., 2016). Furthermore, as Åhlberg and

Granada (2022, p. 128) emphasise, the introduction of this offence has also strengthened 'one of the main tools exploitative employers use to coerce and control migrants in exploitative situations: the threat of reporting them to the authorities'.

The 2016 Immigration Act made 'illegal working' a criminal offence punishable by an unlimited fine, a six-month custodial sentence, and the confiscation of any income earned during the relevant working period. Therefore, with its adoption, the status of irregular migrant de facto negates a worker's right to be paid for their work (Åhlberg & Granada, 2022). By contrast, as highlighted in Chap. 4, EU countries must ensure that employers are liable for retroactive payments (such as outstanding wages and social security contributions) to migrant workers in irregular conditions, as provided by the Employer Sanctions Directive (see also FRA, 2011).

The UK government's focus on immigration policy and enforcement over and above the enforcement of labour rights has helped produce an 'hostile environment'—the term used by Theresa May in 2012 (Kirkup & Winnett, 2012)—for migration to the UK. Fostering the idea of migrants as dangerous/criminals and as a threat to society and interests has increased fear and stigma (Balch, 2016; Griffiths & Yeo, 2021), consequently obscuring exploited migrant workers' awareness of their right to work and dissuading them from seeking help (Dwyer et al., 2016). This, in turn, has favoured abusive employers and traffickers who exploit these workers' vulnerabilities (Weatherburn & Toft, 2018).

By placing the 2016 Immigration Act in the context of neo-liberal globalisation, Judy Fudge has compellingly underscored that the Act should be interpreted in relation to the UK government's objective of preserving the national regime of 'light-touch' labour market regulation. This is achieved by convincing citizens that 'irregular migrants exploited by rogue employers and criminal gangs, and not the deregulated labour market, pose the greatest threat to labour standards and working conditions' (Fudge, 2018, p. 7). As Fudge points out, this approach raises questions about how UK institutions frame and consider the issue of labour exploitation. In this sense, Fudge highlighted how the use of the dominant narrative around 'illegal workers' and 'unscrupulous employers' as the 'objects of legal opprobrium' have contributed to obfuscating the real issues behind labour exploitation while preserving the UK socio-economic model. Indeed, like the narratives surrounding the *caporali* (illegal gangmasters) dominating Italian political and legal discourse on labour exploitation (Chap. 6), the rhetoric of 'illegal workers' and 'unscrupulous employers' has diverted attention away from the structural causes of labour exploitation, while framing exploitation only in terms of abusive individual relationships. This approach, as discussed below, also informs the 2015 Modern Slavery Act.

The restrictive and punitive migration regime supported by the 2014 and 2016 Immigration Acts has been further intensified by recent stringent legislative measures such as the 2022 Nationality and Border Act (c. 36) and the 2023 Illegal Migration Act (c 37). These Acts have reinforced the 'hostile environment' approach and associated culture of disbelief (Anti-Slavery International, 2023), extending it to the UK modern slavery support system and consequently to victims of trafficking and exploitation.

Being informed by the narrative of 'dangerous individuals' abusing the modern slavery system (Haynes, 2023) and that consequently this system is an incentive for irregular migration to the UK, the 2022 Nationality and Border Act was adopted to tackle the growing numbers of individuals claiming to be victims of trafficking and to prevent the 'misuse' of protection mechanisms in the UK. In this sense, the Act, in place since January 2023, introduced provisions aimed at tightening and selecting access to the protection system for victims of modern slavery, as discussed below.

In line with this approach, the latest 2023 Illegal Migration Act represents an additional and most severe intervention of deterrence applied to both the asylum and modern slavery support systems. Aimed at preventing and deterring 'unlawful migration, and in particular migration by unsafe and illegal routes', the Act provides, with 'radical' and temporary measures, for the denial of support, and for detention and deportation of irregular migrant individuals who have irregularly entered the UK, including asylum seekers and potential victims of trafficking and modern slavery. As human rights and migrant rights organisations have denounced, the 2023 Illegal Migration Act measures, in particular those concerning victims of modern slavery, contravene the UK's international obligations, including those under ECHR (especially Article 4—Prohibition of slavery and forced labour) and the Council of Europe Convention against Trafficking (Burland & Jovanovic, 2023).

While it is still too early to have data on the effects of these measures, it is highly likely that they will result in a significant weakening of the Modern Slavery Act System. This would increase the situations of vulnerability of many migrant individuals, leaving them without the means to escape dynamics of exploitation and lacking adequate protection and support.

8.2 The 2015 Modern Slavery Act: Between Reality and Rhetoric

Adopted in 2015, between the 2014 and 2016 Immigration Acts, the Modern Slavery Act was presented by the UK as a 'historic milestone' in the fight against modern forms of slavery (Home Office, 2015). Its aim was to a provide a comprehensive response 'in a field which was hitherto dominated by an arguably minimalist approach to the regulation of human trafficking' (Haynes, 2023, p. 1234).

As legal scholar Virginia Mantouvalou (2018) explains, modern slavery entered the UK agenda after the first early case law of the ECtHR highlighting the need to address the most severe instances of labour exploitation. This included *Siliadin v. France* (Application No. 73316/01, 26 July 2005) and *Rantsec v Cyprus and Russia* (Application No. 25965/04, 7 January 2010) recognising state authorities' obligation to enact legislation criminalising slavery, servitude, and forced and compulsory labour and take positive operational measures to protect individuals (see Chap. 1). Following the early ECtHR case law, in 2009 the UK introduced section 71 of the UK Coroners and Justice Act 2009, 'Slavery, servitude, and forced and compulsory labour'. The same year the 2005 Council of Europe Convention against Trafficking came into force.

After period of hesitation, the UK decided to opt into the EU Anti-trafficking Directive 2011/36/EU. Successively, in 2015 the UK adopted the Modern Slavery Act, substantively implementing the UK's obligations under the UN Palermo Protocol, the Council of Europe Convention against Trafficking, and the EU Anti-Trafficking Directive. However, the 2022 National and Borders Act now provides that this Directive be disapplied in so far as it is 'incompatible with provision made by or under this Act' (section 68; see also Haynes, 2023).

The Modern Slavery Act, which applies to England and Wales and with some provisions also in Scotland and Northern Ireland,[1] aims to prevent trafficking in persons, prosecute perpetrators, and protect victims, in line with the holistic approach supported by the Anti-Trafficking Directive. In this sense, the Modern Slavery Act consolidated and codified existing offences, increased the penalties for human trafficking, and introduced provisions concerning victim protection as well as some measures to foster transparency in supply chains.

Before the Modern Slavery Act was adopted existing offences were included in three separate Acts—the 2003 Sexual Offence Act (ss 57–59), the 2004 Asylum and Immigration Act (s 4), as amended by the 2012 Protection of Freedoms Act (ss 109–110), and the 2009 Coroners and Justice Act (s 71). These caused confusion. As Mantouvalou (2018, p. 1119) pointed out, 'the fact that one of the offences (trafficking for non-sexual exploitation) was part of immigration law, rather than criminal law, created further misunderstandings'. The Modern Slavery Act brought together the offences in one piece of criminal legislation (ibid.). It is noteworthy in this regard that while the previous draft of the Modern Slavery Bill produced by the Joint Committee (2014) delineated offences into slavery, trafficking, and exploitation, the final version opted not to recognise exploitation as a standalone offence.

Indeed, the Modern Slavery Act identifies two stand-alone offences: the offence of slavery, servitude, and forced and compulsory labour (Sect. 8.1) and that of human trafficking (Sect. 8.2). The offence of slavery, servitude, or forced labour is constructed in accordance with Article 4 of the ECHR. According to the Act, in determining whether this offence has been committed, regard may be given to all the circumstances, including any of the 'person's personal circumstances…which may make the person more vulnerable than other persons' and 'any work or services provided by the person', especially in exploitative conditions (Section 1(4)). This provision aligns with a situational understanding of vulnerability as it directs attention to the interplay of factors, including personal and contextual factors, that contribute to a person being in a situation of vulnerability to exploitation (Weatherburn, 2016, 2021). The Act also states that consent of the person to any of the acts that

[1] In particular, these include some provisions in respect of maritime enforcement, the Independent Anti-Slavery Commissioner, and the transparency in supply chains (TISC). It is worth noting that Scotland and Northern Ireland each have dedicated laws on human trafficking: the Human Trafficking and Exploitation (Scotland) Act 2015 and the Human Trafficking and Exploitation (Criminal Justice and Support for Victims) Act (Northern Ireland) 2015.

constitute slavery, servitude, forced or compulsory labour does not preclude a determination that they are victims of the crime (Section 1 (5)).

The offence of trafficking occurs instead when 'a person commits an offence if the person arranges or facilitates the travel of another person ("V") with a view to V being exploited' (Sect. 8.2). The consent of the victim to travel is irrelevant. The Act explains that a person may 'arrange or facilitate someone's travel by recruiting, transporting or transferring, harbouring or receiving, or transferring or exchanging control over another person'. Furthermore, Sect. 8.3 of the Act defines exploitation, affirming that 'a person is exploited if that person is subjected to slavery, servitude, forced labour, sexual exploitation, removal of organs, securing services by force, threats or deception, or securing services etc. from children and vulnerable persons'.

While the definition of trafficking contained in the Modern Slavery Act reflects some elements of the definition provided by international and European legislation such as the EU Directive 2011/36, it does differ in other aspects. For instance, an essential component of the offence of trafficking as defined in the Modern Slavery Act is the notion of travel, which as the Act states (Section 2 (5)) may occur either across borders or within a country. As the GRETA (2016, para. 261) notes, in the Modern Slavery Act the 'action' element of the definition of trafficking is viewed through the notion of 'travel'. This is a reductive approach compared to the definition of trafficking provided by relevant international and EU instruments, which include a list of different actions. Furthermore, the Act does not distinguish between the means and the purpose of exploitation or contain the definition of position of vulnerability provided, for instance, by the EU Anti-Trafficking Directive. All this, as it has been argued, may create problems especially in terms of identification of victims and consequently in the application of assistance and protection measures (Haynes, 2015). Lastly, how the Modern Slavery Act defines exploitation seems to refer to a complete list of practices while EU Directive 2011/36, as well as international instruments on trafficking, provide a non-exhaustive list of exploitation purpose (Cavanna et al., 2018).

Data concerning the number of investigations reveals a ten-fold increase after the adoption the Modern Slavery Act. At the end of December 2019, there were around 1821 ongoing live investigations involving 2500 potential victims, compared to 188 investigations in November 2016 (CSJ & Justice and Care, 2020, p. 22). Most investigations concerned sexual exploitation (592 operations) and criminal exploitation (572 operations), followed by labour exploitation (471 operations), domestic servitude (73 operations), and forced marriage (4 operations) (ibid., p. 24).

However, despite these positive steps, the rate of prosecution and convictions is still low and, as key stakeholders interviewed in this research emphasised, data reveal that there is a striking discrepancy between the number of prosecutions, the number of modern slavery crimes that are recorded, and the number of victims of trafficking and forced labour that have been identified through the national referral mechanism (NRM) (see also Mantouvalou, 2018). According to the data provided by a report by the Centre for Social Justice, 'in the year ending March 2019 there were 322 completed prosecutions for modern slavery-related crimes and 219 convictions served. During the same period, 7,525 adults and children were identified as potential victim of modern slavery' (CSJ & Justice and Care, 2020, p. 6). The same report estimated that the number of victims in the UK could be as high as 100,000. Recent data reveal that in 2020 to 2022 there were only 5578 people (adult) confirmed as victims of trafficking and, as further discussed below, only few (364) adults were granted discretionary leave as a result (Helen Bamber Foundation, 2023).

One of the main concerns highlighted by the stakeholders interviewed for this research and confirmed by other studies is judicial authorities' difficulty in understanding and recognising cases of exploitation that do not clearly amount to slavery or human trafficking. This has led to either cases being closed or prosecuted under different legislation (CSJ & Justice and Care, 2020, p. 34). Frequently the complexity of situations of vulnerability related to less evident coercive elements (including, for instance, family-related responsibility and debt bondage) are underestimated or not comprehended by prosecutors. The related issue of the consent to abuse and exploitation plays a key role and is often misunderstood in court. Emblematic is the example mentioned by the Centre for Social Justice about the forced labour cases investigated by Essex police and charged by the Crown Prosecution Service (CPS) and that failed in court because the people involved were not physically restrained during their exploitation (CSJ & Justice and Care, 2020, p. 34). This was considered as a key element evidencing that the individuals were not victims of slavery.

However, over recent years, there has also been an interesting national case law focused on the situations of vulnerability of exploited and trafficked persons that has paid attention to the various factors creating and amplifying them.[2] Indeed, although the above-mentioned offences in the Modern Slavery Act do not include the abuse of a position of vulnerability as a constituent element, some court decisions refer to it when assessing the level of coercion, control, or deception by the exploiter and when discussing the victim's difficulties in changing their circumstances (Weatherburn, 2021, p. 199). Interestingly, in her analysis of relevant UK case law in the field, Amy Weatherburn (2021, p. 203) highlights that these judicial decisions also include cases regarding British nationals and EU workers. In the case of EU workers' situations of vulnerability, the focus was on the disadvantage of socio-economic status where they sought work and were involved in exploitative dynamics due to an 'economic imperative' (ibid.). In addition, in some decisions courts consider how the situations of vulnerability are created and amplified by the same exploitative conditions experienced by the concerned person. These encompass, for instance, conditions of dependence and isolation that arise from the exercise of control over the individual (ibid.).

In line with this approach is a recent judgment issued in July 2022 by UK Supreme Court in the case of *Basfar v Wong* [2020] UKEAT/0223/19/BA, in which the Court significantly ruled that diplomatic immunity cannot defeat a claim by a victim of modern slavery (see in this regard Garcianda, 2023). In particular, in their reasoning, the Court relevantly argued that there is a 'material and qualitative

---

[2] See, among others, *Reyes v Al-Malki and another* [2017] UKSC 61; and *Basfar v Wong,* [2022] UKSC 20.

difference' between employment, defined as 'a voluntary relationship, freely entered into and governed by the terms of a contract' and modern slavery, where 'the work is extracted by coercion and the exercise of control over the victim' (para 43). This latter, as the judges pointed out, 'usually involves exploiting circumstances of the victim which make her especially vulnerable to abuse' and 'those constraints generally make it impossible or very difficult for the worker to leave' (ibid.). In line with a situational understanding of vulnerability, the Court underlined that physical and social isolation are a 'major source of vulnerability' increasing migrant domestic workers' risk of exploitation. Such a situation creates a sense of extreme dependency on employers that is augmented by psychological abuses and the withholding of pay, combined with the 'invisibility to the outside world' (para 48) characterising the domestic work.

8.2.1 Protection of Exploited Persons, Legal Barriers, and Obstacles

Part 5 of the Modern Slavery Act is dedicated to victims' protection, including provisions concerning identification and assistance. These include a defence for victims of slavery or trafficking who commit to a crime (non-punishment provision) (section 45); some protection for those victims who act as witness in criminal proceedings (section 46); a provision on migrant domestic workers (section 53); and the establishment of office of an Independent Anti-slavery Commissioner (section 40). It is worth noting that some of these provisions regarding regulation about identifying and supporting victims have been recently affected by the 2022 Nationality and Borders Act which, among others, has raised the evidence thresholds and narrowed the criteria for granting leave to remain thus making it harder for a migrant person to be recognised as a victim and obtain to a permission to stay. Provisions for protection have also undergone recent amendments through the 2023 Illegal Migration Act, which aims to restrict access to the modern slavery protection system for potential victims of trafficking who have entered the UK irregularly (sections 22–29) (Burland & Jovanovic, 2023). The Act provides some exceptions for victims supporting investigations and prosecution. However, its Section 22(5) 'creates a presumption that survivors' presence in the UK is not required to provide this support, unless the Home Secretary determines there are compelling circumstances' (Burland & Jovanovic, 2023, p. 2). All this will significantly undermine the support system under the Modern Slavery Act.

Before illustrating some of the protection provisions of the Modern Slavery Act, it is worth saying a few words about the UK system of identification of victims of trafficking and modern slavery, the National Referral Mechanism (NRM).

The NRM was established in 2009 following the ratification of the 2005 Council of Europe Convention on trafficking. In 2015, after the adoption of the Modern Slavery Act, this system was extended to all victims of modern slavery in the UK, covering both victims of human trafficking and victims of slavery, servitude, and forced or compulsory labour.

According to this system, designated first responders such as police, border force, local authorities, and some NGOs (for instance the domestic workers' charity Kalayaan) who have encountered a person suspected to a be a victim of trafficking should present a referral to the NRM. The referral is then considered by the Single Competent Authority (SCA), based in the Home Office or, since 2021, by the Immigration Enforcement Competent Authority (IECA), which is specifically in charge of identification decisions for adults who are subject to forms of immigration control. More specifically, once a referral is made, there is a two-stage process for identifying victims of modern slavery. The first consists of the SCA and IECA making a reasonable grounds decision within five working days, affirming that there are 'reasonable grounds' to believe the person concerned has been a victim of modern slavery. If the decision is positive, the person is entitled to at least a 30-day 'reflection and recovery' period (originally it was 45 days, but the 2022 Nationality and Borders Act reduced it to 30), while their claim is being considered for the second and final grounds decision. Guidance for decisionmakers recommends that this decision be reached promptly, ideally within 45 days. At Conclusive grounds stage, the individual is either recognised as a victim of trafficking or slavery, servitude, and forced or compulsory labour or not if there is insufficient evidence. Such a decision can be formally challenged by way of judicial review.

It is worth mentioning that a person who has been referred to the NRM before seeking international protection can apply for asylum and other kinds of protection at any point after the referral has been made. Likewise, if at any time during the asylum process the applicant self-identifies as a victim of trafficking or slavery/forced labour or there are indicators that it is reasonable to think that they have been trafficked or severely exploited, a referral can be made to the NRM. However, all this will be affected by recent stringent asylum reforms, including the 2023 Illegal Immigration Act, which seeks to prevent migrants arriving irregularly to the UK from being able to apply for asylum and receive assistance as victims of trafficking.

Official data reveal that the number of potential victims referred to the NRM by the police and local authorities has risen significantly since 2015 (CSJ & Justice and Care, 2020, p. 21). To some extent, this reveals an increased awareness about modern slavery. However, as highlighted above, the number of victims of modern slavery referred into the NRM who received positive conclusive grounds decisions is still low compared to the estimated number of people exploited in the UK (Walk Free, 2018; CSJ & Justice and Care, 2020). This has been recently confirmed by a Helen Bamber Foundation (2023) report and is likely to worsen due to the latest restrictive national migration and asylum policies.

Over the years, the NRM has showed substantial shortcomings that significantly affect the system limiting the identification of victims and accordingly their access to support and protection (CSJ & Justice and Care, 2020). These weaknesses in the identification and protection of victims persist despite the enactment (with a significant delay) in March 2020—5 years after the Modern Slavery Act was adopted—of

Section 49, a Statutory Guidance on how identify and support victims of modern slavery[3] (Home Office, 2023a).

Firstly, the NRM is a slow and complex bureaucratic system that often results in many people not receiving the protection and help they needed (CSJ & Justice and Care, 2020). Despite government promises to speed up the decision-making process as a part of the NRM reform, many victims still wait for months, sometimes for years, before receiving the NRM conclusive grounds decision (Kalayaan, 2019; GRETA, 2021). Indeed, far from being 45 days, the average waiting time is about 462 days (Anti-Slavery International, 2021).

During this waiting period, people are entitled to state-funded support that includes access to accommodation or outreach support, medical care, financial assistance (£39.60 per week for single survivor), and legal aid (Human Trafficking Foundation, 2018; GRETA, 2021). Permission to work depends their status at the date when the first decision was made. In particular, migrant people who are irregular by the date of the reasonable grounds decision do not have the right to work while they wait for a conclusive grounds decision, which may entitle them to a residence permit (see below). The result, as has been argued, is the production of a class of individuals who are in the UK under regular conditions and must remain here for their trafficking claim to be determined but are not permitted to work (Kalayaan, 2019).

More specifically, as testimonies collected for this research highlighted, this long protected waiting period is experienced by many exploited people involved in the NRM has time of uncertainty linked to anxiety and fear. As Avril Sharp from Kalayaan organisation noted, 'often they feel as though they are being hindered by a system that should be focused on protecting them instead. They spend months with little to do, while they are worried, for instance, over the financial situation of families'.[4] Most of exploited people have to pay off debts or provide economic support their families (or both)—a key motivation for their choice to migrate abroad. The cumulative effect of these pressures significantly impacts their mental health (Lewis et al., 2020). In these situations, individuals find themselves re-exposed to dynamics of abuse and exploitation while still within the NRM (ibid.). In this light, this waiting period results in a sort of limbo that affects and exacerbates individuals' situation of vulnerability, rather than helping them build individual empowerment paths.

Problems persist even after people receive a conclusive grounds decision. As Roberts (2018) underlined, 'no pathways are put in place to protect those with negative decision from further exploitation; nor is there data as to the current situation of those who have received a positive decision'. In particular, GRETA (2021, p. 70) notes that the absence of adequate support for those who have received a negative decision represents a significant barrier to launching juridical review or reconsideration process.

[3] The Modern Slavery Act provision concerning the Statutory Guidance has been amended by the 2022 Nationality and Borders Act (see Haynes, 2023).

[4] Interview with A. Sharp conducted in March 2023.

From the testimonies collected in this research, it emerges that many exploited migrants do not meet the criteria to be identified as victims of trafficking and therefore cannot enter the NRM. This, as Kate Roberts from the charity FLEX argued during our interview,[5] leads many migrants who experience exploitation—especially those who have come through temporary schemes such as the Seasonal Workers Visa scheme and therefore are in a regular condition—to refrain from seeking assistance and, instead, accept exploitative conditions. Indeed, in the absence of support for those who do not meet the criteria of having been trafficked, migrants who leave exploitative working conditions risk being left without work. Similar dynamics were described by Avril Sharp from Kalayaan: 'unless people have been trafficked or enslaved, or unless they can demonstrate that they have been brought to the UK for the purposes of being trafficked or enslaved, then there are no options for them. Despite this, many people choose to remain in the UK anyway, often becoming undocumented, and risking exposure to severe abuse and exploitation. So in the future, at a point in time that I can't predict, they will become a victim of forced labour or domestic servitude'.[6]

Thus, instead of preventing an escalation of exploitation dynamics, this system focused on severe exploitation, in reality contributes to amplifying the vulnerabilities of migrant workers, offering assistance only when their exploitation reaches serious levels. Such dynamics have, in turn, the effect of normalising those forms of exploitation (Giammarinaro, 2020) that do not amount to severe cases, such as trafficking, and therefore do not constitute grounds for victims to have assistance and protection.

At the same time, difficulties are also encountered by those exploited migrants that meet the criteria of having been trafficked. In this regard, it is worth noting that in recent years in the UK there has been an important number of rejected human trafficking claims that have been overturned by courts. Indicatively, in 2020, out of 325 claims in the Home Office-NRM scheme that were appealed, 255 were reversed (Siddique, 2021). As GRETA highlighted in its 2021 evaluation report, the data is 'suggestive of inadequate decision-making' (GRETA, 2021, p. 68). This, as argued by various testimonies gathered for this research, should be read within a growingly hostile migration environment that nurtures a perilous narrative suggesting the 'abuse' of the NRM by false victims.

The situation has worsened since the implementation of the changes introduced by the 2022 Nationality and Borders Act. Indeed, since January 2023, there has been a significant decrease in the percentage of foreign nationals being recognised as potential victims (IOM, 2023). This, as IOM underlines, is mainly due to the fact that the Modern Slavery Statutory Guidance on identifying and supporting victims, as amended by the Act, requires victims to provide 'objective evidence' to competent authorities deciding on their status. This places the burden of identification on the victims themselves (Haynes, 2023) and makes it harder to prove as the victim's

[5] Interview with K. Roberts, conducted in September 2022.

[6] Interview with A. Sharp, conducted in March 2023.

account alone is no longer sufficient. However, this guidance was amended again in 2023 as a result of a legal challenge; the Secretary of State for the Home Department has agreed to withdraw, reconsider, and revise sections requiring a potential victim of trafficking to produce 'objective' evidence.

On the other hand, problems persist even in the case of migrants finally identified as victims of trafficking. These are not automatically entitled to resident permits but may be eligible for a permission to stay. The 2022 Nationality and Borders Act (section 65) has narrowed the criteria for granting leave to remain, providing that a 'Temporary Permission to Stay' is only granted to confirm victims in order to assist the person in their recovery from any physical or psychological harm arising from their exploitation; enable the person to seek compensation if they are unable to pursue this remotely; and enable the person to co-operate with authorities in connection with an investigation or criminal proceedings. The first of these criteria is significantly more restrictive than the one in place before these amendments. Previously, leave could be granted when deemed necessary owing to personal circumstances. The elimination of this broad criteria, which reflects the approach of the Council of Europe Convention on Trafficking (Council of Europe, 2005, p. 184), will prevent a comprehensive assessment of the needs of victims and, consequently, make it harder for them to access the leave.

Recent data reveal that grant rates are already very low. Indeed, in 2020 to 2022, '5,578 adults were confirmed as victims of trafficking but only 364 adults subject to immigration control were granted leave via the NRM' (Helen Bamber Foundation, 2023, p. 3). Those who are granted leave to remain often experience prolonged delays in receiving such status. Furthermore, the majority of grants are issued for a relatively short period, with the average duration being just 12 months (ibid.).

The limited period of support does not ensure any stability in a long-term perspective, significantly impacting victims' prospects for social and labour inclusion, as well as their overall well-being. The lack of a perspective in terms of long-term social inclusion also significantly impacts victims' engagement with the criminal justice system (CSJ & Justice and Care, 2020, 2022). These limitations also explain the low conviction rate of traffickers. Indeed, people are not properly supported to disclose their abuse and cooperate with relevant authorities, meantime risking deportation in case of a negative outcome. All this fosters victims' situations of vulnerability and exposes even those who have received a positive identification to dynamics of homelessness, abuse, re-trafficking, and exploitation as several studies have reported (Commons Select Committee March, 2018; Murphy, 2018).

Many migrant people therefore often decide to make claims for asylum or humanitarian protection in the UK (Roberts, 2018). However, in this case, persons must wait years in a sort of legal limbo before their applications to stay in the UK are processed by the Home Office and the courts—a period when they are not allowed to work, study, or access mainstream benefits. This—as discussed in Chap. 7—exacerbates their situations of vulnerability.

These problems will probably worsen as a consequence of the restrictive provisions introduced by the 2023 Illegal Migration Act which 'will cut off access to the UK asylum and NRM protection system for those arriving "irregularly", removing the asylum "safety net" for thousands of survivors and increasing the risk that people will be kept in their trafficking situation or face further exploitation or harm' (Helen Bamber Foundation, 2023, p. 3).

In this scenario, the number of victims or potential victims of trafficking in long-term detention is likely to increase (Burland & Jovanovic, 2023). Recent data already reveal significant numbers: 4102 individuals detained under immigration powers between January 2019 and September 2020 were referred to the NRM before, during, or after their detention. Among these, 2914 received a positive reasonable grounds decision and 194 received a positive conclusive grounds decision (After Exploitation and Women for Refugee Women (2020). Several studies have reported the effect that detention produces for migrant people in terms of trauma, extreme uncertainty, and long-term psychological repercussions (see for instance Bosworth, 2014).

It is worth mentioning that, in line with the Council of Europe Convention against trafficking and EU Directive 2011/36, Section 45 of the Modern Slavery Act provides for a Statutory Defence to protect victims from being prosecuted for certain crimes that they may have been compelled to commit as a direct result of being exploited/trafficked. While representing a significant instrument to protect victims of exploitation and trafficking, this provision tends to be viewed by relevant authorities such as the police as a threat in the application of the Modern Slavery Act (CSJ & Justice and Care, 2020). Indeed, the primary concern is that criminals may abuse the Statutory Defence by claiming that they themselves are victims of modern slavery, and as a result, argue that they cannot be prosecuted (ibid.). However, this approach—which reiterates the narrative of migrants abusing the system rather than prioritising the protection of their rights—is dangerous as it risks preventing true victims from accessing protection. In contrast to this view, more attention should be dedicated to training the relevant authorities to identify victims of trafficking, ensuring that those victims suspected of committing criminal offences are not unduly deprived of the right to be identified and protected (Marchetti & Palumbo, 2022). The principle of non-punishment is a crucial element for a human rights-based approach to trafficking and exploitation-related issues. It recognises that the freedom of trafficked persons is significantly undermined due to their situation of vulnerability, leaving them with few choices other than those proposed by the exploiters/traffickers (Giammarinaro, 2020).

An important step towards recognising the principle of non-punishment of victims of trafficking and forced labour is the ECtHR judgment in the case of *V.C.L. and A.N. v. the UK* (Applications Nos. 77587/12 and 74603/12, 16 February 2021). The case concerned two Vietnamese nationals who entered the UK as minors (15 and 17 years old, respectively) and were discovered separately by the police on the premises of cannabis factories in 2009. Both were arrested and charged with drug-related offences. The ECtHR recognised the violation of Articles 4 and 6 of the ECHR by the UK, which failed to adopt appropriate operational measures to protect trafficked persons and instead prosecuted and subsequently convicted them, although they had been identified as victims of trafficking by competent authorities. According to the Court, the evidence as to the quality of the applicants as victims of trafficking was clear: the subjects were minors, foreigners, employed in the production of others' drugs, the suspicion of recruitment and exploitation was credible. Consequently, according to the Court, the national authorities should have taken operational measures from the beginning to protect them as potential victims of trafficking.

With this important judgment, the ECtHR, for the first time, ruled on the relationship between the obligations imposed on States in relation to the prohibition pursuant to Art. 4 ECHR and the principle of non-punishment of the victims of trafficking. Interestingly, while this ruling does not focus directly on the notion of vulnerability but limits itself to emphasising the applicant's vulnerability related to their minor age, it certainly represents important progress in terms of protecting victims of trafficking and recognising the mechanisms of exploitation that rely on the abuse of the situations of vulnerability of the individuals involved. However, even in this case, it is likely that implementation of the principle of non-punishment will be undermined by the provisions of the 2023 Illegal Migration Act that prevent from protection those people for whom their entry to the UK is an integral element of the criminal offence of trafficking committed against them.

With regard to other important provisions concerning the protection of victims of trafficking and modern slavery in UK statutory law, the Modern Slavery Act includes a section on domestic workers who enter the UK on the Overseas Domestic Worker (ODW) Visa (section 53), providing that those workers who have been victims of slavery or human trafficking can change employers and apply to renew the visa. However, as already highlighted in Chap. 7, this is a weak provision as it only applies to domestic workers who have received positive conclusive grounds decisions and does nothing in terms of prevention before exploitation reaches the trafficking threshold. As Roberts observed, the Modern Slavery Act 'did not address the elements of the Overseas Domestic Worker Visa which tied domestic workers to employers, facilitating risks of exploitation and trafficking'.[7]

In line with this limited approach, the Modern Slavery Act did not include any provisions addressing the protection of victims from a gender-based perspective, as provided by the Council of Europe Convention on Trafficking and EU Anti-Trafficking Directive 2011/36. Furthermore, the Act did not include a provision on a general civil remedy for victims of modern slavery, as provided by international obligation under the Council of Europe Convention on Trafficking, the EU Anti-Trafficking Directive, and the 2014 ILO Forced Labour Protocol. The UK Government argued that existing civil remedies in tort were sufficient for victims of modern slavery.[8] However, by choosing to refer to remedies available for other wrongs that do not correspond to the same circumstances as modern slavery, the Act risks not effectively addressing the mistreatment and violations that the victims of

[7] Interview with K. Roberts, conducted in September 2022.

[8] See Lord Bates, House of Lords Debate, 23 February 2015, Col 1464 [online], https://publications.parliament.uk/pa/ld201415/ldhansrd/text/150223-0002.htm (Last Access Apr 2024).

this crime suffer. As Mantouvalou (2018, p. 16) underlined, 'civil remedies must also reflect the gravity of the wrong that was suffered by the individual'.

It must be noted that the Modern Slavery Act (section 8) provides that the Court can compensate victims by making a trafficking and slavery reparation order if the perpetrators are convicted and a confiscation order is made against them. However, as the UK Supreme Court pointed out in *Taiwo v Olaigbe and Onu v Akwiwu* [2016] UKSC 31, these remedies are limited in terms of efficacy and significance. In particular, in this decision, the Baroness Hale stressed the responsibility of the legislation in not preventing exploitation and not properly addressing the wrongs that victims of severe exploitation suffered: 'If a person is convicted of such an offence [slavery, forced labour or trafficking] and a confiscation order made against him, the court may also make a slavery and trafficking reparation order under section 8 of the MSA, requiring him to pay compensation to the victim for any harm resulting from the offence. But such orders can only be made after a conviction and confiscation order; and remedies under the law of contract or tort do not provide compensation for the humiliation, fear and severe distress which such mistreatment can cause' (p. 2). Therefore, she suggested amending section 8 of the Modern Slavery Act to allow employment tribunals to properly compensate exploited workers.

Although there are other paths for victims of modern slavery to obtain compensation, as the latest GRETA (2021) report reveals, access to remedies is still alarmingly low.

8.2.2 The Modern Slavery Act and Hostile Migration Environment

By undermining the protection system for victims of modern slavery/trafficking, the latest draconian migration policies, culminating in the 2023 Illegal Migration Act, seems to challenge the idea of the UK as a leader in the fight against modern slavery and its 'historical' steps materialised in the adoption of the Modern Slavery Act. However, with a more careful and critical look, links and continuities between Modern Slavery Act and hostile migration environment emerge (Hodkinson et al., 2021).

As mentioned above, the Modern Slavery Act was adopted between the 2014 and 2016 Immigration Acts, in a context of an intensified hostile environment towards migration. At the same time, these years were marked pivotal judgments from the ECtHRs (Mantouvalou, 2018), directing national, European, and international attention to this slavery and trafficking related issue. The UK then decided to opt into the Anti-Trafficking Directive.

Against this background, the UK Modern Slavery Act was enacted to protect victims, but, above all, to address traffickers and criminal actors/groups facilitating irregular migration (Home Office, 2013; Joint Committee on the Draft Modern Slavery Bill, 2014). Although the Act aims at tackling modern slavery from a comprehensive approach, its main focus is on increasing prosecutions. As discussed earlier, the Act has not introduced solid provisions in terms of assistance and support for victims and their rights, including labour rights. Similar consideration can be made about measures to foster transparency in supply chains, as discussed in the next section. More generally, as Kate Roberts from FLEX stressed during an interview for this research, the 'Modern Slavery Act does not aim to challenge structural injustices or address the root causes of exploitation'.[9] Exploitation, or better say severe exploitation, is framed in the Act mainly in terms of a criminal phenomenon related to irregular migration rather than as a social issue connected to systemic inequalities.

Nonetheless, the number of prosecution in relation to the offences of the Modern Slavery Act continue to be relatively low. Conversely, since 2015 there has been an increase in victims entered in the NRM, and this number has tended to progressively stabilise especially since 2020 (Home Office, 2023b). Recent stringent national migration policies, such as the 2023 Illegal and Migration Act, have focused on this number. As Cameron Thibos (2023) observes, these 'figures do offer a stark indication of why the government today might see little utility in the [Modern Slavery] act. The MSA has delivered on finding victims in need of state support, but not on prosecutions. That wasn't supposed to happen'.

The numbers of victims of modern slavery/trafficking entered into the NRM have formed the basis for narratives that, as Roberts emphasises, 'demonised victims, repeatedly suggesting that people arriving irregularly here are falsely claiming to be victims to gain entry into the UK's generous protection system'.[10] Apart from the fact that the protection system for trafficking victims is anything but generous and often turns into an endless limbo, as several NGOs and charities have underlined, there is no evidence proving the widespread abuse of the NRM nor that this protection serves as incentive for making dangerous journey to the UK (Burland & Jovanovic, 2023).

Informed by such a narrative, recent stringent migration interventions have contributed to progressively extending the hostile migration environment to victims of trafficking. This undermines the protection provisions of the Modern Slavery Act and makes the system more selective and challenging to enter.

This will likely contribute to the creation and exacerbation of that dichotomy—already mentioned with regard to some trends in Italy—between the 'false'/criminal victims and the 'perfect victim', seen as a passive and helpless individual who is willing to self-identify, cooperate, and provide relevant information. Within this frame, as Jason Haynes (2023, p. 1263) pointed out, those considered as 'dangerous'/'folk devils' 'will be automatically stripped of their victimhood, essentialised as "illegal aliens", denied protection, and even punished for exercising agency'.

All this, in turn, contributes to the evisceration of the complexity of exploited people experiences and their situations of vulnerability. Simultaneously, it further

[9] Interview conducted in November 2022.

[10] Interview conducted in October 2023.

exposes them to dynamics of exploitation, while also making it more difficult to escape from such conditions.

8.2.3 Transparency and Compliance in Supply Chains: More Facade than Substance

In addition to the above illustrated provisions, the Modern Slavery Act introduced a specific clause (Section 54 of the Act) aimed at fostering transparency in supply chains. This provisions seeks to encourage 'businesses to be transparent about what they are doing, thus increasing competition to drive up standards' for effective and appropriate response to modern slavery (Home Office, 2017, p. 7). More specifically, the transparency in supply chains clause places a reporting obligation that applies to all 'commercial organisations' with an annual turnover of £36 million or more, which are required to prepare a 'slavery and human trafficking' statement for each financial year. In this statement companies need to outline what steps the company has taken to ensure its supply chains are free of forced labour and slavery-like conditions. The statement must be published on the company's website; approved by the board directors; and signed by a director (or equivalent). As the Home Office has explained, 'producing a regular annual statement will ensure organisations can build upon earlier statements and demonstrate to the public, consumers and investors that they are being transparent, not because they are required to do so but because they consider it important' (Home Office, 2017, p. 7).

The Modern Slavery Act established the mandatory minimum standards of disclosure and transparency for commercial organisations when drafting their modern slavery statement. Therefore, in practice, companies are not required by the Modern Slavery Act to detail the exact policies adopted to prevent exploitation and reduce the situations of vulnerability of workers; they can decide what to include or not and provide general information about the actions they have carried out. Companies are permitted to report that they have done nothing at all. If the companies do not produce a statement or comply with its guidance, the Home Office has the power to apply for an injunction. However, companies do not incur any penalties for disclosing that they have not implemented measures to guarantee that their business is not involved in or supporting exploitation (Cavanna et al., 2018).

The transparency in supply chains clause of the Modern Slavery Act is built on the 2010 Californian Transparency in Supply Chains Act, which requires companies operating within California to report on their efforts to address and combat slavery and trafficking along supply chains. The Californian Act applies exclusively to retail companies and has a higher revenue threshold ($100 million) for companies compared to the UK Act. Nevertheless, the overall framework and prerequisites of both Acts exhibit significant similarities (Falconer, 2016; Mantouvalou, 2018).

The purpose of the supply chain transparency clause is to raise awareness of the prevalence of serious forms of exploitation, including forced labour and trafficking, and the role companies and investors can play in preventing this. However, by not establishing real monitoring and enforcement mechanisms, this provision has so far proven inadequate in terms of driving a systemic corporate action to prevent and combat exploitation, including serious forms of exploitation in high-risk sectors such as agriculture.

Interestingly, a recent report by the Business and Human Rights Centre significantly showed that 6 years after the adoption of the transparency in supply chains clause, the UK Modern Slavery Act has failed in its stated intentions and aims (BHRC, 2021). This is mainly due to the lack of enforcement of reporting requirement itself and the absence of mandatory reporting criteria. The study reveals that only three in five of in-scope companies have published general statements about their risks and efforts and actions taken to address exploitation. In addition, the study noted that multinational companies connected to high-risk sectors fail to disclose notorious risks in their statements. For instance, important issues such as worker engagement, consideration of business practices and incentives, and remedies have been largely missed by companies' statements (ibid., p. 7). This absence of specific and concrete information, especially with regard to key issues, makes it challenging to assess the credibility and real efforts by companies, including where in the supply chain their efforts are targeted (Bloomfield & Lebaron, 2018, p. 4). Lastly, the BHRC study also highlighted that while around two in five in-scope (40%) companies have not complied with the Act, no administrative penalty (including exclusion from lucrative public procurement contracts) or injunction has been applied to compel a company to publish a statement.

Many of the shortcomings illustrated in the BHRC report were already denounced in other reports and documents, including an independent review on a set of recommendations to strengthen the Modern Slavery Act (Home Office, 2019). In response to these critiques, in 2022 the UK government announced the intention to introduce a bill to amend the Transparency in Supply Chains Clause to provide for the extension of Section 54 of the Modern Slavery Act to the public sector; removing the section of the Act that allows organisations to report that they have taken 'no steps' to tackle modern slavery; launching a registry for companies required to publish annual modern slavery statements; establishing mandatory reporting areas; developing a Single Enforcement Body; and setting financial penalties for organisation which fail to meet their statutory obligations under Section 54 of the Act.

This would be an important step forwards in terms of strengthening transparency measures. Yet, as the Business and Human Rights Centre (2021, p. 11) highlighted, a more robust response to tackle exploitation, including severe exploitation, should include tighter legal liability provisions, 'applying on all companies in all sectors which fail to adopt actions to prevent human and labour rights violations' and also including joint liability to cover all the actors of the supply chains (see also on this LeBaron & Gore, 2018). At the same time, another important measure to adopt is that of establishing import bans on products linked to forms of exploitation and human rights violations, in line with what is established in the United States by Section 307 of the Tariff Act (which bans the import of goods suspected of being produced with forced labour) and with what is currently being considered by

European Parliament (ibid.; see also Vanpeperstraete, 2021). Furthermore, to ensure consistent reporting across companies and to monitor the effectiveness of company behaviours and approaches, it would be important to introduce, in addition to mandatory reporting areas, a standardised set of indicators to report on, as suggested by Bloomfield and Lebaron (2018).

More generally, it may be argued that the Modern Slavery Act, especially its current provision on transparency in supply chains, is based on businesses that are inclined and capable of taking meaningful measures to prevent and tackle labour exploitation within their supply chains (Falconer, 2016). Yet transparency measures relying on voluntary disclosure, without enforcement and monitoring mechanisms, do not impact on business and market behaviour in preventing and addressing exploitation. While transparency is fundamental, relying on voluntarily disclosing actions is not sufficient to effectively drive systemic changes and prevent exploitation (LeBaron & Lister, 2016). Industry-led voluntary initiatives (including ethical certification and private auditing) do not provide a clear guarantee in terms of having an impact on labour standard conditions and, ultimately, of tackling exploitation. Rather, company-led voluntary initiatives may 'obscure the structural inequalities that create the conditions under which exploitation takes place' (Bloomfield & Lebaron, 2018, p. 4).

8.3 The Gangmasters and Labour Abuse Authority: A Real Model to Be Followed?

According to the 2014 ILO Forced Labour (Supplementary Measures) Recommendation (No. 203), governments should promote 'coordinated efforts to regulate, license and monitor labour recruiters and employment agencies and eliminate the charging of recruitment fees to workers to prevent debt bondage and other forms of economic coercion' (para. 4(i)). In this regard, the UK Gangmasters and Labour Abuse Authority can be considered, as GRETA (2012) has highlighted in its 2012 report on the UK, an example of good practice that other governments should adopt. Indeed, this is another element that contributes to the UK being regarded, on an international and European level, as a model to be followed in the fight against exploitation.

The Gangmasters Licensing Authority (GLA) was established in 2005, in the wake of the 'Morecambe Bay cockling disaster' in February 2004 when 23 undocumented Chinese cockle pickers were drowned by a tide after picking cockles off the Lancashire coast (Watts, 2007). By revealing the exploitative and unsafe working conditions of migrant workers employed in this field, the dramatic incident brought to light that 'businesses alone would not be able to root out the underworld of criminals who controlled the industry' (Noble, 2020).

The tragedy led to the adoption of the Gangmaster Licensing Act 2004, which made it a criminal offence to supply workers without a licence or to use an unlicensed labour provider. The Act provided for the creation of the GLA as a 'non-departmental public body' regulating the activities of employment agencies, labour providers, or gangmasters through a licensing scheme. This scheme is aimed at protecting vulnerable workers in agriculture, horticulture, shellfish gathering, and any associated processing and packaging industries in the UK. Labour providers are required to have a license to work in these sectors; to obtain the license, labour providers must meet the GLA licensing standards covering health and safety, accommodation, pay, transport, and training. The GLA monitors compliance with the licensing standards and, in cases of non-compliance, revokes the license.

With the adoption of 2016 Immigration Act, the authority was renamed the Gangmasters and Labour Abuse Authority (GLAA) and its remit has significantly expanded. The 2016 Immigration Act appointed a Director of a Labour Market Enforcement in charge of providing strategic direction for those organisations policing and regulating the UK labour market, including the GLAA, National Minimum Wage unit, and the Employment Agency Standards Inspectorate. Under this reform, the GLAA has been given with additional powers under the Police and Criminal Evidence Act 1984 (PACE), allowing it to investigate abuse allegations across the entire UK labour market. In this framework, the GLAA investigates all aspects of labour in England and Wales. Additionally, it collaborates with partner organisations including the police, the National Crime Agency, and other government law enforcement agencies engaged in combatting organised crime across the UK. How the GLAA operates and its partners vary somewhat in Northern Ireland and Scotland.

The GLAA licensing standards cover key critical areas concerning labour exploitation, forced labour, and trafficking. These standards prohibit activities including physical and mental mistreatment; restricting a worker's movement, debt bondage and retaining ID documents; withholding wages; providing poor quality accommodation; and exceeding working hours (GLAA, 2020). Compliance with the licensing standards is assessed through inspections of applicants and licence holders. This may include visiting the clients to check the place of work and interviewing workers.

According to recent data, in 2019/2020, the GLAA conducted over 200 operations across a range of sectors, including construction, agriculture, hand car washes, and hospitality (Home Office, 2020). As a result, the GLAA arrested 29 people for suspected labour market offences. Furthermore, as a First Responder, the GLAA also referred 30 potential victims of modern slavery to the NRM. In 2020/2021, the GLAA referred 92 potential victims of modern slavery into the NRM (Home Office, 2021a). Yet, the number is not so high compared to estimates of at least 100,000 victims of exploitation in the UK (CSJ & Justice and Care, 2020).

As emerged from the testimonies collected for this research, several elements undermine GLAA activities and raise concerns about their effectiveness in terms of protecting victims. One of the main critical aspects concerns the progressive shift of the GLAA from an 'employment-focused approach to regulating sectors in which workers are notoriously vulnerable to abuse to a migration and criminal regulatory regime' (Fudge, 2018, p. 46). Such a shift reflects the growing closeness of the GLAA with the Home Office. Indeed, in 2014 the GLAA was transferred from the Department for Environment, Food and Rural Affairs to the Home Office. This was ultimately consolidated with the 2016 Immigration Act, which, as mentioned above, dramatically expanded the GLAA's remit, providing it with powers and specialist officers to investigate severe exploitation.

As a consequence, although the GLAA operates independently of the government, there is concern that it has shifted from an authority aimed at protecting the rights of workers in situations of vulnerability to one aimed at identifying irregular migrant workers. Indeed, this 'comes from the fact that the outline of the GLAA's Director of Labour Market Enforcement is located within the same piece of legislation that makes undocumented work a criminal offence. Both outline and offence are situated in the 2016 Immigration Act' (Schenger, 2017, p. 372).

Such concerns about the GLAA focusing more on addressing irregular migration and undeclared work rather than protecting exploited workers discourage many victims or potential victims from reporting the abuse they experience. The fear of being deported and possibly re-exploited and trafficked prevents many exploited migrants from contacting relevant authorities (Åhlberg & Granada, 2022). This trend will likely be exacerbated by the latest stringent UK migration and asylum policies.

Another significant limitation undermining the activities of GLAA regards its available resources. While these were increased by the 2016 Immigration Act, this was not proportional to the organisation's role and responsibilities. As Graig (2017) underlines, the GLAA had a 6000% increase in the number of workers it was responsible for, but it only received a 60% increase in its own staff. Moreover, the additional funding was allocated to the GLAA's 'police-style powers' rather than its licensing and regulatory role and related activities (ATMG, 2018, p. 18). The lack of adequate resources clearly affects the potential of the GLAA to effectively conduct proactive investigation or monitor existing licensing holders. This, in turn, as one member of a London-based charity commented, 'affects and further narrows the possibilities for migrant farmworkers, who live in conditions of isolation and marginalisation, to report labour abuses and exploitation'.[11]

In addition, the GLAA does not conduct overseas licence and compliance inspections in the countries of origin of labour providers. This constitutes a significant limitation in terms of addressing structural factors contributing to workers' situations of vulnerability to exploitation as it 'poses a range of risks of workers facing deceptive recruitment, threats at point of recruitment and recruitment linked to debt' in their home countries (FLEX, 2023, p. 10).

According to one of the trade union representatives interviewed for this research, the GLAA tends to go for the easy targets: 'they go for the targets of the nail bars and the carwashes and things like that where, don't get me wrong, there's people being exploited in these industries, but it's usually a one man band that's bringing these people over. In the agricultural sector they should be going for the mister big because there's a lot of people involved, and again it's government cuts that [mean that] the GLAA cannot deal with it'.[12]

[11] Interview conducted in July 2021.

[12] Interview conducted in September 2021.

All these aspects significantly affect the innovative character and potential of the GLAA model, making it more of a model to be followed in theory than in practice. Moreover, all these limitations clearly emerged during the Covid-19 pandemic, which impacted institutional activities and simultaneously increased the situations of vulnerability of workers to exploitation and abuse. Similar to other organisations, in 2020, the GLAA conducted most of its work, particularly inspection work, online (GLAA, 2020), and this inevitably affected their working practices in a situation of already limited capacity and finances.

From July 2019 to October 2019, there was a public consultation on creating a Single Enforcement Body for Employment Rights. The Government's response to the consultation was supposed to be published in October 2019. However, a series of successive events—the general election in December 2019, Brexit, and the pandemic—delayed the publication of the government's position in response to the consultation until June 2021 (Home Office, 2021b). The government confirmed the its commitment to create such a body, which not only will bring together three existing bodies—the GLAA, the minimum wage inspector, and the employment agency standard inspector—into a single organisation but also deliver a significantly expanded remit (Home Office, 2021b, p. 3). As the official document notes, 'the overriding objective behind the creation of the new body is to significantly improve the government's ability to protect vulnerable workers and ensure they receive their employment rights' (ibid., p. 10). Creating this new body will require a government approval process and also primary legislation; it was supposed to be enacted in 2023, but has not happened as of this writing.

Another key concern about these changes pertains to the legal status of this single body—whether it will be an independent entity or an agency that is part of the government department structure. More generally, the concern is that this change will be a further step aimed at strengthening that assemblage of repressive instruments (Fudge, 2018) designed to target irregular migration and exploitative employers, leaving aside what should be at centre, that is, the protection of exploited migrants (FLEX, 2023).

8.4 Concluding Remarks

In the last decades, amidst an increasingly hostile environment toward migration and asylum, the UK has implemented various legal and policy measures primarily focused on addressing irregular migration through a repressive migration control approach. The 2015 Modern Slavery Act fits into this context. While widely celebrated as an important step forward in the fight against severe exploitation, the effectiveness of this Act, especially with regard to the protection of victims, is questionable. As this chapter has pointed out, by mainly focusing on prosecuting traffickers and abusers and, consequently, on preventing related irregular migration, the Act has primarily addressed the issue of exploitation from a repressive approach rather than a rights- and social-based approach.

The Modern Slavery Act frames labour exploitation mainly in terms of abusive individual relationships, without tackling the interplay of structural factors that create and amplify migrants' situations of vulnerability to exploitation. At the same time, by focusing on severe exploitation, the Act does not cover all those forms of exploitation that do not amount to slavery or trafficking and that are widespread in sectors such as agriculture and domestic work.

Those victims who manage to enter the NRM often navigate a protracted and uncertain journey that does not always result in obtaining permission to remain in the UK. On the other hand, those people, including regular migrant workers, who experience exploitation that does not reach severe forms, such as trafficking, are left without adequate protection, with the likely risk of being exposed again and again to dynamics of exploitation and abuse.

While entities such as the GLAA can potentially play a crucial role in preventing exploitation and protecting the rights of workers, the limited resources of the GLAA, coupled with the perception that this authority has progressively shifted from safeguarding the rights of workers to identifying irregular migrant workers, significantly restrict its effectiveness.

In line then with the approach dominant in countries such as Italy, even in the UK, labour exploitation has been mainly framed and addressed as a criminal law and migration containment issue, leaving untouched the protection of the rights of workers and systemic factors such as selective and restrictive migration regimes that produce inequalities and foster vulnerabilities. While undermining the protection provisions of the Modern Slavery Act, the latest restrictive legislative reforms, such as the 2022 Nationality and Borders Act and the 2023 Illegal Migration Act, align with the restrictive approach of this Act. In this sense, they aim to address the 'gaps' in the Act that, according to the dominant narrative, create opportunities for irregular migration.

References

After Exploitation and Women for Refugee Women. (2020). *Survivors behind bars: Nearly 3,000 potential trafficking victims detained since 2019*. Report [online], https://afterexploitation.com/2021/02/03/survivors-behind-bars-nearly-3000-potential-trafficking-victims-detained-since-2019/ (Last Access Apr 2024).

Åhlberg, M., & Granada, L. (2022). The making of irregular migration: Post-Brexit immigration policy and risk of labour exploitation. *Journal of Poverty and Social Justice, 30*(2), 120–140.

Anti-Slavery International. (2021). *Access to work for survivors of slavery to enable independence and sustainable freedom*. Briefing [online], https://www.antislavery.org/wp-content/uploads/2021/03/Coalition_AccessToWork_report_v3.pdf (Last Access Apr 2024).

Anti-Slavery International. (2023). *Anti-slavery day: The 'Illegal Migration' Act 2023 and its implications for survivors in the UK*. Blog Post, 12 October 2023, https://www.antislavery.org/latest/illegal-migration-act-2023-implications-anti-slavery-day/ (Last Access Apr 2024).

ATMG. (2018). *Before the harm is done: Examining the UK's response to the prevention of trafficking. Report*. Anti-Trafficking Monitoring Group.

Balch, A. (2016). *Immigration and the state: Fear, greed and hospitality*. Palgrave Macmillan.

BHRC. (2021). *Modern Slavery Act: Five years of reporting. Conclusions from monitoring corporate disclosure*. Report by Patricia Carrier. Business and Human Rights Reporting Centre and Modern Slavery Registry.

Bloomfield, M., & Lebaron, G. (2018). Transparency through disclosure in global governance. *E-International Relations* [online], https://www.e-ir.info/2018/09/21/the-uk-modern-slavery-act-transparency-through-disclosure-in-global-governance/ (Last Access Apr 2024).

Bosworth, M. (2014). *Inside immigration detention*. Oxford University Press.

Burland, P., & Jovanovic, M. (2023). *Explainer: The Illegal Migration Act modern slavery provisions*. Report. Modern Slavery & Human Rights and Policy and Evidence Centre.

Calò, F., Baglioni, S., Montgomery, T., & Biosca, O. (2021). Regulating fortress Britain: Migrants, refugees and asylum applicants in the British labour market. In V. Federico, & S. Baglioni (Eds.), *Migrants, refugees and asylum seekers' integration in European labour markets* (pp. 235–258). IMISCOE Research Series. Springer.

Cavanna, P., Valverde-Cano, A. B., & Weatherburn, A. (2018). Securing the prohibition of labour exploitation in law and practice: Slavery, Servitude, forced labour and human trafficking in Italy, Spain and the UK. *Slavery Today Journal, 4*(1), 20–47.

Commons Select Committee. (2018). *Inexcusable lack of support for modern slavery victims*. UK Parliament.

Council of Europe. (2005). *Explanatory report to the Council of Europe Convention on action against trafficking in human beings*. Council of Europe Treaty Series No 197.

CSJ & Justice and Care. (2020). *It still happens here: Fighting UK slavery in the 2020s*. Report, Modern Slavery Policy Unit. Centre for Social Justice (CSJ) and Justice and Care.

CSJ & Justice and Care. (2022). *A path to freedom and justice: A new vision for supporting victims of modern slavery*. Report, Modern Slavery Policy Unit. Centre for Social Justice (CSJ) and Justice and Care.

Dwyer, P., Hodkinson, S., Lewis, H., & Waite, L. (2016). Socio-legal status and experiences of forced labour among asylum seekers and refugees in the UK. *Journal of International and Comparative Social Policy, 32*(3), 182–198.

Falconer, C. (2016). Carrots and sticks: Increasing corporate accountability for 'modern slavery'. *Open Democracy, beyond trafficking and slavery* [online], https://www.opendemocracy.net/en/beyond-trafficking-and-slavery/carrots-and-sticksincreasing-corporate-accountability-for-modern-slav/ (Last Access Apr 2024).

FLEX. (2023). *A single enforcement body: What an effective single enforcement body looks like*. Policy Briefing [online], https://labourexploitation.org/app/uploads/2023/12/FLEX-Single-Enforcement-Body-Briefing-2023.pdf (Last Access Apr 2024).

FRA. (2011). *Fundamental rights of migrants in an irregular situation in the European Union*. Report, European Union Agency for Fundamental Rights. Luxembourg.

Fudge, J. (2018). Illegal working, migrants and labour exploitation in the UK: Liminal legality and the Immigration Act 2016. *Oxford Journal of Legal Studies, 38*(3), 557–584.

Garciandia, R. (2023). Domestic servitude and diplomatic immunity: The decision of the UK Supreme Court in Basfar v Wong. *Industrial Law Journal, 52*(2), 451–462.

Giammarinaro, M. G. (2020). *Beyond law enforcement, towards social justice: A human rights based-approach to trafficking in persons*. Report of the Special Rapporteur on trafficking in persons, especially women and children. A/HRC/44/45. United Nations [online], https://documents-dds-ny.un.org/doc/UNDOC/GEN/G20/086/90/PDF/G2008690.pdf?OpenElement (Last Access Apr 2024).

GLAA. (2020). *Licensing standards*. Gangmasters & Labour Abuse Authority [online], www.gla.gov.uk/media/9590/licensing-standards-october-2018-final-reprint-jan-2020-v22023.pdf (Last Access Apr 2024).

Graig, G. (2017). The UK's modern slavery legislation: An early assessment of Progress. *Social Inclusion, 5*(2), 16–27.

GRETA. (2012). *Report concerning the implementation of the Council of Europe Convention on action against trafficking in human beings by the United Kingdom*. First evaluation round. Group of Experts on Action Against Trafficking in Human Beings.

GRETA. (2016). *Report concerning the implementation of the Council of Europe Convention on action against trafficking in human beings by the United Kingdom*. Second evaluation round. Group of Experts on Action Against Trafficking in Human Beings.

GRETA. (2021). *Evaluation report: United Kingdom*. Third evaluation round. Group of Experts on Action Against Trafficking in Human Beings.

Griffiths M. & Yeo C. (2021). The UK's hostile environment: Deputising immigration control. *Critical Social Policy, 41*(4), 521–544.

Haynes, J. (2015). The Modern Slavery Sct (2015): A legislative commentary. *Statute Law Review, 37*(1), 33–56.

Haynes, J. (2023). Human trafficking: Iconic victims, folk devils and The Nationality and Borders Act 2022. *Modern Law Review, 86*, 1232–1264.

Helen Bamber Foundation. (2023). *Leave in Limbo: Survivors of trafficking with uncertain immigration status*. Report [after], https://www.helenbamber.org/sites/default/files/2023-08/Leave%20in%20limbo_Final_Aug23.pdf (Last Access Apr 2024).

Hodkinson, S. N., Lewis, H., Waite, L., & Dwyer, P. (2021). Fighting or fuelling forced labour? The Modern Slavery Act 2015, irregular migrants and the vulnerabilising role of the UK's hostile environment. *Critical Social Policy, 41*(1), 68–90.

Home Office. (2011). *Written statement to Parliament: EU Directive on sanctions against employers of illegally staying thirdcountry nationals*. Statement laid in the House of Commons on 24 May 2011 by the Rt Hon Damian Green MP [online], https://www.gov.uk/government/speeches/eu-directive-on-sanctions-against-employers-of-illegally-staying-third-countrynationals (Last Access Apr 2024).

Home Office. (2013). *Draft modern slavery bill*. Presented to Parliament by the Secretary of State for the Home Department by Command of Her Majesty [online], https://assets.publishing.service.gov.uk/media/5a7c8afae5274a0bb7cb7bb6/Draft_Modern_Slavery_Bill.pdf (Last Access Apr 2024).

Home Office. (2015). *Historic law to end modern slavery passed*. News story [online], https://www.gov.uk/government/news/historic-law-to-end-modern-slavery-passed (Last Access Apr 2024)

Home Office. (2017). *Transparency in supply chains etc. A practical guide*. Guidance issued under section 54(9) of the Modern Slavery Act 2015 [online], https://assets.publishing.service.gov.uk/media/61b7401d8fa8f5037778c389/Transparency_in_Supply_Chains_A_Practical_Guide_2017_final.pdf (Last Access Apr 2024).

Home Office. (2019). *Independent Review of the Modern Slavery Act. Second report from the independent review of the Modern Slavery Act 2015 covering transparency in supply chains* [online], https://www.gov.uk/government/publications/modern-slavery-act-2015-review-second-interim-report (Last Access Apr 2024).

Home Office (2020). *2021 UK annual report on modern slavery*. Modern Slavery Unit [online], https://www.gov.uk/government/publications/2020-uk-annual-report-on-modern-slavery/2020-uk-annual-report-on-modern-slavery-accessible (Last Access Apr 2024).

Home Office. (2021a). *2021 UK annual report on modern slavery* [online], https://www.gov.uk/government/publications/2021-uk-annualreport-on-modern-slavery/2021-uk-annual-report-on-modern-slavery-accessible-version (Last Access Apr 2024).

Home Office (2021b). *Establishing a new single enforcement body for labour rights: Government response*. Department for Business, Energy & Industrial Strategy [online], https://assets.publishing.service.gov.uk/media/60be1b47e90e0743a210de29/singleenforcement-body-consultation-govt-response.pdf (Last Access Apr 2024).

Home Office. (2023a). *Modern slavery: Statutory guidance for England and Wales (under s49 of the Modern Slavery Act 2015) and Non-Statutory Guidance for Scotland and Northern Ireland*. Version 3.5 [online], https://assets.publishing.service.gov.uk/media/6659a22316cf36f4d63ebcc3/Modern+Slavery+Statutory+Guidance+_EW_+and+Non-Statutory+Guidance+_SNI_+v3.10.pdf (Last Access Apr 2024).

Home Office. (2023b). *Official statistics. Modern Slavery: National Referral Mechanism and Duty to Notify statistics UK, Quarter 1 2023—January to March* [online], https://www.gov.

uk/government/statistics/modern-slavery-national-referral-mechanism andduty-to-notify-statistics-uk-january-to-march-2023/modern-slavery-national-referral-mechanism-and-duty-to-notify-statistics-ukquarter-1-2023-january-to-march (Last Access Apr 2024).

Human Trafficking Foundation. (2018). *The slavery and trafficking survivor care standards*. Human Trafficking Foundation.

IOM. (2023). *IOM's analysis of National Referral Mechanism data following the introduction of the Nationality and Borders Act*. News - Local, 18 October 2023. IOM United Kingdom. [online], https://unitedkingdom.iom.int/news/ioms-analysis-national-referral-mechanism-data-following-introduction-nationality-and-borders-act (Last Access Apr 2024).

Joint Committee on the Draft Modern Slavery Bill. (2014). *Draft modern slavery bill*. Report, Session 2013–14, HL Paper 166, HC 1019. House of Commons and House of Lords.

Kalayaan. (2019). *Dignity, not destitution. The impact of differential rights of work for migrant domestic workers referred to the national referral mechanism*. Kalayaan – Justice for Migrant Domestic Workers.

Kirkup, J., & Winnett, R. (2012). Theresa May interview: 'We're going to give illegal migrants a really hostile reception'. *The Telegraph*. 25 May 2012 [online], https://www.telegraph.co.uk/news/0/theresa-may-interview-going-give-illegal-migrants-really-hostile/ (Last Access Apr 2024).

LeBaron, G., & Gore, E. (2018). *The global business of forced labour*. Policy Brief 1: Key Findings and Recommendations for UK Policymakers. SPERI & University of Sheffield.

LeBaron, G., & Lister, J. (2016). *Ethical audits and the supply chains of global corporations*. Sheffield Political Economy Research Institute SPERI. Global Political Economy Brief No. 1 [online], https://eprints.whiterose.ac.uk/96303/1/Global-Brief-1-EthicalAudits-and-the-Supply-Chains-of-Global-Corporations.pdf (Last Access Apr 2024).

Lewis, H., Lonergan, G., Murray, R. Tomalin, E., & Waite, L. (2020). *Faith responses to modern slavery*. Report [online], https://jliflc.com/wp-content/uploads/2020/02/Faith-reponses-to-modern-slavery-2020-Uni-Sheffield-and-Leeds_LowRes.pdf (Last Accessed Apr 2024).

Mantouvalou, V. (2018). The UK modern slavery act 2015 three years on. *The Modern Law Review, 81*(6), 1017–1045.

Marchetti, S., & Palumbo, L. (2022). *10 Years After the Directive 2011/36/EU: Lights and shadows in addressing the vulnerability of trafficked and exploited migrants*. Population and Policy Brief, 33. Max Planck Society/Population Europe.

Murphy, C. (2018). *A game of chance? Long-term support for survivors of modern slavery*. Centre for Modern Slavery.

Noble, V. (2020). Revealed: How the UK's agriculture sector relies on modern slavery. *Open Democracy* [online], https://www.opendemocracy.net/en/oureconomy/revealed-how-the-uks-agriculture-sector-relies-on-modern-slavery/ (Last Access Apr 2024).

Roberts, K. (2018). Life after trafficking: A gap in the UK's modern slavery efforts. *Anti-Trafficking Review, 10*, 164–168.

Schenger, J. (2017). The Gangmaster licensing authority: An institution able to tackle labour exploitation? *Food Economy, 19*(3), 357–381.

Siddique, H. (2021). Four out of five rejected trafficking claims were overturned in UK last year. *The Guardian*, 2 July 2021 [online], https://www.theguardian.com/uk-news/2021/jul/02/four-out-of-five-rejected-trafficking-claims-overturned-uk-last-year (Last Access Apr 2024).

Sumption, M., Forde, G. A., & Walsh, P. W. (2022). How is the end of free movement affecting the low-wage labour force in the UK? *University of Oxford: The Migration Observatory* [online]. Available at: https://migrationobservatory.ox.ac.uk/resources/reports/how-is-the-end-of-free-movement-affecting-the-low-wage-labour-force-in-the-uk/ (Last Access Apr 2024).

Thibos, C. (2023). Why have the Tories abandoned migrant victims of modern slavery? *Open Democracy*, Beyond Trafficking and Slavery [online], https://www.opendemocracy.net/en/beyond-trafficking-and-slavery/why-have-the-tories-abandoned-migrant-victims-of-modern-slavery/ (Last Access Apr 2024).

Vanpeperstraete, B. (2021). *Towards an EU import ban on forced labour and modern slavery*. Discussion paper commissioned by the Greens/EFA Group in the European Parliament [online], https://www.annacavazzini.eu/wp-content/uploads/Towards_an_EU_import_ban_on_forced_labour_and_modern_slavery_February.pdf (Last Access Apr 2024).
Walk Free. (2018). *The global slavery index 2018*. Walk Free Foundation.
Watts, J. (2007). Going under. *The Guardian*, Crime, 20 June 2007 [online], https://www.theguardian.com/uk/2007/jun/20/ukcrime.humanrights (Last Access Apr 2024).
Weatherburn, A. (2016). Using an integrated human rights-based approach to address modern slavery: The UK experience. *European Human Rights Law Review, 10*, 184–194.
Weatherburn, A. (2021). *Labour exploitation in human trafficking law*. Cambridge University Press.
Weatherburn, A., & Toft, A. (2018). Managing the risks of being a victim of severe labour exploitation: Before and after the modern slavery act 2015. In M. Boretti (Ed.), *Labour migration in Europe* (Vol. II, pp. 99–138). Palgrave Macmillan.

Chapter 9
Taking Vulnerabilities to Exploitation Seriously: Concluding Remarks

9.1 Differential Inclusion, Differential Vulnerabilities

Far from considering vulnerability as something static, abstract, or fixed this book has mobilised the concept of 'situational vulnerabilities' to refer to the interplay of personal and structural factors that render a person vulnerable to forms and dynamics of exploitation. This 'situational' understanding of vulnerabilities requires adopting a perspective attentive to the intersection of various personal, contextual, and material factors that determine situations of vulnerability in a framework marked simultaneously—to use an expression of Iris Marion Young (Young, 1990)—by 'structural forms of oppression' (gender, class, nationality, ethnicity, race, and so on). The situational vulnerabilities of migrant workers cannot be assessed without considering the impact of restrictive and selective asylum, migration and labour policies, related social reproduction regimes (Rigo, 2022), shortcomings in the reception and protection systems, and, more generally, regulatory mechanisms that create and amplify scales and dynamics of power and oppression.

Despite differences in the migration regimes and labour market regulations of Italy and the UK, in both countries labour mobility have contributed to the sustainment of key labour market sectors such as agricultural and domestic work, lowering the cost of production by compressing the rights of workers. Supported by relevant EU policies and legislation, restrictive and selective policies on labour migration have generated and amplified migrants' situational vulnerabilities, which are utilised and exploited, each one in a particular way, within agricultural and domestic work sectors, which in both countries are characterised by exceptional legal and regulatory regimes that weaken workers' rights compared to workers in other sectors.

In the case of the UK, the sponsorship and points-based system, extended to EU citizens in 2021, significantly restricts access channels for those considered 'low-skilled' migrant workers. In addition to the recent changes to the Health and Social Care Visa, the only other migration channels for 'low-skilled' workers are the

L. Palumbo, *Taking Vulnerabilities to Labour Exploitation Seriously*, IMISCOE Research Series, https://doi.org/10.1007/978-3-031-55424-7_9

Seasonal Workers Visa and the Overseas Domestic Worker Visa. These latter schemes grant temporary residence permits to migrant workers, prioritising migration control over workers' rights and protection. While both seasonal migrant workers and domestic workers under these visas are theoretically allowed to change employers, practical factors, including the duration of their stay, often hinder the effective exercise of this right. Furthermore, by denying workers access to various social benefits and the right to family reunification, these schemes ensure the temporary status of these workers, effectively controlling and containing their social reproduction sphere.

In the case of Italy, the national entry route system based on the so-called Flows Decree relies on an employer-driven mechanism, tethering migrants' legal permission to work and reside in the Italy to employers' needs. Moreover, migrant seasonal workers have access to limited rights and protection. In line with the approach of the Seasonal Workers Directive 2014/36/EU, the Italian legal regime on migrant seasonal workers maintains their temporary status by preventing them from accessing social supports such as unemployment benefits for agricultural workers. Furthermore, it denies them access to their right to family reunification, thereby constraining migrant workers' reproduction sphere.

Drawing on feminist analyses of social reproduction and migration (Rigo, 2022; Bhattacharya, 2017; Picchio, 1992), this book has argued how, despite their differences, in both the UK and Italy, workers are recruited through temporary migration channels—such as seasonal migration visa schemes or, in the case of the UK, overseas domestic work programmes—where the containment and control of workers' living and social reproduction conditions play a crucial role. This ensures the temporary stay of these workers to meet the needs of national economic and labour market systems. In this context, migrant workers are less likely to raise issues about employment and working conditions and change employers due to their temporary and precarious legal status. This dynamic leads to workers being more 'docile' and willing to accept abusive work conditions (Corrado & Caruso, 2022; Giammarinaro, 2022) In practice, the ever-present threat of losing permission to stay and work, and related difficulties in finding another job in a limited period, have a disciplinary effect on the behaviour of migrant workers, eroding their bargaining power and exacerbating their situations of vulnerability.

On the other hand, due to the lack of effective national entry channels for 'low-skilled' migrant workers—especially in sectors such as agriculture and domestic work—labour demand has been fulfilled by undocumented migrants, regular migrants with a residence permit but not for work reasons, and EU citizen migrants (the latter in the case of the UK, as known, before Brexit). This has challenged the prevailing categories in legal and policy discourses on migration, particularly underscoring the clear limitations of a rigid distinction between 'economic migration' and 'forced migration' in understanding and addressing the complexity of migratory movements (Mezzadra, 2013).

The various situational vulnerabilities in which migrant persons find themselves—for instance, with respect to legal status, nationality, class, and gender—are translated into different possibilities for their exploitation in these two sectors.

In the case of undocumented migrants—as stressed above in the *Chowdury* case of the ECtHR (Chap. 2)—the condition of irregularity represents a crucial element in creating and exacerbating situations of vulnerability to exploitation and abuse. In the case of regular migrants, such as asylum seekers, the conditions of precarity and uncertainty make them particularly vulnerable to exploitation. In the UK, asylum seekers could only apply for permission to work after waiting 12 months for an initial decision on their asylum claim. Given that it is extremely difficult for asylum seekers to meet the conditions required for UK's Shortage Occupation List (the only employment option available to asylum seekers), accessing the UK labour market after the 12-month period is quite challenging. The de facto exclusion of asylum seekers from the labour market and therefore from employment makes them fully dependent on the state for their means of subsistence. This condition of dependence—as the ECtHR pointed out in *M.S.S. v. Greece and Belgium* (see Chap. 3)—creates, fosters, and exacerbates asylum seekers' situations of vulnerability, and therefore their exposure to exploitation and abuse. This is likely destined to worsen due to the recent and increasingly draconian migration and asylum policies adopted by the UK government, particularly the 2023 Illegal Migration Act, which is informed by the narrative of 'fake' asylum seekers and victims of trafficking abusing the national protection system (Chap. 7).

Even in Italy, particularly since the so-called refugee crisis, there has been a progressive erosion of the right to asylum (Sciurba, 2021), which has faced continuous curbs, fuelled by the narrative of alleged bogus asylum seekers and reaching their peak with the 2017 Memorandum of Understanding between Italy and Libya (renewed in 2020 and 2022); Law Decree No. 113/2018 and Law Decree No. 53/2019, known as the 'Security/Salvini' decrees; and the recent Law Decree 20/2023, 'Cutro Decree'. The interplay between the inadequate implementation of asylum procedures and the absence of appropriate hosting and inclusion measures in the country has produced a 'hyper precarity'—to borrow an expression by Lewis and Waite (2015)—that contributes to creating and amplifying their vulnerabilities to dynamics of exploitation. Moreover, the fact of being hosted in a reception centre often constitutes an element used by employers to further lower asylum seekers' wages, considering that workers do not need to pay for accommodation. These dynamics clearly show the systemic nature of exploitation, which also relies on the compression of the costs of social reproduction of workers (Chap. 5).

As discussed in the Italian context, dynamics of exploitation also involve EU migrant workers, particularly those workers coming from eastern European Countries, who represent an important pillar of agriculture and domestic labour. The ability of EU migrant workers to easily cross EU internal borders produces a 'circular migration' that exposes these workers to irregular work and exploitation, especially in low protected sectors such as agriculture and domestic work. In fact, EU workers can be easily employed on a seasonal basis or according to the contingent needs of the employer, becoming competitive in terms of wages and contractual conditions (Chap. 5).

All of this unfolds in a scenario where, in the case of both non-EU migrant workers' labour migration and intra-EU mobility, the EU legal framework provides room for restricting equal treatment and curbing workers' rights and protection (Chap. 3). As Bogoeski and Costamagna (2022, p. 661) observe, 'while EU law has increasingly become crucial in shaping the conditions of production directly affecting work and labour conditions, the protective responses have remained at national or local level'.

Emblematic in this regard is the Seasonal Workers Directive, which is de facto the main EU instrument regulating labour migration of 'low-skilled' third-country nationals and provides Member States with wide discretionary powers over implementation of the provisions concerning the rights of seasonal workers, especially with regard to social rights. Furthermore, according to the Directive, non-EU migrant seasonal workers cannot rely on to the right of family reunification. These limited rights granted to seasonal workers under this legal regime, based on their perceived low 'economic value', impacts these workers' social reproduction dimension, constraining and containing it (Chap. 3). This, in turn, contributes to processes of the migrant force labour's subordination based on gender, nationality/ethnicity, and class.

Adopting a gender and intersectional perspective (Crenshaw, 1989; Yuval-Davis, 2015), this book has paid specific attention to the working and living conditions of migrant women employed in the agricultural and domestic work sectors. Building on extensive fieldwork conducted in Italy, particularly in Sicily, I have shed light on the wage disparities, irregularities, and denied rights (including reproductive rights) constantly experienced by migrant women workers in these sectors (Chap. 5). For them, irregular working conditions also result in a lack of protections related to pregnancy and maternity benefits, making it even more challenging to combine work with family and social reproductive-related activities and responsibilities. All of this, in turn, is exacerbated by the conditions of isolation and dependence on employers and intermediaries/contractors, in both the agricultural and domestic work sectors.

The labour conditions experienced by women migrant workers are persistently tainted by gender-based harassment and violence within a system that relies on the specific vulnerabilities of these women and their need for employment. In these circumstances, family and related social reproduction responsibilities may increase their situational vulnerabilities to exploitation and abuse (Chap. 5). For migrant women considered 'low-skilled', employment options are restricted to unprotected sectors such as domestic work, agriculture and sexual work. This translates into a simultaneity and constrained circularity among such work, and often results in dynamics of transition from one form of exploitation to another.

However, the complexity of the gender dimension is often overlooked by most relevant EU and national legal and policy instruments, reducing it to a mere 'flag' to be inserted into documents and political and legal discourses.

9.2 Challenging a Mere Repressive Approach to Labour Exploitation

This book has highlighted how, parallel to increasingly stringent migration and asylum policies contributing to the production and amplification of migrants' situations of vulnerability, Italy and the UK have adopted several legal and policy instruments aimed at addressing exploitation of migrant workers and protecting them. However, in both countries, exploitation has primarily been framed and addressed through a repressive and migration containment approach, failing in preventing vulnerabilities to exploitation and contributing instead to intensifying these.

In the case of the UK, as discussed in Chap. 8, the 2015 Modern Slavery Act is considered, at the international and European levels, a landmark instrument in tackling exploitation. However, far from introducing substantial protection and support provisions for victims, the Act aims mainly at increasing prosecutions of traffickers and other abusive actors. Moreover, by centring on severe instances of exploitation captured under the umbrella term 'Modern slavery', the Act falls short of addressing all types of exploitation that do not rise to the level of grave forms, such as slavery or trafficking. In this context, those exploited people who are identified as victims and manage to enter the National Referral Mechanism system often undergo a prolonged and uncertain process, which does not always lead to securing a permission to stay in the UK—and if it does, it is often for a short period of time. On the other hand, those people, including regular migrant workers, who have experienced forms of exploitation that do not reach severe forms such as trafficking are left without protection. This often occurs in the case of many exploited migrants who have migrated through the Seasonal Workers Visa or the Overseas Domestic Worker Visa scheme and do not meet the criteria to be identified as victims of trafficking. The lack of protection and support exposes these migrant workers to additional dynamics of exploitation and abuse, with the probable risk of successively falling into the 'category' of victims allowed to access adequate protection. Therefore, by focusing only on serious forms of abuse, the Modern Slavery Act system tends to normalise less severe but not nonetheless pressing exploitative practices. This overlooks the complexity of related situational vulnerabilities, and instead of preventing it contributes to exposing the persons to dynamics of exploitation, often escalating to severe forms.

Many exploited migrants have thus been reliant on the asylum system as a way of being granted protection. However, the asylum 'safety net' will be significantly undermined by recent, progressively restrictive UK migration policies such as the 2023 Illegal Migration Act, which seeks to prevent asylum seekers and potential victims of trafficking from accessing the national protection system. By extending the hostile migration environment to victims of trafficking, the 2023 Illegal Migration Act will probably exacerbate the dichotomy between the 'false'/criminal victims slated for removal and the 'perfect victims' willing to self-identify as such, cooperate, and provide relevant information, thus deserving protection.

The Italian legal framework on exploitation and trafficking has innovative elements compared to the UK model, but even in its case, there are many limitations regarding the effective protection of exploited people and, more generally, the understanding of the structural dimension of exploitation and the situational dimension of vulnerabilities.

As highlighted in Chap. 6, Italian Law 199 of 2016 has brought institutional attention to the issue of labour exploitation, primarily in the agricultural sector. Importantly, this Law has approached labour exploitation as a stand-alone offence, amending Article 603-bis of the Italian Criminal Code. For the offense to be established, two conditions are required: the exploitation of the worker and the taking advantage of their state of need. By reflecting the notion of labour exploitation contained in the Employer Sanctions Directive 2009/52 (Article 2), Article 603-bis of, as amended by Law 199 of 2016, defines exploitation through indicators related to payment, working hours, safety, degrading working conditions, methods of surveillance, and accommodation conditions. These indicators are conceived in reference to all aspects of work protected by Italian Constitution, particularly by Article 36, and therefore fall within the broader scope of safeguarding human dignity in the exercise of work activities. As this book has argued, these indicators offer a definition of labour exploitation that acknowledges the dignity of working and living conditions as a criterion for setting limits on contractual freedom, particularly on the freedom of private economic initiative. This implies a notion of human dignity that, far from being an abstract and moral value, relates to its social dimension (Marella, 2007), and therefore to the material conditions ensuring a dignified life.

In general, the definition of labour exploitation offered by Art. 603-bis represented an important change introduced by Law 199/2016 as legislation in most countries in Europe, including the UK, does not include a definition of labour exploitation per se. Furthermore, relevant national case law has provided an interpretation of the concept of 'state of need' contained in the provision of Art. 603-bis that emphasises the diverse and variable material circumstances that can influence the will of workers and the extent to which their contractual self-determination is compromised. Such an approach aligns with a situational conception of vulnerability that takes into account the complex and different forms of vulnerabilities depending on the individuals and contexts in which they are situated (Chap. 6).

However, despite these important and positive aspects, the impact of Law 199/2016 has been predominantly in the repressive dimension to exploitation. Numerous projects have been funded under the National Plan against labour exploitation and illegal gangmastering (*caporalato*) to implement the provisions of Law 199/2016 aimed at improving the working and living conditions of migrant workers, especially in the agricultural sector. Yet almost nothing has been done in terms of structural interventions to enforce and strengthen the rights of migrant workers or enhance their access to adequate housing and transportation. Most of the projects have mobilised humanitarian infrastructures relying on an emergency-based approach that in many cases reproduced dynamics of marginalisation, isolation, and invisibility for workers (Caruso & Corrado, 2021). For instance, interventions on accommodation have mainly resulted in models (i.e., cargo containers) that rely on the compression of migrant workers' reproduction spheres, thereby supporting a production system in which exploitation is also based on the reduction of the reproduction costs of workers. Furthermore, most of these projects have overlooked the gender dimension, failing to consider the complexity of migrant women's situational vulnerabilities and the factors that contribute to exposing them to dynamics of exploitation and abuse.

Italy has been acclaimed at international and European level for having adopted a regularisation scheme for undocumented migrant workers employed in agriculture and domestic work following the outbreak of the Covid-19 pandemic. However, as underlined in Chap. 6, this scheme resulted in failure. In line with the previous regularisation plans, it has mainly relied on an employer-driven approach, providing a limited space of action for migrant workers. Being primarily aimed at responding to market needs and pressures rather than fulfilling the declared purpose of protecting irregular migrant workers, this regularisation scheme has clearly revealed how temporary, selective, emergency-based, and excessively bureaucratic measures cannot be the solution to address situations of vulnerability in their complexity.

Italy is also considered a model for the protection system for victims of exploitation and trafficking, especially regarding the system under Article 18 of the Immigration Consolidation Act. But even this instrument and related practices have displayed shortcomings, particularly in the case of labour exploitation. On the one hand, Article 18, especially its so-called social path—which provides assistance to victims irrespective of their participation in the criminal proceedings—has been inadequately implemented. This means that most victims of exploitation, especially victims of labour exploitation, are de facto required to cooperate with relevant authorities to obtain a residence permit. On the other hand, Article 18 and related practices have demonstrated difficulties in addressing changes and complexities in the dynamics of labour exploitation, related situational vulnerabilities, and the corresponding needs of exploited workers. Even in this system, the assessment by competent authorities of requests for protection and situations of vulnerability is often affected by the stereotypical idea of the 'perfect victim', that is expected to clearly show their vulnerabilities and related 'dangerous' situations and willingness to be 'collaborative'. In addition to this, the requirement of participation in Article 18 integration programmes, often isolating and disciplining, discourages many migrants, whose urgency is to work and earn money for their subsistence and that of their family, from applying for this protection.

The other instrument providing a residence permit for exploited undocumented migrant workers is Article 22 of the Immigration Consolidation Act, introduced to implement the Employer Sanctions Directive. But the issuance of this permit is linked to the victims' co-operation in criminal proceedings against the employer. This requirement prevents many exploited workers from applying for this permit.

Similar to the dynamics in the UK, many exploited migrants in Italy have turned to the asylum system to regularise their status. However, the asylum channels have been progressively restricted through increasingly stringent legal reforms such as the recent 'Decreto Cutro' that has narrowed the conditions for granting the 'special protection' (Article 19 of Consolidate Act on Immigration), which has replaced the former humanitarian protection.

Therefore, even in the case of Italy, although its protection system extends to situations that may not necessarily involve extreme cases like trafficking, exploitation tends to be predominantly addressed within the context of criminal law. In this framework, the structural factors contributing to migrant workers' vulnerabilities and undermining their labour and social rights are inadequately addressed, if not overlooked. Little attention is also paid to exploitation in other sectors, such as domestic work.

Drawing from relevant legal and feminist literature on this matter (Marks, 2008; Kotiswaran, 2017; Mantouvalou, 2018), this book has pointed out how social issues with systemic characteristics, such as labour exploitation, cannot be defined, understood, and addressed solely through the instrument of criminal law. From this latter perspective, exploitation and its severe forms (such as trafficking) are considered mainly as a contingent event, and, in any case, are seen only at the level of abusive interpersonal relationships between victims and exploiters. This view overlooks the pervasive and systemic character of labour exploitation, including severe exploitation, in contemporary capitalist systems. At the same time, it also tends not to take into account the background conditions and structures—economic, social and legal factors—that lead to instances of injustice and exploitation at work.

Moreover, as emerged from both the cases of Italy and the UK, reductive representations of exploitation reflecting a mere repressive vision of this phenomenon often constitute the conceptual framework for securitarian interventions and restrictive migration policies, which have the effect of increasing situations of vulnerability to exploitation for the very same people that these measures are intended to protect.

Far from being reduced to exceptional facts and to a pathological dimension of contractual relationships, exploitation should be considered as a structural component of capitalist systems developed exponentially in the current neo-liberal era—an era characterised by deregulation of the markets, as well as by increasingly exclusive and selective migration and social policies. In this sense, in line with notion of 'intersectional exploitation' mobilised by legal scholar Laura Calafà (2021), this book has highlighted that exploitation has to be addressed beyond the limited confines of criminal law, taking into account legal and policy regimes regulating migration, employment and working conditions, and access to justice and citizenship. This perspective, as feminist analysis on social reproduction has highlighted (Rigo, 2022), should also pay attention to the entanglements between mobility and social reproductive regimes and the role these play in the dynamics of labour exploitation.

At the heart of this reflection is therefore the need to treat exploitation in its complexity from a social and rights-based approach. This involves moving beyond dichotomies such as victims vs. exploiters-perpetrators, public vs. private, productive vs. reproductive, ordinary vs. extreme violence or exploitation, and consensus vs. exploitation that are inadequate for comprehending the complexity of exploitation dynamics and the multitude of their effects, especially in the experiences of individuals, particularly migrant workers.

9.3 The Right to Decent Work and Dignified Life

By challenging the aforementioned dichotomies and aligning with a perspective attentive to the intricacy of exploitation, this book has considered exploitation as a structural continuum (Skrivankova, 2010) wherein varying degrees of vulnerability to exploitation exist. Indeed, along this continuum, various forms of exploitation are linked to different 'situational' vulnerabilities resulting from the interplay of personal and structural elements, in line with an intersectional approach. This creates situations where the individual's choices are so limited that they are led to 'accept' exploitation. Especially in cases of severe exploitation, this is often the only alternative available to support themselves and their families.

Far from embracing a victimising view of vulnerable subjects fuelled by the neo-abolitionist feminist narratives (Chap. 4), such a conception of vulnerability—which pays attention to the specificities of the context within which a given person acts and makes choices—does not exclude or oppose individual agency: instead, it recognises the elements of agency and, in particular, the ways in which people act (or try to act), negotiate, and make their choice within a framework of economic, social, affective, and power relationships. Vulnerability and agency are two sides of the same coin (Giammarinaro & Palumbo, 2021; see also, Mackenzie et al., 2014; Giolo & Pastore, 2018). There are various combinations of vulnerability and agency along the continuum of exploitation, depending on the possibilities/capacity for action and bargaining of the person concerned (Chap. 2).

Chapter 5 underlined how the agency of migrant women workers employed, for instance, in the agricultural sector in Ragusa (Sicily) is never completely annulled by exploitation, even if in extreme situations the range of choices is so severely limited they are led to accept exploitation itself as a preferable option. By compressing the social reproduction sphere of these women workers, the poor and exploitative working and living conditions experienced by many of these women significantly limit their possibilities to have and organise their lives beyond the work dimension and related power relationships. Women migrant workers must thus navigate a complex interplay of responsibilities (in particular family responsibilities), constraints, pursuit of freedom, exploitation, violence, and tactics of resistance.

As this book has discussed, in recent years there has been relevant case law of the ECtHR (in particular *Chowdury and others v. Greece*) and national courts that, in line with a situational approach to vulnerabilities, have considered the structural factors that create and amplify situations of vulnerability to exploitation. Although the gender dimension is lacking in most of these decisions (Giammarinaro & Palumbo, 2021), the European and respective national judges have importantly focused on the material conditions in which the concerned person gave their consent to certain exploitative practices, paying attention to the dynamics and contextual elements generating situations of vulnerability that significantly affect the freedom of choice of the people concerned and in which labour exploitation becomes the only feasible choice in the face of a worse alternative.

Indeed, the forms and gradations of agency and contractual bargaining for workers depend on the structure of power relationships and the resources they actually have in a context marked by substantial inequalities, persistent patriarchal legacies, stringent migration regimes, and genderised and racialised labour market segmentation.

In this light, taking vulnerabilities to exploitation seriously requires structural interventions that prioritise the social dignity of persons, viewed in its material/social dimension (Marella, 2007). As discussed in Chap. 2, this social conception of dignity arises in the Constitutions of several European countries, including Italy's (Articles 3(1), 36 and 41), as well as in the EU Charter of Fundamental Rights, and entails a view of human dignity as a guarantee of minimum living conditions that allow a person a dignified life. As Maria Rosaria Marella (2007) and Stefano Rodotà (2012) have pointed out, the social conception of dignity, which is strongly related to the principle of equality, encompasses the materiality of social relationships thereby addressing the material needs and living conditions of individuals. Therefore, it entails an obligation on States to ensure that each person makes their own decisions in conditions of freedom and responsibility, and, consequently, to ensure that no one lives and works in exploitative and degrading conditions.

This obligation of States to guarantee that nobody falls below a 'dignified' level of existence has been also expressly recognised by the ECtHR, including in decisions regarding migrants' rights (such as *M.S.S. v Belgium and Greece* of 2011, App no 30696/09) and by national constitutional courts (Resta, 2014). Furthermore, in Italy the protection of right to a dignified life occupies a central role in a significant case law in the field of international protection and former humanitarian protection (former art. 5(6) of the Consolidated Act on Immigration),[1] including decisions concerning the protection of exploited migrant workers (Giammarinaro & Palumbo, 2021).

With specific regard to working conditions, the principle of dignity entails an obligation of States to ensure that individuals do not make their choice under conditions of vulnerability that can be easily exploited by others (Santoro & Genovese, 2018, p. 553). In other words, it entails preventing persons from being and making decisions in situations of vulnerability that significantly curtail their freedom of choice, lead them to 'accept' work in exploitative conditions as one of the few—and in some cases only—viable practical choices available to them.

During the Covid-10 pandemic the recognition that 'no one is saved alone' seemed to entail a revision of national and European social and economic models, putting at the centre the principles of social dignity, solidarity, and a relational conception of freedom. Yet, both EU and national initiatives have largely left the structural factors producing and intensifying social and economic inequalities mostly untouched (Triandafyllidou, 2022).

At the EU level, there have been some important initiatives to bolster its social dimension. These include, as underlined above, the reform of the Common

[1] See for instance, Court of Cassation, Civil Section, Decision No. 4455/2018.

Agricultural Policy (CAP) – which has approved a social conditionality mechanism making CAP payments conditional on respect for labour standards – the adoption of the Directive on Minimum Wage, and negotiations for a Directive on Corporate Sustainability Due Diligence.

All these actions constitute important steps for the protection of social and labour rights. However, this response is not enough. A more profound change on European and national legal and political regimes on migration, labour, and social-related issues is necessary. These interventions should be aimed, among other things, at: creating safe and legal entry routes for so-called low and medium-skilled workers and supporting their social and labour inclusion on a long-term perspective; promoting fair and sustainable supply chains by ensuring that businesses effectively implement both human rights and environmental due diligence; fostering the strengthening of the enforcement of labour and social rights; and, more generally, guaranteeing migrant workers the conditions to have a free and dignified existence, for instance by ensuring them the right to social and housing assistance in accordance with the EU Charter of Fundamental Rights (in particular article 34 (3)) and irrespective of legal migration status. Only by moving in this direction is it possible to ensure that individuals can act and make choices in conditions of equality and avoid situations where some persons accept abusive and exploitative conditions as the only option for their subsistence and survival.

References

Bhattacharya, T. (Ed.). (2017). *Social reproduction theory. Remapping class, recentering oppression*. Pluto Press.

Bogoeski, V., & Costamagna, F. (2022). Law and the production of precarious work in Europe: An introduction. *European Law Open, 1*(3), 660–668. https://doi.org/10.1017/elo.2022.44

Calafà, L. (2021). Per un approccio multidimensionale allo sfruttamento lavorativo. *Lavoro e diritto, 35*(2), 193–213.

Caruso, F. S., & Corrado, A. (Eds.). (2021). *Essenziali ma invisibili. Analisi delle politiche e delle iniziative di contrasto allo sfruttamento e per l'inclusione dei lavoratori migranti in agricoltura nel sud Italia*. Rosenberg and Sellier.

Corrado, A., & Caruso, F. S. (2022). Essential but exploitable: Migrant agri-food workers in Italy and Spain. *European Journal of Migration and Law, 24*(2), 193–216.

Crenshaw, K. (1989). Demarginalizing the intersection of race and sex: A black feminist critique of antidiscrimination doctrine, feminist theory and antiracist politics. *University of Chicago Legal Forum, 1*, 139–167.

Giammarinaro, G. M. (2022). Understanding severe exploitation requires a human rights and gender-sensitive intersectional approach. *Frontiers in Human Dynamics, 4*, 861600. https://doi.org/10.3389/fhumd.2022.861600.

Giammarinaro, M. G., & Palumbo, L. (2021). Vulnerabilità situazionale, genere e dIrIttI umanI. AnalIsI della normatIva e della gIurIsprudenza ItalIana e sovranazIonale sullo sfruttamento lavoratIvo. In G. Gioffredi, V. Lorubbio, & A. Pisanò (Eds.), *Diritti umani in crisi? Emergenze, disuguaglianze, esclusioni* (pp. 45–62). Pacini Giuridica.

Giolo, O. & Pastore, B. (Eds.). (2018). *Vulnerabilità. Analisi multidisciplinare di un concetto*. Carocci.

Kotiswaran, P. (2017). *Revisiting the law and governance of trafficking forced labor, and modern slavery*. Cambridge University Press.
Lewis, H., & Waite, L. (2015). Asylum, immigration restrictions and exploitation: Hyper-precarity as a lens for understanding and tackling forced labour. *Anti-Trafficking Review, 5*, 50–68.
Mackenzie, C., Rogers, W., & Dodds, S. (Eds.). (2014). *Vulnerability: New essays in ethics and feminist philosophy*. Oxford University Press.
Mantouvalou, V. (2018). Legal construction of structures of exploitation. In H. Collings, G. Lester, & V. Mantouvalou (Eds.), *Philosophical foundations of labour law* (pp. 188–204). Oxford University Press.
Marella, M. R. (2007). Il fondamento sociale della dignità umana. Un modello costituzionale per il diritto europeo dei contratti. *Rivista Critica del Diritto Privato, XXV*(1), 67–103.
Marks, S. (2008). Exploitation as an international legal concept. In S. Marks (Ed.), *International law on the left: Re-examining Marxist legacies* (pp. 281–307). Cambridge University Press.
Mezzadra, S. (2013). Moltiplicazione dei confine e pratiche di mobilità. *Ragione Pratica, 41*, 413–422.
Picchio, A. (1992). *Social reproduction. The political economy of the labour market*. Cambridge University Press.
Resta, Giorgio (2014) *Dignità, Persone, Mercati*. Giappichelli Editore.
Rigo, E. (2022). *La straniera. Migrazioni, asilo, sfruttamento in una prospettiva di genere*. Carocci Editori.
Rodotà, S. (2012). *Il diritto di avere diritti*. Editori Laterza.
Santoro, E., & Genovese, D. (2018). L'articolo 18 (t.u. immigrazione) e il contrasto allo sfruttamento lavorativo: la fantasia del giurista tra libertà e dignità. *Giornale di Diritto del Lavoro e di Relazioni Industriali, 159*, 543–579.
Sciurba, A. (2021). *Le parole dell'asilo: un diritto di confine*. Giappichelli Editore.
Skrivankova, K. (2010). *Between decent work and forced labour: Examining the continuum of exploitation*. JRF.
Triandafyllidou, A. (2022). *Migration and pandemic. Spaces of solidarity and spaces of exception*. Springer.
Young, I. M. (1990). *Justice and the politics of difference*. Princeton University Press.
Yuval-Davis, N. (2015). Situated intersectionality and social inequality. *Raisons politiques, 58*, 91–100.

The manufacturer's authorised representative in the EU is Springer Nature Customer Service Centre GmbH, Europaplatz 3, 69115 Heidelberg, Germany. If you have any concerns regarding our products, please contact ProductSafety@springernature.com

Printed and bound by CPI Group (UK) Ltd, Croydon, CR0 4YY
01/10/2026
02225909-0009